DATA ANALYSIS

PSYCHONOMIC PERSPECTIVES

a series edited by Judson S. Brown, University of Iowa

DATA ANALYSIS

a statistical primer
for psychology students

Edward L. Wike

UNIVERSITY of KANSAS at LAWRENCE

ALDINE · ATHERTON
Chicago & New York

First published 1971 by
Aldine·Atherton, Inc.
529 South Wabash Avenue
Chicago, Illinois 60605

Library of Congress Catalog Card Number 78-131048

ISBN 202-25036-9, cloth; 202-25037-7, paper

Printed in the United States of America

Preface

As the title indicates, this book is concerned with the analysis of data. It is primarily aimed at undergraduate psychology students who are trying for the first time to do research. It is hoped, however, that parts of the book may be of some value to graduate students and research workers.

The bulk of the text is devoted to a presentation of some elementary statistical techniques. Students in introductory research courses often do simple investigations with small numbers of subjects. The statistical techniques, which are included, are suitable for such limited experimental undertakings. In addition, a few more complicated statistical methods are incorporated for the benefit of instructors who require their students to perform more elaborate experiments.

The question might be raised: why call the subject matter "data analysis"? This title stems from a desire to put statistical techniques in their proper research context. Data analysis is a broader endeavor than the application of statistics and may even be carried out without statistics. The phrase, data analysis, also serves as a reminder that the analyses are on data *from experiments*.

Although there is a focus on data analysis and "how to do it," one goal of the book is to impart a philosophy of data analysis. That is to say, there is concern with the function of data analysis and the interpretations that can legitimately be drawn from data analysis. This viewpoint has been influenced by the writings of various individuals such as J. W. Tukey, R. G. Miller, W. L. Hays, B. J. Underwood, P. E. Meehl, D. T. Lykken, and others.

It will be readily apparent that the writer is not a statistician. Being an experimental psychologist, I am interested in the kinds of questions that experimental psychologists ask. Thus there is a heavy emphasis throughout the book upon techniques for performing multiple comparisons. Likewise there is a concern with interactions and what to do with them. The interaction problem is presently in a most unsatisfactory state. Perhaps the stress herein will prompt others to turn their attention to it.

With one exception the examples in the book are based on actual investigations. Some of the problems draw upon the same data. This tactic of including actual data was employed deliberately to make students aware of the fact that statistics is not an abstract discipline but a tool in research.

The present book is a social product. I wish to thank my colleague, Dr. Anthony J. Smith, for his thoughtful reading of Chapter 6 and his helpful comments. Discussions with two other colleagues, Drs. Juliet Shaffer and George Kellas, were most beneficial in resolving a number of difficult problems. Thanks are due to Joan Fixsen, Karen Schank, and Elsie Pinkston for the typing of drafts and the final manuscript and to Walter Hicks for the preparation of figures. I am grateful to Verne Bacharach for checking all of the calculations — any errors that remain are, of course, his fault. Although my wife, Dr. Sharron S. Wike, was responsible for my undertaking this project, she was thereafter a dependable source of assistance at every stage. Finally, I wish to thank Dr. Judson S. Brown, editor of Aldine's Psychonomic Series, and Mr. Robert Wesner, associate publisher, for their sustained interest, useful suggestions, and encouragement.

I am grateful to the many research workers who kindly permitted the use of their original data as examples. Their generosity affords students an opportunity to face genuine problems and actual data rather than the usual contrived examples. Another debt is to statisticians, editors, and publishers who kindly permitted the reprinting of tables, figures, etc. Specific acknowledgement is made to the following sources to quote and reproduce materials:

Psychological Reports—Table 2.1 (Maier, Thurber, & Janzen, 1968).
American Psychological Association—Table 2.3 (Reynolds, 1949); Figures 3.2–3.4 (Boneau, 1960); Tables 3.1, 3.2, and 3.3 (Klein, 1959); Tables 3.10 and 3.11 (Petrinovich & Hardyck, 1969); Table 3.12 (Overstreet & Dunham, 1969); Table 4.1 (Levinson & Sheridan, 1969); Table 6.3 (Grice & Saltz, 1950); and Table 6.5 (Welker, 1956).
Butterworths—Figure 2.5 (Quenouille, 1950) and Tables U and V (Quenouille, 1952).
Houghton Mifflin Company—Figure 3.5 and Table 3.6 (Lindquist, 1953).
John Wiley & Sons—Table 3.7 (Scheffé, 1959).
McGraw-Hill Book Company—Table 3.9, Figures 3.7–3.9, and Table C (Winer, 1962); and Tables O and S (Miller, 1966).
Science—Tables 3.13 and 3.14 (Weil, Zinberg, & Nelsen, 1968).
Dr. Earl D. Scott—Tables 3.17, 3.21, and 3.25 (Scott, 1960).
Biometrics—Tables 4.4 and 4.6 (Steel, 1961) and Table D (Dixon, 1953).
Dr. Elizabeth A. Beale—Tables 5.1, 5.3, 5.4, and 5.6 (Beale, 1956).
Dr. Rebecca Snyder—Table 5.9 (Snyder, 1956).

Psychological Record—Table 6.6 (Lynch, 1968).

Drs. Jack W. Dunlap and Albert K. Kurtz—Table A (Dunlap & Kurtz, 1932).

The Chemical Rubber Company—Table B (Weast, 1969).

Professor E. S. Pearson and the Biometrika Trustees—Tables E–G and M (Pearson & Hartley, 1966) and Table T (Finney, 1948).

Dr. H. Leon Harter—Table H (Harter, Clemm, & Guthrie, 1959).

Journal of the American Statistical Association—Table I (Dunn, 1961); Table L (Kruskal & Wallis, 1952, 1953); Table Q (MacKinnon, 1964); and Table R (Friedman, 1937).

American Cyanamid Company—Tables J and P (Wilcoxon, 1949; Wilcoxon & Wilcox, 1964).

The RAND Corporation—Table K (The RAND Corporation, 1955).

The Macmillan Company—Table N (Wallis & Roberts, 1956).

Charles Griffin & Company—Table W (Kendall, 1962).

Contents

Preface   v

1. Opening Shots   1
    *Bird Watching — The Place of Statistics in Research —
    Answering Questions vs Hypothesis Testing — Research
    Errors — Pilot Experiments — Summary*

2. The Search for Indications   7
    *Multiple-Analysis — Empirical Distributions — Measures
    of Central Tendency — Measures of Variability — "Spotty"
    Data — Reviewing the Bidding — Problems*

3. Steps to Inference: I. Numbers   26
    *A Single Mean — The Means of Two Independent Groups
    — The Means of k Independent Groups — Multiple Com-
    parisons of Means and Variances from k Independent
    Groups — The Means of Two Matched Groups — The
    Means of k Matched Groups — Multiple Comparison of
    Means from k Matched Groups — Three More Complex
    Experimental Designs — A Quick Review — Problems*

4. Steps to Inference: II. Ranks and Signs   105
    *A Location Test for Two Independent Groups — A Loca-
    tion Test for k Independent Groups — Multiple-Compari-*

son Location Tests for k *Independent Groups — A Loca-*
tion Test for Two Matched Groups — A Location Test for
k Matched Groups — Multiple-Comparison Location Tests
for k *Matched Groups — A Quasi-Summary and a Few*
Words-To-Live-By — Problems

5.   Steps to Inference: III. Classes   123
     Class Frequencies of Two Independent Groups — Class
     Frequencies of k *Independent Groups — Partitions with* k
     Independent Groups — Class Frequencies of Two Matched
     Groups — Class Frequencies of k *Matched Groups — Mul-*
     tiple Comparisons of Class Frequencies with k *Matched*
     Groups — A Mini-Summary and More Words-To-Live-By
     — Problems

6.   Steps to Inference: IV. Relationships   140
     The Case of Harvey, Traffic Engineer — Linear Relation-
     ships: Numbers — Curvilinear Relationships: Numbers —
     Monotonic Relationships: Ranks — A Nonsummary —
     Problems

7.   Closing Shots   164
     Testing Statistical Hypotheses vs. Confidence Intervals —
     Multiple-Analysis Revisited — Some Tactics for Research
     and Data Analysis — Final Remarks

Answers to the Even-Numbered Problems   177

References   181

Appendix   187

Index   249

CHAPTER ONE

Opening Shots

Statistical techniques serve a useful function but they have acquired a purely honorific status which may be troublesome. Their presence or absence has become a shibboleth to be used in distinguishing between good and bad work. — B. F. Skinner

Bird Watching

One warm, breezy afternoon I was at my office window happily engaged in the pleasant activity of bird watching. The window overlooks the library and a large busy yard. I deliberately selected the office because of its view of the yard. (I'm not a "library man" like some university types who spend most of their lives in libraries. Rather, I associate libraries with signs commanding silence and no smoking, an empty shelf where "the book" should be, books lost and in the bindery, people tiptoeing around, fines for overdue books, and other dreary events. I'm not putting down the library man — if he likes it, let him do it. I just never found much action there). But to return to the yard, it's a different story. Between classes the yard comes alive with splendid displays of beautiful young birds. And, with the advent of the mini-skirt, they're becoming even more splendid and more beautiful. The great quest in bird watching is, of course, to find a "hummer." A hummer is a rare avian specimen whose passage by a group of men is accompanied by a universal comment of "hmm."

This particular afternoon my work was interrupted by an occupational hazard — a student. I maintain an open-door policy on students: if they can get into the door before I can slam it, they come in. This bright undergraduate student, being a former vacuum cleaner salesman, won easily by means of the old foot-in-the-door trick. He talked about this and that, but I was thinking about other things like an improved open-door policy.

1

However, he caught my attention when he said: "I'm trying to design an experiment so I can apply statistics to the data." That sentence not only woke me, but it has continued to haunt me.

The Place of Statistics in Research

What's wrong with the student's statement? What's wrong is that the tail is wagging the dog. In the simplest terms science is devoted to answering questions. We go through the difficult, time-consuming, and expensive process of doing research in order to answer questions. We don't do research to "apply statistics to the data." Statistics is a *tool* — and an imperfect one — which may help us to analyze the data generated by experiments. The thesis that statistics is an imperfect tool is a central idea in the present book. This thesis and its implications for research will, accordingly, be developed throughout.

If we are going to de-emphasize the importance of statistics in research, then why devote any time to statistics? There are at least two significant reasons for a concern with statistics. First, statistical techniques can be useful tools in realizing the scientific goal of answering questions. Second, we need an understanding of statistics to evaluate the research of others. Although an occasional experiment will result in data that are so compelling that no formal analysis is necessary, most research in the behavioral sciences ends with highly variable data that have to be subjected to statistical analysis in order to arrive at some indications. Regarding the second justification, an examination of the current literature of psychology makes it obvious that a research worker would be seriously handicapped without some knowledge of statistics. But we should not, like the student, confuse statistical analysis with the aim of the research process.

Answering Questions vs Hypothesis Testing

We have asserted that in simplest terms it is the business of science to answer questions. The big trick is to ask "good" questions. Unfortunately, there is no cookbook or handy set of rules to tell us how to formulate research questions. The questions that direct research arise from diverse sources, there are different kinds of experiments, and the motivation of research workers is complex. Some research workers get ideas from theories, some from studying the research of others, some from everyday observations, some from laboratory accidents, and so on. Plutchik (1968) has distinguished four types of experiments: (a) those aimed at determining the relationship between two or more variables; (b) studies which attempt to explore the limits of a variable; (c) replication studies which have as their goal the establishment of reliability of findings; and (d) those oriented towards the testing of theories. This classification is not exhaustive and other types of experiments have been proposed by Sidman (1960). The complexity of the scientist's motivation is evident. Research is done to satisfy the investigator's curiosity, to establish the truth, to secure fame, promotions, and monetary rewards, etc. Whatever the roots of the research question, the type of study, or motivation of the researcher, in the last analysis progress in science rests upon asking "good" questions.

We have stressed that there is no cookbook or handy set of rules to inform us how to formulate questions for research. Likewise there is no set of criteria that permits us to say that a given question is indeed a good one. Judgments as to the goodness of questions ultimately rest with the scientific community or even with historians of science. At the very least, a question ought to be testable in principle. And if we want to do the research now, the question must have reference to technical manipulations that are presently possible.

The view that science is devoted to answering questions should not be construed to mean that we regard science simply as a collection of facts. Obviously, besides a foundation of facts, the development of comprehensive theories is a major focus of science (McCain & Segal, 1969). However, theoretical development does not occur in a vacuum — it can only take place when some well-established empirical relationships exist. The emphasis here is upon the empirical substratum rather than upon theory construction.

There is a widely circulated notion to the effect that research *must* begin with an "hypothesis." Unfortunately, the term hypothesis does not have invariant meaning. Sometimes in everyday life it is used as an idea, an untested idea, a question, or a hunch. In a more technical sense an hypothesis is a proposition (or group of propositions), which has been derived from a theory, and which provides an explanation for a set of phenomena. Often an hypothesis (more properly termed a working hypothesis) is a proposition, stemming from a provisional theory, that we tentatively assume to be correct in order to use it as a guide for research. If the dictum that "research must begin with an hypothesis" refers to the latter two formal meanings of the term hypothesis, then this dictum is absurd. It bears little relation to the actual behavior of most scientists. In addition, it is a dangerous pre-scription because it acts as a deterrent to research by throwing up an un-necessary and unrealistic road block. It would rule out research of potential value in which an investigator merely asks: Is X related to Y? Or if I did this, what would happen? Experiments that test hypotheses derived from theories are both exciting and impressive, but this type of experiment is only a small part of the science game. Furthermore, research directed at answering questions has its moments of excitement and often leads to results of enduring value. It should also be recognized that scientists do not always know clearly what they are doing. And that sometimes an explicit formulation of the research question may occur *after* the research is done rather than before. This does not imply that we should discourage students from specifying with as much precision as possible what they intend to do, but we should certainly be aware of the fact that research doesn't always follow a simple one-way path from an hypothesis, to an experiment, to conclusions. It should also be remembered that beneath that crisp white laboratory coat there dwells a primate.

Research Errors

Having formulated a question, the next steps in the scientific process are designing and executing an experiment. While we cannot specify criteria for triviality with which to evaluate the quality of research questions, we can with some assurance say that an experiment is unsound. An experiment is unsound to the degree that it includes research errors. Regarding the detection of errors, Underwood says:

> To determine whether or not there is an error in an investigation requires a comparison of what the investigator does and what he concludes was found as a consequence of this doing. Experimental research involves the manipulation of a variable in some fashion; the intent is to discover if this manipulation is related to behavioral changes. What the investigator said or implied he has found in light of what he did are two critical focal points in determining whether a research error does or does not exist (1957, p. 89).

Underwood has presented an organizational scheme for research errors, described these errors concretely, and pointed out which errors are most common in psychological research. Another classification of errors has been offered by Campbell and Stanley (1966). They have divided errors into those which jeopardize *internal* validity and those which jeopardize *external* validity. These writers assert:

> *Internal validity* is the basic minimum without which any experiment is uninterpretable. Did in fact the experimental treatments make a difference in this specific experimental instance? *External validity* asks the question of *generalizability*. To what populations, settings, treatment variables, and measurement variables can this effect be generalized? (1966, p. 4).

There are many possible errors in research. For example, were the groups being compared equivalent prior to the introduction of the experimental variable? Do the measuring instruments produce different results with continued use? Does a loss of subjects occur so as to bias the results? Are the results due to the experimental treatments per se or to the sequence in which the treatments are imposed? And so on. Despite the intricacies of experimental design, a basic paradigm of research is to vary one factor and to hold all others constant. Departures from this paradigm are research errors. One way of detecting errors is to lay out an experiment on paper schematically. What treatment(s) will be given to whom and when? Will only one factor be varied? Will all others be held constant? This technique is of value too in assessing the soundness of published research. The statement, all published studies are sound, is false.

While some benefit may be derived from reading about errors and from considering the advice of specialists in conducting research in specific areas (cf. Sidowski, 1966; Aronson & Carlsmith, 1968), there is probably no substitute for actually doing research and receiving feedback, painful as it may sometimes be. In view of the possibility of errors that invalidate research, the student is well-advised to put considerable care and effort into the planning of research. He must ask himself over and over: Am I studying what I intend to investigate? What's wrong with this experiment? Have I overlooked something that will invalidate the investigation?

Pilot Experiments

An experiment that looks good on paper may crash when launched. Murphy's law (if something can go wrong, it will) is no joke. It is a principle with strong empirical grounding! One possible way of forestalling disasters is to run a preliminary or pilot experiment with a few subjects. Sidman (1960, ch. 7) has considered the problem of pilot studies in great detail. He is strongly opposed to pilot experiments as a device to get a sneak preview of results. He is likewise opposed to pilot studies that are executed in a sloppy manner or under conditions which differ from those which the investigator intends to impose in the real study. Quite properly he asserts: "A deliberate pilot experiment, in which the experimenter purposely fails to maintain the most rigorous conditions, can never rise above itself" (1960, p. 233). There can be no quarrel with this position or with Sidman's insistence upon carrying out the pilot study under the conditions of the real experiment. Obviously a pilot experiment which differs greatly can yield little information of value.

Do these considerations imply that pilot studies are of no value? Certainly not. A pilot study may give the experimenter information about the adequacy of the instructions, the difficulty of the task, the time required to run a subject, the experimental procedures and equipment, etc. On the basis of a pilot study the experimenter may sometimes make changes that improve his experiment. And a pilot study may also serve as a useful training experience for a neophyte research worker. It's better for him to break the apparatus during a pilot study than in the course of a full-scale investigation.

Are pilot studies always advisable? Again, certainly not. If an experienced research worker is going to perform experiments using familiar techniques, it would probably be a waste of time to do a pilot study. If he's familiar with his apparatus, methods, etc., it is doubtful if anything can be gained from a pilot study. If, however, he's on an unfamiliar track – investigating a new variable or a new technique – then like the neophyte research worker he may secure valuable information from a rigorously conducted pilot study done under the conditions of the "real thing."

Summary

Let us recapitulate. One aim of science is to answer questions. One way of doing this is to perform experiments. Experiments lead to data which we must analyze. One technique of data analysis is statistics. The critical steps in the research process are those of formulating a question, and designing and executing a sound experiment. A bad experiment is just that, and it cannot be salvaged in some magical manner by statistical gyrations. We need to secure data that are worthy of analysis. Accordingly, the student should think "long and hard" about the questions that he is asking and how he is going to answer them. If he can do a sound experiment – that is, one free of research errors – a way can surely be found to deal with the resulting data. If getting "hung up" is inevitable, let's get hung up on the design and execution of the experiment, not on the statistics.

At this point, let us permit an imaginary critic to speak. He might say that you talk as if experimental design is unrelated to statistical analysis. Can't statistics, for example, help us to design more efficient experiments? While we agree with this position, we believe that especially in the case of beginning research workers the main emphasis should be focussed upon the goal of science, i.e., seeking answers to questions. A pioneer in educational research, W. A. McCall, wrote over four decades ago (1923): "There are excellent books and courses of instruction dealing with the statistical manipulation of experimental data, but there is little help on the methods of securing adequate and proper data to which to apply statistical procedure." Today our statistical textbooks are bigger and better, and giant computers are performing analyses that are beyond human capabilities. These developments do not obviate the need for "adequate and proper data." It doesn't help to run the data from a bad experiment through a computer – it's not a washing machine. The student's attention is properly directed toward the execution of a sound experiment.

CHAPTER TWO

The Search for Indications

I usually think it is a good idea to analyze the data of completed experiments in many different ways. One may make analyses on subgroups within the general groups or fractionate the data in many other ways to obtain all the information possible from a single experiment. – B. J. Underwood

Multiple-Analysis

The advice above comes from a very able and active experimental psychologist. For a long time this approach to data analysis seemed unsound to me. The concern was this: Is it not possible that in the course of analyzing and reanalyzing the data, relationships will be discovered which in reality are merely chance occurrences? Would it not be more prudent for the experimenter to approach the data only in terms of his initial research questions? These reservations with respect to multiple-analysis of data were based on the naive view that in an experiment questions are asked and that as a consequence of the analysis of the data pertinent to these questions conclusions are drawn.

The next attitude taken towards multiple-analysis involved a double standard: (a) conclusions could be drawn in the case of the questions proposed by the experimenter prior to the investigation; but (b) relationships observed after "inspection" of the data were to be regarded as *hypotheses* that would be tested in further experiments.

The position to be advocated here is an even more extreme one. It is the view that one never draws conclusions from a single psychological experiment. All that a single experiment provides is, to use Tukey's term (1962), *indications*.

Tukey has commented on the use of multiple-analysis in the physical sciences:

7

The physical sciences are used to "praying over" their data, examining the same data from a variety of points of view. This process has been very rewarding, and has led to many extremely valuable insights. Without this sort of flexibility progress in physical science would have been much slower (1962, p. 46).

Regarding the interpretation of such analyses, he has proposed:

Flexibility in analysis is often only to be had honestly at the price of a willingness not to demand that what has *already* been observed shall establish or prove, what analysis *suggests*. In the physical sciences generally, the results of praying over the data are thought of as something to be put to further tests in another experiment, as indications rather than conclusions (1962, p. 46).

Perhaps the tactic of multiple-analysis will prove equally rewarding in psychology.

It should also be stressed that the preselected experimental questions can serve as a set of filters that close our eyes to "what's in the data." Furthermore, "what's in the data" can sometimes be more important than the initial questions. Skinner (1956) has stressed the importance of serendipity in science – finding one thing while looking for something else. Serendipitous discoveries are not limited to observations made during the course of data collection; they can occur too in the process of "praying over" data.

If an experiment yields only indications, then how are conclusions ever achieved? Indications become conclusions when they turn up time and time again in experiments. In other words, conclusions are dependent upon experimental replication.

Let us leave the problem of the meaning of data analysis. We shall return to this issue in the final chapter. For the moment we will accept the tactic of multiple-analysis and regard the results of this procedure as generating indications rather than conclusions.

Empirical Distributions

In examining data it is often useful to look at their form or distribution. Here we are asking the question: How frequently do different scores occur? Consider the following observations (Table 2.1) from a study of creativity by Maier, Thurber, and Janzen (1968). The scores are the numbers of pairs of words, learned earlier singly, appearing in the stories of 32 male and 32 female Ss.[1] Inspection of Table 2.1 shows that the *range* of scores or the

1. In this book we shall restrict ourselves to experiments in which the numbers of Ss (subjects) in the treatments are equal. The reason for this strategy will be described later. If one treatment lacks an observation, the mean or median score for that treatment should be substituted for the missing observation. A less desired procedure is to equalize the number of scores per treatment by randomly discarding the excess observations.

Table 2.1.*   Pairs of Words Used in Stories
(Maier, Thurber, and Janzen, 1968)

Males	12	11	7	7	9	8	1	4
	7	6	7	9	5	8	7	5
	7	3	5	3	5	4	4	6
	9	6	6	11	2	7	10	8
Females	5	3	5	7	6	8	6	6
	7	7	13	5	5	6	8	6
	9	8	4	4	6	6	4	6
	4	6	4	6	5	6	3	5

*Reprinted by permission of the publisher from Maier et al., *Psychological Reports*, 23, p. 1012, 1968.

Table 2.2.   Tallies of Scores for Male and Female Subjects

Score	Males	f	Females	f
1	1	1		0
2	1	1		0
3	11	2	11	2
4	111	3	⊬⊬	5
5	1111	4	⊬⊬ 1	6
6	1111	4	⊬⊬ ⊬⊬ 1	11
7	⊬⊬ 11	7	111	3
8	111	3	111	3
9	111	3	1	1
10	1	1		0
11	11	2		0
12	1	1		0
13		0	1	1

highest score–lowest score is $12 - 1 = 11$ for the males and is $13 - 3 = 10$ for the females. In Table 2.2 the scores have been tallied and the frequencies of occurrence, f, for each score are shown. We can graph these frequencies to produce a figure termed a *histogram* (Figure 2.1). The class interval, i, used for this bar graph is 1. It yields 12 classes for the male Ss and 11 classes (3 empty) for the female Ss. A rough rule of thumb is to employ a class interval size that will generate about 10 to 20 classes (Hays, 1963). To decide what i to use, divide the range of scores, i.e., highest score–lowest score, by the number of classes desired. In the case of the males, suppose we wanted 12 classes, then:

$$i = \frac{\text{range of scores}}{\text{no. of classes}} = \frac{12 - 1}{12} \cong 1.$$

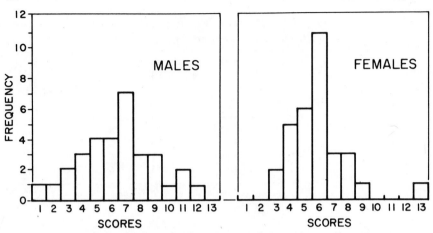

Figure 2.1. Histograms representing the frequencies of scores for male and female subjects.

The symbol, $\cong$, means is approximately equal to. What do the histograms in Figure 2.1 show us? First, the bulk of the scores for the males appears to be more spread out than for the females. Second, even though we have a fair-sized number of cases (32 for each sex), the data do not form normal bell-shaped curves.[2] For example, there are gaps in the histogram for the female Ss and one observation (13) is out in the tail of the distribution by itself.

Let us examine another set of data. Reynolds (1949) reported the numbers of trials to extinction made by 32 rats in a simple instrumental conditioning apparatus. Half of the Ss had been trained under high drive (HD) and half under low drive (LD). Reynold's data, arranged according to score size, are summarized in Table 2.3. Reynolds presented his data in histogram form,

Table 2.3.*   *Trials to Extinction for LD and HD Groups*
(Reynolds, 1949)

LD				HD			
6	17	33	42	7	10	13	26
7	19	35	45	7	10	15	28
10	22	41	59	7	11	18	33
11	30	42	68	8	13	22	47

2. The normal curve is a symmetrical bell-shaped frequency distribution. It is referred to as bell-shaped because the frequencies of scores are the greatest at the middle and decrease at the extremes.

using an $i = 1$. These figures revealed that the scores for the HD group piled up at the low-score end, while the scores for the LD group were generally without peaks (rectangular distribution).[3] For practice sake, we will group these data into fewer classes. The range of scores for LD is $68 - 6 = 62$ and for HD is $47 - 7 = 40$. If we want about 10 classes and use the data from the LD group, then $i = 6$:

$$i = \frac{\text{range of scores}}{\text{no. of classes}} = \frac{62}{10} \cong 6.$$

Having selected i, where shall we start our classes? Conventionally, multiples of the class interval are utilized as the lower limits of each class, i.e., 6–11, 12–17, 18–23, etc. If $i = 10$, then we would have: 0–9, 10–19, 20–29, and so on. Let us tally the Reynolds data and then plot two histograms. It will be noted that we said $i = 6$; yet the limits of the first class are 6–11, the next 12–17, and so on. The discrepancy is due to the fact that the *true* class interval extends from 0.5 unit below the lower limit (e.g., 6) to a 0.5 unit above the upper limit (e.g., 11). Thus the true limits for the first class are 5.5–11.5, and the size of i is indeed 6. The resulting histograms, Figure 2.2,

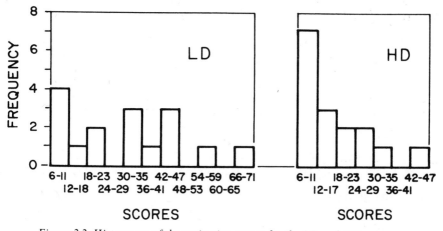

Figure 2.2. Histograms of the extinction scores for the LD and HD groups.

suggest that these distributions are clearly not bell-shaped and that the LD scores may be more variable than those for the HD group.

Another technique for depicting a distribution of data is termed a *frequency polygon*. Instead of representing the frequency of scores in each class by a bar as we did for a histogram, we plot the frequencies in each class *at the midpoint* of the class and connect the adjoining points by a straight line.

3. A rectangular distribution is a frequency distribution in which each score occurs with equal frequency.

In the Reynolds example the midpoint or average of the class 6–11 is 8.5, for the class 12–17 it is 14.5, and so on. Whether we use these apparent class intervals or the true class intervals does not affect the midpoint; the midpoint of 5.5–11.5 is also 8.5. A frequency polygon for the extinction scores of the LD group in the Reynolds experiment is shown in Figure 2.3. It should be

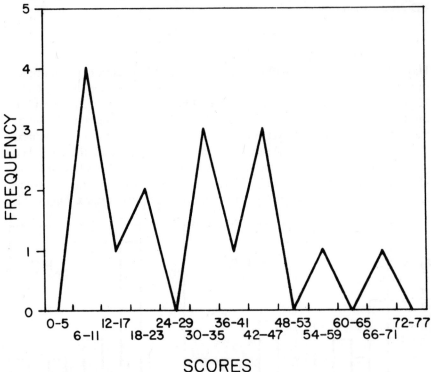

Figure 2.3. A frequency polygon of the extinction scores for the LD group.

noted that in the construction of this frequency polygon that an extra class, 0–5, has been added to the low end of the distribution and another class, 72–77, to the high end and that the straight line was drawn down to the baseline for these two classes. Guilford (1956) had discussed the advantages and disadvantages of histograms and frequency polygons. He prefers the frequency polygon because it reveals the contour of the data better and provides a clearer picture when two distributions are plotted on the same baseline. Whenever one has a number of observations, say 30 or more, it is often valuable to take a few moments and "plot the data" with either a histogram or frequency polygon. These representations give indications as to the scatter of the scores, their central tendency, and the shape of the distribution. In constructing these figures, time may be saved by using graph paper.

Measures of Central Tendency

While a histogram or frequency polygon may impart considerable information, we want a single number that describes the center of the distribution.
The most commonly-used number is the mean (M) or "average". Since the
so-called average is well understood in everyday life, we may proceed to its
determination. The formula is:

$$M = \frac{\Sigma X}{N}.$$

The Greek letter Σ (Sigma) denotes the operation of summing. X refers to
our scores and N signifies the number of scores. Thus the formula says:
Add all of the scores and divide by the number of scores. If we apply this
procedure to the LD scores in Table 2.3, we have:

$$M = \frac{6 + 7 + 10 + \dots + 68}{16} = \frac{487}{16} = 30.44.$$

Except when there are a great many observations, this formula is convenient.
If a desk calculator or adding machine is available, ΣX can readily be obtained.

Another average or measure of central tendency is the *median* (Mdn). It
is that *point* in a distribution at or below which half of the cases fall. There
are nongrouped- and grouped-data methods for finding the median. The
grouped-data method is useful when there are a large number of observations
or when duplication of scores occurs near the median.

In the nongrouped method the scores are first arranged in order of their
size. For example, the data in Table 2.3 are presented in this fashion. If the
number of scores, N, is *odd*, then the Mdn is the $(N + 1)/2$ score. If the number
of scores, N, is *even*, then the median is the point halfway between the
$(N/2)$ and $(N/2) + 1$ scores. In the data for LD in Table 2.3 the $N = 16$. The
$(N/2)$ or 8th score is 30. The $(N/2) + 1$ or 9th score is 33. The Mdn of this set
of scores is $(30 + 33)/2$ or 31.5.

To exemplify the determination of the median when N is odd, let us imagine
that the first observation, 6, is missing from the LD group. Now N is 15.
The $(N + 1)/2$ or 8th score in the ordered series is the Mdn and it is 33.

This is a good place to point out one important advantage of the median
over the mean as an indication of central tendency. The median is less
affected by extreme scores than the mean. Suppose that we replace the last
observation, 68, in the LD group by a score of 200. The Mdn value remains
the same. It is still the half-way point between the $(N/2)$ and $(N/2) + 1$ scores
or 31.5. The mean, on the other hand, is now greatly increased:

$$M = \frac{\Sigma X}{N} = \frac{619}{16} = 38.69.$$

The lesson is clear: extreme scores have profound effects upon the mean. This is a critical statistical problem but since extreme scores also influence measures of variability, we shall consider this problem in detail after measures of variability are examined.

In order to apply the grouped-data method of calculating the median, a new column of cumulative frequencies, *cf*, will be added to the frequency distribution of scores for the LD group (Table 2.4). The *cf* for each class is

Table 2.4.   Cumulative Frequency Distribution for the LD Group

Class	f	cf
6–11	4	4
12–17	1	5
18–23	2	7
24–29	0	7
30–35	3	10
36–41	1	11
42–47	3	14
48–53	0	14
54–59	1	15
60–65	0	15
66–71	1	16

the frequency for that class plus the frequencies for the prior classes. Note that the *cf* value for the last class is 16 which is the same as N. The median is the point half way between the $(N/2)$ and $(N/2)+1$ scores. Since these values are the 8th and 9th scores, respectively, the median is somewhere in the 30–35 class, which is termed the *median class*. Let us assume that the scores in the median class; fMdn, are evenly distributed in this class. Then the Mdn can be determined by the following formula:

$$Mdn = l + \frac{(N/2) - cfa}{f\,Mdn}\, i.$$

The symbol l is the lower limit of the median class, *cfa* is the cumulative frequency above the median class, and i is the class interval size. The median is:

$$Mdn = 29.5 + \left(\frac{(16/2) - 7}{3}\right)6 = 31.5.$$

Another average is the *mode*. It is defined as the most frequently occurring score. Thus in Figure 2.1 the mode is 7 pairs of words for the male Ss and 6 pairs for the female Ss. The mode is little used except as a quick indication of the central tendency. Like the median it has the advantage of not being affected by extreme scores. However, modern analysis is generally oriented towards the mean and we shall follow this trend.

Measures of Variability

The above measures, the mean, median, and mode, describe the center of a distribution. They do not, however, provide any information regarding the spread or scatter of the scores. Consider the hypothetical frequency polygrams in Figure 2.4. In Figure 2.4 A the two groups have the same means but

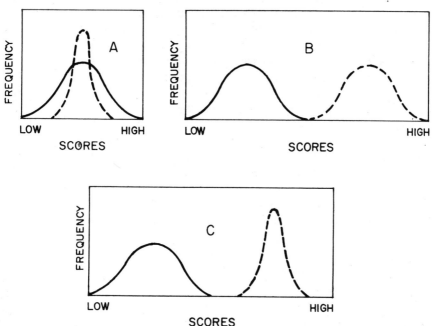

Figure 2.4. Hypothetical frequency polygons showing (A) equal means and unequal variances, (B) unequal means and equal variances, and (C) unequal means and variances.

the scores scatter more for the group designated by the solid line. In Figure 2.4 B the variability is the same in the two groups but the mean for the group denoted by the dashed line is larger. In Figure 2.4 C the groups differ in both central tendency and variability; the mean of the dash-line group is larger but its scores are less variable.

Older books on statistics often include a number of indices of variability: the range, interquartile range, the average deviation, and the standard deviation. Today, the most important and widely used index of variability is the standard deviation, s, and, accordingly, it will be considered in detail below.

The first index of variability, the range, has already been mentioned. It is of limited value because it is derived from only the highest and lowest scores. As a general principle, indices based on fewer scores are less reliable than those based on all of the scores.

The median was previously defined as the point in a distribution at or below which half of the cases fall. The median can also be designated as the second quartile, Q_2. Following the logic for the calculation for Q_2, Q_1, and Q_3 can be determined. Q_1 is defined as the point in a distribution at or below which one-quarter of the cases fall. And Q_3 is the point at or below which three quarters of the cases fall. The difference between Q_3 and Q_1 is another index of variability, the *interquartile range*.

These ideas are often encountered in reports of test scores. The 90th percentile is the point at or below which 90 % of the cases fall. Similarly, Q_1, Q_2, and Q_3 can be called the 25th, 50th, and 75th percentiles, respectively. And various percentile ranges can be employed as indices of variability, e.g., the difference between the 90th and 10th percentile, etc. The advantage of percentile ranges as measures of variability is the same as that of the median: they are unaffected by extreme scores. Despite this advantage, the current trend in data analysis is to eliminate extreme scores in some way so as to utilize the standard deviation as an index of variability.

The *average deviation, AD*, is the average of the absolute deviations or differences of the mean from the scores. Absolute is symbolized by two heavy vertical bars and refers to the operation of ignoring the signs of the differences. The reason for ignoring the signs is that the algebraic sum of the differences would be equal to 0 and thereby provide no meaningful measure of variability. The formula for the *AD* is:

$$AD = \frac{\Sigma \, |X - M|}{N}.$$

The formula says: subtract the mean from every score; regard all the differences as positive; sum the absolute differences; and divide by the number of scores.

At this point, let us raise two questions about the average deviation. First, what interpretation can be made of the average deviation? Second, what is wrong with the average deviation as a measure of variability? The average deviation tells us how the scores scatter about the mean. More precisely, approximately 58 % of the cases are included within the limits of the mean plus or minus one average deviation, $M \pm AD$, (Guilford, 1956). The qualification "approximately" is added because this statement is true only in the case of large samples whose distributions are bell-shaped. In Table 2.1 the mean pairs of words for male Ss is 6.5 and the *AD* is (66/32) or 2.1. We would anticipate that about 58 % of the scores would fall between 6.5

± 2.1 or between 4.4 and 8.6. Second, the average deviation has three weaknesses: (a) it is affected by extreme scores; (b) it is a less reliable index than the standard deviation; and (c) while the standard deviation is a part of more elaborate and useful statistical techniques, the average deviation is not. Regarding the second deficiency (b), if an experiment were repeated a large number of times, then the average deviations, calculated for each replication, would be found to vary more than the standard deviations for the same experiments.

The most common measure of variability is the *standard deviation, s*. Computationally, s resembles the AD which, as we have seen, is an average of absolute deviations from the mean. There are, however, important differences between AD and s. In the case of s, the problem of the signs of deviations is solved by squaring the deviations and thereby rendering them all positive. To provide a better estimate of the *population standard deviation*, σ, from which the sample was randomly drawn, the squared deviations are divided by $N-1$ rather than N. Finally, the square root of the result is taken. The formula for s is then:

$$s = \sqrt{\frac{\Sigma(X - M)^2}{N - 1}}.$$

This formula says: subtract the mean from a score; square the difference; repeat for all scores; sum the squared deviations; divide by the number of scores minus one; and take the square root of the result.

Subtracting the mean from every score is tedious unless the samples are small. Accordingly, this step can be by-passed by employing a longer but handier formula. Since $\Sigma(X - M)^2 = \Sigma X^2 - (\Sigma X)^2/N$, then a formula for s, which does not require obtaining deviations is:

$$s = \sqrt{\frac{\Sigma X^2 - (\Sigma X)^2/N}{N - 1}}$$

This formula says: square every score; sum the squared scores; sum the scores; square the sum of the scores; divide the square of the summed scores by the number of scores; subtract this quantity from the sum of the squared scores; divide the result by the number of scores minus one; and take the square root of the answer. The verbal description sounds forbidding but with a table of squares the actual procedure is not. And with a simple desk calculator, squaring the scores by the cumulative multiplication key yields both ΣX and ΣX^2 in one operation. Let us calculate (see Table 2.5) the standard deviation for the LD group in Table 2.3 using a table of squares (Table A, Appendix).

*Table 2.5.   Table for Calculation of
the Standard Deviation for LD Group*

S	X	X^2
1	6	36
2	7	49
3	10	100
4	11	121
5	17	289
6	19	361
7	22	484
8	30	900
9	33	1089
10	35	1225
11	41	1681
12	42	1764
13	42	1764
14	45	2025
15	59	3481
16	68	4624
	$\Sigma X = 487$	$\Sigma X^2 = 19993$

$$s = \sqrt{\frac{19993 - (487)^2/16}{16 - 1}}$$

$$= \sqrt{344.66}$$

$$= 18.57$$

As was true for the average deviation, the mean plus or minus one standard deviation will include a certain percentage of the scores. In the case of the standard deviation, if N is large and the scores are normally distributed, then 68.26% of the scores will fall within the limits, $M \pm s$. Thus in the LD group approximately two-thirds of the scores would be expected to fall between 30.44 ± 18.57 or between 11.87 and 49.01. The estimate, two-thirds, is a useful one to remember. Since many distributions observed in research are not normal, the two-thirds figure is precise enough.

At this point, it is appropriate to introduce three fundamental concepts that we will encounter frequently later on. These concepts are the *sum of squares*, *degrees of freedom*, and *variance*. The sum of squares, SS, is equal to the sum of the squared deviations from the mean, i.e., $SS = \Sigma(X - M)^2$. Or to employ the more convenient formula, $SS = \Sigma X^2 - (\Sigma X)^2/N$. Degrees of freedom, *df*, is a divisor that yields a modified average of the sum of the squared deviations. As a general principle, the *df* is one less than the number of squared deviations $(N - 1)$. The variance, s^2, is the result of dividing the SS, by *df*. The s^2 is, of course, the square of the standard deviation, *s*. Like *s*, s^2 is an index of variability. In the next chapter, we will be concerned with the determination of the total variance of a set of observations, the partitioning of this total variance into its components, and relating these components to one another.

Previously it was pointed out that indices of variability like Q_3-Q_1 and percentile ranges like the 90th percentile–the 10th percentile are relatively unaffected by extreme scores. The obvious reason for this statement is that the magnitudes of the extreme scores are not included in the calculation of interquartile or percentile ranges. On the other hand, the average deviation, which incorporates every score in its determination, is influenced by extreme observations. In a like manner the standard deviation and variance are affected by unusually large and small observations in the tails of the distribution of scores. In fact, these indices of variability are weighted heavily by such "outliers" because the deviations from the mean are squared (Guilford, 1956). We may document this assertion by replacing the largest score of 68 in the LD group in Table 2.5 with a score of 200 and recalculating the standard deviation. Under these conditions *s* is 45.77. Thus this single extreme observation results in a standard deviation that is over twice the size of the original standard deviation (45.77 vs 18.57). If we consider the s^2 instead of *s*, then the extreme score has produced over a six-fold increase in variance. Not only is the magnitude of the standard deviation greatly increased but also rather strange things occur. If we find the limits, $M \pm s$, they now are: 38.69 ± 45.77 or between -7.08 and 84.46. Rather than the expected one-third of the scores falling between the *M* and $M-s$ (38.69 and -7.08), over half of the scores fall between these values.

As we said in the beginning of this section, we are seeking numbers that describe the center of a distribution of scores and the variability of the distribution. The two most reliable indices are the mean and the standard deviation. However, to repeat, these indices are badly distorted by the presence of even a single extreme observation. On the other hand, indices like the median and interquartile range are unaffected by extreme scores, but they are less reliable. We shall examine this dilemma more fully in the next section.

A further related difficulty involves the assumptions which must be made in applying certain statistical techniques. Later we shall be interested in comparing the means of two or more groups. In certain statistical tests it is assumed: (a) that the sets of observations being compared come from normally distributed populations; and (b) that the variances of the scores in these populations are equal. The latter assumption implies that the variances do not vary beyond chance deviation. The presence of extreme observations in certain groups can greatly distort variances in these groups. Having stated these problems, let us turn to a discussion of the kinds of data that are commonly encountered in research, the use of transformations to normalize data and equalize variances, the detection of extreme observations, and how to deal with them.

"Spotty" Data

The pretty bell-shaped distributions that decorate statistical textbooks are rarely encountered in the world of research. Tukey (1962) has aptly described much actual data as "spotty." The distributions of such scores frequently lack symmetry, there are "holes" in distributions, and extreme scores, termed outliers or "wild shots," are seen. Mosteller and Tukey have commented: "Real distributions often straggle a lot compared to a

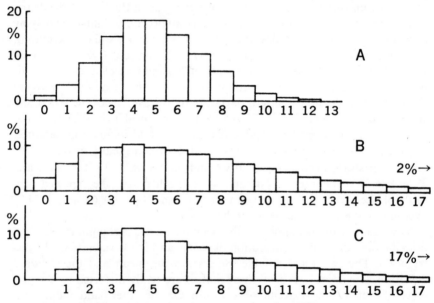

Figure 2.5. Types of skew distributions (Quenouille, 1950).

*Reprinted by permission of the publisher from M. H. Quenouille, *Introductory Statistics,* p. 174. Copyright 1950, Butterworths.

normal distribution" (1968, p. 89). In other words, real data are frequently not peaked enough, there are too many observations in the tails, and often some of these observations are wild shots.

Mosteller and Tukey (1968) have described four kinds of departures from normality: (a) discreteness and irregularity; (b) gross differences in shape; (c) minor differences in central shape; and (d) behavior in the tails. The problem of discreteness often arises because the scores are multiples of some count rather than being scores that take on an infinite number of values. For example, the scores in Table 2.1 and 2.3 are whole numbers like 6, 9, 11, etc. rather than numbers like 2.74, 6.41, and so on. Irregularity or "jaggedness" in moderate form is revealed in Figure 2.3.

Some examples of gross differences in shape are rectangular distributions in which each score occurs with equal frequency and skewed distributions of various kinds. A rectangular distribution is symmetrical. If the distribution is folded at its middle, nothing hangs out. If an asymmetrical or skewed distribution is folded at the middle, the two halves do not coincide. Skewed distributions can often be detected by "eyeballing" or visually inspecting them. Another method is to compare the mean to the median of the distribution. The mean is pulled by extreme scores in the tail of a distribution toward that tail. If the mean is greater than the median ($M >$ Mdn), the distribution is skewed positively or skewed to the right. If the mean is less than the median ($M <$ Mdn), the distribution is skewed negatively or skewed to the left.

In Figure 2.5 are three positively skewed distributions from Quenouille (1950). As we go from Figure 2.5 A to 2.5 C the distributions are increasingly skewed. Instead of analyzing the original skewed data, data can sometimes be normalized by a transformation, which means changing the scale of measurement. Quenouille suggests that a square-root transformation should be applied to distributions like 2.5 A, a logarithmic transformation to 2.5 B, and a reciprocal transformation to 2.5 C. The effect of these transformations is, in varying degrees, to pull in the extreme scores on the right hand tails.

Table 2.6.   Transformed Scores for
Female Ss in Table 2.2

X	$\sqrt{X+0.5}$	$log_{10}X$	$1/X$
3	1.871	0.4771	0.3333
4	2.121	0.6021	0.2500
5	2.345	0.6990	0.2000
6	2.550	0.7782	0.1667
7	2.739	0.8451	0.1429
8	2.915	0.9031	0.1250
9	3.082	0.9542	0.1111
13	3.674	1.1139	0.0769

In Table 2.6 the scores for the female Ss in Table 2.2 have been transformed to $\sqrt{X+0.5}$, $log_{10}X$, and $1/X$ by using Tables A and B from the Appendix.

When the data from more than one group are available, comparisons of the groups' means and variances or standard deviations offer clues as to the most suitable transformation to apply. The following rules have been suggested by Edwards (1960). (a) When the mean in each group is equal to the variance, then a $\sqrt{X+0.5}$ transformation is appropriate. (b) When the means and standard deviations tend to be proportional, then a $\log_{10} X$ transformation is applicable. In instances in which there are scores of 0, $\log_{10}(X+1)$ is used. (c) If the variance increases with the mean but out of proportion, then $1/X$ transformation is called for. This situation is often evident when the behavioral measures are time scores, e.g., running times for rats. The presence of some extremely long response times will induce a disproportionality in the increase of means and variances. It should be noted that the scale of measurement is reversed with a reciprocal transformation. Very large raw scores are transformed into very small reciprocal scores and vice versa. Although it is uncommon to find 0 scores, when they appear the transformation $1/(X+1)$ is necessary.

In Table 2.7 some hypothetical data are presented for which $\sqrt{X+0.5}$ (condition A), $\log_{10} X$ (condition B), and $1/X$ (condition C) are the appropriate transformations.

Table 2.7. *Hypothetical Data for (A)*
$\sqrt{X+0.5}$, *(B)* $\log_{10} X$, *and (C)* $1/X$
Transformations

Condition		Groups		
		1	2	3
A	M	2	8	16
	s^2	2	8	16
B	M	2	8	16
	s	4	16	32
C	M	2	8	16
	s^2	4	20	60

Another transformation, an arcsin or $2 \sin^{-1} \sqrt{X}$, is applied to data that are in the form of percentages or proportions (see Table C, Appendix). When the X scores are proportions, they have a potential range from .001 to .999 while the transformed scores range from .0633 to 3.0783. All of the foregoing transformations, properly applied, may produce two desired consequences: (a) normalizing distributions; and (b) equalizing variances.

The third type of departure from normality listed by Mosteller and Tukey (1968) is minor differences in central shape. This form of normality is said to be inseparable from (a) discreteness and irregularity and (b) gross departures from normality, above, and relatively unimportant in its own right. Accordingly, we shall proceed to the fourth type of departure, (d) behavior in the tails. Regarding this type of departure. Mosteller and Tukey say: "[it is] hard to detect, yet often important because a few straggling values scattered far from the bulk of the measurement can, for example, alter a sample mean drastically, and a sample s^2 catastrophically" (1968, p. 93). It should be made clear that we are not concerned here with skewed distributions but with wild shots, isolated observations in the tails. Such aberrant scores can, as was demonstrated earlier, displace means and greatly enlarge variances.

In coping with wild shots, there are three important questions: (a) How to detect a wild shot? (b) What to do with a wild shot? (c) What does a wild shot mean? As we shall learn, the latter two questions are intimately related. Although the problem of detecting wild shots has worried statisticians since the turn of the century, there is no generally agreed-upon method of detection. We shall employ a test for extreme scores which was devised by Dixon (1953; see Dixon & Massey, 1957, pp. 275 ff.). One virtue of Dixon's test is its simplicity. The test consists of finding the ratio of two ranges. The range in the numerator is the difference between the second score in the ordered series of scores and the suspected wild shot, $X_2 - X_1$. The range in the denominator is the total range of scores, the difference between last score in the ordered series and the suspected wild shot, $X_k - X_1$. As the number of scores increases, the two ranges that are compared are modified slightly. For example, if there are 14 to 30 scores, the ratio is: $X_3 - X_1/X_{k-2} - X_1$. Again, X_1 is the possible outlier, X_3 is the third score in the ordered series and X_{k-2} is the next-to-the-next-to last score. If the obtained ratio of the ranges, R, is sufficiently large as determined by comparing it with the critical values in Dixon's table (Table D, Appendix), then we would conclude *provisionally*, that the wild shot is indeed a wild one! If the obtained ratio is less than the critical value, then we have no evidence to treat the wild shot as being any different from any other observation in the set.

Let us apply this procedure to the data in Table 2.3 for the HD group. Is the observation, 47, a wild shot? Before doing this, it is important to point out that X_1 *always* denotes the suspected extreme observation. If the extreme observation, X_1, is the smallest score, then X_k is the largest score in the ordered set. Conversely, if the extreme observation, X_1, is the largest score, then X_k is the smallest score in the ordered set. In the present example, X_1 is the largest score, therefore, X_k is the smallest. Thus $X_1 = 47, X_3 = 28$, and $X_{k-2} = 7$. Since $N = 16$, the appropriate ratio formula (cf. Table D) is:

$$R = \frac{X_3 - X_1}{X_{k-2} - X_1} = \frac{28 - 47}{7 - 47} = \frac{-19}{-40} = .475.$$

Since the obtained R value of .475 does not equal or exceed the critical 5% R value of .507 for $N = 16$ in Dixon's table, we would not be justified in treating the observation of 47 as a wild shot.

Suppose, however, the last observation were 67 instead of 47. Now we would have:

$$R = \frac{X_3 - X_1}{X_{k-2} - X_1} = \frac{28 - 67}{7 - 67} = \frac{-39}{-60} = .650.$$

This R value of .650 does exceed the critical 5% R value of .507. In fact, it is larger than critical 1% value of .595. Therefore, we would deem the observation of 67 to be a wild shot.

It's one thing to locate a wild shot but another to know what to do with it! Miller has summarized the three main courses of action towards wild shots that have been proposed by Tukey (1962) and others (Mosteller & Tukey, 1968):

1. *Ignore:* Simply forget that the outlier is strange as compared with the other observations and proceed with the analysis.

2. *Trim:* Discard the outlier from the sample and proceed with the analysis.

3. *Winsorize:* Replace the value of the outlying observation by the nearest non-outlying observation and proceed with the analysis (Miller, 1966, p. 214).

Prior to discussing these alternative ways of handling wild shots, let us consider the third question: What does a wild shot mean? This is a troublesome question but the answer is simple: we don't know! Dixon and Massey assert: "Such extreme observations, or *outliers*, may occur because of *gross errors*, or *blunders*, or may be from a population other than the population from which the rest of the data comes, or may result from the fact that the population under investigation contains a certain proportion of extreme cases and our sample happens to include one" (1957, p. 275).

Imagine an hypothetical experiment in which a wild shot, as assessed by Dixon's test, is observed. Suppose further that it results from an experimenter's erroneous reading of an instrument. In this case the correct solution is *trim* – throw out the wild shot. On the other hand, the wild shot might represent a genuine effect of the experimental variable. That is, the variable in question may reliably produce some extreme scores. In this case, the correct solution is to *ignore*. If we trimmed, we would be discarding a "real" effect. The point is that the meaning of a wild shot is often indeterminate for a single experiment. In view of this uncertainty, how shall we proceed? (a) We will avoid the *ignore* solution because the presence of outliers greatly distorts such indices as the mean and variance. The sole exception is when replications of the experiment, and especially independent replications, keep reporting the same wild shots. (b) The *trim* tactic may be employed in a modified form by dropping the same number of cases from each end of the distribution (Tukey, 1962). (c) The *Winsorize* solution (named in honor of the late Charles P. Winsor) consists of replacing the outlier by the nearest nonsuspect observation. In the earlier hypothetical example, 67 was found to be a wild shot. The nearest observation to it is 33 which, by inspection does not deviate from the bulk of scores in Table 2.3. Therefore, we would replace 67 with 33 and proceed with the analysis. If the score nearest to the outlier appeared to be a long way from the bulk of the scores, we could test it by Dixon's method. If it were also a wild shot, then it would also be replaced. If not, it would be substituted for the outlier of 67. One appealing feature of Winsor's treatment of wild shots is that the N is not altered. It should be stressed that the application of solution (b) or (c) is contingent upon a demonstration by Dixon's test that the outliers are aberrant observations.

Reviewing the Bidding

In this chapter we have covered considerable ground: the strategy of multiple-analysis; pictorial and numerical representations of data; and the problem of spotty data. Let us return for a moment to multiple-analysis. The student should feel free to wander through his data. While he may benefit from seeing how other research workers have dealt with similar observations, he should feel no constraints about trying new ways of looking at the data. Is there another way to graph the data? If the data were "broken" along another variable, would some new relationship emerge? We mentioned transformations above as devices to normalize data and equalize variances. Transformations can also be utilized to produce simpler relationships. Does one of those transformations lead to a simpler relationship? In short, the student should be encouraged to be bold and creative in his analysis of data, but cautious with respect to drawing conclusions.

PROBLEMS

1. Using the 72 scores in Table 3.3 (p. 40) and an $i = 1$, make a histogram.
2. Given the 16 scores in Table 2.3 (p. 10) for the HD group, find the M, Mdn, and Mode.
3. Is this distribution skewed? How do you know?
4. With the same data as for problem 2, find s.
5. With the same data as for problem 2 and an $i = 4$, make a frequency polygon.
6. Using the 12 scores for the CR–pr Ss in Table 3.17 (p. 76), test the score 114 for extremeness ($p = .05$). Is the score 62 a wild shot? How would you Winsorize this set of scores?
7. Consider the data in Table 3.3 (p. 40). Should these scores be transformed? If so, how? If not, why?

CHAPTER THREE

Steps to Inference:
I. Numbers

... the experimenter and statistician find themselves, willing or not, being pushed in the direction of multiple inference. – R. G. Miller

A Single Mean

A common undertaking in research is to compare the means of two or more groups. Prior to an examination of these kinds of comparisons, we shall look at a simpler case in which we want to test the mean of a group, M, against a theoretical mean, M_T. The theoretical mean might be the known mean of the population from which the sample in question was randomly drawn or it might be a value expected on the basis of a particular theory.

Let us consider a concrete example. Klein (1959) reported the numbers of turns to a particular goal box in a T-maze for a group of 12 rats. Since 20 trials were run, the Ss, if responding by chance, would be expected to turn toward the particular goal box 10 times and to turn 10 times to the alternative box. Thus the theoretical mean would be 10. The question being asked is: Was the actual mean significantly larger than the $M_T = 10$? The actual M found by Klein (see Table 3.1) was $\Sigma X/N = 134/12 = 11.17$. Since the Mdn is 11.5, the distribution is only slightly skewed to the left (i.e., Mdn > M) and it appears to be approximately rectangular in shape. Calculating the standard deviation by the longer formula from Chapter 2, we have:

$$s = \sqrt{\frac{\Sigma X^2 - (\Sigma X)^2/N}{N-1}} = \sqrt{\frac{1544 - (134)^2/12}{12-1}} = 2.08.$$

As was indicated earlier, we would anticipate that about two-thirds of the observed scores would fall within the limits of $M \pm s$ or 11.17 ± 2.08. This statement would not, however, answer the question that has been raised.

To deal with the question we must introduce a fundamental concept, *the standard error of the mean, s_M*. If the student grasps the meaning of a standard error, he will have taken a major step in understanding the process of statistical inference. Let us first define s_M and then try to make this definition more explicit. *The standard error of the mean is the standard deviation of a sampling distribution of means*. We know what a standard deviation is, but what is a sampling distribution of means? A sampling distribution of means is a fre-

Table 3.1.* Number of Entries into
Training Box (Klein, 1959)

S	100% Group X	X^2
1	14	196
2	14	196
3	13	169
4	12	144
5	12	144
6	12	144
7	11	121
8	11	121
9	10	100
10	9	81
11	8	64
12	8	64
	$\Sigma X = 134$	$\Sigma X^2 = 1544$

*Reprinted by permission of the publisher and author from R. M. Klein, "Intermittent Primary Reinforcement as Parameter of Secondary Reinforcement." *Journal of Experimental Psychology*, 58, p. 424. Copyright 1959, American Psychological Association.

quency distribution of means that would be obtained from a large number of replications of an experiment. For example, we might randomly select samples of 12 Ss and repeat the Klein experiment 1000 times. Each time the experiment is done, we could calculate a mean number of turns to the particular goal box for the 12 Ss. We could then construct a frequency distribution of these 1000 means. This hypothetical distribution is termed a *sampling distribution*. We could also calculate the standard deviation of the sampling distribution of 1000 means. The standard deviation of the 1000 means *is* the standard error of the mean.

Luckily, we don't have to carry out this laborious task to obtain s_M

because statisticians have provided a simple formula for estimating s_M:

$$s_M = \frac{s}{\sqrt{N}}.$$

In this formula s is based on our sample of 12 scores and N is 12. Thus for Klein's data: $s_M = 2.08/\sqrt{12} = .60$.

At this point, let us sum up what we know in Figure 3.1. This hypothetical figure represents a sampling distribution of means with $M_T = 10$ and

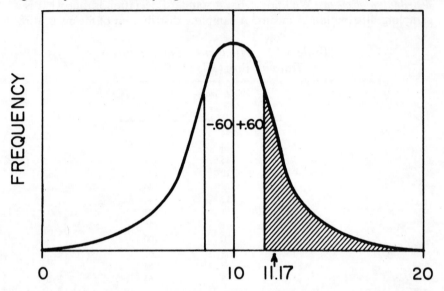

MEAN NUMBER OF TURNS TO GOAL BOX

Figure 3.1. Hypothetical sampling distribution of means.

$s_M = .60$. We know that about two-thirds of the means would fall within $M_T \pm s_M$, $10 \pm .60$ or between 9.40 and 10.60. The $M = 11.17$ found by Klein falls well outside of these limits and, therefore, it is unusually large. Is it sufficiently large for us to say that it deviates significantly from $M_T = 10$?

Suppose the $M = 10.60$. Then how often would a value this large or larger occur? "How often" is determined by the frequency of means in the shaded area in the right-hand tail of Figure 3.1. One-third of the means would be expected to fall in the two tails. Therefore, one-sixth (one-third/2) of the means would be expected to fall at or beyond 10.60. In other words, to decide whether or not an event (e.g., $M = 10.60$) is significant, we have to know how often it might happen by chance. If it occurs 1 out of 6 times, we aren't too impressed. But if it happens say, 5 times out of 100 or 1 time out of 100 or less, we are inclined, conventionally, to regard the outcome as quite unusual and, therefore, significant.

Thus the question now becomes: How often would a $M = 11.17$ be expected to occur when $M_T = 10$ and $s_M = .60$? We know that it is less than one-sixth of the time, but precisely how often?

Once again, a statistician, W. S. Gosset, has come to our rescue. Gosset (1927), writing under the name of "Student," proposed a formula for this situation:

$$t = \frac{M - M_T}{s_M}.$$

By calculating t and referring the obtained t value to a table, it is possible to learn how often M would be expected to occur. In this instance $t = (11.17 - 10)/.60 = 1.95$. The t table (Table E, Appendix) summarizes a family of curves, the horizontal axis of which corresponds to t values and the vertical axis to their frequencies of occurrence. The curves, for various degrees of freedom, df, are symmetrical, approximately bell-shaped, and have mean t – values $= 0$. Previously we defined df as one less than the number of squared deviations; with Klein's group of $N = 12$ the df would be $N - 1$ or 11. To evaluate the $t = 1.95$ we have to enter the t table with df of 11. The probability of $t = 1.95$ falls between .05 ($t = 1.796$) and .025 ($t = 2.201$). This means that between 5 and 2.5 times out of 100 by chance we would expect a t value as large or larger than 1.95. (Or that between 5 and 2.5 times out of 100 we would expect a $M = 11.17$ from a population with $M_T = 10$). If we decide to call an event unusual when it happens 5 or less times by chance in a 100, then the $M = 11.17$ is an unusual event. We may assert that the $M = 11.17$ is significantly different from a $M_T = 10$. In statistical parlance, we would accept the hypothesis being assessed, *viz.*, $M > M_T$.

In this example we have performed what is referred to as a *one-tailed test* of significance. This type of test is appropriate only under two conditions: (a) when assessing the results of a replication experiment; and (b) when testing a specific directional prediction derived from a well-articulated theory. In each condition we are interested in a difference between means in a specific direction. The Klein example is an instance of (a) and a difference in the other direction, i.e., $M < M_T$, would immediately falsify the hypothesis, $M > M_T$, under investigation. In a one-tailed test only one particular tail of the t distribution is employed to assess the frequency of occurrence by chance of the event in question. In effect, we are asking the question: Is a difference in means *in a specified direction* significant?

A more frequently used test of significance is a *two-tailed test*. Here we are asking the question: Is a difference in means, *whatever its direction*, significant? Instead of testing the hypothesis, $M > M_T$, we would test both

$M > M_T$ and $M < M_T$. In the case of a two-tailed test of significance, both tails of the t distribution are utilized in the determination of the unusualness of the event. For our problem, the two-tailed probability of a $t = 1.95$ with $df = 11$ falls between .10 and .05. That is to say, a t this large would be expected by chance between 10 and 5 times out of 100 occasions. Since we have decided that an event is rare, if and only if it is observed 5 or fewer times in 100, we have found no convincing evidence that $M > M_T$. The two-tailed test is disadvantageous because it requires a larger t value than a one-tailed test for a comparable level of significance but possesses a decided advantage in generality. A large difference in either direction, either $M > M_T$ or $M < M_T$, can be taken by the experimenter as an indication. In the one-tailed procedure, on the other hand, a difference in the wrong direction, no matter how large, falsifies the hypothesis. In view of the immature state of theoretical development in most areas of psychology, it follows that for the bulk of research two-tailed tests of significance are appropriate.

Every experiment embodies a lot of hypotheses which have been called *auxiliary hypotheses* (Mandler & Kessen, 1959). For example, the physical principles underlying the operation of the electronic and mechanical apparatus used are presumed to hold and the apparatus is presumed to perform reliably. Furthermore, various statistical techniques embody assumptions. For instance, the t test involves the assumptions that: (a) the sample has been randomly selected from a normally distributed population; and (b) the observations are independent of one another. Sometimes a third assumption is stipulated: (c) that the observations are made with at least an *interval* scale (Stevens, 1951).

Let us consider these assumptions briefly. Since the shape of the parent population is generally not known, various stances have been taken towards (a). First, some investigators have relied upon the *central limit theorem* to minimize the importance of (a). According to this theorem, indices such as the mean tend to be normally distributed as N increases regardless of the shape of the parent population. The crucial question here is: Is our N large enough that we can assume that the probability values obtained from tables of test distributions, like the t table, are correct? If the t table reveals that a difference is significant at the .05 level, or could occur by chance 5 times in 100, is this information accurate? Suppose instead, that 10 times in 100 is the true state of affairs? Second, these matters have been approached by sampling studies to determine actually how various shapes of populations affect the tabled probability values. We shall consider some of these sampling studies in the next section. Third, faced with these uncertainties some research workers have elected to apply another class of statistical techniques termed *distribution-free* or *nonparametric* methods, which entail different assumptions. We shall describe some of these methods in later chapters.

The assumption of independence (b) means simply that one observation is not affected by another. For example, it means that the score for S1 in Klein's experiment is not influenced by the score for S2, etc. Actually in Klein's experiment there were 72 rats, and we have selected the data for only one group. Regarding the Ss, Klein states: "They were randomly divided into six groups of 12 each" (1959, p. 424). Because of this random-assignment procedure we would not anticipate that the independence assumption was violated. As we shall see shortly, dependence among observations may exist when the repeated observations from the same Ss are analyzed or when the Ss are matched on some variable. Later we shall take up techniques for analyzing such dependent data. Although the tenability of the independence assumption may be readily checked by finding out whether or not the Ss were randomly assigned to the experimental treatments, the importance of this assumption should not be minimized. Violation of the independence assumption can lead to gross errors in inference (Hays, 1963).

A few additional comments are in order concerning assumptions (a) and (b). In most psychological experiments the notion of a "random" sample is a myth. A research worker who orders rats from an animal dealer does not receive a random sample of all 90–120-day-old Sprague-Dawley rats, he gets what the supplier selects from his available supply. Likewise, a research worker in verbal learning does not employ a random sample of this semester's supply of introductory psychology students – instead his sample is a group of Ss who happen to "volunteer" for this particular experiment. What complex of variables prompts these Ss to "volunteer" or the animal supplier to select a batch of rats is unknown, but we can be sure that they are not random samples. Once we have a sample, we can fulfill the assumption of independence (b) by randomly assigning our Ss to the various experimental conditions. But randomly assigning a nonrandom sample of Ss to the treatments is *not* the same operation as obtaining a random sample.

Stevens (1951) and others (e.g., Siegel, 1956) have argued (c) that the use of certain statistical techniques requires that our dependent or behavioral variable must be measured on at least an interval scale. The classification of scales into *nominal, ordinal, interval,* and *ratio* was originally proposed by the physicist, N. R. Campbell (1938). In nominal measurement, the most primitive form, we have classes into which persons or objects are placed. Examples of two nominal scales would be political party affiliation and the diagnostic groups assigned by psychiatrists. In ordinal scales the classes may be ordered. For example, the hardness of a set of minerals can be determined by finding which specimens can scratch other specimens. A final scale might look like this: specimen $A >$ specimen $B >$ specimen C, etc. Here the symbol $>$ means "can scratch" or "is harder than." Note that we cannot say anything about the distance in hardness between the specimens. In interval scaling we not only have ordered classes, but also equal units and an arbitrary zero point. Thus, if one had an interval scale of hardness, it might be possible to say that the hardness of specimen A is, for example, 3, B is 5, C is 6, and so on. That is, we would say that two units of hardness separate A and B but only one unit of hardness separates specimens B and C. Common examples of interval measurement are Fahrenheit and centigrade temperature scales. In the highest form of measurement, ratio scales, we have, in addition to the characteristics of nominal, ordinal, and interval measurement, a "true" or absolute zero point. Examples of such scales are absolute temperature, length, weight, etc. Stevens has nicely summarized the requirements of the four types of scales as possessing four relations: "equality, rank order, equality of intervals, and equality of ratios" (1951, p. 28). In nominal scales we have only the single operation of equality – the things in a class are alike. Whereas for the highest form of measurement, a ratio scale, all four relations exist.

How concerned should we be with these scaling problems in relation to data analysis? Not too much! As Tukey has put it: "Campbellian measurement has scared us far too long" (1969, p. 87). Rather than worrying about whether or not we have an interval scale, attention should be directed to two other matters: (a) establishing the replicability of findings; and (b) seeking simplicity of relationships. Regarding (b) Tukey has commented: "our data analysis must stress reexpressing variables for simplicity of behavior" (1969, p. 86). In accord with this attitude, we have simply termed the subject matter of this chapter "numbers." If we have data in the form of numbers with a range of 8–12 and can meet the other assumptions of the particular statistical test being used, we shall, like most experimental psychologists, proceed with the analysis. We won't ask whether or not our scale is an interval scale. Given a choice between "doing research or studying our instruments," we will take the first track. Our only partial concession to measurement assumptions will be made in Chapters 4 and 5 in which we shall consider statistical techniques for dealing with data in the form of ranks and signs, and a limited number of unordered classes, respectively. Also in Chapter 6 a section on relationships with ranks is included.

We have devoted a lot of time to this simple example because it is prototypic of the general problem of statistical inference. In succeeding pages we will play this same game over and over. From an experiment we obtain certain indices, e.g., M's. We inquire whether or not these obtained values are significant. We calculate further indices, e.g., t, by relating our obtained indices to an estimate of random variability, e.g., s_M. We assess the unusualness of the obtained index by reference to a test distribution, e.g., the t distribution. If the outcome is sufficiently unusual, say it happens by chance only 5 times out of 100, then we assert the results are "significant." While we may ask about the significance of different indices and employ a variety of test distributions like t, χ^2, F, and so on, the rationale of the procedure remains basically the same.

Before leaving this topic, we need to stress again the uncertainty of statistical inference. Even though the various auxiliary hypotheses embedded in an experiment are valid, we have to remember always that a significant difference can occur, say 5 times out of 100, *by chance*. A single experiment yields indications not firm conclusions. However, when a series of independent experiments reliably produces the same results, the likelihood of such a concatenation occurring by chance becomes extremely small. This combination of results is all the scientist means by "truth."

The Means of Two Independent Groups

One of the simplest types of experiments is that involving two independent groups. Usually one group, termed the experimental group, is given a certain treatment while the other, termed the control group, is not. An alternative to the treatment vs no treatment paradigm is to impose two levels of a treat-

Table 3.2.* Number of Entries into Training Box (Klein, 1959)

S	100% and 80% Groups 100%	S	80%
1	14	13	19
2	14	14	19
3	13	15	18
4	12	16	17
5	12	17	15
6	12	18	15
7	11	19	14
8	11	20	14
9	10	21	12
10	9	22	11
11	8	23	11
12	8	24	9
ΣX	134		174
ΣX^2	1544		2644
M_2	11.2		14.5
s	4.3		11.0

*Reprinted by permission of the publisher and author from R. M. Klein, "Intermittent Primary Reinforcement as Parameter of Secondary Reinforcement" *Journal of Experimental Psychology*, 58, p. 424. Copyright 1959, American Psychological Association.

ment, e.g., two amounts of reward, two intensities of a stimulus, etc. Then the research worker asks (a) whether the means of the two groups differ in either direction (two-tailed test), or (b) whether the means differ in a predicted direction (one-tailed test). To illustrate the appropriate test for comparing the means of two independent groups, we will arbitrarily select another group from the Klein data and contrast it with the group studied previously (see Table 3.2). Following Klein's analysis, a two-tailed test will be performed between M_1, the mean of the 100% group, and M_2, the mean of the 80% group. The statistical hypothesis to be tested is termed the *null hypothesis*: $M_1 = M_2$[1]. If a difference is found equal or less than the 5% level of significance (a probability of .05 or less), we will reject this null hypothesis in favor of an alternative hypothesis.

As in the test of a single mean, we need an estimate of error or random variation. In this case it is called the *standard error of the difference in means*, $s_{M_1-M_2}$. And as before, it is a standard deviation of a sampling distribution; only this time it is a standard deviation of a sampling distribution of differences in means. That is, hypothetically, a large number of replications of the two-group experiment could be done by randomly drawing pairs of samples. For every replication a difference in the two means, $M_1 - M_2$, could be found and a sampling distribution of these differences could be constructed. The $s_{M_1-M_2}$ is the standard deviation of this sampling distribution. The index for assessing significance is t, as determined by the formula below, and the obtained t is referred to the t table for $df = [(N_1-1) + (N_2-1)] = [(12-1)+(12-1)] = 22$. The formula for t is:

$$t = \frac{M_1 - M_2}{s_{M_1-M_2}} = \frac{M_1 - M_2}{\sqrt{\dfrac{s_1^2}{N_1} + \dfrac{s_2^2}{N_2}}}$$

After calculating the s^2 values for the two groups with the previous formula for a single group, the t for our two-sample problem is found to be -3.0:[2]

$$t = \frac{11.2 - 14.5}{\sqrt{\dfrac{4.3}{12} + \dfrac{11}{12}}} = \frac{-3.3}{1.1} = -3.0$$

From the t table for *df* of 22 the probability of t this large occurring by chance is observed to be less than .01. In light of the unusualness of this

---

1. Technically, the null hypothesis refers to population means, μ_1 and μ_2. Throughout, however, we shall oversimplify the inference process by casting nullity in terms of sample indices like means (M's), variances (s^2's), and the like.

2. The negative t value signifies that the t falls in the left-hand tail of the t distribution and is the consequence of $M_2 > M_1$. The sign of the t is, of course, crucial in one-tailed tests of significance.

outcome the null hypothesis that $M_1 = M_2$ would be rejected, and an alternative hypothesis, that $M_2 > M_1$, would be entertained.

Once more we must be concerned about the assumptions underlying this test of two independent means. They are: (a) the samples have been randomly selected from normally distributed populations; (b) the observations are independent of one another; and (c) the variances of populations, σ^2's, are equal. We already asserted that assumption (b) can be readily evaluated by determining that the Ss were randomly assigned to the treatments. Since Klein did this, the critical assumption of independence of observations would appear to be satisfied.

The third assumption (c) *homogeneity of variance*, is a new notion. Generally we do not know what the variances of the populations are. However, we can estimate them, and $s_1{}^2$ and $s_2{}^2$ represent the best guesses of the population variances. The two variances, 4.3 and 11.0, are obviously not equal but is the difference merely due to chance variation? To answer this question we need a significance test. The formula for the significance test is:

$$F = \frac{\text{larger } s^2}{\text{smaller } s^2}.$$

The larger $s_2{}^2$, 11.0, is divided by the smaller $s_1{}^2$, 4.3, and the resulting F value is assessed by a new test distribution, the F distribution (Table F, Appendix). Once more, the F table represents a family of curves, only in this case the table is entered with two degrees of freedom: (a) for the horizontal entry the df for the larger variance $(N_2 - 1)$ is used; and (b) for the vertical entry the df for the smaller variance $(N_1 - 1)$. F is: $11.0/4.3 = 2.56$. Entering the table for $df = 11$, 11 we find that our $F = 2.56$ has a probability of between .10 $(F = 2.25)$ and .05 $(F = 2.85)$. (In this case there is no horizontal entry of $df = 11$ so we have looked under $df = 10$. If $df = 12$ is used, the result is the same). However, because the test for homogeneity of variance is a two-tailed test, we must *double the tabled probability values* for F. Thus our obtained F has a probability of between .20, i.e., 2 (.10), and .10, i.e., 2 (.05). Since the probability of F is greater than .05, we have no convincing evidence for rejecting the null hypothesis that $s_1{}^2 = s_2{}^2$.

In evaluating the tenability of the homogeneity of variance assumption, we employed a two-tailed test of significance. While investigators are generally interested in comparing means, comparing the variances of two groups is a legitimate and important undertaking and probably a matter that is not investigated sufficiently. If we had a well-developed theory that led to the prediction that the scores of one group should be more variable than the scores of another group, then a one-tailed test would be appropriate and the probability values listed in the F table would *not* be doubled. A word of caution is in order regarding the F test for homogeneity of variance: this test is strongly affected by nonnormality. In fact, Scheffé (1959) has labelled its use as "dangerous" under these conditions. Once more the specter of uncertainty haunts us. Not only do we have the uncertainty that is an integral part of all statistical inference, but this uncertainty is compounded by the fact that after testing variances for equality we cannot always trust the probability values read from the F tables. Again we shall belabor our themes: (a) a single experiment yields indications rather than firm conclusions; and (b) conclusions are the product of experimental replications.

Suppose assumptions (a) and (c) do not hold; that is, imagine that the parent populations are nonnormal and possess unequal variances. What are the consequences of these violated assumptions for the t test of the means of two independent groups? Some answers to this question have been provided by Boneau (1960) who with the aid of a computer drew repeated random samples of two sizes of groups, 5 and 15, from three different populations, normal, rectangular, and exponential. Every population had a mean of 0 but variances of 1 or 4. In each sub-study, e.g., normal population, $\sigma^2 = 4$, N per group of 5 vs normal population, $\sigma^2 = 1$, N per group of 15, 1000 t's were obtained and the empirical distribution of these t's was compared with the theoretical t distribution for the appropriate degrees of freedom. Then comparisons were carried out between the percentages of t's obtained empirically and critical values like the 5 % and 1 % levels in the theoretical t distribution. For example, in the sub-study above with normal populations, unequal N's, and the larger variance associated with the smaller N, 16 % of the obtained t's fell beyond the 5 % level in the theoretical t distribution and 6 % fell beyond the 1 % level. Thus an experimenter dealing with such populations would obtain too many significant differences. He would commit what is called a *Type I error* of inference – he would be rejecting the null hypothesis when he should accept it.

The opposite error of inference, *Type II*, involves the acceptance of the null hypothesis when it is false. When Boneau repeated the above sub-study but had the larger variance, 4, associated with the larger samples of $N = 15$ and the smaller variance, 1, with the smaller samples of $N = 5$, the percentages of t's falling outside of the 5 % and 1 % levels of significance were 1.0 and 0.1, respectively. Thus an experimenter, working under these conditions, would find too few significant differences; i.e., he would often commit a Type II error. The results of these two parts of Boneau's investigation are shown in Figures 3.2 and 3.3.

The encouraging thing about Boneau's study is that the two examples above are the worst results he found. These results and those from other substudies with equal N's per group yield an important principle for research – *use equal sample sizes*. When samples of equal size were studied, the effects of unequal variances were minimal. As stated earlier, throughout this book

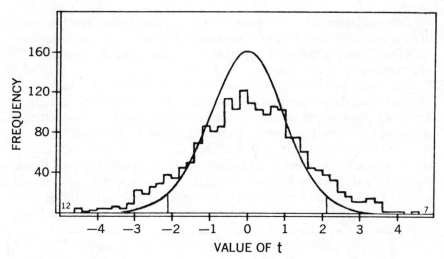

Figure 3.2. Empirical distribution of t's from N(0, 4)5 − N(0, 1)15 and theoretical distribution with 18 df (Boneau, 1960).

*Reprinted by permission of the publisher and author from C. Alan Boneau, "The Effect of Violations of Assumptions Underlying the *t*-Test," *Psychological Bulletin*, 57, p. 56. Copyright 1960, American Psychological Association.

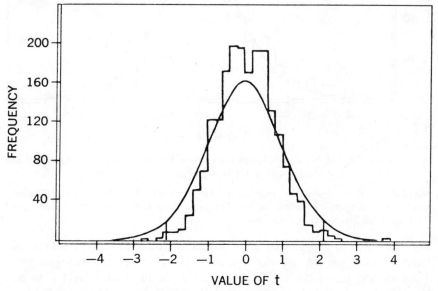

Figure 3.3. Empirical distribution of t's from N(0, 1)5 − N(0, 4)15 and theoretical distribution with 18 df (Boneau, 1960).

*Reprinted by permission of the publisher and author from C. Alan Boneau, "The Effect of Violations of Assumptions Underlying the *t* Test," *Psychological Bulletin*, 57, p. 55. Copyright 1960, American Psychological Association.

the data and formulas that are given are for experiments with equal numbers
of Ss in each treatment. This procedure was followed because (a) it simplifies
the calculations and (b) more importantly, it reduces the deleterious effects
of heterogeneity of variance.

So far then we have seen that the effects of inequality of variances are
minimal when the populations have the same shapes and the N's per group
are equal. Another critical finding emerged when populations of different
skewness, e.g., normal vs exponential, were sampled. Under these conditions,
the empirical distributions of t's were not symmetrical. One such case is
shown in Figure 3.4. What is the implication of the results displayed in this
figure? It is that one-tailed tests of significance may lead to pronounced
errors of inference. Furthermore, the type of error differs depending upon
which tail of the distribution is being employed to assess significance. From

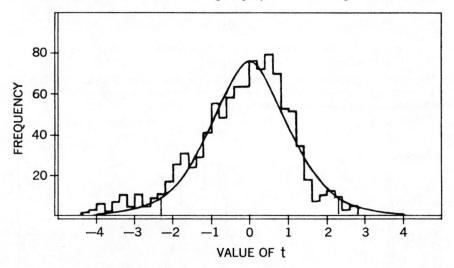

Figure 3.4. Empirical distributions of t's from $E(0, 1)5 - N(0, 1)5$ *and theoretical
distribution with 8* df *(Boneau, 1960).*

*Reprinted by permission of the publisher and author from C. Alan Boneau, "The Effect of
Violations of Assumptions Underlying the *t* Test," *Psychological Bulletin*, 57, p. 59. Copyright
1960, American Psychological Association.

Figure 3.4 we can discern that the investigator would make Type I errors of
inference when the left tail was used and Type II errors with the right tail.
Thus, as was stated before, the unrestricted use of one-tail tests is to be
strongly discouraged. They should only be applied: (a) when replicating a
previous finding; or (b) when testing a specific directional prediction derived
from a well-articulated theory. Finally, it should be stressed that Boneau
observed that all of the above errors of inference became less serious as the

sample sizes were increased. This finding is to be expected on the basis of the central limit theorem.

Boneau summarized his excellent study as follows:

Having violated a number of assumptions underlying the *t* test, and finding that, by and large, such violations produce a minimal effect on the distribution of *t*'s we must conclude that the *t* test is a remarkably *robust* test in the technical sense of the word. This term was introduced by Box (1953) to characterize tests which are only inconsequentially affected by a violation of the underlying assumptions (1960, p. 61).

While the results of Boneau's study are decidedly encouraging for *t* test users, we believe that his major conclusion should be tempered somewhat. First, Boneau included only three different distribution shapes. This obviously does not exhaust the range of nonnormality and combinations of nonnormality. It should also be pointed out that unless a variable has been widely investigated, we do not know what kind of a population we are sampling from. Therefore, we cannot compensate for the type and degree of inference error being made. If the *t* test were *totally* independent of the shapes of the populations and their variances, then there would be no problem. Unfortunately, the *t* test is not. Second, the violations built into the Boneau study are not as extreme as those which may be encountered out in the jungle of research. For example, any research worker who has led a few safaris in *that* jungle has met variance ratios greater than the four-fold ratio investigated by Boneau. Third, as Boneau carefully notes, under certain population conditions, *t* may not be the most *powerful* test. Roughly speaking, *power* refers to the potentiality of a test in detecting a difference when a difference is present. More precisely, Edwards says: "The power of a statistical test is defined as $1 - P$ (Type II error) or, equivalently, as the probability of rejecting a null hypothesis when it is false and should be rejected" (1968, p. 23). When all the assumptions are fulfilled, the *t* test is maximally powerful. However, when the assumptions are not fulfilled, nonparametric tests may sometimes be more powerful (Bradley, 1968). The fact that the *t* test displays considerable robustness does not necessarily mean that it is the best test to use under *all* conditions.

In the early fifties many psychologists swung sharply to the widespread application of nonparametric methods of data analysis. But the later empirical and theoretical work of Norton (1952), Box (1953), Scheffé (1959), Boneau (1960), and others revealing the robust character of classical tests like the *t* and *F* test for means, has swung research workers back just as sharply to these tests. It is our uneducated hunch that the truth lies between these extreme strategies of the exclusive use of either classical or nonparametric methods. Obviously, much more research is called for to find the optimal tests for various situations. In the meantime, the research worker will be where he usually is — sitting quietly but bravely on a cloud of un-certainty.

The Means of k Independent Groups

While the two-group experiment may provide an indication that a treatment may have an effect, this type of experimental design cannot disclose what the nature of the functional relationship is between the independent and dependent variables. This question must be attacked by a design in which several levels of the independent variable are manipulated. As a consequence, the investigator has k means $(k > 2)$, and he usually wants to know whether or not they are significantly different. As in a previous example, we are concerned at this point with independent groups.

Once more we will draw upon the Klein experiment and this time the data from all of his conditions will be examined. The independent variable manipulated by Klein was the percentage of times the Ss were fed in a particular goal box after running there in training. The dependent variable was the number of turns to the particular goal box in 20 T-maze test trials. Our initial question about the data in Table 3.3 is: Did the six means observed by Klein differ significantly?

Table 3.3.*   *Number of Entries into Training Box*
(Klein, 1959)

| | Percentage of Reinforcement | | | | | | |
	100%	*90%*	*80%*	*60%*	*40%*	*20%*	
	14	16	19	20	20	20	
	14	15	19	20	20	20	
	13	14	18	19	20	20	
	12	14	17	19	19	20	
	12	13	15	19	19	20	
	12	13	15	16	19	19	
	11	12	14	16	17	18	
	11	11	14	14	16	15	
	10	10	12	12	0	14	
	9	10	11	10	0	12	
	8	10	11	10	0	10	
	8	6	9	0	0	0	
ΣX =	134	144	174	175	150	188	$965 = \Sigma\Sigma X$
ΣX^2 =	1544	1812	2644	2935	2828	3350	$15113 = \Sigma\Sigma X^2$
M =	11.17	12.00	14.50	14.58	12.50	15.67	

*Reprinted by permission of the publisher and author from R. M. Klein, "Intermittent Primary Reinforcement as Parameter of Secondary Reinforcement," *Journal of Experimental Psychology,* 58, p. 424. Copyright 1959, American Psychological Association.

Thus the null hypothesis is: $M_1 = M_2 = M_3 = M_4 = M_5 = M_6$.

To answer the question we need to describe a statistical technique termed analysis of variance. The technique suitable for our example is usually called "a simple analysis of variance." The label, analysis of variance, is fitting because it describes precisely what is done. First, the total sum of squares, SS_T, based on all 72 scores is found. Second, this quantity is analyzed into two additive components: a between-groups (treatments) portion, SS_B, and a within-groups portion, SS_W. The $SS_T = SS_B + SS_W$. Third, variance estimates, s_B^2 and s_W^2, are obtained by dividing SS_B and SS_W by their respective degrees of freedom. Fourth, if the ratio, s_B^2/s_W^2, is sufficiently large, as ascertained from the table of the F distribution, the null hypothesis is rejected.

Let us first analyze the Klein data and then provide a little intuitive rationale for the procedure. The SS_T represents the variation of all 72 scores about their mean. Since "their mean" is the mean of all scores, it is termed the grand mean, M_G. The formula for SS_T is the same formula used before:

$$SS_T = \Sigma\Sigma X^2 - \frac{(\Sigma\Sigma X)^2}{N}.$$

The only modification in this formula is use of the double summation sign, $\Sigma\Sigma$. It says: sum the scores (or scores squared) for each group and then sum the groups' sums. Applying this formula to the data in Table 3.3, we have:

$$SS_T = 15113 - \frac{(965)^2}{72} = 2179.32.$$

The SS_B represents the weighted deviations of group means, M_1, M_2, ..., M_6, from the grand mean, M_G. Weighted signifies that the deviations are multiplied by the number of observations in each group. The computational formula for SS_B is:

$$SS_B = \frac{(\Sigma X_1)^2}{N_1} + \frac{(\Sigma X_2)^2}{N_2} + ... + \frac{(\Sigma X_k)^2}{N_k} - \frac{(\Sigma\Sigma X)^2}{N}.$$

Note that we have already calculated the last term, $(\Sigma\Sigma X)^2/N$, in finding SS_T, and that k is the number of groups or 6. Thus SS_B is:

$$SS_B = \frac{(134)^2}{12} + \frac{(144)^2}{12} + \frac{(174)^2}{12} + \frac{(175)^2}{12} + \frac{(150^2)}{12} + \frac{(188)^2}{12} - \frac{(965)^2}{72}.$$

Because the number of observations in groups is equal, i.e., $N_1 = N_2 = N_3$, etc., we can sum all of the squared group totals and divide once by the number of observations in each group:

$$SS_B = \frac{157437}{12} - \frac{(965)^2}{72} = 186.07.$$

We can then obtain the SS_W by subtraction:

$$SS_T = SS_B + SS_W, \quad SS_W = SS_T - SS_B,$$

$$SS_W = 2179.32 - 186.07 = 1993.25.$$

The SS_W represents the variation of scores within each group about the group mean, summed across all groups. At this stage of the analysis it often pays to become slightly paranoid! We have carried out a number of calculations – how do we know that our answers are correct? One method of checking the analysis is simply to do it again. This procedure provides a check, but there is always the danger that one may simply repeat errors made in the original analysis. Another check is to have someone else analyze the data and compare the two sets of answers. A third mode of checking is to calculate *directly* a value like SS_W that was found by subtraction. Since checking and rechecking of calculations is an essential part of data analysis, we will employ the third type of check:

$$SS_W = \left[\Sigma X_1^{\,2} - \frac{(\Sigma X_1)^2}{N_1} \right] + \left[\Sigma X_2^{\,2} - \frac{(\Sigma X_2)^2}{N_2} \right] + \cdots + \left[\Sigma X_k^{\,2} - \frac{(\Sigma X_k)^2}{N_k} \right]$$

$$SS_W = \left[1544 - \frac{(134)^2}{12} \right] + \left[1812 - \frac{(144)^2}{12} \right] + \left[2644 - \frac{(174)^2}{12} \right] +$$

$$\left[2935 - \frac{(175)^2}{12} \right] + \left[2828 - \frac{(150)^2}{12} \right] + \left[3350 - \frac{(188)^2}{12} \right]$$

$$SS_W = 47.67 + 84.00 + 121.00 + 382.92 + 953.00 + 404.67 = 1993.26.$$

Thus the SS_W's obtained directly and by subtraction agree within the limits of rounding error. The direct calculation also reveals marked differences among the SS_W's for the six groups. We shall return to this important observation shortly.

Just as the SS values sum to produce a total SS, so are the corresponding degrees of freedom additive:

$$df_T = df_B + df_W.$$

The df_T are equal to the number of deviations minus one or $N - 1 = 72 - 1 = 71$. In the case of the df_B we are concerned with the deviations of k means about the grand mean. Therefore, the df_B are $k - 1 = 6 - 1 = 5$. By subtraction the df_W may be found:

$$df_W = df_T - df_B = 71 - 5 = 66.$$

We can also obtain the df_W directly. The SS_W for the 100% group is the variation of 12 scores about M_1. Accordingly, the *df* for this group are equal to $N_1 - 1 = 12 - 1 = 11$. Because the *N*'s are equal for each treatment and the SS_W's for the *k* treatments are pooled to form SS_W, the $df_W = k(N_1 - 1) = 66$.

Having found the SS_B and SS_W and their *df*'s, we are ready to complete the significance test. The $s_B^2 = SS_B/df_B = 186.07/5 = 37.21$ *and* $s_W^2 = SS_W/df_W = 1993.25/66 = 30.20$. The significance test is:

$$F = \frac{s_B^2}{s_W^2} = \frac{37.21}{30.20} = 1.23.$$

Entering the table for the *F* distribution with df_B or 5 for the horizontal entry and df_W or 66 for the vertical entry, we observe that an $F = 2.37$ is required for significance at the 5% level.[3] Because our obtained $F = 1.23$ is less than this required *F* value, we would have no reason to reject the null hypothesis that Klein's six means were equal. The discerning reader will have noticed that in this simple analysis of variance procedure for evaluating *k* means, we have read the probability value from the *F* table rather than doubling it as was done in testing two variances for homogeneity. Hays has commented on this procedure:

> The *F* ratio used in the analysis of variance always provides a *one-tailed* test of H_0 [the null hypothesis] in terms of the sampling distribution of *F*. Evidence for H_1 [the alternative hypothesis] must show up as an *F* ratio greater than 1.00, and an *F* ratio less than 1.00 can signify nothing except sampling error (or perhaps non-randomness of the samples or failure of the assumptions). Therefore, for the analysis of variance, the *F* ratio obtained can be compared directly with the one-tailed values given . . . (1963, p. 369).

Let us deal briefly with the intuitive rationale of analysis of variance and then turn to a more detailed consideration of the assumptions underlying analysis of variance. Klein's experiment is an example of what is called a *fixed-effects model*. Another kind of statistical model, which occurs infrequently in psychological research, is a *random-effects model*. The distinction between these two models depends upon how the levels of the *independent* variable are selected. In Klein's study the six percentages of reward in training, ranging from 100% to 20%, were *arbitrarily* selected by the experimenter. Therefore, his design fits a fixed-effects model. On the other hand, if Klein had taken the total population of percentages of reward, ranging from 100% to 0% and *randomly* selected six values like 89%, 74%, 48%, 41%, 39%, and 4%, then this design would correspond to a random-effects model.

What are the consequences of this distinction between fixed- and random-

---

3. Since there is no entry for $df = 66$, the nearest entry $df = 60$ has been used.

effects models?[4] They are these: (a) the interpretation of the variance estimates (e.g., $s_B{}^2$) is affected; (b) in certain complex designs as a result of
(a) what error term is used to evaluate some effects varies with the model;
and (c) the generality of the conclusions that can be drawn is related to the
model. Since the fixed-effects model is encountered most often, we will
consider implication (a) only with respect to this model. This discussion
constitutes a terse intuitive rationale for a simple analysis of variance paradigm. With a fixed-effects model, which is appropriate to Klein's design,
the $s_B{}^2$ is an estimate of error or random variation *plus* the variation due to
the effects of the treatments. The $s_W{}^2$, on the other hand, is an independent
estimate of error only. If there is no treatment effect, i.e., the means of treatments are the same, then F should be approximately 1.00 because one independent error estimate is being divided by another. On the other hand,
when the means do differ, the treatment component of $s_B{}^2$ should increase
and the F ratio should become larger than 1.00. The occurrence of an F
ratio less than 1.00 represents, as Hays has indicated, a chance occurrence
or nonindependent groups or some other failure to meet the assumptions for
analysis of variance.

The second implication, of the two models, (b) regarding error terms, does
not concern us because we are limiting our presentation to simple designs of
the more frequently used fixed-effects type. In the case of the generality of
interpretation (c), the conclusions from a fixed-effects design are limited to
those values of the independent variable that the experimenter has arbitrarily
selected. With a random-effects design, the conclusions are more general;
they concern the population from which the experimenter has randomly
selected his levels of the independent variable (Hays, 1963). Although the
third implication (c) is important to us, we should stress again that we contend that a single experiment yields indications rather than conclusions.

What assumptions are made when using the simple analysis of variance
paradigm? The assumptions are the same as those for the t test for two independent means, *viz*, (a) the samples have been randomly selected from normally distributed populations; (b) the observations are independent of one
another; and (c) the variances of the populations, σ^2's, are equal. We have
already talked at length about the first two assumptions, and there is no
need to repeat this discussion. Instead we will concentrate on (c), homogeneity of variance. Since the F test for homogeneity of variance is suitable
only for the situation in which there are two groups, another test is required
for our present problem. For the case of k groups, tests of homogeneity of
variance have been devised by Bartlett (1937; see Edwards, 1950), Cochran
(1941; see Dixon & Massey, 1951) and Hartley (1950; see Walker & Lev,

4. A third type of statistical model, *mixed-effects*, contains both random and fixed-effects
components.

1953). Unfortunately all of these tests suffer from the same malady as the F test for homogeneity – they are extremely sensitive to nonnormality (Box, 1953; Scheffé, 1959). Box has proposed an alternative approximate test to solve this problem. The procedure consists of randomly "breaking" the scores for each group into c subsamples of m scores each. (No rules are given for selecting the values of c and m). Next the variances of the sub-samples are calculated and their logs are found.[5] Then a simple analysis of variance is performed upon the resulting logs of the subsample variances. If the F test is significant, the variances are regarded as heterogeneous. Thus Box's test translates a variance problem into a test of mean variances.

As a computational example of the Box test for homogeneity of variance we will again use the Klein data from Table 3.3. For each group, 3 subsamples ($c = 3$) of 4 observations each ($m = 4$) were selected by a table of random numbers (see Table 3.4). Although there are no clearly prescribed rules for

Table 3.4. Breakdown of Entries into Subsamples

| | Percentage of Reinforcement | | | | | |
	100%	90%	80%	60%	40%	20%
	14	16	19	20	20	20
	12	15	18	16	17	18
	12	14	15	10	16	15
	11	11	11	0	0	10
ΣX	49	56	63	46	53	63
ΣX^2	605	798	1031	756	945	1049
	14	14	19	19	20	20
	12	10	17	14	20	20
	10	10	14	12	19	20
	9	6	12	10	0	0
ΣX	45	40	62	55	59	60
ΣX^2	521	432	990	801	1161	1200
	13	13	15	20	19	20
	11	13	14	19	19	19
	8	12	11	19	0	14
	8	10	9	16	0	12
ΣX	40	48	49	74	38	65
ΣX^2	418	582	623	1378	722	1101

5. Why should the scale be changed to logs? Miller has commented: "Statistical lore tells us that applying the log transformation to s^2 very often produces beneficial results. It stabilizes the variance, creates a more normal-looking distribution, etc." (1968, p. 569).

obtaining the subsamples, two obvious limiting conditions are that both c and m must be at least equal to 2. It is also desirable to have more than 2 subsamples for every treatment so that the df_w will be reasonably large. For example, if we used $c = 2$ in the present problem, then the df_w would only be 6. In Table 3.5 are presented the SS, s^2, and $\log s^2$ values for the 18 subsamples in Table 3.4. Although Scheffé (1959, p. 84) advises transforming the s^2 values to $\log_e$, we will use $\log_{10}$ because the two transformations produce exactly the same F ratio. The resulting 18 $\log s^2$ were then treated as scores

Table 3.5. *Sums of Squares, Variances, and Log Variances of the Subsamples*

Measure	Percentage of Reinforcement					
	100 %	90 %	80 %	60 %	40 %	20 %
	4.75	14.00	38.75	227.00	242.75	56.75
SS	14.75	32.00	29.00	44.75	290.75	300.00
	18.00	6.00	22.75	9.00	361.00	44.75
	1.58	4.67	12.92	75.67	80.92	18.92
s^2	4.92	10.67	9.67	14.92	96.92	100.00
	6.00	2.00	7.58	3.00	120.33	14.92
	0.1987	0.6693	1.1113	1.8789	1.9080	1.2770
$\log s^2$	0.6920	1.0282	0.9854	1.1738	1.9819	2.0000
	0.7782	0.3010	0.8797	0.4771	2.0802	1.1738
ΣX	1.6689	1.9985	2.9764	3.5298	5.9701	4.4508
ΣX^2	1.1239	1.5958	2.9799	5.1357	11.8956	7.0085

and subjected to a simple analysis of variance by applying the formulas from the first part of this section:

$$SS_T = \Sigma\Sigma X^2 - \frac{(\Sigma\Sigma X)^2}{N} = 29.7394 - \frac{(20.5945)^2}{18} = 6.1764.$$

$$SS_B = \frac{(\Sigma X_1)^2}{N_1} + \frac{(\Sigma X_2)^2}{N_2} + \cdots + \frac{(\Sigma X_k)^2}{N_k} - \frac{(\Sigma\Sigma X)^2}{N}.$$

$$SS_B = \frac{(1.6689)^2}{3} + \frac{(1.9985)^2}{3} + \cdots + \frac{(4.4508)^2}{3} - \frac{(20.5945)^2}{18}$$

$$SS_B = \frac{83.5494}{3} - \frac{(20.5945)^2}{18} = 4.2868.$$

$$SS_W = SS_T - SS_B.$$

$$SS_W = 6.1764 - 4.2868 = 1.8896.$$

The $df_B = k - 1 = 6 - 1 = 5$ and $df_W = k(N_1 - 1) = 6(3 - 1) = 12$. Then:

$$s_B^2 = SS_B/df_B = 4.2868/5 = 0.8574$$

$$s_W^2 = SS_W/df_W = 1.8896/12 = 0.1575$$

$$F = \frac{s_B^2}{s_W^2} = \frac{0.8574}{0.1575} = 5.44.$$

For df's $= 5$ and 12 the obtained $F = 5.44$ is found to be significant by the F table at less than the .01 level. Accordingly, the null hypothesis that $s_1^2 = s_2^2 = s_3^2 = s_4^2 = s_5^2 = s_6^2$ would be rejected. Since there is a clear indication of heterogeneity of variance, secured from a test which is believed to be unaffected by nonnormality, a basic assumption for our original analysis of variance of Klein's data is violated. Faced with such a state of affairs, what courses of action are open to an investigator? They are three: (a) to inquire as to the consequences of unequal variances upon simple analysis of variance; (b) to attempt to transform the original data so as to stabilize the variances and normalize the distributions; and (c) to analyze the data with some nonparametric test. The last course of action (c) was the one taken from Klein, and we will consider it in detail in Chapter 4. Option (b) includes deciding upon the proper transformation, transforming the data, checking for equality of variances by inspection or test, and rerunning the analysis of variance on the transformed scores. The student should be warned that some data may be encountered which cannot be "straightened out" by any of the usual transformations (Lindquist, 1953). Since we talked about various transformations earlier, we will examine the first alternative (a), the consequences of unequal variances.

Prior to this discussion, we should make it clear that when we have random samples from known normal populations, Hartley's test (1950) permits a quick indication regarding homogeneity of variance. Hartley's test consists of finding the largest and smallest variances from the set of k variances, forming a ratio of these two variances, and then assessing this ratio in Hartley's table for the F_{max} distribution (Table G, Appendix). Let us pretend that Klein's data (Table 3.3) come from normally distributed populations. From the previous direct calculation of SS_W we note that the largest s^2 is $953/11 = 86.64$ for the 40% group and the smallest s^2 is $47.67/11 = 4.33$ for the 100% group. The F_{max} test is:

$$F_{max} = \frac{\text{largest } s^2}{\text{smallest } s^2} = \frac{86.64}{4.33} = 20.01.$$

Like the F table, the F_{max} table is of the double-entry type. It is entered for $k = 6$, the number of variances in the initial set, and $df = 11$, one less than the number of observations that each variance is based upon. Whether we enter the table with $df = 10$ or $df = 12$ (there is no $df = 11$), the obtained $F_{max} = 20.01$ is significant at less than .01. In agreement with the result of the Box test, the hypothesis of equal variances would be rejected. Once more

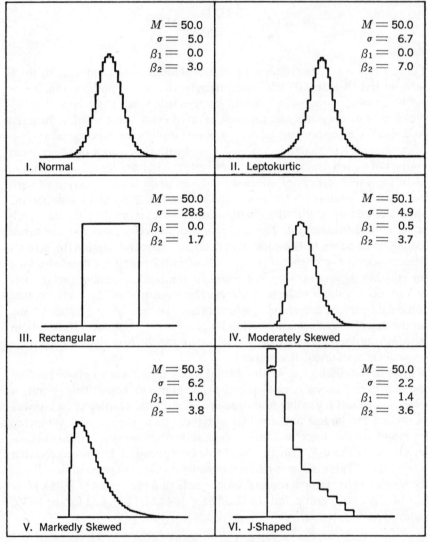

Figure 3.5. Histograms of populations for which empirical F distributions were obtained in Phase 1 of the Norton study (Lindquist, 1953).

*Reprinted by permission of the publisher from E. F. Lindquist, *Design and Analysis of Experiments in Psychology and Education,* p. 80. Copyright 1953, Houghton Mifflin Company.

it should be stressed that Hartley's test is strongly influenced by nonnormality, and we are applying it to Klein's data simply to present a computational example.

What are the consequences of violating the equal variances assumption upon the *F* test? One sampling investigation on the assumptions for analysis of variance has been carried out by Norton (see Lindquist, 1953). In the first phase, Norton studied the effects of distribution shape with six populations ranging from approximately normal to J-shaped (see Figure 3.5). All populations had almost the same mean but differed in variance (σ's ranged from 2.2 to 28.8). Norton randomly drew 3000 sets of $k = 3$ or 4 samples and N's per group of 3 or 5 from each population of 10,000 scores. *F* values were found for each set and the percentages of these *F*'s falling beyond critical points in the theoretical *F* distribution for the appropriate *df*'s were obtained.

Table 3.6.*   *Results of the Norton Study on Violations of Assumptions upon the F Test (Lindquist, 1953)*

No. Sets	Population(s)	k	n	Per Cents from F Distribution		
				5%	1%	0.10%
3000	Normal	4	5	5.61	1.44	0.17
3000	Leptokurtic	3	3	7.83	2.76	0.80
3000	Leptokurtic	4	5	6.56	1.63	0.37
3000	Rectangular	3	3	6.07	1.77	0.13
3000	Moderate Skew	4	5	5.15	1.32	0.13
3000	Extreme Skew	3	3	4.77	0.80	0.13
3000	Extreme Skew	4	5	4.76	1.00	0.10
3000	J-Shape	3	3	4.80	1.00	0.20
3333	Heterogeneous	3	3	7.26	2.13	0.36
3000	Variances	3	10	6.56	2.00	0.37
3333	Heterogeneous	3	3	6.72	1.65	0.15
3333	Forms	3	6	6.81	1.98	0.39
3333	Both	4	3	10.02	3.57	0.84
3000	Heterogeneous	4	10	8.10	2.93	0.87

**Reprinted by permission of the publisher from E. F. Lindquist, *Design and Analysis of Experiments in Psychology and Education*, pp. 82 and 84. Copyright 1953, Houghton Mifflin Company.*

These results shown in Table 3.6 suggest that, within the limits investigated by Norton, when such samples are obtained from the same nonnormal populations, the investigator would not make serious errors of inference even with very small numbers of observations in each group. For example, Norton's data reveal that the worst inference errors would occur when small samples were drawn from a leptokurtic population, which is a symmetrical distribution that is too peaked. With $k = 3$ and N per group of 3, 7.83% of the *F* ratios fell beyond 5% point in the theoretical *F* distribution, 2.76% exceeded the 1% point, and 0.80% were found beyond the 0.10% point.

Under these conditions then, an investigator would make Type I errors, i.e., reject the null hypothesis too often. As in the case of Boneau's study, increasing the N per group serves to improve the "fit" between the empirical and theoretical distributions of F and thereby to reduce the errors of inference. We should also point out that in four instances where the populations were extremely skewed or J-shaped that some Type II errors of inference might occur.

In the second phase of the investigation, the effect of heterogeneity of variance was studied by drawing samples from three normal populations whose variances were about 35, 100, and 225. From Table 3.6 it can be seen that Type I errors of inference would be made and that these generally decrease as the N per group is increased.

The third phase investigated heterogeneity of form by drawing samples from three different populations. The first population was markedly skewed to the *right* with a variance of 25, the second was approximately normal with a variance of 54.76, and the third was markedly skewed to the *left* with a variance of 25. These heterogeneous populations produced Type I errors of inference but possibly less frequently than those observed with heterogeneous variances.

In the final phase, the effects of heterogeneous forms and variances were explored by drawing random samples from four different populations. The first population was J-shaped with a variance of 4.84; the second was markedly skewed to the right with a variance of 38.44; the third was moderately skewed to the right with a variance of 100; and the last was normal with a variance of 222.01. It is notable in light of our remarks on the small ratio of variances included in Boneau's study that Norton had a ratio of over 45 between the largest and smallest variance. With samples of $k = 4$ and N per group of 3 and $k = 4$ and N per group of 10 the percentages of F's obtained empirically exceeded the critical 5%, 1%, and 0.10% points of the theoretical F distributions to a greater degree than any other conditions which were investigated by Norton (see Table 3.6).

Summarizing the first phase of Norton's study Lindquist asserts: "Unless the departure from normality is so extreme that it can be easily detected by mere inspection of the data, the departure from normality will probably have no appreciable effect on the validity of the F test and the probabilities read from the F table may be used as close approximations to the true probabilities" (1953, p. 86). With regard to the other conditions in Norton's study, Lindquist concludes:

> The findings of the Norton study are not quite so encouraging with reference to situations in which the treatment populations are *heterogeneous*, either in form, or in variance, or in both. However, the heterogeneity must be quite extreme to be of any serious consequence (1953, p. 86).

Lindquist does not advocate tests for homogeneity of variance. Where marked heterogeneity in form or variance prevails, he suggests either setting a higher significance level or transforming the data to another scale. In the first case, instead of the experimenter regarding a difference at the 5% level as significant, he might require the 2.5% level. This advice is probably based upon the fact that in most instances Norton observed higher percentages of F's empirically. It should be noted, however, that this correction procedure would compound the inference errors in the few cases in which the percentages of F's from sampling were less than the theoretical percentages (e.g., the result for the J-shaped distribution, row 8 of Table 3.6, for the 5% level).

Other evidence of a *theoretical* nature regarding the effects of heterogeneity of variance has been summarized by Scheffé (1959). Box (1954) has calculated the probabilities for a Type I error for a few conditions of unequal variances with a simple analysis of variance design. These results, shown in Table 3.7, are congruent with Boneau's finding that with equal N's in each

Table 3.7.* *Probabilities of Type I Error with F Test for Means at the Nominal 5% Level (Scheffé, 1959)*

No. of Groups	Variance Ratios	Group Sizes	N	Probability of Type I Error
3	1 : 2 : 3	5, 5, 5	15	0.056
		3, 9, 3	15	0.056
		7, 5, 3	15	0.092
		3, 5, 7	15	0.040
3	1 : 1 : 3	5, 5, 5	15	0.059
		7, 5, 3	15	0.110
		9, 5, 1	15	0.170
		1, 5, 9	15	0.013
5	1 : 1 : 1 : 1 : 3	5, 5, 5, 5, 5	25	0.074
		9, 5, 5, 5, 1	25	0.140
		1, 5, 5, 5, 9	25	0.025
7	1 : 1 : ... : 1 : 7	3, 3, ..., 3, 3	21	0.12

*Reprinted by permission of the publisher from Henry Scheffé, *The Analysis of Variance*, p. 354. Copyright 1959, John Wiley & Sons, Inc.

group and unequal variances Type I errors occur, while with unequal N's per group and unequal variances either type of error is possible. Box's last condition (row 12, Table 3.7) which produces a large positive bias, 12% vs a nominal 5%, is atypical both in its design (i.e., $k = 7$, N per group $= 3$) and in the pattern of variances (i.e., six variances of 1 and one of 7).

Let us return to the original question: What are the consequences of violating the equal variances assumption upon the F test? On the basis of the present evidence it appears that the F test displays considerable robustness. This conclusion is especially true when the N's in the groups are equal. Furthermore, increasing these N's improves the fit between the observed and theoretical probability values. Despite this optimism, we should read carefully the comments that introduce Scheffé's chapter on "The Effects of Departures from the Underlying Assumptions":

> A study of this kind cannot be exhaustive, for one reason, because assumptions like this [normality of errors, equality of variances, and independence of errors] can be violated in many more ways than they can be satisfied . . . Some of our conclusions will have to be inductions from rather small numerical tables. However, we must tackle the important questions . . . even though the evidence is incomplete . . . (1959, p. 331).

At this juncture, we must stress once more that although the F test for means displays considerable robustness, this does not imply that it is the most powerful test under all conditions. While it is an optimal test when the assumptions can be met, other tests may be more appropriate for situations in which the assumptions are violated to a marked degree. We shall deal with some alternative tests in Chapters 4 and 5.

Finally, let us comment on the advisability of testing variances for homogeneity. In view of the robustness of the t and F tests and the lack of robustness of the early homogeneity of variance tests, many writers (e.g., Lindquist, 1953; Hays, 1963; and Edwards, 1968) have advised against the testing of variances. Box (1953) put the advice most charmingly: "To make the preliminary test on variances is rather like putting to sea in a rowing boat to find out whether conditions are sufficiently calm for an ocean liner to leave port."

We shall, however, take a contrary position on this problem and urge that variances be investigated for homogeneity. First, the evidence on the robustness of the F test for means is not complete. Lyle V. Jones comments:

> It would be in error to conclude, on the basis of these and other sampling studies, that one can ignore the normality and equal variance assumptions in the F-test. There are a multitude of aberrant conditions, combinations of departures from normality and heterogeneous variances, which have not been subjected to scrutiny; existing results do not provide generalized conclusions to most such conditions. Further, even among conditions investigated, the differences between apparent and actual significance levels are often sufficiently large to be of practical importance in terms of the increased probability of erroneous rejection of the null hypothesis (1955, p. 413).

Jones' remarks were made over a decade ago, but they are still defensible today. Second, there now exist a number of tests for homogeneity of variance which, like Box's test above, are far more robust than the earlier tests (Miller, 1968). Third, while an experienced worker can often detect the possibility of heterogeneity by "eyeballing" his data, a neophyte cannot. Accordingly, it would seem advisable for students just beginning in research to rely upon a statistical test for equal variances rather than an untrained eyeball. Fourth, it should be emphasized again that testing variances is just as legitimate as testing means. To learn that one experimental treatment produces greater variability than another is not unimportant. With nonnormal data, of course, this problem should be tackled by a test like Box's. In this context, it should be pointed that Box's test can be applied also to evaluate the variances of two independent groups when the distributions of scores depart from normality. In this case the logs of variances of the randomly selected samples within the two groups can be compared by a *t* test for independent groups or an *F* test for means. One possible difficulty with this procedure is that the *df* for the error will be relatively small unless N_1 and N_2 are each fairly large, say 20 to 25 or larger.

Multiple Comparisons of Means and Variances from k Independent Groups

The problem of multiple comparisons is an outgrowth of a problem considered earlier — the detection of extreme observations. If an investigator performs an experiment with *k* independent groups ($k > 2$), does an analysis of variance, and finds a significant *F*, then he has an indication that one or more comparisons of means are significant. However, the problem that most investigators are interested in is: What means are significantly different from what other means?

Let us suppose that an investigator has $k = 10$ treatments. He then has 10 *M*'s and if he only examines the *M*'s in a pairwise fashion, he can make $k(k-1)/2 = 10(10-1)/2 = 45$ pairwise comparisons of means. Suppose further, that instead of initially performing an *F* test for the whole batch of *M*'s, he simply selected the largest and smallest means and did a *t* test upon these two means using the .05 level of significance. With 45 possible comparisons and such a selection procedure, it is obvious that by chance alone significance would be observed rather often. Some protection against this type of an error (Type I) is provided by obtaining a significant *F* from an analysis of variance *before* comparing the means. Nevertheless, it still seems reasonable that in making subsequent comparisons of means, the significance level should be adjusted in some manner to take into account the number of comparisons being carried out.

What procedure should be used to make pairwise comparisons of means after significance is found in an analysis of variance? Unfortunately, a variety of methods is available, the inventors are partial to their own methods, and textbook writers usually present the methods without advocating the use of a particular method. The last difficulty stems, in turn, from a lack of knowledge about the properties of the various multiple-comparison techniques, e.g., their power, their susceptibility to nonnormality, the influence of heterogeneity of variance upon them, etc. (Miller, 1966).

Since the existent multiple-comparison techniques have been examined carefully by Miller (1966) and one detailed sampling investigation has recently appeared (Petrinovich & Hardyck, 1969), we shall try to reach an answer to the question that we have posed and recommend a multiple-comparison method. It should be emphasized that the answer must be provisional because the evidence is quite incomplete.

A further complication to the multiple-comparison problem concerns a reference against which to judge errors of inference. Two extreme positions on this matter have been described by Miller:

> A nonmultiple comparisonist regards each separate statistical statement as a family, and does not give increased protection to any groups of statements through group error rates. At the other extreme is the ultraconservative statistician who has just a single family consisting of every statistical statement he might make during his lifetime (1966, p. 31).

Thus the first individual might employ the .05 level of significance for every comparison; while the latter individual, knowing that he is going to perform an enormous number of significance tests in his lifetime, might therefore require a fantastically high level of significance. Tukey, who has made important contributions to the multiple-comparisons problem, has suggested three references for errors and thereby delineated three error rates:

1. *Error rate per comparison:* This is the probability that any particular one of the comparisons will be incorrectly considered to be significant.
2. *Error rate per experiment.* This is the long-run average number of erroneous statements per experiment . . . it is the *expected number* of errors per experiment.
3. *Error rate experimentwise.* This is the probability that *one or more* erroneous conclusions will be drawn in a given experiment. In other words, *experiments* are divided into two classes: (a) those in which all conclusions are correct and (b) those in which some conclusions are incorrect. The error rate experimentwise is the probability that a given experiment belongs in class (b) (Ryan, 1959, p. 29).

Which conception of error is most reasonable is a matter of some controversy. For example, Petrinovich and Hardyck (1969) favor the error rate experimentwise. Miller contends: "The natural family for the author *in the majority of instances* is the *individual experiment* of a *single-researcher*" (1966, p. 34). But after noting that even a single complex experiment might entail a great many comparisons, Miller takes a more relativistic stand: "*There are no hard-and-fast rules for where the family lines should be drawn and the statistician must rely on his own judgments for the problem at hand*" (1966, p. 35). Thus, besides the problem of different error rates, there is the additional difficulty as to their merits.

One approach to the evaluation of the various multiple-comparison tests is to examine them from the point of view of their rationale, range of application, assumptions, and the like. Miller (1966) has followed this approach, and on the basis of his analysis we can eliminate certain techniques as not suited to our goal of selecting a technique for the pairwise comparisons of means. The most general multiple-comparison method has been proposed by Scheffé (1953). It is general in the sense that it is designed to test *any* and *all* possible contasts among a set of means. As Edwards (1968) has shown, if we have $k = 4$ treatments, then 25 contrasts can be done with the 4 means (see Table 3.8). The first six two-mean contrasts in Table 3.8 are what we

Table 3.8. The 25 Possible Contrasts of 4 Treatment Means

1 vs. 2	1 vs. 2 + 3
1 vs. 3	1 vs. 2 + 4
1 vs. 4	1 vs. 3 + 4
2 vs. 3	2 vs. 1 + 3
2 vs. 4	2 vs. 1 + 4
3 vs. 4	2 vs. 3 + 4
1 + 2 vs. 3 + 4	3 vs. 1 + 2
1 + 3 vs. 2 + 4	3 vs. 1 + 4
1 + 4 vs. 2 + 3	3 vs. 2 + 4
1 vs. 2 + 3 + 4	4 vs. 1 + 2
2 vs. 1 + 3 + 4	4 vs. 1 + 3
3 vs. 1 + 2 + 4	4 vs. 2 + 3
4 vs. 1 + 2 + 3	

have termed pairwise comparisons. If an investigator wishes to test any and all possible contrasts, the Scheffé method is ideal. The reader can find a lucid presentation of the application of this technique in Edwards (1968, pp. 180–183). As a test of pairwise comparisons, however, it is far too conservative. That is to say, the differences required for significance are so large that investigators would likely be distressed by the infrequency with which they observed significant differences.

Another multiple-comparison technique, Duncan's multiple range test (1955), has been designed to permit systematic comparisons of pairs of means. This test has been criticized (Scheffé, 1959; Miller, 1966) on the opposite grounds from the Scheffé test — namely, for being too liberal, i.e., for leading to too many Type I errors. In fact, if the different multiple-comparison techniques are collated, it is readily apparent that the magnitudes of the differences which are required for significance by the various techniques vary greatly. These gross disparities are revealed clearly in a table from Winer (1962). Although this table (Table 3.9) is for group *totals* rather than for

Table 3.9.*   *Differences in Treatment Totals Required for the*
.01 Level of Significance (Winer, 1962).

Method	k:	2	3	4	5	6	7
Scheffé		13.02	13.02	13.02	13.02	13.02	13.02
Tukey A		10.90	10.90	10.90	10.90	10.90	10.90
Tukey B		9.36	9.93	10.29	10.54	10.74	10.90
Newman–Keuls		7.82	8.96	9.68	10.18	10.56	10.90
Duncan		7.82	8.16	8.36	8.56	8.68	8.78
Ind. Comparisons		7.82	7.82	7.82	7.82	7.82	7.82

*Reprinted by permission of the publisher from B. J. Winer, *Statistical Principles in Experimental Design*, p. 88. Copyright 1962, McGraw-Hill Book Company.

means, it is obvious that the application of different methods would often yield widely disparate indications. In using multiple comparisons, the sums (or means) are first ranked in magnitude. Then the most extreme values, in Winer's example the first and seventh sums, are compared. With the Scheffé method a difference of 13.02 would be necessary for significance at the .01 level. With Tukey A method the necessary difference is 10.90. At the bottom of the column, $k = 7$, it can be seen that 8.78 and 7.82 would be needed with the Duncan test and individual comparisons (t tests), respectively. If the first extreme comparison was significant, then the difference between the smallest and the next-to-the-largest sum is tested using a critical difference under $k = 6$ and so on. Finally, the values under $k = 2$ are applied for evaluating adjacent sums in the ranked series of sums.

We have already suggested that the Scheffé technique is probably too conservative for pairwise comparisons and that the Duncan method may be too liberal. If the latter supposition is true, then doing t tests (individual comparisons) would be even more liberal than Duncan's test, since the required critical difference for t is smaller than Duncan's critical differences for all comparisons except $k = 2$. Before leaving Winer's informative table, three other observations are in order. First, in the case of Scheffé's test, Tukey's A test, and the individual-comparison method, the required difference is a constant value for every comparison. Second, for the remaining tests, the Tukey B, the Newman-Keuls, and the Duncan, the required difference increases as sums (or means) farther apart in an ordered series are contrasted. Third, the Tukey B test is a compromise between the Tukey A and the Newman-Keuls test (Winer, 1962):

$$\text{crit. diff. (Tukey B)} = \frac{\text{crit. diff. (Tukey A)} + \text{crit. diff. (Newman-Keuls)}}{2}.$$

For example, for $k = 2$:

$$\text{crit. diff. (Tukey B)} = \frac{10.90 + 7.82}{2} = 9.36.$$

The foregoing discussion yields hints and hunches about some of the multiple-comparison techniques, but we need more solid information as to how they actually perform. Fortunately, an impressive beginning step in this regard has been taken in a sampling investigation by Petrinovich and Hardyck (1969). The purpose of their study was to evaluate seven multiple-comparison methods: the Duncan test; the Scheffé test; the Tukey A test; the Tukey B test; the Newman-Keuls test; t_1; and t_2. The t_1 test is simply doing conventional t tests between pairs of means, while t_2 is the same procedure except that $\sqrt{s_w{}^2}$ from the prior analysis of variance is employed as a best estimate of s for the t tests. Two basic populations were included: a normal population with a mean of 50 and a variance of 225; and an exponential distribution with a mean of 5.25 and a variance of 64. The results were based on 1000 sets of samples with k from 2 to 10 and with the numbers of replicates per group ranging from 5 to 50.

For the first phase, samples were drawn from within each of the two populations so that the means were identical. In general, the Tukey A and B and Newman-Keuls tests led to results which were satisfactorily close to the .05 level when this significance level was imposed. As would be expected from the remarks above, the t_1, t_2, and Duncan tests yielded too many significant differences, and the Scheffé test disclosed too few differences. These conclusions are valid for equal sample sizes of 30, 10, and 5 and population changes, normal or exponential. When unequal sample sizes (5, 10, and 15) were combined with either of two unequal variance conditions (1, 2, and 4 or 4, 2, 1), the various methods tended to yield *too few* significant differences when the larger variance was associated with larger number of subjects and to produce *too many* significant differences when the larger variance was associated with smaller number of subjects. Once again, as in the Boneau study, the implication is clear: use equal sample sizes. Finally, when k was increased from 3 to 6, the t_1, t_2, and Duncan tests became worse instead of better and disclosed far too many significant differences. This result suggests that these tests lack adequate protection against larger numbers of comparisons. In contrast, the Tukey A and B and Newman-Keuls tests were all quite close to the proper .05 level of significance.

For the second phase, the authors drew samples from populations in which there *were* differences among the means. Thus these tests are informative about power and Type II errors. As would be anticipated from our earlier discussion and from the representative critical differences shown earlier in Table 3.9, the Duncan, t_1, t_2, and Newman-Keuls tests were better at detecting the differences.

At this point we appear to be caught in a double-bind: one set of multiple-comparison methods works best with respect to Type I errors and another set functions better with regard to Type II errors. It is indeed fortunate that Petrinovich and Hardyck included one more phase in their study, for this series of tests serves in part to modulate the dilemma. Acting upon a suggestion by Ryan (1959), the authors ask, in effect: What happens to error rates for the different techniques when samples are drawn from various populations, some of which differ in their means and some of which do not? In brief,

Table 3.10.* Populations Investigated in the Multiple-Null Tests
(Petrinovich and Hardyck, 1969)

Set 1 (k = 5)	Set 2 (k = 6)
a. $NP, n = 5$	a. $NP, n = 5$
b. $NP, n = 15$	b. $NP, n = 15$
c. $NP, n = 5, 15, 5, 15, 5$	c. $NP, n = 5, 15, 5, 15, 5, 15$
d. $NP, n = 5, 15, 5, 15, 5$	d. $NP, n = 5, 15, 5, 15, 5, 15$
$V = 4, 1, 4, 1, 4$	$V = 4, 1, 4, 1, 4, 1$
e. $NP, n = 5, 15, 5, 15, 5$	e. $NP, n = 5, 15, 5, 15, 5, 15$
$V = 1, 4, 1, 4, 1$	$V = 1, 4, 1, 4, 1, 4$
f. $NP, EP, NP, EP, NP, n = 5$	f. $NP, EP, NP, EP, NP, EP, n = 5$
g. $NP, EP, NP, EP, NP, n = 15$	g. $NP, EP, NP, EP, NP, EP, n = 15$
h. $NP, EP, NP, EP, NP, n = 5$	h. $NP, EP, NP, EP, NP, EP, n = 5$
$V = 4, 1, 1, 4, 4$	$V = 4, 1, 1, 4, 4, 1$
i. NP, EP, NP, EP, NP	i. NP, EP, NP, EP, NP, EP
$n = 5, 15, 15, 5, 5$	$n = 5, 15, 15, 5, 15, 15$
$V = 4, 1, 4, 1, 8$	$V = 4, 1, 4, 1, 8, .5$

NP = normal population
EP = exponential population
n = replicates/group
V = variance

*Reprinted by permission of the publisher and authors from L. Petrinovich and C. D. Hardyck, "Error Rates for Multiple Comparison Methods: Some Evidence Concerning the Frequency of Erroneous Conclusions," *Psychological Bulletin*, 71, p. 51. Copyright 1969, American Psychological Association.

in phase three conditions resembling those from phases one and two were investigated simultaneously. Two sets of conditions were studied. In Set 1, populations 1 and 2 had the same mean; populations 3 and 4 had the same mean but it was considerably higher than the mean for 1 and 2; and the mean for population 5 was considerably higher than the mean for 3 and 4. In Set 2 the mean was the same for populations 1–4, and the mean of populations 5 and 6 was the same but considerably higher than the mean for 1–4. Within each set various combinations of sample sizes, variances, and shapes were included (see Table 3.10).

To simplify the results from phase three, we have abstracted the findings for the five conditions with equal numbers in the subgroups, i.e., conditions a, b, f, g, and h. Then the median proportions of errors across these five conditions for the two sets and seven methods were obtained. These median values are shown in Table 3.11. In the case of Type I errors, the t_1, t_2, Newman-

*Table 3.11.** Median Errors for Multiple-Null Hypothesis at the .05 Level (modified from Petrinovich and Hardyck, 1969)

Set	t_1	t_2	Type I Scheffé	Tukey A	Tukey B	N-K[a]	Duncan
1	.097	.089	.005	.008	.033	.097	.097
2	.243	.242	.009	.029	.051	.093	.184
			Type II				
1	.079	.031	.367	.206	.092	.039	.032
2	.032	.104	.698	.472	.276	.144	.108

[a]Newman-Keuls

*Reprinted with modifications by permission of the publisher and authors from L. Petrinovich and C. D. Hardyck, "Error Rates for Multiple Comparison Methods: Some Evidence Concerning the Frequency of Erroneous Conclusions," *Psychological Bulletin*, 71, p. 51. Copyright 1969, American Psychological Association.

Keuls, and Duncan tests produced too many significant differences; while the Scheffé and Tukey A methods revealed too few. Considering both sets of population conditions, the Tukey B method stands out as the best test with median Type I error values of .033 and .051 for the .05 level of significance. As was seen before, a general reversal of results occurs in the case of Type II errors. Here the simple t_1 test had the lowest proportions of errors, followed by the t_2, the Duncan, and the Newman-Keuls. The Scheffé test produced the greatest incidence of errors, followed by the Tukey A and B with fewer.

Taking into account the results from all three phases of the Petrinovich-Hardyck investigation as well as weighting Type I errors as more important than Type II, our choice of the multiple-comparison methods is the Tukey B test. Across all three phases of the investigation it has a Type I error rate closely approaching .05. Its use will, of course, result in accepting the null hypothesis incorrectly somewhat too often, but generally this is the direction in which we prefer to err. Another consideration entering into this choice is the earlier recommendation for multiple-analysis of data. Multiple-analysis should not be viewed as *data-snooping* for which the Scheffé test was designed. "Data-snooping is mucking around in the data to see if anything significant turns up" (Miller, 1966, p. 62). Rather, multiple-analysis includes partitioning data in terms of different variables, trying appropriate transformations to simplify relationships, and so on. However, the significance tests used in multiple-analysis should be multiple-comparison tests which are done only after significant overall F tests. Since the multiple-analysis strategy would involve far fewer comparisons than are possible with the Scheffé test (see Table 3.8), we would not favor the Scheffé technique for the post-F comparisons.

How do Petrinovich and Hardyck stand on the choice of a multiple-comparison technique? First, they eliminate the t_1, t_2, Duncan, and Newman-Keuls tests because of their high Type I error rates. Second, they argue that if the sample size is 15 or more, it does not matter whether the Tukey A, B, or Scheffé test is used as they differ little in their Type II error rates. Then they say:

> Perhaps the simplest approach would be to argue for the use of the Scheffé as the initial test of choice. If differences among groups are found to be significant by the Scheffé method, the possibility of drawing erroneous conclusions is extremely unlikely. If differences are not found to be significant by the Scheffé, the method of choice would seem to be the Tukey B, which fixes the *experimentwise* error rates at conventional levels and which shows little deviation as a result of the violations of assumptions. The Tukey B is also somewhat more sensitive to real differences between the groups (1969, p. 53).

While we would agree with the authors' assessment of the Tukey B test, their rationale for suggesting the prior use of the Scheffé test escapes us. If they are thinking of any and all possible contrasts, then the Scheffé test is *the* test to employ. But for pairwise comparisons it is simply far too conservative.

The choice of the Tukey B for pairwise comparisons, is a provisional one, being based largely on the Petrinovich-Hardyck study. This study, while an excellent one, represents the first of many sampling investigations that need to be done using other distribution shapes, variance conditions, etc. Finally, two other major findings from the Petrinovich-Hardyck study should not be overlooked: (a) abnormal conditions – unequal sample sizes, unequal variances, etc. — which affect F test probabilities also distort the percentages of significant differences found with multiple-comparison tests; and (b) the power of these multiple-comparison tests is extremely low when the sample sizes are less than 10.

Having selected the Tukey B method, we will now present an example of its application (see Ryan, 1959, pp. 45–46; Winer, 1962, pp. 87f.). In Table 3.12 some data are displayed from a concept-formation study by Overstreet

Table 3.12.* Dimension Selection Scores in Multiple-Concept Formation (modified from Overstreet and Dunham, 1969)

Condition	ΣX	N	M	s
1	120	11	10.91	9.11
2	148	11	13.45	8.42
3	44	11	4.00	6.93
4	173	11	15.73	7.42

*Reprinted with modifications by permission of the publisher and authors from J. D. Overstreet and J. L. Dunham, "Effect of Number of Values and Irrelevant Dimensions on Dimension Selection and Associative Learning in a Multiple-Concept Problem," *Journal of Experimental Psychology*, 79, p. 266. Copyright 1969, American Psychological Association.

and Dunham (1969). There were four concept-formation conditions with 11 Ss per group and the dependent variable was number of trials required by the Ss to name the correct pair of relevant dimensions in the concept task. The variances appear to be homogeneous by inspection and an F test for conditions is:

$$F = \frac{s_B^2}{s_W^2} = \frac{283.72}{64.24} = 4.42.$$

The obtained F of 4.42 for df's of 3 and 40 is significant at less than the .01 level. Accordingly, we now wish to determine which means differ from one another.

The first step in the Tukey B test is to determine the standard error of an *individual* mean. From the first section of this Chapter the formula is:

$s_M = s/\sqrt{N}$. Since the best estimate of s is $\sqrt{s_W^2}$:

$$s_M = \frac{\sqrt{s_W^2}}{\sqrt{N}} = \frac{\sqrt{64.24}}{\sqrt{11}} = 2.42.$$

Next, the four means are arranged in order of magnitude: 4.00, 10.91, 13.45, 15.73. The first comparison is between the extremes: 15.73–4.00 = 11.73.

The critical difference for this comparison is:

$$crit.\ diff. = \frac{q_r s_M + q_k s_M}{2}.$$

The term q_r is the studentized range value from Table H (Appendix) for r, the number of steps separating the means being compared, and df_w; q_k is the studentized range value for k, the total number of means in the complete set, and df_w. For this comparison $r = k = 4$ and $df_w = 40$. Finding the appropriate studentized ranges for the .01 level in the table, we have:[6]

$$crit.\ diff. = \frac{4.70(2.42) + 4.70(2.42)}{2} = 11.37.$$

As the obtained difference between the extreme means is greater than this critical difference, we have an indication that the extreme means differ at less than the .01 level of significance.

The next comparison is $13.45 - 4.00 = 9.45$. For this comparison, $r = 3$, $k = 4$, and $df_w = 40$:

$$crit.\ diff. = \frac{4.37(2.42) + 4.70(2.42)}{2} = 10.97.$$

As the obtained difference is less than the required critical difference, there is no evidence to reject the null hypothesis. One other comparison, $15.73 - 10.91 = 4.82$, can also be tested with this same critical difference because $r = 3$, $k = 4$, and $df_w = 40$. This comparison is also not significant. Since $M_2 = M_3$ and $M_4 = M_1$, the three other possible comparisons are not done. (See the analysis of the chick data, Table 4.6, for a fuller description of this layer method of making multiple comparisons.) Therefore, the indication from this pairwise analysis of means is that only the two extreme means differ.

This same method of multiple comparisons can be applied to k variances after Box's test for homogeneity of variance reveals a significant overall F. For example, the data in Table 3.5 could be further analyzed by Tukey's B test. The mean log s^2 for each group would be obtained, and the analysis would follow exactly the procedure as that above for the Overstreet-Dunham data. For example, for testing the two extremes mean log s^2 values, the critical difference for $r = k = 6$ and $df_w = 12$ would be calculated, and so on. It should be noted, however, that the indications from this analysis would pertain to comparisons among *variances* rather than means.

In the last two sections we have covered a lot of topics: (a) the testing of k independent means by an analysis of variance; (b) testing k independent variances; (c) the assumptions for analysis of variance; (d) the effect of

---

6. The level of significance used in doing multiple-comparison tests should be the same as the investigator selected as significant for his analysis of variance.

violations of these assumptions on analysis of variance; (e) an evaluation of methods for comparing k independent means after an analysis of variance; (f) the application of Tukey's B test to k means; and finally (g) comparing k independent variances after Box's test for homogeneity of variance. Next we shall turn to the problem of testing means resulting from two matched groups and then from k matched groups.

The Means of Two Matched Groups

Our initial task is to specify clearly what "matched" groups are. Matched groups include two experimental designs: (a) the two groups consist of N pairs of Ss and the members of each pair are alike in terms of some variable (which we will term the *matching* variable); and (b) a set of N Ss is tested twice. Suppose an experiment were being done on the effect of two kinds of instructions upon performance in a problem-solving task. Suppose further that it were known from previous research that intelligence is positively related to problem-solving. If the experimenter randomly assigned his 20 Ss to the two instruction conditions, then he would equate his groups on intelligence (and other variables) by randomization. Or he might obtain IQ scores for his Ss prior to the experiment, find pairs with similar IQ scores (e.g., 89 and 90), and assign the members of each pair randomly to the two instruction conditions. Thus the IQ scores of the Ss might look like this:

| | Instructions | |
Pair	A	B
1	89	90
2	107	105
3	122	121
.	.	.
.	.	.
.	.	.
10	135	133

With the matching procedure the experimenter has exerted definite control over intelligence rather than trusting it to randomization. Two practical problems that arise in matching are: the Ss for whom no closely matched mates can be found have to be discarded; and, if in the course of the experiment an S is lost, then his score must either be estimated somehow or else the score of his mate must be discarded.

In the second type of matched group design the matching is even more precise because the *same* Ss are tested twice. Thus we might have 10 Ss and test them with both instructions A and B. This design, which resembles the first design, is much trickier to interpret. If the effects of the first test condition "carry over" into the second test, then the results are not solely a function of the second test conditions but of the unknown amount of carry-over *and* the second test condition. One strategy to alleviate this difficulty is to test half of the Ss in a test 1-test 2 order and the other half with a test 2-test 1 order. This so-called *cross-over* design, which may be subjected to a more complex analysis, provides hints as to possible carry-over effects. Note that there are no carry-over effects in the matched pairs design for the simple reason that each S is exposed to only one condition.

One other design should be mentioned at this time because it resembles a matched group design. Suppose the experimenter randomly assigned his 20 Ss to the two instruction groups. He then checks their IQ scores and observes that the Ss have higher IQ scores in one group. By switching a few Ss between the groups, he is able to equate the means and variances of the IQ's for the two groups. We will call this design an *equated* groups design. This design is a monster and should never be used! Since the experimenter has tampered with his original randomization, he cannot evaluate the results with a *t* test for independent groups. The reason for this is that he cannot trust the obtained probability values from the *t* table, for he has violated (to some unknown degree) the *t* test assumption of independence. Nor can the data from the design be treated as a matched groups study because the Ss are not matched in pairs. Therefore, the equated groups design should always be avoided.

One other feature of the matched group design, its efficiency, needs elaboration. The formula for the standard error of the difference of the means for a matched group experiment is:

$$s_{M_1 - M_2} = \sqrt{\left(\frac{s_1{}^2}{N_1} + \frac{s_2{}^2}{N_2}\right) - 2r\, s_{M_1}\, s_{M_2}}.$$

The part of the formula enclosed in parentheses is identical to the formula for the standard error of the difference of means from two independent groups. The new symbol, r, is the correlation between the scores of the dependent variable for the two groups (see Chapter 6). This index of relationship tells us whether: (a) the scores in the two groups rise together; (b) one set rises while the other falls: or (c) neither. When (a) occurs, r will range from greater than zero to $+1.00$. When (b) occurs r will range from less than zero to -1.00. When (c) occurs, r will be close to zero. Under condition (a) the $s_{M_1 - M_2}$ will be smaller than the $s_{M_1 - M_2}$ for an equivalent independent groups design. It is smaller because the quantity, $2r\, s_{M_1}\, s_{M_2}$, will be subtracted from the error term. Thus the matched group design may be a more *efficient* design than the independent groups design. But when r is negative or zero, the matched group error term will be larger ($2r\, s_{M_1}\, s_{M_2}$ will be *added* to the error term) or remain unchanged, respectively. Thus a matched groups design is a sound undertaking, if and only if a substantial positive correlation exists between the two sets of dependent variable scores. Such a correlation will be found when the *matching* variable is positively correlated with the *dependent* variable. It follows that matching should be done only when we have definite knowledge that there is indeed such a correlation between the matching variable and the dependent variable. Employing a "bad" matching variable can backfire and produce a less efficient design in contrast to an independent groups design.

Let us now turn to the analysis of a matched groups design. We can summarize this analysis quickly because the formula above for the standard error of the difference between two correlated means can be bypassed by reducing the data to N difference scores and testing the mean of these scores, M_D, with the t test for a single group as was done in the first section of this Chapter. The rationale underlying this procedure is that the difference in the two means is equal to the mean of differences between the pairs of scores, i.e., $M_1 - M_2 = M_D$. Most textbooks present special formulas for the t test of correlated means, but we will simply analyze the difference scores with the regular formula for a single mean.

To illustrate this procedure we shall use some data from a marijuana

Table 3.13.* *Change in Heart Rate 15 Minutes after Smoking Tobacco and Low Dose of Marijuana (modified from Weil, Zinberg, and Nelsen, 1968)*

S	Placebo	Low	Difference Low−Placebo
1	+ 16	+ 20	+ 4
2	+ 12	+ 24	+ 12
3	+ 8	+ 8	0
4	+ 20	+ 8	− 12
5	+ 8	+ 4	− 4
6	+ 10	+ 20	+ 10
7	+ 4	+ 28	+ 24
8	− 8	+ 20	+ 28
9	0	+ 20	+ 20
M	+ 7.8	+ 16.9	+ 9.1

*Reprinted with modifications by permission of the publisher and author from A. T. Weil et al., "Clinical and Psychological Effects of Marihuana in Man," *Science*, 162, p. 1234, 1968.

investigation by Weil, Zinberg, and Nelson (1968). "The central group of subjects consisted of nine healthy, male volunteers, 21 to 26 years of age, all of whom smoked tobacco cigarettes regularly but had never tried marijuana previously" (Weil, et al., 1968, p. 1236). The scores in Table 3.13 are changes in heart rate (beats/minute) from base-rate levels before smoking to 15 minutes after smoking two cigarettes of tobacco and flavoring (placebo) and two cigarettes with a low dosage of marijuana (0.25 gram of marijuana mixed with tobacco and flavoring). To evaluate the difference between the means for the placebo and low dose conditions, all we have to do is to treat the nine *difference* scores in Table 3.13 as scores from a single group. The null hypothesis for a two-tailed test is that: $M_D = 0$. (Two one-tailed hypotheses would be: $M_D > 0$ or $M_D < 0$). Applying the formulas from the first of this chapter, we have:

$$s = \sqrt{\frac{\Sigma X^2 - (\Sigma X)^2/N}{N-1}}; \qquad s_M = \frac{s}{\sqrt{N}}; \qquad t = \frac{M_D - M_T}{s_M};$$

$$s = \sqrt{\frac{2180 - (82)^2/9}{9-1}} = 13.38. \qquad s_M = \frac{13.38}{\sqrt{9}} = 4.46. \qquad t = \frac{9.1-0}{4.46} = 2.04.$$

The *df* for this *t* are $N-1 = 9-1 = 8$. From the *t* table the two-tailed probability for a $t = 2.04$ is between .10 and .05. Although 6 out of 9 Ss displayed increased heart rates 15 minutes after a low dose of marijuana, the mean gain was not significant at the .05 level. Parenthetically, it might be noted that 8 other Ss, who were chronic users of marijuana, did display highly significant increases in heart rate 15 minutes after smoking two low-dose cigarettes. Regarding the possibility of carry-over effects in matched group designs mentioned above, the authors reported that they administered the drug treatments to the Ss in three different orders and brought the Ss to high levels of performance on one task, the pursuit rotor, prior to beginning the experiment. This study also reveals one advantage of the matched groups design: it can be employed when, as in this investigation, the supply of Ss is limited.

Another factor bearing on the efficiency of the matched groups design relative to an independent groups design is the *df* for the two designs. In the matched group design the *df* are number of differences minus one or $N-1$. In the independent group design the *df* are $[(N_1-1)+(N_2-1)]$. Thus the latter design has twice as many *df*. For the matched group design to be more efficient, the reduction in the error term as a result of a substantial positive correlation between the scores for the two groups must be large enough to offset the loss in *df*.

What are the assumptions underlying the *t* test for correlated means? It is important to point out that the assumptions are made regarding the *difference scores* rather than the scores for the two treatments themselves. Siegel says: "The *t* test assumes that these difference scores are normally and independently distributed in the population from which the sample was drawn, and requires that they be measured on at least an interval scale" (1956, p. 62). As these assumptions were dealt with in some detail in the section on the *t* test for a single sample, it is unnecessary to examine them again. Regarding the independence assumption, it might be mentioned that although the paired scores are dependent when the matching variable is a well-selected one, the difference scores are independent. Lastly, let us re-iterate our opposition to Siegel's assumption that the difference scores must be measured on an interval scale or better.

The Means of k Matched Groups

This design is simply an extension of the foregoing matched group design. Instead of having N pairs of matched Ss, we now have N sets of k matched Ss. As in the previous design, the same N Ss may be tested k times or they may be N sets of triplets or quadruplets, etc., of Ss, who are alike on some matching variable and are randomly assigned to the k treatments. This latter design is termed a *randomized blocks* design. And, as before, the problem of carry-over effects constitutes an ever-present danger to causal analysis when the same Ss are tested more than once. Whenever possible, the sounder tactic of randomly assigning matched Ss to single treatments should be

Table 3.14.*   Pursuit-Rotor Scores for Naive Subjects after Three Dosages of Marijuana (modified from Weil, Zinberg, and Nelsen, 1968)

S	Placebo	Low	High	ΣX
1	+ 1.20	− 1.04	− 4.01	− 3.85
2	+ 0.89	− 1.43	− 0.12	− 0.66
3	+ 0.50	− 0.60	− 6.56	− 6.66
4	+ 0.18	− 0.11	+ 0.11	+ 0.18
5	+ 3.20	+ 0.39	+ 0.13	+ 3.72
6	+ 3.45	− 0.32	− 3.56	− 0.43
7	+ 0.81	+ 0.48	− 0.79	+ 0.50
8	+ 1.75	− 0.39	− 0.92	+ 0.44
9	+ 3.90	− 1.94	− 2.60	− 0.64
ΣX	+15.88	− 4.96	−18.32	− 7.40 = ΣΣX
M	+ 1.76	− 0.55	− 2.04	

*Reprinted with modifications by permission of the publisher and author from A. T. Weil et al., "Clinical and Psychological Effects of Marihuana in Man," Science, 162, p. 1240, 1968.

followed. Like the simple matched group design, the efficiency of the k matched groups design rests upon the selection of a "good" matching variable.

To provide an example, we will select some other data on the effects of marijuana on pursuit rotor performance from the Weil et al. study (1968). This task requires the S to keep a stylus in contact with a small dot on a moving turntable. The scores in Table 3.14 represent the changes in performance for 9 naive Ss 15 minutes after the different dosages of marijuana. These data may be assessed by an analysis of variance. As in the case of a simple analysis of variance design, the first step is to determine the SS_T with the usual formula:

$$SS_T = \Sigma\Sigma X^2 - \frac{(\Sigma\Sigma X)^2}{N} = 131.55 - \frac{(-7.40)^2}{27} = 129.52.$$

This SS_T has df_T of $N-1 = 27-1 = 26$. Likewise we can calculate a SS_B for dosage level with the previous formula:

$$SS_B = \frac{(\Sigma X_1)^2}{N_1} + \frac{(\Sigma X_2)^2}{N_2} + \frac{(\Sigma X_3)^2}{N_3} - \frac{(\Sigma\Sigma X)^2}{N},$$

$$SS_B = \frac{(15.88)^2}{9} + \frac{(-4.96)^2}{9} + \frac{(-18.32)^2}{9} - \frac{(-7.40)^2}{27} = 66.01.$$

The df_B are $k-1 = 3-1 = 2$. For this design a new source of variation due to Ss or blocks can be determined using the totals for Ss:

$$SS_{Ss} = \frac{(\Sigma X_{S1})^2}{k} + \frac{(\Sigma X_{S2})^2}{k} + \cdots + \frac{(\Sigma X_{SN})^2}{k} - \frac{(\Sigma\Sigma X)^2}{N},$$

$$SS_{Ss} = \frac{(-3.85)^2}{3} + \frac{(-0.66)^2}{3} + \cdots + \frac{(-0.64)^2}{3} - \frac{(-7.40)^2}{27} = 22.81.$$

Since this SS_{Ss} is based upon the number of S totals minus one and $N_1 = N_2 = N_3$, the $df_{Ss} = N_1 - 1 = 9-1 = 8$. Finally, by subtraction a sum of squares for error can be found:

$$SS_E = SS_T - SS_B - SS_{Ss},$$

$$SS_E = 129.52 - 66.01 - 22.81 = 40.70.$$

The df_E will be $(N_1 - 1)(k-1) = (9-1)(3-1) = 16$ or it can be obtained by subtraction:

$$df_E = df_T - df_B - df_{Ss} = 26 - 2 - 8 = 16.$$

It is convenient to put these quantities together in what is called a *summary table* (Table 3.15). By dividing each *SS* by its appropriate *df*, the s^2's are obtained. We are now ready to assess the significance of dosage level:

$$F = \frac{s_B^2}{s_E^2} = \frac{33.00}{2.54} = 12.99.$$

For *df* of 2 and 16 the $F = 12.99$ has a probability of less than .001.

Table 3.15. Summary Table for Analysis of Variance of the Pursuit Rotor Results

Source of Variation	SS	df	s^2	F
Dosage Level	66.01	2	33.00	12.99
Ss	22.81	8	2.85	
Error	40.70	16	2.54	
Total	129.52	26		

Once more the question of the relative efficiency of this design can be raised. If an independent groups design had been employed instead of matched groups, the SS_T and SS_B values would be the same. The error term, SS_W, would be:

$$SS_W = SS_T - SS_B = 129.52 - 66.01 = 63.51.$$

The df_W would be:

$$df_W = df_T - df_B = 26 - 2 = 24.$$

Accordingly, the error term for an independent groups design would be $SS_W/df_W = 63.51/24 = 2.65$, and the F would be $s_B^2/s_W^2 = 33.00/2.65 = 12.45$. The df for this F would be 2 and 24 and again the probability of this F for treatments is less than .001. The relative efficiency of the *k* matched group design depends upon how much variation is due to SS_{Ss} since:

$$SS_W = SS_{Ss} + SS_E.$$

In the present example the error term has been reduced slightly in the matched groups design ($s_E^2 = 2.54$) as against that from the independent groups design ($s_W^2 = 2.65$). However, at the same time we have lost brownie points for *df* with the matched groups design in contrast to the independent groups design, $df = 2$ and 16 vs 2 and 24, respectively. As before the efficiency of the matched groups design rests ultimately on the correlations among the scores. The SS_{Ss} will be large only when the matching variable correlates substantially and positively with the dependent variable. In the Weil et al. example it is questionable whether or not the matching has increased the efficiency of the design because the decrease in the error term was not large enough to offset the loss in df. Once more we should caution that matching is only a sound tactic when the matching variable is *known* to correlate highly with the dependent variable. However, the matched groups design can still be defended in the Weil et al. study on the grounds that as a result of the controversial nature of the research the supply of Ss was limited.

We have already indicated that matched groups designs may suffer from a possible confounding of carry-over effects with treatment effects. A further major difficulty concerns the assumptions underlying the design. Two of these assumptions are that: (a) the variances of the treatment populations are homogeneous; and (b) the correlations among the treatment populations are homogeneous. As Box (1953) has shown that assumption (b) is more critical, we will devote our attention to it. It means that all possible correlations among the k sets of treatment scores are alike within the limits of sampling fluctuation. One correlation would be between the scores for the placebo and low dosage, another between placebo and high dosage scores, and another between the low and high dosage scores. Furthermore, the testing of assumptions (a) and (b) is a very tedious procedure.

Box (1953) has investigated the consequences of the violation of these assumptions and concluded that when the assumptions are violated too many Type I errors are made in evaluating the effects of treatments. Since the F test bias is positive, Box has proposed a "conservative" F test for treatments. This test consists of assessing the obtained F ratio with reduced df. More precisely, the obtained F is looked up in the table for 1 and $N_1 - 1$ df instead of the usual df of $k - 1$ and $(N_1 - 1)(k - 1)$. That is, the regular df's are divided by $k - 1$ for the conservative test. To perform the conservative F test on the Weil et al. example, the F of 12.99 is looked up in the F table with 1 and $N_1 - 1$ df or 1 and 8. Myers (1966) advises the application of both the regular and conservative F tests and reaching a decision regarding the null hypothesis for treatments on the basis of the outcome of the two tests. Three outcomes are possible: (a) if the regular F test is not significant, there is no point in doing the conservative test, and the null hypothesis would not be rejected; (b) if the regular test is significant but the conservative test is not, then a decision is difficult; (c) if both tests are significant, the null hypothesis may be safely rejected. In the present case, where the regular test attains significance at less than .001 and the conservative test is significant somewhere between .01 and .005, the decision to reject the null hypothesis is easy.

In view of the difficulty of evaluating the assumptions for the k matched groups test and the pronounced bias introduced by the violation of these assumptions, Myers' method of arriving at a decision on the null hypothesis, by contrasting the outcomes of regular and conservative F tests, seems like a sound procedure. Having rejected the null hypothesis in this case, we are faced by the same old question: Which treatment means are different from one another? In the next section we shall consider the problem of multiple comparisons of k means from matched groups.

Multiple Comparisons of Means from k Matched Groups

At the outset we must acknowledge that the methods proposed in this section are offered with considerable uncertainty. There are two reasons for this uncertainty: (a) competent specialists have proposed the application of different multiple-comparison techniques; and (b) little is known about the power and robustness of the techniques. Regarding (a), Edwards says:

> Additional tests concerning the treatment means may be made in terms of the procedures discussed previously under the heading multiple comparisons [Duncan's test, Scheffé's test, etc.]. For the randomized block design, s^2, the error mean square is the block × treatment mean square $[s_E^2]$ (1968, p. 160).

The same advice is offered by Winer (1962, p. 114) for testing the treatment means from an example in which five Ss were exposed to four drugs. On the other hand, Miller, in discussing another multiple-comparison technique, Bonferroni t statistics, asserts: "Let $Y_1, ..., Y_k$ be normally distributed random variables with means $\mu_1, ..., \mu_k$ and variances $\sigma_1^2, ..., \sigma_k^2$, respectively. The Y's may or may not be independent" (1966, p. 67). At a later point in describing Tukey's test, Miller comments: "Note in contradistinction to the Bonferroni t that the variables $Y_1, ..., Y_k$ *must be independent*" (1966, p. 71, emphasis added). Thus Edwards and Winer have proposed that multiple-comparison methods like the Tukey B, Newman-Keuls, and Duncan tests are appropriate for comparisons of dependent treatment means; while Miller argues that these techniques are only suitable for testing the means of independent groups.

Following the analysis of Weil et al., let us apply the Tukey B method to the means in Table 3.14. The standard error of an individual mean is:

$$s_M = \frac{\sqrt{s_E^2}}{\sqrt{N}} = \frac{\sqrt{2.54}}{\sqrt{9}} = 0.53$$

Note that we have employed the $\sqrt{s_E^2}$ as an estimate of s rather than $\sqrt{s_W^2}$ as in the case of independent groups. The means for the treatments in order are: -2.04, -0.55, and 1.76. The critical difference at the .05 level of significance for the extreme means when $r = k = 3$ and $df_E = 16$ is:

$$crit. \; diff. = \frac{q_r s_M + q_k s_M}{2}$$

$$\text{crit. diff.} = \frac{3.65\,(0.53) + 3.65\,(0.53)}{2} = 1.93.$$

Since the difference in the extreme means, $1.76 - (-2.04) = 3.80$, is greater than the critical difference of 1.93, the difference between the placebo and high dosage of marijuana treatment means is significant. For the other two comparisons, $1.76 - (-0.55) = 2.31$ and $-0.55 - (-2.04) = 1.49$, the critical difference for $r = 2$, $k = 3$, and $df_E = 16$ is:

$$\text{crit. diff.} = \frac{3.00\,(0.53) + 3.65\,(0.53)}{2} = 1.76.$$

Accordingly, the difference between the placebo and the low dosage means is significant but that between the high and low dosage is not.[7]

Another technique of testing the means, suggested by Miller (1966) and Dunn (1959; 1961), is the Bonferroni t statistic. These statisticians contend that this class of statistics is applicable to either independent or dependent treatment means. The Bonferroni t method is a simple one that incorporates the t distribution rather than studentized ranges. More precisely, the constant critical difference for making C comparisons is:

$$\text{crit. diff.} = t_{df_E}^{\alpha/2C} \sqrt{\frac{2s_E^2}{N}}.$$

In this formula $t_{df_E}^{\alpha/2C}$ is the t value for df_E at the $\alpha/2C$ significance level. For example, suppose we wished to make five pairwise comparisons of means ($C = 5$) at the .01 level ($\alpha = .01$) when df_E was 20. Then $t_{df_E}^{\alpha/2C}$ would be t for $20df$ corresponding to the $\alpha/2C$ level of significance or $.01/2(5) = .001$. Obtaining this t value directly necessitates extended t tables, but Dunn (1961) has provided tables for directly obtaining these $t_{df_E}^{\alpha/2C}$ values. From her table (Table I, Appendix) the value is 3.55. It should be pointed out that the Bonferroni t method, like other multiple-comparison techniques, requires a higher significance level as C, the number of comparisons of means, increases. In this example instead of a t corresponding to the .01 level, with $C = 5$ the t is for the .001 level.

To illustrate Bonferroni t statistics, let us apply the method to the Weil, et al. problem. The critical difference for $C = 3$, $\alpha = .05$, and $df_E = 16$ would be:

$$\text{crit. diff.} = t_{df_E}^{\alpha/2C} \sqrt{\frac{2s_E^2}{N}} = 2.67 \sqrt{\frac{2(2.54)}{9}} = 2.01.$$

---

7. Actually Weil et al. found that all three contrasts were significant. This discrepancy is probably due to the fact that they had a smaller error term and greater df because they apparently included other data for 90 minutes after smoking in their analysis.

The t value was found by linear interpolation in Dunn's table:

df	$t_{df_E}^{\alpha/2C}$
15	2.69
20	2.61

Since $df_E = 16$ is one-fifth of the distance from $df = 15$ to $df = 20$, the t for $.05/2(3) = 2.67$. When the differences among the means are compared with the critical difference of 2.01, the indications are the same as those observed above with the Tukey test. The difference between the placebo and high dosage (3.80) and between placebo and low dosage (2.31) are both significant, but the difference between high and low dosage (1.49) fails to equal or exceed the required critical difference of 2.01.

Another approach to the pairwise testing of the k means would be to run simple t tests. In the Weil et al. example the constant t value needed with this method would be the t for $df = 8$ at the .05 level or 2.306. This value is, of course, smaller in magnitude than the studentized ranges for the Tukey method and the Bonferroni t. Since the simple t method includes no adjustments in the probability values for the number of comparisons, we would suspect that it would probably produce a high Type I error rate.

Considering the other two techniques, the Tukey B and Bonferroni t, we would advise applying Bonferroni t's for making tests of treatment means from a k matched group design. This suggestion is based upon the fact that when the same Ss undergo k treatments, the obtained data may be highly correlated and the methods utilizing studentized ranges are for independent variates. Perhaps, the Tukey B method could be applied to the k matched groups design when each S experiences only a single treatment. For such a randomized blocks design, Hays (1963, pp. 454f.) has proposed that independence of errors is a more tenable possibility than for a repeated measurements design. Again let us stress that the suggestion to apply the Bonferroni t to the treatment means from k matched groups is offered with considerable uncertainty. We badly need sampling studies to see how the Tukey B, Bonferroni t, and other techniques actually perform.

Three More Complex Experimental Designs

In the previous portions of this chapter some methods for analyzing data from two and k independent and matched groups were described. These designs were relatively simple. However, by a few extensions and combinations of these techniques we can achieve some more elaborate experimental designs that are often encountered in psychological research. More specifically, in this section we shall consider in an elementary fashion three more complicated designs: (a) *a factorial design*, (b) *an independent groups design with repeated measurements*, (c) *a factorial design with repeated measurements*.

A factorial design represents an extension of the independent groups design. An independent groups design with repeated measurements may be viewed as a combination of the independent and matched groups designs. And a factorial design with repeated measurements is like a combination of a factorial design and a matched groups design. Faced with such extrapolations, students often panic. This reaction is unwise. Imagine, if you will, that the previous sections have provided us with a few Tinker Toys. Now let's play Tinker Toys — let's build something.

Independent groups designs were discussed earlier in which two or k groups were exposed to different levels of a variable or factor and the Ss were randomly assigned to the groups. For example, the independent variable manipulated by Klein was the percentage of trials which was reinforced in a particular goal box, and the six levels of this variable were 100, 90, 80, 60, 40, and 20 %. We may denote a variable as A and the levels of the variable as $A_1, A_2, ..., A_k$. Suppose an investigator were also interested in the influence of a second variable, B. He might perform one experiment in which A was varied and a second study in which B was varied. He would then be able to ascertain how A and B *separately* affected some dependent variable. That is, by performing two independent groups experiments the investigator could gain some indications regarding the two variables. However, a more efficient procedure would be to "cross" one variable with the other. When two (or more) variables are crossed, the resulting design is termed a factorial design. This design is not only informative regarding the main effects of A and B, but also it tells us about the effect of *combining* A and B. The latter information is technically known as the *interaction* of A and B and the concept of interaction will be examined in greater detail later.

What do we mean by crossing one variable with another? It means simply that *every level of a variable is combined with every level of the other variable.* Let's reduce the abstractness of this statement by means of a table. Suppose we have an experiment with three levels of A and three levels of B. This 3×3 factorial design can be represented as in Table 3.16. Note that this

Table 3.16. A 3×3 Factorial Design

	A_1	A_2	A_3
B_1	Group A_1B_1	Group A_2B_1	Group A_3B_1
B_2	Group A_1B_2	Group A_2B_2	Group A_3B_2
B_3	Group A_1B_3	Group A_2B_3	Group A_3B_3

factorial design includes nine groups. At this time it is inevitable that some wide-awake and slightly compulsive student will raise the following instructive question: "The factorial design requires nine groups. But two separate experiments with three levels each of A and B would require only six groups. How can the factorial design be said to be more efficient if it takes more groups?"[8] What is crucial here is not the number of groups but the df's in the error terms for testing the variables. Assume that the investigator had randomly assigned 15 Ss to each level (A_1, A_2, and A_3) of the A experiment and an equal number to each level (B_1, B_2, and B_3) of the B experiment. Then he would need 90 Ss for the two separate experiments. For each experiment the df_T would be $N-1 = 45-1 = 44$, the df_B would be $k-1 = 3-1 = 2$, and df_W would be $df_T - df_B = 44-2 = 42$. Thus, the error terms for assessing factors A and B would each be based upon $df_W = 42$.

If, by way of contrast, the experimenter had followed a factorial plan, he could randomly and equally assign the 90 Ss to the nine groups. In this case, although he would have more groups (9 vs 6) and fewer Ss per group (10 vs 15), his df_W would actually be greater. In fact, the df_W would be 81. (With the factorial design the $df_T = N-1 = 90-1 = 89$. The $df_B = N_G - 1 = 9-1 = 8$; where N_G = the number of groups. The $df_W = df_T - df_B = 89-8 = 81$). Both of the main effects, A and B, as well as their interaction, $A \times B$, would be tested against an error term s_W^2 based on 81 df. Since this error term has a larger number of df than the df's for the s_W^2 from the two separate experiments, it should yield a more precise estimate of random variability. In addition to the efficiency that accrues to a factorial design as a consequence of the larger df for an error estimate, two other favorable characteristics of a factorial design should be mentioned. First, the estimations of variation due to the main effects, A and B, are based on more observations when a factorial plan is followed rather than a separate experiment plan. Second, as indicated above, a factorial design provides information about the interaction of A and B, while a two experiment plan does not. Regarding the first advantage, in our imaginary two experiment example the variation between the levels A_1, A_2, and A_3 would be estimated from the observations on 15 Ss in each level. In the factorial version the variation would be estimated from the scores of 30 Ss at each level. The greater number of observations in a factorial design result from a *pooling* of the B levels when determining the variation due to A. That is, A_1 includes the observations from groups A_1B_1, A_1B_2, and A_1B_3; A_2 includes scores from A_2B_1, A_2B_2, and A_2B_3; and A_3 includes

8. Questions like this one often evoke defensive ploys on the part of instructors. These ploys are designed to give the instructor time in which to attempt to devise a reasonable answer. One ploy is to tell the student: "That's an interesting question!" Another is to throw the question to the class: "Does anyone know the answer to Bunkie's question?" A desperation ploy is for the instructor to knock all his notes on the floor. This is a messy ploy but quite time-consuming.

scores from A_3B_1, A_3B_2, and A_3B_3. Likewise in calculating the variation due to B, the A levels are pooled. Thus in this particular example the estimates of variation of the main effects, A and B, would be obtained from twice as many observations when a factorial design was applied.

Now let us look at an actual experiment in which a factorial design was used. Scott (1960) investigated the learned reward value of a light for 48 rats in a Skinner box. Two of the variables studied by Scott were (a) the percentage of times the occurrence of the light was associated with primary reward in training, and (b) the percentage of times the light followed a bar press in test. Each factor, in turn, had two levels: 100% and less than 100%. We shall denote the training conditions as CR (100% primary reward) and PR (less than 100% primary reward) and the test conditions as cr (100% secondary reward) and pr (less than 100% secondary reward). The dependent variable was the total number of bar presses made by the 48 Ss during four

Table 3.17.*   *Total Bar Presses during Tests (Scott, 1960)*

Test	Training CR		PR	
cr	23	19	10	15
	5	24	19	8
	8	22	35	17
	14	3	32	8
	12	11	4	18
	15	12	8	21
	$\Sigma X_1 = 168$		$\Sigma X_2 = 195$	
pr	46	114	24	36
	42	45	30	3
	29	22	25	2
	17	18	14	21
	62	1	4	9
	25	15	21	19
	$\Sigma X_3 = 436$		$\Sigma X_4 = 208$	
		$\Sigma\Sigma X = 1007$		

*Derived from Earl Scott, "The Effects of Reward Schedules and Drive Conditions on Secondary Reinforcement," pp. 62–63. Ph.D. dissertation, The University of Kansas, 1960.

daily 10-minute tests. These data are displayed in Table 3.17. It should be noted that the 48 Ss were randomly and equally assigned to the four groups in Table 3.17.

We may begin the analysis by calculating the total variation, the variation between the four groups, and the variation within the groups (SS_T, SS_B, and

SS_W) by means of the formulas for an independent groups design:

$$SS_T = \Sigma\Sigma X^2 - \frac{(\Sigma\Sigma X)^2}{N},$$

$$SS_T = 37555 - \frac{(1007)^2}{48} = 16428.98.$$

$$SS_B = \frac{(\Sigma X_1)^2}{N_1} + \frac{(\Sigma X_2)^2}{N_2} + \frac{(\Sigma X_3)^2}{N_3} + \frac{(\Sigma X_4)^2}{N_4} - \frac{(\Sigma\Sigma X)^2}{N},$$

$$SS_B = \frac{(168)^2}{12} + \frac{(195)^2}{12} + \frac{(436)^2}{12} + \frac{(208)^2}{12} - \frac{(1007)^2}{48},$$

$$SS_B = \frac{299609}{12} - \frac{1014049}{48} = 3841.40.$$

As before, SS_W can be obtained by subtraction:

$$SS_W = SS_T - SS_B,$$

$$SS_W = 16428.98 - 3841.40 = 12587.58.$$

The $df_T = N - 1 = 48 - 1 = 47$, the $df_B = N_G - 1 = 4 - 1 = 3$, and $df_W = df_T - df_B = 47 - 3 = 44$.

The next problem is to partition the SS_B with 3 df into three additive parts: the SS due to the training variable, SS_{Tng}; the SS due to the test variable, SS_{Test}; and the SS due to the interaction of the training and test variables, $SS_{Tng \times Test}$. Each of these components will have a single df. In computing the SS_{Tng}, the scores of the 24 Ss with CR training will be contrasted with the scores of the 24 Ss with PR training. As a consequence of pooling the test groups, there are two training groups and the $df_{Tng} = N_G - 1 = 2 - 1 = 1$. Similarly, in calculating SS_{Test}, the scores of the 24 Ss with cr test are compared with the scores of the 24 Ss with pr test and so $df_{Test} = N_G - 1 = 2 - 1 = 1$. To determine the df for the interaction of training $\times$ test, we will invoke a rule: the df for any interaction are equal to the *product* of the df's of the variables involved in the interaction. Therefore, $df_{Tng \times Test} = (1)(1) = 1$.

The SS_{Tng} and SS_{Test} can be calculated by pooling the appropriate groups and applying the formula for SS_B. The total number of responses for the 24 Ss with CR training was $168 + 436 = 604$; the total for 24 Ss with PR training was $195 + 208 = 403$. Using these totals, the SS_{Tng} can be found:

$$SS_{Tng} = \frac{(\Sigma X_{CR})^2}{N_1 + N_3} + \frac{(\Sigma X_{PR})^2}{N_2 + N_4} - \frac{(\Sigma\Sigma X)^2}{N},$$

$$SS_{Tng} = \frac{(604)^2}{24} + \frac{(403)^2}{24} - \frac{(1007)^2}{48} = 841.69.$$

The corresponding totals for the test groups were $168 + 195 = 363$ for cr and $436 + 208 = 644$ for pr.

$$SS_{Test} = \frac{(\Sigma X_{cr})^2}{N_1 + N_2} + \frac{(\Sigma X_{pr})^2}{N_3 + N_4} - \frac{(\Sigma\Sigma X)^2}{N},$$

$$SS_{Test} = \frac{(363)^2}{24} + \frac{(644)^2}{24} - \frac{(1007)^2}{48} = 1645.02.$$

As always, the squared totals, e.g., $(\Sigma X_{CR})^2$, are divided by the number of observations contributing to the totals.

Finally, the problem of obtaining the SS due to the interaction of training and test remains. Let us construct what is termed an *interaction table* by entering the totals for the four groups into a 2×2 table (Table 3.18). The

Table 3.18.   Interaction Table for Training × Test

Test	Training		Totals
	CR	PR	
cr	168 (a)	195 (b)	363
pr	436 (c)	208 (d)	644
Totals	604	403	1007

$SS_{Tng \times Test}$ is equal to the variation of the four cell entries (i.e., 168, 195, 436, and 208) about the grand total (i.e., 1007) *minus* the variation of the column totals (i.e., 604 and 403) and the variation of the row totals (i.e., 363 and 644). Fortunately, in this instance we have already found these three needed quantities: the cell variation $= SS_B$; the column variation $= SS_{Tng}$; and the row variation $= SS_{Test}$. Therefore, the interaction is:

$$SS_{Tng \times Test} = SS_B - SS_{Tng} - SS_{Test},$$

$$SS_{Tng \times Test} = 3841.40 - 841.69 - 1645.02 = 1354.69.$$

In the case of a 2×2 factorial design, such as Scott's, a shortcut formula is available for determining the interaction. Just as it is useful to directly calculate SS_W as a check upon the accuracy of an analysis, it also is helpful to apply this formula as a check:

$$SS_{Tng \times Test} = \frac{[(a+d) - (b+c)]^2}{4N_C}.$$

Here a, b, c, and d denote the totals for the four cells (see Table 3.18) and N_C is the number of observations that each cell total is based upon. Applying the formula, we have:

$$SS_{Tng \times Test} = \frac{[(168 + 208) - (195 + 436)]^2}{4(12)},$$

$$SS_{Tng \times Test} = \frac{(-255)^2}{48} = 1354.69.$$

This result is identical to that observed with the subtraction method above.

The analysis can be completed by finding the variance estimates, s_{Tng}^2, s_{Test}^2, $s_{Tng \times Test}^2$, and s_w^2, by dividing the appropriate SS's by their df's. The s_w^2 is the error term for evaluating the training, test, and training $\times$ test sources of variation. Again, it is convenient to put these quantities into a summary table (Table 3.19). The F value for test of 5.75 and the F value for

Table 3.19. *Summary Table for Analysis of Variance of Bar Presses during Tests*

Source of Variation	SS	df	s^2	F
Training	841.69	1	841.69	2.94
Test	1645.02	1	1645.02	5.75
Training × Test	1354.69	1	1354.69	4.74
Within Groups (Error)	12587.58	44	286.08	
Total	16428.98	47		

training $\times$ test of 4.74 are both significant, as seen in Table F, at less than the .025 and .05 level for 1 and 44 df, respectively. While the F for training of 2.94 failed to achieve the F value of 4.08 required for significance at the .05 level.

Inspection of Table 3.18 reveals that the Ss under the pr test condition made significantly more bar presses, averaged across the two training conditions, than the Ss under the cr test condition. This F test corresponds to a t test for two independent groups. (Actually an F for 1 and 44 $df = t^2$ for 44 df). However, because the interaction of training $\times$ test is significant, we become less interested in the significant main effect of test and are forced to consider the interaction. Conversely, if the interaction were nonsignificant, then our concern would be with the main effect. Moreover, if there had been more than two levels of the test variable, then multiple comparisons of the k test means would be in order. The appropriate multiple comparison test for such a situation would be Tukey's B test and the $\sqrt{s_w^2}$ would serve as an estimate of s.

In view of the fact that the interaction of training and test is significant, let us turn our attention to the interaction. What is the meaning of this inter-

action? What do we do about it? Notions as to the meaning of the interaction
can be gained by re-examining the operations that were used to compute
the interaction. It will be recalled that the interaction *SS* were the *SS* that
were "left over" after the variation due to the main effects, training and test,
was subtracted from the variation between the cells of the interaction
table, i.e., $SS_{Tng \times Test} = SS_B - SS_{Tng} - SS_{Test}$. When the main effects are
additive, then there is no interaction. Or, to say this in another way, if there
is no interaction, the variation between the cells can be fully predicted from
the main effects. Inspection of an interaction table like Table 3.18, or of
graphs of means for different levels of the interacting variables, yields information about the likelihood and the nature of an interaction. The possibility of finding an interaction exists when *the differences between the levels
of a variable are unequal for different levels of the other variable.* For example,
in Table 3.18 the difference between the test conditions pr − cr for the CR
level of training is $436 - 168 = 268$. The difference between the same test
conditions for the PR level of training is $208 - 195 = 13$. Because these
differences are grossly unequal, the possibility of an interaction would be
anticipated. (Note also that CR − PR for cr differs greatly from CR − PR
for pr: $168 - 195 = -27$ vs $436 - 208 = 228$).

Let us digress for a moment to consider some hypothetical results in

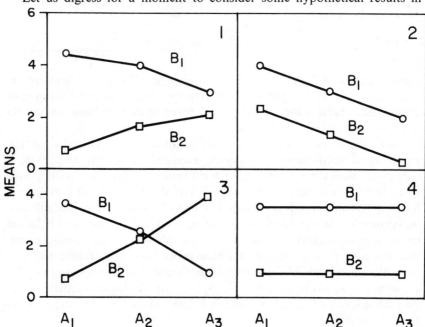

Figure 3.6. Graphs showing nonzero A × B interactions (panels 1 and 3) and zero
A × B interactions (panels 2 and 4).

Figure 3.6. The left-hand panels, 1 and 3, depict cases in which an $A \times B$ interaction might be expected, while in the right-hand panels, 2 and 4, no $A \times B$ interaction would be found. In panels 1 and 3 the differences between B_1 and B_2 are unequal for A_1, A_2, and A_3, but in panels 2 and 4 these differences are equal. Inspection of the figure also suggests the possibilities of various main effects: in panels 1 and 4 there might be a main effect of B; in panel 2 a main effect of A and B; and in panel 3 no main effect.

We have seen that interactions occur when the differences between the levels of a variable are unequal for different levels of the other variable. What is the implication of a significant interaction? It is that a significant main effect must be regarded with considerable caution. The presence of a significant interaction often demands that a statement about the main effect must be qualified. For example, although Scott's pr rats made more bar presses, averaged across training conditions, than the cr rats, this description is accurate only for Ss with CR training. The small difference between the pr and cr Ss with PR training was probably only a chance difference. If we had to predict what another batch of rats would do, we would be imprudent if we bet much money on a large difference being observed between pr and cr for Ss with PR training. Thus the presence of interactions limits the scope of the indications regarding the main effects.

Given a significant interaction, what can an investigator do about it? One tactic rests on the knowledge that interactions may be dependent upon the scale of measurement for the dependent variable. Sometimes it is possible to eliminate an interaction by transforming the original data into logs. A second tactic is to inquire as to the genuineness of an interaction. Lindquist (1953) has drawn an important distinction between *intrinsic* and *extrinsic* interaction. In intrinsic interaction there is a genuine interaction between the variables. That is to say, the *combination of variables* produces unequal differences between levels of a variable for different levels of another variable. In addition, the observed unequal differences are too large to be accounted for on the basis of random variation. In extrinsic interaction the differences are not the result of the experimental variables but of *some extraneous variable* that distorts all of the scores of a treatment combination. For example, if a different experimenter tested one particular treatment combination and this group's scores were aberrant, then we might suspect that the experimenter's technique was faulty or different. Or if the out-of-line group had been tested at an unfavorable time of day, then this procedure could be the suspected extraneous variable. The detection of extrinsic interaction requires a careful assessment of the investigation's experimental procedures. It should also be emphasized that interactions may be some combination of intrinsic and extrinsic effects. In the last analysis, the genuineness of an interaction is demonstrable by replications of an investigation and, particularly, by replications by other investigators. A third tactic is to "live with" the interaction and to explore its nature by further analysis. For didactic purposes we shall adopt the third tactic with respect to Scott's data. The method of analysis (Winer, 1962) we shall follow is to determine what are called the *simple main effects* of test. Then the significance of these simple main effects is tested against an error estimate. In this problem the error is the s_W^2 from the original analysis of variance. The SS_{Test} for CR training is calculated (see Table 3.18) by the regular SS_B formula:

$$SS_{Test\ for\ CR} = \frac{(436)^2}{12} + \frac{(168)^2}{12} - \frac{(604)^2}{24} = 2992.66$$

In a like manner, the SS_{Test} for PR training is calculated:

$$SS_{Test\ for\ PR} = \frac{(208)^2}{12} + \frac{(195)^2}{12} - \frac{(403)^2}{24} = 7.04.$$

Each of these SS's has, of course, a single df. These simple main effects and

Table 3.20.   Summary Table for Simple Main Effects

Source of Variation	SS	df	s^2	F
Test for CR	2992.66	1	2992.66	10.46
Test for PR	7.04	1	7.04	< 1
Within Groups (Error)	12587.58	44	286.08	

the error term may be entered into a summary table (Table 3.20). The F tests of the simple main effects confirm what was obvious from an inspection of the interaction table (Table 3.18): the difference between pr and cr is significant at less than the .05 level for the Ss with CR training but not for Ss with PR training. It is time once more for a student with a good head on his shoulders but with a background of early and severe toilet training to raise another instructive question.[9] "The SS for the interaction of training × test was 1354.69 and it had a single df. If the SS's and df's for the simple effects are added together, they yield a total SS of 2999.70 and 2 df. Why the discrepancies?" That's certainly an interesting question! However, it should be noted that if the SS_{Test} and $SS_{Tng \times Test}$ (see Table 3.19) are added, their sum is 2999.71 with 2 df. Thus the analysis of simple main effects is not simply a partitioning of the variation resulting from the interaction, but a splitting of the variation due to the interaction *and* the main effect of test.

---

9. Is this an indictment of such training? Certainly not! Our simple formula for the bright-eyed and bushy-tailed scientist is: 3 (jiggers) of intelligence + 4 of frustration tolerance + 1 of paranoia + 2 of compulsiveness. Shake well.

If the interaction table for training × test (Table 3.18) is re-examined, it is apparent that the significant interaction could be broken into another set of simple main effects, i.e., the variation between the training conditions for each of the two levels of test. Should this procedure be followed instead of or in addition to what was done? Quite frankly it must be admitted that we do not know the answer to this question. Beset by ignorance, certain suggestions — which should be viewed with considerable caution — will be offered. (a) In a case like the present one in which a main effect and an inter-action are significant, then only the simple main effects for the significant main effect (i.e., test) should be analyzed. (b) If the interaction alone is signi-ficant, then the choice of the set of simple effects to be analyzed should be dictated by the investigator's interest. We are reluctant to break down the interaction into two sets of simple main effects because it seems like these two partitions of the data would greatly exceed the *df* that are available for the interaction. (c) Unfortunately, a third possible case in which both main effects and the interaction are significant poses a formidable problem. In this instance it appears that both sets of simple effects should be tested, despite the fact that this procedure of necessity involves exceeding the *df* for the interaction. We will leave the problem of what simple main effects should be analyzed in this unsatisfactory state and hope that an ominiscient Saint Bernard (complete with brandy cask) will come forth.

The simple main effects analysis completes the factorial analysis of the Scott data. If, however, there had been *k* levels of the test factor rather than two levels, then multiple comparisons would be performed on the means of the significant simple main effect by Tukey's B test.

The matter of the assumptions underlying a factorial design can be disposed of quickly. The assumptions are the same as those for an indepen-dent groups design: (a) the samples have been randomly selected from normally distributed populations; (b) the observations are independent of one another; and (c) the variances of the populations, σ^2's, are equal. Were these assumptions fulfilled in our computational example? We shall leave this question as an exercise for the students — especially for those students who ask instructive questions — to answer!

Finally, it should be mentioned that factorial designs are not limited to two factors. Several factors may be crossed to form more complicated factorial designs. While these designs are efficient, the number of groups and Ss required increases rapidly. Furthermore, there are genuine practical problems in doing experiments with a large number of treatment combina-tions (Lindquist, 1953, p. 256). Lastly, if any of the resulting higher-order interactions (e.g., $A \times B \times C \times D$) are significant, they present grave problems of interpretation.

The next design to be considered is an independent groups design with repeated measurements. In the independent groups design discussed earlier, each S had one score. In the present design two or more measures are available for each S. Moreover, since these measures are the result of repeated tests upon the same Ss, the measures are likely to be correlated. Thus an independent groups design with repeated measurements is like a combination of the independent and matched groups designs which were previously examined.

Part of Scott's data (1960) may be used as an example of this type of experimental plan. In Table 3.21 are shown the number of bar presses made during

Table 3.21.* Bar Presses in Daily Tests for cr and pr Test Groups Trained under CR (Scott, 1960)

						Test Groups						
		cr							pr			
		Days							Days			
S	1	2	3	4	Totals		S	1	2	3	4	Totals
1	7	6	7	3	23		13	6	4	19	17	46
2	2	1	1	1	5		14	10	12	5	15	42
3	4	3	0	1	8		15	4	14	6	5	29
4	6	2	3	3	14		16	0	3	7	7	17
5	6	2	3	1	12		17	11	8	25	18	62
6	4	8	3	0	15		18	8	9	6	2	25
7	4	0	8	7	19		19	13	22	30	49	114
8	4	7	5	8	24		20	12	12	5	16	45
9	9	6	4	3	22		21	5	5	0	12	22
10	3	0	0	0	3		22	0	5	4	9	18
11	7	1	1	2	11		23	1	0	0	0	1
12	5	1	4	2	12		24	1	1	7	6	15
Total 61	37	39	31	168 = $\Sigma\Sigma X_{cr}$			Total 71	95	114	156	436 = $\Sigma\Sigma X_{pr}$	

*Derived from Earl Scott, "The Effects of Reward Schedules and Drive Conditions on Secondary Reinforcement," pp. 62–63. Ph.D. dissertation, The University of Kansas, 1960.

four daily 10-minute tests by the 24 Ss that were trained under CR but tested under cr and pr conditions. In this arrangement cr and pr are the independent groups and the daily test scores are the repeated measurements.

The first step in the analysis is to determine the total variation among the 96 test scores:

$$SS_T = (\Sigma\Sigma\Sigma X^2) - \frac{(\Sigma\Sigma\Sigma X)^2}{N},$$

$$SS_T = (7^2 + 2^2 + 4^2 + \cdots + 6^2) - \frac{(604)^2}{96}$$

$$= 8730.00 - 3800.17 = 4929.83.$$

Next, the total variation of the total scores for the 24 Ss is found:

$$SS_{Ss} = \frac{(\Sigma X_{S1})^2}{k} + \frac{(\Sigma X_{S2})^2}{k} + \cdots + \frac{(\Sigma X_{S24})^2}{k} - \frac{(\Sigma\Sigma\Sigma X)^2}{N},$$

$$SS_{Ss} = \frac{(23)^2}{4} + \frac{(5)^2}{4} + \cdots + \frac{(15)^2}{4} - \frac{(604)^2}{96}$$

$$= 7103.00 - 3800.17 = 3302.83.$$

The SS_{Ss} can be partitioned into two components: the variation between the test groups, SS_{Test}, and the variation within groups, SS_W. The SS_{Test} is:

$$SS_{Test} = \frac{(\Sigma\Sigma X_{cr})^2}{N_1 k} + \frac{(\Sigma\Sigma X_{pr})^2}{N_2 k} - \frac{(\Sigma\Sigma\Sigma X)^2}{N},$$

$$SS_{Test} = \frac{(168)^2}{(12)(4)} + \frac{(436)^2}{(12)(4)} - \frac{(604)^2}{96}$$

$$= 4548.33 - 3800.17 = 748.16.$$

Inasmuch as the SS_{Ss} and SS_{Test} correspond to SS_T and SS_B, respectively, in an independent groups design, the SS_W can be secured by subtraction:

$$SS_W = SS_{Ss} - SS_{Test},$$

$$SS_W = 3302.83 - 748.16 = 2554.67.$$

The df_T are $N - 1 = 96 - 1 = 95$, the $df_{Ss} = N_1 + N_2 - 1 = 12 + 12 - 1 = 23$, and the $df_{Test} = N_G - 1 = 2 - 1 = 1$. Accordingly,

$$df_W = df_{Ss} - df_{Test}$$

$$df_W = 23 - 1 = 22.$$

The SS_T include the variation resulting from both independent and correlated observations. The SS_{Ss} is the total variation of the independent observations. If the SS_{Ss} are subtracted from the SS_T, a residual source of variation, SS_C, due to the correlated observations, remains:

$$SS_C = SS_T - SS_{Ss},$$

$$SS_C = 4929.83 - 3302.83 = 1627.00.$$

This variation will have $df_C = df_T - df_{Ss} = 95 - 23 = 72$. The next task is to divide the SS_C into its three parts. The first component is the variation due to the four days' totals. These daily totals are: $61 + 71 = 132$ for day 1; $37 + 95 = 132$ for day 2; $39 + 114 = 153$ for day 3; and $31 + 156 = 187$ for day 4. The SS_{Days} is then:

$$SS_{Days} = \frac{(\Sigma\Sigma X_{Day\ 1})^2}{N_1 + N_2} + \cdots + \frac{(\Sigma\Sigma X_{Day\ 4})^2}{N_1 + N_2} - \frac{(\Sigma\Sigma\Sigma X)^2}{N},$$

$$SS_{Days} = \frac{(132)^2}{24} + \frac{(132)^2}{24} + \frac{(153)^2}{24} + \frac{(187)^2}{24} - \frac{(604)^2}{96}$$

$$SS_{Days} = 3884.42 - 3800.17 = 84.25.$$

The $df_{Days} = k - 1 = 4 - 1 = 3$.

The second component is the variation due to the interaction of test × days. To obtain this quantity, it is necessary to arrange a 2 × 4 interaction table and to enter the daily totals for each group in the cells (Table 3.22). The method

Table 3.22.   *Interaction Table for Test × Days*

Test	Days 1	2	3	4	Totals
cr	61	37	39	31	168
pr	71	95	114	156	436
Totals	132	132	153	187	604

of finding the interaction is the same that was used in case of the factorial design: obtain the variation due to cells and then remove the row and column variation from it.

$$SS_{Cells} = \frac{(\Sigma X_{Cell\ 1})^2}{N_1} + \cdots + \frac{(\Sigma X_{Cell\ 8})^2}{N_8} - \frac{(\Sigma\Sigma\Sigma X)^2}{N},$$

$$SS_{Cells} = \frac{(61)^2}{12} + \cdots + \frac{(156)^2}{12} - \frac{(604)^2}{96}$$

$$= 4914.17 - 3800.17 = 1114.00.$$

The variation of the row totals is, of course, the variation due to the test groups, SS_{Test}, and the variation of the column totals is that resulting from days, SS_{Days}. Therefore, the interaction is:

$$SS_{Test \times Days} = SS_{Cells} - SS_{Test} - SS_{Days},$$

$$SS_{Test \times Days} = 1114.00 - 748.16 - 84.25 = 281.59.$$

Following the rule that the df for an interaction are the product of the df's for the interacting variables, the $df_{Test \times Days} = (N_G - 1)(k - 1) = (2 - 1)(4 - 1) = 3$.

The third component of the total variation due to correlated observations, SS_C, is an estimate of random variation or error, SS_E. This SS_E and its df_E may be obtained by subtraction:

$$SS_E = SS_C - SS_{Days} - SS_{Test \times Days}$$
$$SS_E = 1627.00 - 84.25 - 281.59 = 1261.16,$$
$$df_E = df_C - df_{Days} - df_{Test \times Days}$$
$$df_E = 72 - 3 - 3 = 66.$$

Although we have attained the SS_E by subtraction, it is possible to obtain it directly. The $SS_E = SS_{Ss \times Days}$ for cr $+ SS_{Ss \times Days}$ for pr. These interactions would be found in the customary manner and they would have df's of $(N_1 - 1)(k - 1) = (12 - 1)(4 - 1) = 33$ and $(N_2 - 1)(k - 1) = (12 - 1)(4 - 1) = 33$, respectively.

In this analysis the s_E^2 serves an error term for evaluating the correlated sources of variation of days and test $\times$ days; the s_W^2 is the appropriate error estimate for evaluating the independent factor of test. The complete analysis is summarized in Table 3.23. The F ratio of 6.44 for test ($F = s_{Test}^2/s_W^2$) is

Table 3.23. *Summary Table for Analysis of Variance of Bar Presses during Four Days*

Source of Variation	SS	df	s^2	F
Test	748.16	1	748.16	6.44
Within Groups	2554.67	22	116.12	
(Total Between Ss	3302.83	23)		
Days	84.25	3	28.08	1.47
Test $\times$ Days	281.59	3	93.86	4.91
Error	1261.16	66	19.11	
(Total Correlated Observations	1627.00	72)		
Total	4929.83	95		

significant at less than the .025 level, as seen in Table F, for 1 and 22 df. The F of 1.47 for days ($F = s_{Days}^2/s_E^2$) is not significant, but the $F = 4.91$ for the interaction ($F = s_{Test \times Days}^2/s_E^2$) with 3 and 66 df is significant at less than the .005 level. As in the previous example, the Ss with pr test produced more responses, averaged across days, than the Ss with cr test. But again the presence of a significant interaction forces us to turn our attention away from the main effect and toward the interaction. Before examining the interaction, it is important to review the assumptions for this design.

At the beginning of this section it was proposed that an independent groups design with repeated measurements could be seen as a combination of an independent and a matched groups design. Accordingly, we would expect that the assumptions for an independent groups design with repeated measurements would be an amalgam of the assumptions for the two kinds of designs. For the independent observations, consisting of the totals for Ss, the assumptions are the same as those for independent groups design, viz., (a) the samples have been randomly selected from normally distributed populations, (b) the observations are independent of one another, and (c) the variances of the populations, σ^2's, are equal. In the case of the correlated observations, consisting of the Ss' daily scores, the assumptions are like those for a matched groups design, viz., (d) both the variances of treatment populations, and (e) the correlations among the treatment populations must be homogeneous. Thus the variances of daily tests and all possible correlations among the daily tests have to be homogeneous.

In performing significance tests on the correlated factors of days and test × days, we will follow Myers' strategy used earlier for a matched group design. That is, decisions about significance will be made by applying *both* a regular and a conservative F test proposed by Box (1953). The conservative F test is done by dividing the usual df's by $k-1$, where k is number of levels of the correlated factor of days. Instead of the regular df of 3 and 66, the df's for the conservative test would be 1 and 22. Since days was not significant by even a regular F test, it is unnecessary to apply the conservative F test. The interaction of test × days is significant at less than .005 by the regular F test ($df = 3, 66$) and at less than .05 by the conservative test ($df = 1, 22$). Since both procedures point to the same indication, we are faced again with the problem of partitioning an interaction.

Once more the simple main effects procedure will be applied by determining the variation between the pr and cr groups on the different days. Using the cell totals in Table 3.22 and the usual formula for SS_B, these simple main effects may be calculated:

$$SS_{\text{Test on Day 1}} = \frac{(61)^2}{12} + \frac{(71)^2}{12} - \frac{(132)^2}{24} = 4.17,$$

$$SS_{\text{Test on Day 2}} = \frac{(37)^2}{12} + \frac{(95)^2}{12} - \frac{(132)^2}{24} = 140.17,$$

$$SS_{\text{Test on Day 3}} = \frac{(39)^2}{12} + \frac{(114)^2}{12} - \frac{(153)^2}{24} = 234.37,$$

$$SS_{\text{Test on Day 4}} = \frac{(31)^2}{12} + \frac{(156)^2}{12} - \frac{(187)^2}{24} = 651.04.$$

Each of these SS's is based on a single df and they add up to 1029.75 which equals the $SS_{Test} + SS_{Test \times Days}$. What is the proper error term for assessing these simple effects? Winer (1961, pp. 310f.) advises using a pooled error term: $(SS_W + SS_E)/(df_W + df_E)$. The $SS_{Pooled\ E} = 2554.67 + 1261.16 = 3815.83$ and $df = 22 + 66 = 88$. The simple main effects and the pooled error estimate are summarized in Table 3.24. From Table F it may be observed that the pr

Table 3.24. Summary Table for Simple Main Effects

Source of Variation	SS	df	s^2	F
Test on Day 1	4.17	1	4.17	<1
Test on Day 2	140.17	1	140.17	3.23
Test on Day 3	234.37	1	234.37	5.41
Test on Day 4	651.04	1	651.04	15.01
Pooled Error	3815.83	88	43.36	

group made significantly more responses than the cr group only on days 3 and 4. Again it is apparent that the occurrence of a significant interaction has exerted a limiting effect upon a main effect.

Before leaving this design, a few other comments are in order. If there were more than two test groups, then Tukey's B test would be applied to the means within the significant simple main effects with the $\sqrt{s_{Pooled\ E}^2}$ serving as an estimate of s. If the investigator elected to evaluate simple main effects of days for the different groups, then these simple main effects would be tested against the usual error for correlated factors, s_E^2, and comparisons of the k correlated means within the significant simple main effects (e.g., $M_{Day\ 1}$ for pr vs $M_{Day\ 2}$ for pr, etc.) could be performed by Bonferroni t tests (which were described in the section on matched groups).

The last complex design to be examined is a factorial design with repeated measurements. This design, as the name implies, is like a factorial design except that repeated measurements are available for each S. Once more Scott's investigation provides a computational example. In this case, the data for the 48 Ss with CR and PR training conditions, cr and pr test conditions, and four daily tests will be analyzed (see Table 3.25).

As always, calculating an SS_T with 191 df is the first step:

$$SS_T = (\Sigma\Sigma\Sigma\Sigma X^2) - \frac{(\Sigma\Sigma\Sigma\Sigma X)^2}{N},$$

$$SS_T = (7^2 + 2^2 + 4^2 \cdots + 9^2) - \frac{(1007)^2}{192}$$

$$SS_T = 11747 - 5281.51 = 6465.49.$$

Table 3.25.* Bar Presses in Four Daily Tests for Rats Trained under CR and PR and Tested under cr and pr (Scott, 1960)

	S	1	2	3	4	Total	S	1	2	3	4	Total
			CR Days						PR Days			
	1	7	6	7	3	23	25	1	3	3	3	10
	2	2	1	1	1	5	26	13	3	3	0	19
	3	4	3	0	1	8	27	10	3	18	4	35
	4	6	2	3	3	14	28	3	4	12	13	32
	5	6	2	3	1	12	29	4	0	0	0	4
cr	6	4	8	3	0	15	30	0	0	3	5	8
	7	4	0	8	7	19	31	5	3	5	2	15
	8	4	7	5	8	24	32	4	2	2	0	8
	9	9	6	4	3	22	33	7	3	3	4	17
	10	3	0	0	0	3	34	3	2	1	2	8
	11	7	1	1	2	11	35	9	4	2	3	18
	12	5	1	4	2	12	36	1	6	3	11	21
	Total	61	37	39	31	168 = $\Sigma\Sigma X_1$	Total	60	33	55	47	195 = $\Sigma\Sigma X_2$
	13	6	4	19	17	46	37	10	7	5	2	24
	14	10	12	5	15	42	38	4	3	8	15	30
	15	4	14	6	5	29	39	5	10	6	4	25
	16	0	3	7	7	17	40	4	4	1	5	14
	17	11	8	25	18	62	41	3	0	0	1	4
pr	18	8	9	6	2	25	42	5	7	3	6	21
	19	13	22	30	49	114	43	13	8	6	9	36
	20	12	12	5	16	45	44	0	1	1	1	3
	21	5	5	0	12	22	45	0	1	0	1	2
	22	0	5	4	9	18	46	4	4	3	10	21
	23	1	0	0	0	1	47	7	1	1	0	9
	24	1	1	7	6	15	48	3	4	6	6	19
	Total	71	95	114	156	436 = $\Sigma\Sigma X_3$	Total	58	50	40	60	208 = $\Sigma\Sigma X_4$

*Derived from Earl Scott, "The Effects of Reward Schedules and Drive Conditions on Secondary Reinforcement," pp. 62–63. Ph.D. dissertation, The University of Kansas, 1960.

Next the total variation of the total scores for the 48 Ss and 47 *df* is found:

$$SS_{Ss} = \frac{(\Sigma X_{S1})^2}{k} + \frac{(\Sigma X_{S2})^2}{k} + \cdots + \frac{(\Sigma X_{S48})^2}{k} - \frac{(\Sigma\Sigma\Sigma\Sigma X)^2}{N},$$

$$SS_{Ss} = \frac{(23)^2}{4} + \frac{(5)^2}{4} + \cdots + \frac{(9)^2}{4} - \frac{(1007)^2}{192}$$

$$= 9388.75 - 5281.51 = 4107.24.$$

As before, the SS_{Ss} can be divided into two components, SS_B and SS_W:

$$SS_B = \frac{(\Sigma\Sigma X_1)^2}{N_1 k} + \frac{(\Sigma\Sigma X_2)^2}{N_2 k} + \frac{(\Sigma\Sigma X_3)^2}{N_3 k} + \frac{(\Sigma\Sigma X_4)^2}{N_4 k} - \frac{(\Sigma\Sigma\Sigma\Sigma X)^2}{N},$$

$$SS_B = \frac{(168)^2}{(12)(4)} + \frac{(195)^2}{(12)(4)} + \frac{(436)^2}{(12)(4)} + \frac{(208)^2}{(12)(4)} - \frac{(1007)^2}{192}$$

$$= 6241.85 - 5281.51 = 960.34.$$

By subtraction, the SS_W with 44 *df* may be obtained:

$$SS_W = SS_{Ss} - SS_B,$$

$$SS_W = 4107.24 - 960.34 = 3146.90.$$

Next, the SS_B with $df_B = N_G - 1 = 4 - 1 = 3$ are separated into three portions, SS_{Tng}, SS_{Test}, and $SS_{Tng \times Test}$, each with a single *df*. The SS_{Tng} and SS_{Test} are:

$$SS_{Tng} = \frac{(\Sigma\Sigma\Sigma X_{CR})^2}{(N_1 + N_3)(k)} + \frac{(\Sigma\Sigma\Sigma X_{PR})^2}{(N_2 + N_4)(k)} - \frac{(\Sigma\Sigma\Sigma\Sigma X)^2}{N},$$

$$SS_{Tng} = \frac{(604)^2}{(12+12)(4)} + \frac{(403)^2}{(12+12)(4)} - \frac{(1007)^2}{192},$$

$$= 5491.93 - 5281.51 = 210.42.$$

$$SS_{Test} = \frac{(\Sigma\Sigma\Sigma X_{cr})^2}{(N_1 + N_2)(k)} + \frac{(\Sigma\Sigma\Sigma X_{pr})^2}{(N_3 + N_4)(k)} - \frac{(\Sigma\Sigma\Sigma\Sigma X)^2}{N},$$

$$SS_{Test} = \frac{(363)^2}{(12+12)(4)} + \frac{(644)^2}{(12+12)(4)} - \frac{(1007)^2}{192},$$

$$= 5692.76 - 5281.51 = 411.25.$$

The interaction of training × test may be arrived at directly by the short-cut formula for a 2×2 factorial design or by subtraction. By the latter method it is:

$$SS_{Tng \times Test} = SS_B - SS_{Tng} - SS_{Test},$$

$$SS_{Tng \times Test} = 960.34 - 210.42 - 411.25 = 338.67.$$

This completes the analysis of the independent portion of the data.

The total variation of the correlated observations, SS_C, is:

$$SS_C = SS_T - SS_{Ss},$$

$$SS_C = 6465.49 - 4107.24 = 2358.25.$$

The *df* for the correlated portion of the data are:

$$df_C = df_T - df_{Ss},$$
$$df_C = 191 - 47 = 144.$$

Next the SS_C has to be split into five sources of variation: (a) days, (b) training × days, (c) test × days, (d) training × test × days, and (e) residual or error. The days variation is:

$$SS_{Days} = \frac{(\Sigma\Sigma\Sigma X_{Day\ 1})^2}{(N_1 + N_2 + N_3 + N_4)} + \cdots + \frac{(\Sigma\Sigma\Sigma X_{Day\ 4})^2}{(N_1 + N_2 + N_3 + N_4)} - \frac{(\Sigma\Sigma\Sigma\Sigma X)^2}{N},$$

$$SS_{Days} = \frac{(250)^2}{48} + \frac{(215)^2}{48} + \frac{(248)^2}{48} + \frac{(294)^2}{48} - \frac{(1007)^2}{192},$$

$$= 5347.19 - 5281.51 = 65.68.$$

The two-factor interactions are computed as before and the required interaction tables are presented in Table 3.26. The variation of the cell totals in subtable *A* is:

$$SS_{Cells} = \frac{(132)^2}{24} + \frac{(118)^2}{24} + \cdots + \frac{(107)^2}{24} - \frac{(1007)^2}{192},$$

$$= 5604.71 - 5281.51 = 323.20.$$

Table 3.26. Interaction Tables for
(A) Training × Days and (B) Test × Days

(A)

		Days			
Training	1	2	3	4	Totals
CR	132	132	153	187	604
PR	118	83	95	107	403
Totals	250	215	248	294	1007

(B)

		Days			
Test	1	2	3	4	Totals
cr	121	70	94	78	363
pr	129	145	154	216	644
Totals	250	215	248	294	1007

The interaction of training × days is:

$$SS_{\text{Tng} \times \text{Days}} = SS_{\text{Cells}} - SS_{\text{Tng}} - SS_{\text{Days}},$$

$$SS_{\text{Tng} \times \text{Days}} = 323.20 - 210.42 - 65.68 = 47.10.$$

The variation of the cell totals in subtable *B* is:

$$SS_{\text{Cells}} = \frac{(121)^2}{24} + \frac{(129)^2}{24} + \cdots + \frac{(216)^2}{24} - \frac{(1007)^2}{192},$$

$$= 5937.46 - 5281.51 = 655.95.$$

The interaction of test × days is:

$$SS_{\text{Test} \times \text{Days}} = SS_{\text{Cells}} - SS_{\text{Test}} - SS_{\text{Days}},$$

$$SS_{\text{Test} \times \text{Days}} = 655.95 - 411.25 - 65.68 = 179.02.$$

The determination of the three-factor interaction, training × test × days, requires a new computational method.[10] In brief, what is done is to calculate the two-factor interactions for every level of the third factor, sum these interactions, and remove the two-factor interaction previously obtained on

Table 3.27. Interaction Tables for Training × Test × Days

CR Training

Test	Days 1	2	3	4	Totals
cr	61	37	39	31	168
pr	71	95	114	156	436
Totals	132	132	153	187	604

PR Training

Test	Days 1	2	3	4	Totals
cr	60	33	55	47	195
pr	58	50	40	60	208
Totals	118	83	95	107	403

10. See Edwards (1968, pp. 237–240) for a lucid description of methods for calculating interaction *SS*'s for three or more factors.

the basis of all of the data. The required interaction tables are given in Table 3.27. The $SS_{Test \times Days}$ for CR training are obtained in the usual manner:

$$SS_{Cells} = \frac{(61)^2}{12} + \frac{(71)^2}{12} + \cdots + \frac{(156)^2}{12} - \frac{(604)^2}{96},$$

$$= 4914.17 - 3800.17 = 1114.00.$$

$$SS_{Test} = \frac{(168)^2}{48} + \frac{(436)^2}{48} - \frac{(604)^2}{96},$$

$$= 4548.33 - 3800.17 = 748.16.$$

$$SS_{Days} = \frac{(132)^2}{24} + \cdots + \frac{(187)^2}{24} - \frac{(604)^2}{96},$$

$$SS_{Days} = 3884.42 - 3800.17 = 84.25.$$

$$SS_{Test \times Days} = 1114.00 - 748.16 - 84.25 = 281.59.$$

The $SS_{Test \times Days}$ for PR training are:

$$SS_{Cells} = \frac{(60)^2}{12} + \frac{(58)^2}{12} + \cdots + \frac{(60)^2}{12} - \frac{(403)^2}{96},$$

$$= 1748.92 - 1691.76 = 57.16.$$

$$SS_{Test} = \frac{(195)^2}{48} + \frac{(208)^2}{48} - \frac{(403)^2}{96},$$

$$= 1693.52 - 1691.76 = 1.76.$$

$$SS_{Days} = \frac{(118)^2}{24} + \cdots + \frac{(107)^2}{24} - \frac{(403)^2}{96},$$

$$= 1720.29 - 1691.76 = 28.53.$$

$$SS_{Test \times Days} = 57.16 - 1.76 - 28.53 = 26.87.$$

As stated above, the interaction of training $\times$ test $\times$ days is equal to the sum of the interactions of test $\times$ days for the two levels (CR and PR) of training less the interaction of test $\times$ days based upon all of the data. Thus the three-factor interaction is:

$$SS_{Tng \times Test \times Days} = \Sigma SS_{Test \times Days} - SS_{Test \times Days},$$

$$= (281.59 + 26.87) - 179.02 = 129.44$$

The final component of SS_C is SS_E. This source of variation may be found by subtraction:

$$SS_E = SS_C - SS_{Days} - SS_{Tng \times Days} - SS_{Test \times Days} - SS_{Tng \times Test \times Days},$$
$$SS_E = 2358.25 - 65.68 - 47.10 - 179.02 - 129.44 = 1937.01.$$

The SS_E is equivalent to the pooled interactions of subjects $\times$ days for the four groups and can, therefore, be calculated directly. Each component interaction has 33 df [e.g., $(N_1 - 1)(k - 1) = (12 - 1)(4 - 1) = 33$] and thus the df_E are $4(33) = 132$ df. While the analysis could be checked by calculating SS_E directly, we have found this error term by subtraction. By the rule for interactions, the two-factor and three-factor interactions have 3 df. The df_{Days} are also 3. Therefore, df for SS_E are:

$$df_E = df_C - df_{Days} - df_{Tng \times Days} - df_{Test \times Days} - df_{Tng \times Test \times Days},$$
$$df_E = 144 - 3 - 3 - 3 - 3 = 132.$$

The complete analysis is summarized in Table 3.28. The indications from

Table 3.28. *Summary Table for Factorial Design with Repeated Measurements*

Source of Variation	SS	df	s^2	F
Training	210.42	1	210.42	2.94
Test	411.25	1	411.25	5.75
Training × Test	338.67	1	338.67	4.74
Within	3146.90	44	71.52	
(Total Between Ss	4107.24	47)		
Days	65.68	3	21.89	1.49
Training × Days	47.10	3	15.70	1.07
Test × Days	179.02	3	59.67	4.07
Training × Test × Days	129.44	3	43.15	2.94
Error	1937.01	132	14.67	
(Total Correlated Observations	2358.25	144)		
Total	6465.49	191		

the independent part of the design are the same as those observed above in the section on the factorial design, viz., significant F values at less than the .025 and .05 level for test and training × test, respectively. The outcomes are not surprising since the same data, the response totals for Ss, were subjected to analysis. As we have previously partitioned the significant training × test interaction, there is no reason to repeat the procedure. It will be recalled that the pr group with CR training, averaged across days, bar pressed significantly more often than the cr group with CR training, averaged across days, but that the groups did not differ under the condition of PR training.

Evaluation of the correlated factors will again be performed by the joint application of regular and conservative F tests. By regular F tests ($df = 3$ and 132), two factors, test × days and training × test × days, are significant at less than the .01 and .05 level respectively. But applying a conservative F test (dividing the df's by $k-1$), only the interaction of test × days is significant for $df = 1$ and 44.[11] Following the same method used in the section on an independent groups design with repeated measurements, we shall break down this significant interaction to conclude the analysis. The relevant interaction table is the B subtable in Table 3.26. The SS due to the differences between the test groups on different days (simple main effects) are:

$$SS_{\text{Test on Day 1}} = \frac{(121)^2}{24} + \frac{(129)^2}{24} - \frac{(250)^2}{48}$$

$$SS_{\text{Test on Day 1}} = 1303.42 - 1302.08 = 1.34$$

$$SS_{\text{Test on Day 2}} = \frac{(70)^2}{24} + \frac{(145)^2}{24} - \frac{(215)^2}{48}$$

$$SS_{\text{Test on Day 2}} = 1080.21 - 963.02 = 117.19$$

$$SS_{\text{Test on Day 3}} = \frac{(94)^2}{24} + \frac{(154)^2}{24} - \frac{(248)^2}{48}$$

$$SS_{\text{Test on Day 3}} = 1356.33 - 1281.33 = 75.00.$$

$$SS_{\text{Test on Day 4}} = \frac{(78)^2}{24} + \frac{(216)^2}{24} - \frac{(294)^2}{48}$$

$$SS_{\text{Test on Day 4}} = 2197.50 - 1800.75 = 396.75.$$

It is worthy of note that these simple main effects each have a single df and add up to 590.28 which, within the limits of rounding error, is equal to $SS_{\text{Test}} + SS_{\text{Test} \times \text{Days}}$. The pooled error term for evaluating these simple effects is:

$$s^2_{\text{Pooled E}} = (SS_W + SS_E)/(df_W + df_E),$$

$$s^2_{\text{Pooled E}} = (3146.90 + 1937.01)/(44 + 132),$$

$$= 28.89.$$

11. Since Box's conservative test is for the extreme case of heterogeneity of variance and correlation and an $F = 4.08$ for 1 and 40 df is required for the .05 level, we may reject the null hypothesis with an obtained $F = 4.07$ for 1 and 44.

The simple main effects analysis of the test × days interaction is collated in Table 3.29. The pr rats made significantly more bar presses on days 2 and 4

Table 3.29.   Summary Table for Simple Main Effects Analysis of Test × Days Interaction

Source of Variation	SS	df	s^2	F
Test on Day 1	1.34	1	1.34	< 1
Test on Day 2	117.19	1	117.19	4.06
Test on Day 3	75.00	1	75.00	2.60
Test on Day 4	396.75	1	396.75	13.73
Pooled Error	5083.91	176	28.89	

than the cr rats, but not on days 1 and 3. Thus the complete analysis of Scott's data indicates that: (a) the pr group with CR training, averaged across days, bar pressed significantly more often than the cr group with CR training, averaged across days; and (b) the pr group, averaged across training conditions made significantly more bar presses on days 2 and 4 than the cr group, averaged across training conditions.

Before leaving this design, we need to talk some about the three-factor interaction. First, it should be made clear that this interaction can be calculated directly in two other ways. (a) The interactions of training × days for the two levels of test can be found, added together, and the interaction of training × days based on all of the data subtracted from the sum:

$$SS_{\text{Tng} \times \text{Test} \times \text{Days}} = \Sigma SS_{\text{Tng} \times \text{Days}} - SS_{\text{Tng} \times \text{Days}}$$

(b) The interactions of training × test for the four days can be found, added together, and the interaction of training × test based on all of the data subtracted from the sum:

$$SS_{\text{Tng} \times \text{Test} \times \text{Days}} = \Sigma SS_{\text{Tng} \times \text{Test}} - SS_{\text{Tng} \times \text{Test}}$$

The necessary interaction tables for (a) are shown in Table 3.30 and those for (b) are shown in Table 3.31. Methods (a) and (b) as well as the method used with Table 3.27 will all yield the same value for the three-factor interaction. That is to say, the three formulas for the three-factor interaction are equivalent. While this is a happy outcome, it implies that a significant three-factor interaction could be looked at in three different ways. This troublesome implication will be considered more fully below.

Second, what does a three-factor interaction mean? To begin with, it can be said that the SS for the three-factor interaction are what are left over when the appropriate two-factor interaction based on all the data is removed from the sum of the two-factor interactions at different levels of the third

Table 3.30.   Alternate Interaction Tables for Training × Test × Days

cr Test

Training	Days				
	1	*2*	*3*	*4*	*Totals*
CR	61	37	39	31	168
PR	60	33	55	47	195
Totals	121	70	94	78	363

pr Test

Training	Days				
	1	*2*	*3*	*4*	*Totals*
CR	71	95	114	156	436
PR	58	50	40	60	208
Totals	129	145	154	216	644

Table 3.31.   Alternate Interaction Tables for Training × Test × Days

Day 1

Test	Training		Total
	CR	*PR*	
cr	61	60	121
pr	71	58	129
Totals	132	118	250

Day 2

Test	Training		Total
	CR	*PR*	
cr	37	33	70
pr	95	50	145
Totals	132	83	215

Day 3

Test	Training		Total
	CR	*PR*	
cr	39	55	94
pr	114	40	154
Totals	153	95	248

Day 4

Test	Training		Total
	CR	*PR*	
cr	31	47	78
pr	156	60	216
Totals	187	107	294

factor. Since this is a verbal statement of the computational formula, it is correct but it is not a very revealing answer. A more satisfying answer emerges from a graphic analysis. Winer (1962) has provided three enlightening graphs of three cases of three-factor interactions. In the first two panels of Figure 3.7 the means for a two-factor interaction $(A \times B)$ are plotted for

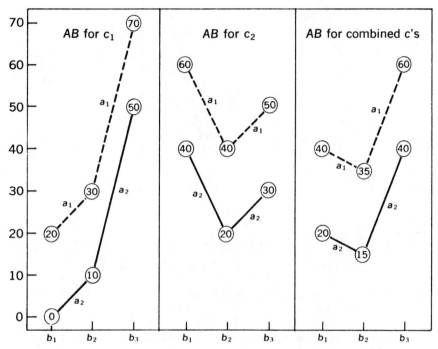

Figure 3.7. Graphs depicting a zero $A \times B \times C$ interaction and a zero $A \times B$ interaction (modified from Winer, 1962).

*Reprinted by permission of the publisher from B. J. Winer, *Statistical Principles in Experimental Design*, p. 179. Copyright 1962, McGraw-Hill Book Company.

two levels of a third factor, C. In the third panel the $A \times B$ interaction, based on all the data, is presented. Since the differences between the levels of A for all C levels are almost equal, all three of the $A \times B$ interactions and the $A \times B \times C$ interaction would be zero:

$$SS_{A \times B \times C} = \Sigma SS_{AB} - SS_{AB},$$
$$SS_{A \times B \times C} = (0+0)-0 = 0.$$

In Figure 3.8 the differences between the levels of A for every C level are markedly unequal. But since the profiles are parallel in all panels, there will not be a three-factor interaction. However, there will be an $A \times B$

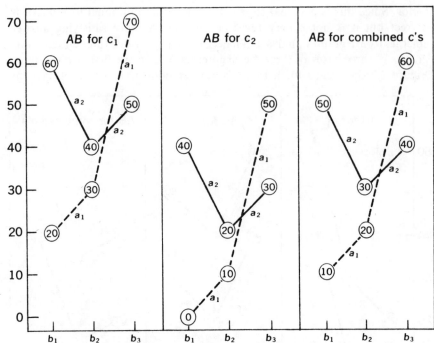

Figure 3.8. Graphs depicting a zero A × B × C interaction, but a nonzero A × B interaction (Winer, 1962).

*Reprinted by permission of the publisher from B. J. Winer, *Statistical Principles in Experimental Design*, p. 181. Copyright 1962, McGraw-Hill Book Company.

interaction. Using some made-up values for the SS's, we have here:

$$SS_{A \times B \times C} = (10 + 10) - 20 = 0.$$

In Figure 3.9 the differences between the levels of A are unequal for the two levels of C, but are equal in the combined graph. In this case an $A \times B \times C$ interaction will be found but not an $A \times B$ interaction. Employing hypothetical SS values, we have:

$$SS_{A \times B \times C} = (10 + 5) - 0 = 15.$$

Third, suppose Scott's three-factor interaction had been significant. How would the interaction be broken down? Most books are not very explicit regarding this situation. We will provisionally propose some extensions of the method employed earlier. Once more these proposals should be viewed with extreme caution. It seems reasonable to look first at the simple *interaction* effects. That is, one might test (a) the interaction of test × days for CR, and (b) the interaction of test × days for PR against $s^2_{\text{Pooled E}}$. Then simple *main* effects tests could be performed within the significant simple interaction effects. One complication here is that the simple interaction effects of training × days for cr and pr and the simple interaction effects of training × test for different days could also be tested. Perhaps, the decision as to what set of simple interaction effects should be tested could be made on the basis of what other effects, main or interaction, were significant or in terms of the investigator's interests. This discussion of a three-factor interaction serves to document the assertion made earlier that experimental designs incorporating too many factors may terminate with uninterpretable higher-order interactions.

The assumptions underlying a factorial design with repeated measurements do not require any discussion. As would be expected, the assumptions are the same as those for an independent groups design with repeated measurements.

The three complex designs that have been described in this section are a micro-sample of the many experimental plans that are available. The interested reader should consult advanced texts (e.g., Lindquist, 1953; Winer, 1962; Myers, 1966; Edwards, 1968) for treatments of other designs. It needs to be stressed, however, that the elaborateness of a design is not a defensible criterion as to the soundness of an experiment.

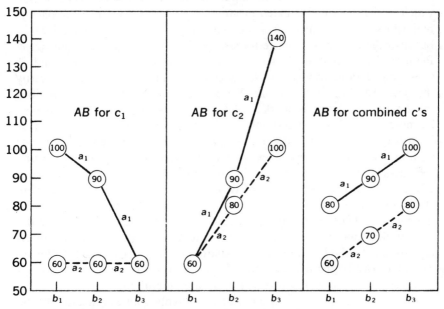

Figure 3.9. Graphs depicting a nonzero A × B × C interaction, but a zero A × B interaction (*Winer, 1962*).

A Quick Review

There is no point rehashing the chapter. However, a number of tactics for research that have emerged should be emphasized. (a) The use of equal numbers of Ss in groups is strongly advised – it greatly simplifies the analysis and modulates the effects of departures from homogeneity of variance, etc. (b) After significant overall F tests, comparisons between means should be done by techniques with built-in protection for the number of contrasts. More particularly, we have suggested that the Tukey B method be employed for making comparisons with k independent groups and the Bonferroni t technique for k matched groups. (c) In general, we would urge the use of independent groups designs as these are more defensible and better understood. Matching produces a more efficient design, if and only if, a high positive correlation is present between the matching variable and the dependent variable. Furthermore, a negative or zero correlation can even produce a less efficient design in contrast to independent groups. Thus matching should only be introduced when the investigator knows from past research that the necessary high positive correlation exists. Another case where matching is a reasonable tactic is when the supply of Ss is restricted. (d) The design, which we have termed equated groups, should be avoided like the plague, bad whiskey, and leaky lifeboats. Not only are the data unanalyzable, but also the design is a masterful strategy for finding nothing (Boneau & Pennypacker, 1961). (e) While the classical statistical tests, like t and F, show considerable robustness, this does not mean that they are necessarily the best tests for all conditions. When departures from the assumptions for the classical tests are marked, then the possibility that other tests may be more suitable should certainly be entertained. (f) We have argued that inexperienced research workers should rely on homogeneity of variance tests rather than on a visual inspection of variances. Furthermore, testing variances is just as legitimate an aim as testing means. (g) Factorial designs, which result from the crossing of two or more independent variables are efficient plans for research. In contrast to independent experiments, factorial designs provide estimates of main effects and random error based on more df as well as information regarding the interactions of variables. (h) Interactions may be the result of the combination of experimental factors (intrinsic), they may be the consequence of some extraneous variable affecting a treatment group's scores (extrinsic), or a combination of intrinsic and extrinsic. Detection of an extraneous factor involves an examination of the procedure of the investigation. (i) Some interactions can be "made to disappear" by rescaling the dependent variable, e.g., by a log transformation. If an interaction is accepted as "real," its nature should be explored by further tests. There is no consensus as to how this should be done. We advocated tests of simple main effects and simple interaction effects followed by appropriate multiple comparison tests when necessary. (j) If factorial designs include more than several factors, they require many groups and Ss, they become difficult to carry out, and they may result in higher order interactions that present serious problems of interpretation.

PROBLEMS

1. Given the information in Table 3.2 (p. 33) for the 80% group. Is the $M = 14.5$ different from $M_T = 10.0$ at the .01 level of significance with a two-tailed test?

2. Do the means for the 20% ($M = 15.67$) and 100% ($M = 11.17$) groups in Table 3.3 (p. 40) differ significantly? Do a two-tailed test and require a $p = .01$.

3. Assume that the data for problem 2 come from normally distributed populations. Are the variances for the 20% and 100% groups equal? Require a $p = .01$. Under what conditions is a one-tailed test appropriate for such a problem?

4. Assume that the scores in Table 3.25 (p. 90) for Day 4 came from a k independent groups design rather than a factorial design. Is there an overall difference among the four means at the .01 level of significance?

5. Assume that the data in problem 4 came from normally distributed populations. Do the variances differ significantly at the .01 level of significance?

6. Perform pairwise comparisons of the means in problem 4, using the .01 level of significance.

7. Using the data for Ss 13–24 for Days 1 and 4 in Table 3.25 (p. 90), test the hypothesis that: $M_{Day\ 4} - M_{Day\ 1} = 0$. Do a two-tailed test with $p = .05$.

8. With the data for Ss 13–24 for Days 1 through 4, determine whether or not there is an overall difference in the means of the four days at the .05 level.

9. Perform pairwise comparisons of the means in problem 8 at the .05 level.

10. Given the Day 4 scores for all Ss in Table 3.25 (p. 90), find out if the number of bar presses on Day 4 differed at the .05 level as a function of the training conditions, test conditions, and their interaction.

11. An investigator does a study with 90 rats in which factor A is three levels of drive, factor B is three levels of reward, and factor C is five blocks of test trials. A and B are fully crossed, 10 Ss are randomly assigned to each treatment combination, and every S undergoes five blocks of test trials. Present a summary table showing the sources of variation and their df's.

12. With the data provided in Table 3.31 (p. 98), calculate the $SS_{\text{Training} \times \text{Test} \times \text{Days}}$.

13. From the data given in Table 3.30 (p. 98), calculate $SS_{\text{Training} \times \text{Days}}$ for cr test.

14. An experimenter studies the effects of three levels of meaningfulness upon serial learning with 30 Ss. Ten Ss are randomly assigned to each of the three levels of meaningfulness and every S receives 10 learning trials. Present a summary table showing the sources of variation and their df's. How should the experimenter do significance tests upon the effects of trials and meaningfulness × trials?

15. A study involving four independent groups of rats with 0, 10, 20, and 40 seconds delay of reward, respectively, yields a significant F for groups. How many pairwise comparisons of means are possible? The investigator employs simple t tests to make these comparisons. Comment on this procedure.

16. A factorial design with factor A (three levels), B (four levels), and C (two levels) is done. The factors are independent and fully crossed. Five Ss are randomly assigned to each treatment combination. Present a summary table showing the sources of variation and their df's. Suppose that the $A \times B$ interaction was the only significant source of variation. How should the investigator proceed? Suppose instead that the $A \times B \times C$ interaction was the only significant source of variation. What should the investigator do next?

CHAPTER FOUR

Steps to Inference:
II. Ranks and Signs

Data analysis is never going to be basically nonparametric. The costs of nonparametrism usually substantially exceed the advantages. – J. W. Tukey

A Location Test for Two Independent Groups

In this chapter we will be concerned with some alternative tests, termed *nonparametric* or *distribution-free* tests, for analyzing data from some of the kinds of experimental designs examined in the previous chapter. The first test to be presented is a randomization-of-ranks test which was first proposed by Wilcoxon (1945). This test must be a reasonable one because it has been invented by a number of individuals. Thus Walsh (1965) labels it the "Wil coxon-Mann-Whitney-Festinger test."

   In order to demonstrate Wilcoxon's test, let us apply it to some data from Levinson and Sheridan (1969) who were concerned with monocular acquisition and transfer of a discrimination habit to the other eye. Half of the Ss (rats) had their corpus callosum sectioned and half were sham-operated controls. The trials to a learning criterion for one discrimination problem are shown in Table 4.1, and we wish to know whether or not the two groups differed in learning. The first step in analysis is to arrange *all* ten of the scores in order of magnitude from smallest to largest: 67, 95, 192, 200, 240, 277, 326, 336, 370, 465. Next the ordered scores are assigned ranks with the lowest score getting a rank of 1, the next score 2, and so on. In columns 5 and 6 of Table 4.1 the ranks corresponding to the scores are listed. It may be noted that the sum of the ranks (ΣR) for the Sham group is 18, for the Callosum

105

Table 4.1.*. Trials to a Learning Criterion and Ranks for Sham and Callosum Sectioned Rats (Levinson and Sheridan, 1969)

	Trials				Ranks	
S	Sham	S	Callosum		Sham	Callosum
2	192	3	240		3	5
8	336	5	326		8	7
10	200	9	465		4	10
14	67	11	277		1	6
16	95	19	370		2	9
				ΣR	18	37

*Reprinted by permission of the publisher and authors from D. M. Levinson and C. L. Sheridan, "Monocular Acquisition and Interocular Transfer of Two Types of Pattern Discrimination in Hooded Rats," *Journal of Comparative and Physiological Psychology*, 67, p. 470. Copyright 1969, American Psychological Association.

group it is 37, and that $\Sigma\Sigma R = 18 + 37 = 55$. Since $\Sigma\Sigma R = N(N+1)/2 = 10(11)/2 = 55$, the rank totals check. The critical index is the smaller sum of the ranks, 18, which Wilcoxon calls T. To evaluate the $T = 18$, we enter Wilcoxon's table (Table J) for an N per group of 5. The obtained $T = 18$ is found to be significant at the .05 level with a two-tailed test. Accordingly, this test indicates that the scores of the Callosum population are stochastically larger than the scores of the Sham population. "Stochastically larger" means that the "bulk" of the Callosum population is larger than the

Table 4.2.   Assignment of Ranks To Maximize and Minimize the Difference in Rank Sums

	Group		Maximum		Minimum	
100%	80%		100%	80%	100%	80%
14	19		16	24	16	24
14	19		15	23	15	23
13	18		14	22	14	22
12	17		12	21	13	21
12	15		11	20	12	20
12	15		10	19	11	19
11	14		7	18	9	18
11	14		6	17	8	17
10	12		5	13	5	10
9	11		3	9	4	7
8	11		2	8	2	6
8	9		1	4	1	3
		ΣR 102		198	110	190

bulk of the Sham population (Siegel, 1956). While the Wilcoxon test is technically a test of distributions, it is generally interpreted in terms of location, i.e., indications are drawn regarding the averages of the two groups as in the t test for independent groups.

In order to contrast Wilcoxon's test with the t test and to disclose a formidable problem, the problem of tied scores, let us analyze the Klein data from Table 3.2. Again, all 24 scores are ordered in terms of magnitude and ranked. At this point (see Table 4.2) we run head-on into a difficult problem in rank statistics — the problem of tied scores. The two smallest· scores are 8 and 8 — what ranks shall be assigned to these two observations? Furthermore, inspection of the data reveals six other sets of ties: 9, 9; 11, 11, 11, 11; 12, 12, 12, 12; 14, 14, 14, 14; 15, 15; and 19, 19. Bradley (1968) has discussed a number of approaches to the problem of tied scores. We shall consider four of these solutions: (A) obtain probability limits; (B) obtain an average probability; (C) randomize the ranks; (D) assign midranks.

Method A involves assigning ranks to the tied scores twice — once to make the difference in rank totals between the groups as large as possible and a second time to make the difference as small as possible. Then the probability value for each outcome is found and both probability values are reported by the investigator. In the Wilcoxon test, significance is achieved when the smaller ranks are in one group and the larger ranks are in the other. Ties within a group are not important but across groups they are. Accordingly, the scores 8 and 8 would be assigned ranks 1 and 2. In case of 9 and 9, which would normally get ranks of 3 and 4, we will assign a rank of 3 to the 9 score in the 100% group and a rank of 4 to the 9 score in the 80% group to maximize the difference in rank sums. In the case of the four 11's we would assign ranks of 6 and 7 to the two 11's in the 100% group and 8 and 9 to the 11's in the 80% group. To minimize the difference in the rank sums, we would reverse this process. In columns 3 and 4 of Table 4.2 the ranks have been assigned to all scores to maximize the difference in the rank sums and in columns 5 and 6 to minimize the differences. The critical values are the T's, the smaller sum of the ranks (ΣR). Note again that $\Sigma\Sigma R = N(N+1)/2 = 24(24+1)/2 = 300$ for each method of breaking the tied scores. For the maximum procedure of assigning the ranks $T = 102$, and for the minimum $T = 110$. From Wilcoxon's table of T (Table J) the probabilities for a two-tailed test of significance lie between .02 and less than .01. Therefore, we would reject the null hypothesis, if we had elected to employ the .05 or .02 level of significance.

The second technique of breaking ties is (B) assign the ranks to the tied scores in all possible ways. Then the T values and their probabilities are obtained for each assignment. Finally, the mean or median probability value is calculated and reported. We will reject this method on the grounds that it is unduly laborious. Also if only the maximum and minimum assignment of ranks are done (as in method A) and the average of these two probability values is calculated, then method B reduces to a variant of method A except that the average probability value is reported instead of the range of probability values. Method A has greater intuitive appeal – the experimenter "tells it as it is" by informing his readers that the probability value lies between two limits, depending upon how the ties are broken.

In method C the ranks of the tied scores are assigned by using a table of random numbers (Table K). Whether the 9 in the 100% group receives a rank of 3 or 4 is dependent upon randomly drawing a number from Table K: e.g., if an odd digit is drawn 9 gets a rank of 3; if an even digit, 9's rank is 4. Finally, in the last method D the midranks are assigned. For example, the two 9 scores would *each* receive a rank of $(3+4)/2 = 3.5$, and so on. Because of its convenience, the midranks method has been used most frequently with many ranking tests. In Table 4.3 method C has been applied in columns 1 and 2, and method D in columns 3 and 4. The obtained T values

Table 4.3. Use of Random and Midranks Methods for Tied Scores

Random		Midranks	
100%	*80%*	*100%*	*80%*
17	23	16.5	23.5
18	24	16.5	23.5
14	22	14	22
13	21	11.5	21
10	20	11.5	19.5
11	19	11.5	19.5
9	15	7.5	16.5
6	16	7.5	16.5
5	12	5	11.5
3	8	3.5	7.5
2	7	1.5	7.5
1	4	1.5	3.5
ΣR 109	191	108.0	192.0

of 109 and 108 for methods C and D, respectively, are significant at less than the .02 level (Table J, N per group of 12). Thus methods A, C, and D all lead to essentially the same indications. In agreement with Bradley (1968), we would recommend the application of method A – finding the probability limits. However, in point of fact, the use of either method A, C, or D will probably produce about the same outcome. It is also possible to correct for the presence and extent of tied scores (Siegel, 1959, pp. 124 ff.). But the effects of correction are slight and always increase significance. Therefore, the correction of T for the presence of ties is unnecessary when the T is significant. In our examples of Wilcoxon's test we have employed two-tailed significance tests. For one-tailed tests the probability values in Table J should be halved, i.e., the values would be for the .025, .01, and .005 levels of significance. For extended tables of T, see Wilcoxon, Katti, and Wilcox (1963).

Let us now examine (a) the intuitive rationale for Wilcoxon's test and (b) the assumptions underlying the test. Regarding (a), Bradley has aptly termed Wilcoxon's test a "rank-randomization" test. In Table 4.1 we have the ranks from 1 to 10. If the ranks in the groups were completely random, we would expect a rank total (ΣR) of 27.5 (i.e., $\Sigma\Sigma R/2$) for each treatment. As the rank totals begin to deviate from these expected values, the outcome becomes more unusual and we begin to suspect that the treatments are having effects. The maximum difference in rank sums that can occur with N per group of 5 is where one sample receives the ranks of 1 to 5 ($\Sigma R = 15 = T$) and the other sample gets the ranks from 6 to 10 ($\Sigma R = 40$). The probability values in Table J are based on finding all possible combinations of the ranks 1 to 10 taken 5 at a time. The probability equals the number of ways a given T can occur divided by the total number of combinations. Thus Wilcoxon's test is indeed a "rank-randomization" test.

(b) The assumptions for Wilcoxon's test are two (Siegel, 1956; Walsh 1965; Bradley, 1968). First, that the samples have been randomly and independently drawn. And, second, that the samples come from continuous population distributions. Regarding the continuity assumption Siegel says:

> An underlying continuous variable is one that is not restricted to having isolated values. It may have any value in a certain interval . . . Frequently grossness of our measuring devices obscures the underlying continuity that may exist. If a variate is truly continuously distributed, then the probability of a tie is zero. However, tied scores frequently occur. Tied scores almost invariably are a reflection of the lack of sensitivity of our measuring instruments . . . Therefore even when ties are observed it may not be unreasonable to assume that a continuous distribution underlies our gross measures (1956, pp. 25f.).

It may also be noted (Walsh, 1965) that when ranks are assigned at random to tied scores, continuity is imposed.

It is important to mention that the normality and equal variance assumptions necessary for the t test are *not* required for the Wilcoxon test. There is considerable evidence (Bradley, 1968, pp. 108 ff.; Boneau, 1962) to suggest that the Wilcoxon's test, despite its calculational simplicity, is highly efficient. When the assumptions for the t test are questionable, the student should feel no constraints against the application of Wilcoxon's test to his data.

A Location Test for k Independent Groups

We are now concerned with the case of k independent groups. In Chapter 3 the data from this type of experimental arrangement were analyzed by means of a simple analysis of variance. Now we shall look at a nonparametric test for this situation — the Kruskal-Wallis test. This test (Kruskal & Wallis, 1952) is a simple extension of Wilcoxon's test to k independent groups. As in the procedure for the Wilcoxon test, all N scores are ordered, ranked, and the sums of ranks, R_j, for the separate treatments are found. This information is then "plugged into" the following formula:

$$H = \frac{12}{N(N+1)} \sum_1^k \frac{R_j^2}{n_j} - 3(N+1),$$

where k = number of groups,

n_j = total number of cases in jth group,

N = total number of cases,

R_j = sum of ranks in jth group,

$\sum_1^k$ = a summation over the k groups.

The obtained H, when based on small samples ($k = 3$ and up to N per group of 5), is evaluated by consulting Table L. For larger samples, H is assessed as a χ^2 with $df = k - 1$ (see Table M). The probability values in Table L are exact, being based on combinations of ranks; those in Table M are approximate because with more observations H follows the well-known χ^2 distribution.

To illustrate the Kruskal-Wallis test, some data from Steel (1961) on the effects of protein supplements upon the growth of chicks will be used. First, the weights of all 60 chicks are ordered in magnitude and ranked (Table 4.4).[1] Next the sums of the ranks (R_j) for the various dietary treatments are found and H is calculated:

$$H = \left[\frac{12}{60(61)} \frac{(88^2 + 190^2 + \cdots + 454^2)}{10} \right] - 3(61)$$

$$= 216.51 - 183 = 33.51.$$

Since the k and N per group values exceed the limits of Table L, $H = 33.51$ is evaluated as a χ^2 with $df = k - 1 = 6 - 1 = 5$. From Table M it can be seen that the χ^2 is significant at less than the .001 level of significance. Like Wilcoxon's test this result indicates that the distribution of *at least* one group

1. Since there are only two sets of tied scores with two scores in each set, the ties, have been broken simply by applying the midranks method.

is stochastically larger than that of another group. Although, again, a significant H is usually interpreted to signify a difference in location or central tendency. As H is significant, we are faced with the familiar multiple-

*Table 4.4.** *Final Chick Weights in Grams and Ranks for Six Protein Supplements (Steel, 1961)*

H	L	Sb	M	C	Sf
108 (1)	141 (5)	193 (14)	153 (8)	216 (18)	226 (21)
124 (2)	148 (7)	230 (24)	206 (16)	222 (20)	295 (36)
136 (3)	169 (11)	243 (26)	242 (25)	260 (31.5)	320 (42)
140 (4)	181 (13)	248 (27)	257 (29.5)	318 (41)	322 (43)
143 (6)	203 (15)	250 (28)	263 (33)	352 (52)	334 (47)
160 (9)	213 (17)	267 (34)	303 (37)	359 (53)	339 (48)
168 (10)	229 (23)	271 (35)	315 (39)	368 (54)	340 (49)
179 (12)	257 (29.5)	316 (40)	325 (44)	379 (55)	341 (50)
217 (19)	260 (31.5)	327 (45)	344 (51)	390 (57)	392 (58)
227 (22)	309 (38)	329 (46)	380 (56)	404 (59)	423 (60)
R_j 88	190	319	338.5	440.5	454

*Reprinted by permission of the publisher from R. G. D. Steel, "Some Rank Sum Multiple Comparisons Tests," *Biometrics,* 17, p. 542, 1961.

comparison problem of localizing the difference(s) among the groups. This problem will be discussed in the next section.

The assumptions for the Kruskal-Wallis test are identical to those for Wilcoxon's test: (a) the samples must be random and independent; and (b) the samples must come from continuous distributions. In common with the Wilcoxon test, there are no assumptions of normality and equal variances and the Kruskal-Wallis test is a highly efficient one (Bradley, 1968, pp. 131 f.). In this respect, it might be noted that the Klein data, which were far from significant with an F test, were found to be significant by a Kruskal-Wallis test. Finally, mention should be made of the beneficial effect of ranking upon extreme observations. An extreme observation, no matter how deviant it is, receives a rank of 1 or N depending upon which end of the distribution it falls.

Multiple-Comparison Location Tests for k Independent Groups

For a long time investigators have been testing comparisons, after a Kruskal-Wallis test, by applying Wilcoxon's test (or the Mann-Whitney test). This procedure is equivalent to performing simple t tests among treatment means following an analysis of variance. Like the t test procedure, doing multiple Wilcoxon tests probably errs on the side of leniency because no protection is provided for the number of comparisons. This multiple-comparison situation has improved recently with the emergence of a number of procedures (Ryan, 1960; Steel, 1960, 1961; Dwass, 1960; Nemenyi, 1963; Dunn, 1964). As the logic of Nemenyi test, which involves multiple Kruskal-Wallis tests, has been criticized by Miller (1966, pp. 168f.), we will turn our attention to the remaining tests for evaluating the data in Table 4.4.

The simple procedure of performing multiple Wilcoxon tests, without adjustments for the number of comparisons, requires a critical T' value of 131, where $T' = N(N+1)/2 - T = 20(21)/2 - 79 = 131$, for the pairwise

Table 4.5.   *Required Larger Rank Totals (T') for Various Multiple-Comparison Tests When k = 6 and N = 10 per Group*

Test	k				
	2	3	4	5	6
Wilcoxon	131	131	131	131	131
Dunn	146.5	146.5	146.5	146.5	146.5
Ryan	136	140	142	143	144
Steel	144	144	144	144	144

comparisons for two-tailed tests at the .05 level of significance (see Table 4.5). Throughout this section we will use T' instead of T for making comparisons.

The Dunn Test (1964, Procedure II) is a normal deviate test:

$$Z = \frac{\dfrac{T_1}{N_1} - \dfrac{T_2}{N_2}}{\dfrac{^{\sigma}T_1}{N_1} - \dfrac{T_2}{N_2}}$$

$$\frac{^{\sigma}T_1}{N_1} - \frac{T_2}{N_2} = \left[\frac{N(N+1)}{12}\left(\frac{1}{N_1} + \frac{1}{N_2}\right)\right]^{\frac{1}{2}}$$

In order for the difference in the *average* ranks of any two groups to be significant, Z must be larger than $Z^{\alpha/2C}$, where $\alpha = .05$ (two-tailed) and $C =$ number of comparisons. Because $C = 15$, i.e., $k(k-1)/2 = 6(5)/2 = 15$, the critical Z for $.05/2(15)$ (Edwards, 1950) is 3.14. Substituting the quantities N, N_1, N_2 and $T_2 = 210 - T_1$, into the formulas above, the obtained T' for Dunn's method is found to be 146.5.

Ryan's test (1960), an extension of Tukey's B test, reduces to performing Wilcoxon (or Mann-Whitney) tests among the k groups with different probability values being required for significance as a function of how far the groups are apart when they have been ordered in terms of their medians.

For the extreme groups, the required probability value is $2\alpha/k(k-1) = 2(.05)/6(5) = .0033$. For the groups 5 apart in the ordered series the probability value is $2\alpha/k(k-2) = 2(.05)/6(4) = .0042$. For groups 4, 3, and 2 apart, the required probability values are .0056, .0083, and .0167, respectively. By use of the Mann-Whitney tables (Siegel, 1956), the extended Wilcoxon tables (Wilcoxon, Katti, and Wilcox, 1963), and the normal deviate formula for the Mann-Whitney test (Ryan, 1960) the required T' values for Ryan's test in Table 4.5 have been calculated.

The Steel test (Steel, 1960, 1961; Dwass, 1960) likewise entails multiple Wilcoxon tests but with a *single* critical T' value. The Steel test is more convenient than Ryan's test because tables are available which make it unnecessary to calculate the critical T' values. Steel's original exact tables for small k and N have recently been extended by Miller (1966) and Miller's tables are reproduced in Table 0.

In Table 4.5 the required T's for the four multiple-comparison tests are summarized *for the problem in question* (Table 4.4). The simple pairwise application of Wilcoxon's test, of course, yields the smallest required larger rank sum. It is likely that the common use of this technique in the past has filled the research literature with some Type I errors of inference. The Dunn method, on the other hand, appears to be most conservative in that the required T' is larger at every k value than those for the Ryan and Steel techniques. Perhaps Dunn suspects this difficulty, for she comments: "On the general subject of choice of α, I believe that in making multiple tests and contrasts, one might tend to use a value of α considerably larger than the traditional .05" (1964, p. 248). While the Dunn test might be advantageous for evaluating a few *a priori* comparisons from a larger set of possible comparisons, it would seem to be a little conservative for pairwise testing.

The Ryan and Steel tests also require different critical T' values. For testing the extreme groups the T' value is the same for the two tests. With groups closer together, the critical T' values for the Ryan test are smaller. Provisionally, we would recommend the use of Steel's test for making pairwise comparisons after a significant overall H has been obtained. This advice must be tentative as nothing is known as yet about the power of these multiple-comparisons tests. Our preference for the Steel test over Ryan's is based on the irrational ground of laziness — Steel has tables! Once more it is apparent that sampling studies are badly needed to assess the properties of the various new multiple-comparison methods based on ranks. It should be stressed, too, that these methods possess a decided advantage over the studentized range tests in Chapter 3 in that they do not assume normality.

To complete this section we will apply the Steel test to the chick data using the T' value from Table 4.5. For each of the 15 pairs of groups a Wilcoxon test was performed and the larger sum of the ranks, T' was found.

These T' values are shown in Table 4.6 where the six groups are ordered in terms of increasing sums, R_j. First, the extreme groups, Sf and H, are contrasted. Because the obtained T' is greater than the required T' (154 > 144) for $k = 6$, group Sf is stochastically larger than H. Next Sf is compared to

Table 4.6.* Steel Multiple-Comparison Tests of the Chick Data (modified from Steel, 1961)

	Group				
	H	L	Sb	M	C	Sf
H	—	135	153	148	152	154
L		—	135	134.5	145.5	150
Sb			—	110	130	139
M				—	126	128
C					—	107
Sf						—

*Reprinted with modifications by permission of the publisher from R. G. D. Steel, "Some Rank Sum Multiple Comparisons Tests," *Biometrics*, 17, p. 543, 1961.

L and this difference is also significant (150 > 144). As the difference between Sf and Sb is not significant (139 < 144), no further tests of Sf are done and the nonsignificant differences are underlined. Now C is contrasted with H and then with L and both of these comparisons are significant (152 > 144; 144.5 > 144). Since C is not greater than Sb (130 < 144), this comparison and C–M are underscored. Continuing this process of columnwise tests, six significant differences are detected.

Finally, an interesting question warrants discussion: Why not employ the Steel test of the two extreme groups (e.g., Sf vs H) as an overall test instead of the Kruskal-Wallis test? This procedure is a legitimate one, but it incorporates only the data from two groups while the Kruskal-Wallis test is based upon all N scores. As a consequence of this procedural difference, the two tests do not always yield the same result. For example, with Klein's data (Table 3.3) Kruskal-Wallis test produces significance but the Steel test of the extreme groups does not. A parallel situation exists with an F test for k independent groups and a test of extreme groups by a studentized range test like Tukey's B. Winer, who has discussed this issue and provided examples, says:

> Use of the F statistic generally leads to a more powerful test with respect to a broader class of alternative hypotheses than does the use of the q statistic [studentized range test]. However, there are some alternative hypotheses for which the q statistic leads to a more powerful test (1962, pp. 78f.).

We would guess that the Kruskal-Wallis test would function as a more omnibus test than the Steel test of the two extreme groups and for this reason we have recommended it as an overall test. Nevertheless, in view of Winer's remarks the student should not suffer an anxiety attack if, on occasion, Kruskal-Wallis and Steel tests give different overall results – it can happen!

A Location Test for Two Matched Groups

We shall now return to the problem of matched groups. Usually textbooks describe two nonparametric techniques for comparing the locations of two matched groups – the Wilcoxon signed-ranks test (1949) and the Sign test. The procedure for the Wilcoxon test (Siegal, 1956) is first to find the difference scores for the matched Ss as was done with the t test for paired replicates. However, instead of dealing with the *absolute* magnitude of the differences, only their *relative* magnitude is taken into consideration by ranking the differences but *ignoring their signs*. Once ranked, the signs are noted and the index T, the sum of the ranks for the less-frequently occurring sign, is obtained. This T is evaluated by reference to Wilcoxon's table for the distribution of T in Table P (for an extended table, see Wilcoxon, Katti, & Wilcox, 1963).

Table 4.7. Applying the Wilcoxon Signed-Ranks Test to the Heart Rate Data

S	Placebo	Low	Differences Low– Placebo	Ranks of Differences	Ranks for – Sign
1	+ 16	+ 20	+ 4	1.5	
2	+ 12	+ 24	+ 12	4.5	
3	+ 8	+ 8	0	—	
4	+ 20	+ 8	− 12	4.5	4.5
5	+ 8	+ 4	− 4	1.5	1.5
6	+ 10	+ 20	+ 10	3	
7	+ 4	+ 28	+ 24	7	
8	− 8	+ 20	+ 28	8	
9	0	+ 20	+ 20	6	
					$\Sigma R = T = 6$

This procedure can better be understood with an example. Let us, therefore, apply the signed-ranks test to the Weil et al. data (Table 4.7) which were analyzed earlier by a t test. The difference scores are found as before but they are then ranked, ignoring the signs. The zero difference for S3 is eliminated from the sample, and N now becomes 8. Tied differences are treated by the midranks method. Since there are six positive differences and two negative differences, the ranks for the negative differences are listed in the last column of Table 4.7. (If there had been six negative differences and two positive differences, the ranks for the positive differences would have been collected in the last column). The sum of the ranks for the negative differences (ΣR) is T. Looking up the $T = 6$ for the $N = 8$ differences in Table P, we observe that the two groups do not differ at .05 level by a two-tailed test. This outcome is in accord with the earlier t test result.

What are the assumptions for Wilcoxon's signed-ranks test? These assumptions have been described most carefully by Bradley in contrasting the t test, Wilcoxon's test, and the Sign test: "The essential population conditions which must be met if the three test statistics are to have their null distributions, and which are therefore the population characteristics that are actually being tested, are as follows: for the t test — that the difference-score population is normally distributed about a median of zero; for the Wilcoxon test — that the difference-score population is symmetrically distributed about a median of zero; for the Sign test — that the difference-score population has a median of zero" (1968, pp. 192 f.). Thus it is apparent that the signed-ranks test is not completely distribution-free (see Bradley, 1968, pp. 96–105; Miller, 1966). As a consequence of this observation, we would concur with Bradley's advice (1968, p. 103) in general to employ the Sign test as a nonparametric test for location in the case of matched groups. Three additional advantages of the Sign test are: (a) its greater simplicity; (b) its high efficiency; and (c) the fact that the Sign test, in contrast to Wilcoxon's test, has been extended to permit the pairwise comparisons of k matched groups (Miller, 1966; Rhyne and Steel, 1967).

The Sign test is ideal for anyone whose mathematical sophistication ends at the level of subtraction! The difference scores are complied as in Table 4.7. This time, however, we ignore the magnitude of the differences entirely and merely count up the number of signs. After tossing out the single zero difference score, six positive difference scores and two negative difference scores remain. The index, r, is the smaller number of signs. The r is assessed by MacKinnon's table (1964), part of which is reproduced in Table Q. From this table, with $N = 8$ (the total number of differences) and $r = 2$, we see no reason at the .05 level to reject the hypothesis that the median difference score is zero.

The rationale of the Sign test derives from the binomial distribution. If chance alone were operating, half of the differences would be positive and half would be negative. If we are flipping a coin with a "friendly" stranger in a dark but friendly bar to see who buys the next round and he keeps calling "heads" and winning, we begin to suspect the stranger's friendliness and *his* coin. Likewise, in playing the science game when a preponderance of differences with the same sign turns up, we begin to doubt chance and entertain an alternative hypothesis. Lest we get too cozy regarding such an alternative hypothesis, we must be slightly paranoid at all times about the possibility of carry-over effects, especially when the same Ss are tested twice. The beautiful simplicity of the Sign test should not blind us to the inherent trickiness of the matched-group design. All previously stated warnings about this design should not be lost in the nonparametric shuffle.

The assumptions for the Sign test match its computational simplicity. They are that: (a) the difference scores are randomly and independently drawn from the difference-score population; and (b) the difference-score population is continuously distributed. Although these assumptions are elegantly simple, the efficiency of the Sign test is most impressive. Bradley, in summarizing the evidence on this matter, asserts: "This test appears to be the most powerful (rank-type) distribution-free test for an hypothesized median when all that is known about the sampled population is that it is continuous" (1968, p. 168).

Finally, we should leave the Sign test with a few words-to-live-by for the ideal type, slightly paranoid research worker. While the Sign test user only looks at the signs of the differences, an occasional peek at the magnitude of differences and the number of zero differences scores can sometimes pay off. Suppose that there is a preponderance of differences of one sign but the magnitudes of the differences with the other sign are unusually large. This should make the investigator a little uneasy and a little cautious. This uneasiness and caution should be even greater when the nature of the experiment has important consequences. For example, suppose it were a study of the effects of a new drug on blood pressure with ten cases showing a beneficial drop in blood pressure and three showing a rise. The warm feeling, induced by tallying the signs, might prove to be heartburn if the three increments were dangerously large ones. Regarding zero differences, it should be noted that the indication, for example, that the median population difference is not zero, can only be defended for the cases remaining after the sample is reduced by tossing out the zero differences. Furthermore, the occurrence of more than a few zero differences should produce uneasiness and cautiousness on the part of the research worker. He might properly be concerned by (a) generalizing from a truncated sample and (b) the validity of the continuity assumption.

A Location Test for k Matched Groups

One of the earliest nonparametric tests (except for χ^2 and rank correlation techniques) was devised by Friedman (1937). It is a ranks test that permits an overall test of k matched means. Instead of ranking all N scores, as in the Wilcoxon and Kruskal-Wallis tests, the ranks from 1 to k are assigned across each row. If the null hypothesis that $M_1 = M_2 = M_3 = \cdots = M_k$ is true, then the sums of ranks for each column (i.e., treatments) should be equal. If these sums are sufficiently disparate, then the null hypothesis is rejected. For illustrative purposes the Friedman test will be applied to the data from Weil et al. (Table 4.8) which were previously analyzed by an F

Table 4.8.   Application of the Friedman Test to the Pursuit-Rotor Scores

S	Placebo	(Rank)	Low	(Rank)	High	(Rank)
1	+1.20	(3)	−1.04	(2)	−4.01	(1)
2	+0.89	(3)	−1.43	(1)	−0.12	(2)
3	+0.50	(3)	−0.60	(2)	−6.56	(1)
4	+0.18	(3)	−0.11	(1)	+0.11	(2)
5	+3.20	(3)	+0.39	(2)	+0.13	(1)
6	+3.45	(3)	−0.32	(2)	−3.56	(1)
7	+0.81	(3)	+0.48	(2)	−0.79	(1)
8	+1.75	(3)	−0.39	(2)	−0.92	(1)
9	+3.90	(3)	−1.94	(2)	−2.60	(1)
	$\Sigma R = R_j = 27$		16		11	54 $= \Sigma\Sigma R$

test for k matched groups. For the first S, the score of -4.01 receives a rank of 1, -1.04 a rank of 2, and $+1.20$ a rank of 3. This ranking process is continued across the rows (Ss) and the sums of ranks for the treatments, R_j, are obtained. Then these values are substituted in Friedman's computational formula:

$$\chi_r^2 = \frac{12}{Nk(k+1)} \sum_1^k (R_j)^2 - 3N(k+1),$$

where N = number of rows,

   k = number of treatments,

   R_j = sum of ranks for the jth column,

   $\sum_1^k$ = operation of summing R_j^2 from 1 to k.

In this instance we have:

$$\chi_r^2 = \left[\frac{12}{9(3)(4)} (27^2 + 16^2 + 11^2) \right] - 3(9)(4),$$

$$\chi_r^2 = 122.89 - 108 = 14.89.$$

The exact probability of a $\chi_r^2 = 14.89$ for $N = 9$ per treatment and $k = 3$ treatments can be ascertained from Friedman's Table (Table R). Since the probability is far beyond the .001 level, the hypothesis of equal treatment means would be rejected. This rejection of the null hypothesis, of course, brings us face-to-face once again with the multiple-comparison issue. For N and k values that exceed the limits of Table R, the χ_r^2 can be treated as a χ^2 with $df = k - 1$ and referred to Table M to obtain its approximate probability. Before leaving the computation of χ_r^2, it should be mentioned that tied observations are broken by the midranks method and that as a check on the ranking, $\Sigma\Sigma R = N(k)(k+1)/2 = 9(3)(4)/2 = 54$.

The literature, in general, does not contain very direct statements regarding the assumptions for Friedman's test. Apparently neither homogeneity of variance nor normality of the parent population is assumed (Walker and Lev, 1953, p. 438; Siegel, 1956, p. 170; Miller, 1966, p. 175). Bradley, in the most explicit account, offers some other assumptions:

> Assignment of the C units from each matching population to the C treatments must be *random*. Alternatively, if a single unit [S] is subjected to all C treatments, it is assumed there is *no carryover effect* . . . In a somewhat broader sense it is assumed that there is independence between the rows, i.e., that the units in the different rows are separate and noninteracting. Finally, it is assumed that there are *no tied observations* within any one row (Bradley, 1968, pp. 124f.).

Finally, Miller mentions that: "Interactions between treatments and blocks are excluded" (1966, p. 175). This statement means that the treatments should have roughly equivalent effects on the different Ss. Inasmuch as these assumptions have already been discussed, this section will be closed with a few comments on the efficiency of Friedman's test.

For some curious reason, even though Friedman's test has been around since 1937, there is little information about its efficiency. Friedman (1937) analyzed 56 sets of data with both an F test and χ_r^2. He found: in 45 cases the two tests gave essentially the same results; in 4 cases the χ_r^2 rejected the null hypothesis when F did not; in 2 cases the reverse occurred; in 1 case the χ_r^2 yielded a lower level of significance than F; and in the remaining 4 cases the reverse occurred. Siegel says " . . . it would be difficult or even impossible to say which is the more powerful test" (1956, p. 172). However, it should be stressed that Friedman used data which were suitable for an F test analysis. What is needed is knowledge about the performance of the two tests when the data are unsuited for an F test. Bradley (1968) points out that for normal data the efficiency of Friedman's test increases as the number of treatments is increased and that with two treatments its efficiency is comparable to that of the Sign test. Let us repeat — it is curious that there is so little information on the efficiency of Friedman's test.

Multiple-Comparison Location Tests for k Matched Groups

In the old days when the West was wild (i.e., when men were men and girls wore flour sack underwear), people didn't know what to do when they met a significant χ_r^2 eyeball to eyeball, so to speak. Being reasonable people, they did what they could do—they ran pairwise tests using Wilcoxon's signed-ranks test or Sign tests. These procedures, as we have said before, are equivalent to running simple t tests after analysis of variance. Fortunately, there has been some work done on this particular multiple-comparison problem in recent years by Nemenyi (1963) and Rhyne and Steel (1967). Miller (1966) has carefully considered the statistical logic for the various techniques.

The Nemenyi test (Miller, 1966, pp. 172–178) involves the determination of a single critical difference for comparing the differences in *mean* sums of ranks. The formula for the critical difference is:

$$crit.\ diff. = [\chi_r^2\alpha]^{\frac{1}{2}}\left[\frac{k(k+1)}{6N}\right]^{\frac{1}{2}}.$$

If the difference between any two treatment mean sums of ranks equals or exceeds the critical difference, it is significant at the α level. The means for the sums of the ranks in Table 4.8 are: $M = R_j/N = 27/9 = 3.00$; $16/9 = 1.78$; $11/9 = 1.22$. The critical difference for $\alpha = .05$ found by inserting the χ_r^2 (for $k = 3$ and $N = 9$) from the Table R, k, and N into the formula, above is:[2]

$$crit.\ diff. = (6.22)^{\frac{1}{2}}\left[\frac{3(3+1)}{6(9)}\right]^{\frac{1}{2}},$$

$$crit.\ diff. = (2.49)(.471) = 1.17.$$

The difference between the Placebo group and High dosage groups ($M_P - M_H = 3.00 - 1.22 = 1.78$) is greater than the critical difference of 1.17, and therefore this contrast is significant. Likewise the difference between the Placebo and Low groups is significant but that between the Low and High groups is not: $3.00 - 1.78 > 1.17$; $1.78 - 1.22 < 1.17$. Thus the Nemenyi test produces the same results as the Bonferroni t tests which were applied to the same data.

A second technique which is suitable for this problem is Multiple-Sign tests (Miller, 1966). Sign tests are performed among all possible groups and S_+, the *larger* number of signs, is counted up for each contrast. These S_+ values are then assessed for the proper k and N values in Table S. The probability values in this table represent approximations that agree closely

2. This test was run at $\alpha = .05$ to contrast the results with those from Chapter 3 where $\alpha = .05$ was used as in the Weil et al. study (1968).

with the exact probabilities for small k and N (for more detailed tables for $k = 3$, see Rhyne & Steel, 1967). Since the pursuit rotor scores in Table 4.8 are greater for all 9 Ss in the Placebo than in the High treatment, $S_+ = 9$ for this contrast. From Table S, $S_+ = 9$ is found to be significant at the .05 level for $k = 3$ and $N = 9$. The $S_+ = 9$ for the Placebo-Low contrast ($k = 3$, $N = 9$) is also significant.[3] And, as was observed with the Nemenyi test, the Low-High contrast is not significant ($S_+ = 7$, $k = 3$, $N = 9$). For this particular problem, then, the two tests – the Nemenyi and Multiple-Sign tests – yield the same indications. Our present preference is for the Multiple-Sign procedure. It entails a minimum of assumptions and nicely fulfills the laziness criterion.[4] In addition, Miller has offered the following critique of the Nemenyi tests:

> Within a block the ranks are assigned with respect to the observations from all the populations. This makes the disparity between the ranks for two other populations. dependent upon the values of the observations from the other populations. The significance or nonsignificance of a comparison between two populations depends upon the other populations not involved in this comparison. This is most distasteful (1966, p. 175).[5]

Nevertheless, the advice to apply Multiple-Sign tests must be tempered by the fact that little is known about the power of either test.

At this point a question posed earlier can again be raised: Why not test the two extreme groups with the Multiple-Sign test as an overall test instead of using a Friedman test? The answer is the same: yes, it is a legitimate procedure. Is the Friedman test a more omnibus test? Possibly. Will the two procedures yield the same results? Probably some of the time!

A Quasi-Summary and a Few Words-To-Live-By

In this Chapter the nonparametric counterparts to some of the tests in Chapter 3 were discussed. Procedures for coping with two and k independent and matched groups were considered as well as techniques for making pairwise comparisons. The nonparametric methods described are eminently suited for data analysis when the data clearly violate the usual assumptions of homogeneity of variance, normality, and so on. However, the implication

---

3. As in the case of the Steel k ranks test above, a *single* critical S_+ value for $k = 3$ and $N = 9$ is required for all three comparisons.

4. This is the second time the laziness criterion has been pressed into service. The use of this criterion here should not be taken as indication of an antiempirical bias on the part of the writer. The grand plan is try out a reasonable method for which tables are available. If the answers it gives don't make sense or if new information on the power of these tests becomes available, then seek a new method.

5. This same criticism was levelled earlier by Miller regarding the Nemenyi multiple Kruskal–Wallis test.

should not be drawn that nonparametric methods, being more assumption-free, should be used exclusively. The classical methods should certainly be applied whenever the assumptions can be met — there's no sense in using a rock to pound nails when a hammer is available. Nor should the implication be drawn that "good" experiments should be analyzed with classical tests, but "bad" ones should be subjected to nonparametric analysis. A bad experiment is a bad experiment and beyond salvaging with any kind of statistics. Finally, the fact that some nonparametric tests are, to use Tukey's phrase, "quick and dirty" tests should not deter investigators from their use. They have a rightful place among the researcher's tools, and their simplicity should not obscure their demonstrated high efficiency when "taken as directed."

PROBLEMS

1. Using the data in Table 3.2 (p. 33), determine whether or not the bulk of the scores is larger in the 80% group at the .05 level (one tail). Apply a test which does not assume homogeneity of variance or normality.
2. Perform a similar overall test on the 100%, 80%, and 20% groups in Table 3.3 (p. 40). Require the .05 level for significance and use the mid-ranks method for tied scores.
3. Make pairwise comparisons of the 100%, 80%, and 20% groups at the .05 level with the appropriate distribution-free tests.
4. With a nonparametric test compare the average performance of Ss 13–24 on Days 1 and 4 in Table 3.25 (p. 90). Require the .05 level of significance (two tail).
5. For the same Ss find out if there was an overall difference in their performance over Days 1 through 4 at the .05 level. Use a nonparametric test.
6. What is the appropriate nonparametric test for making pairwise comparisons in such a situation?
7. Twelve pairs of Ss, matched on their performance on a creativity test, were exposed to a problem-solving task. Half of the Ss were instructed to manipulate the materials of the task "in their mind;" the other half were instructed to actually manipulate the materials. All Ss solved the problem, but 10 out of 12 Ss in the actual manipulation group were faster. Is this a significant difference? Prior to doing the experiment, the investigator *randomly* assigned one S from each matched pair to each treatment. Is this procedure necessary or useful?

CHAPTER FIVE

Steps to Inference: III. Classes

This [Aristotelian] classification often took the form of paired opposites, such as cold and warm, dry and moist, and compared with present-day classification had a rigid, absolute character. In modern quantitative physics dichotomous classifications have been entirely replaced by continuous gradations. Substantial concepts have been replaced by functional concepts. – K. Lewin

Class Frequencies of Two Independent Groups

In Chapter 3 we described some statistical tests which are applicable to the numbers that emerge from certain common experimental designs. These numbers were generally assumed to represent randomly and independently drawn samples from normally distributed populations whose variances were equal. In Chapter 4 several nonparametric tests were presented for analyzing data when the assumptions of population normality and equal variances could not be met. Moreover, the techniques of Chapter 4 do not require numbers – data initially in the form of ranks or signs (+ or −) can be subjected to analysis. However, investigators sometimes end up with even grosser behavioral measures in the form of a limited number of classes like: solved vs did not solve, survived vs died, improved vs no change vs became worse, and so on. The present chapter will be concerned with some nonparametric methods for the analysis of such nominal data. The chapter will follow the previous organizational scheme of examining two and k independent and matched groups. After the discussions of k groups, we will be concerned with the analogue of multiple comparisons – the partitioning of contingency tables.

We can best approach the analysis of class-type data by a concrete example. Beale (1956) confronted nursery-school and grade-school children with a choice between a more desired toy, which the child could have if he waited 20 minutes, and a less desired toy, which he could have immediately. The frequencies of children who delayed for 20 minutes and did not delay in this "temptation" situation are shown in Table 5.1. This arrangement of data is

Table 5.1.*   *Frequencies of Nursery School and*
Grade School Children Who Delayed
or Did Not Delay (Beale, 1956)

	Group		
Response	NS	GS	*Totals*
Delay	15	46	61
No Delay	38	1	39
Totals	53	47	100

*Reprinted by permission of the author from Elizabeth Beale, "A Developmental Analysis of Children's Delay Behavior in a Temptation Type of Conflict Situation," p. 65. Ph.D. dissertation, The University of Kansas, 1956.

termed a 2×2 *contingency table*. The research question is: Did the proportion (or percentage) of Ss who delayed differ in the two groups? The proportion in the NS group is: $15/53 = .28$; in the GS group it is: $46/47 = .98$. To answer this question a χ^2 test is performed and the obtained χ^2 is evaluated by reference to Table M. The *df* for entering the table are $(R-1)(C-1)$, where R denotes the number of rows in the contingency table and C is the number of columns. Thus, $df = (2-1)(2-1) = 1$. The formula for χ^2 is:

$$\chi^2 = \Sigma \frac{(fo - fe)^2}{fe},$$

where fo = the observed frequencies in the cells,
$\quad\;\; fe$ = the expected frequencies in the cells.

The *fe* for the upper left-hand cell is $\Sigma R_1 (\Sigma C_1)/N$ or $61(53)/100 = 32.33$. For the lower left-hand cell it is: $\Sigma R_2 (\Sigma C_1)/N = 39(53)/100 = 20.67$. The other two *fe* values are calculated in the same manner and the four *fe* values are shown in Table 5.2. It may be noted that the *fe*'s sum to produce the original marginal totals and N. For each cell $(fo - fe)^2/fe$ is found, and these squared deviations divided by *fe* are added to give χ^2. Thus χ^2 is:

$$\chi^2 = \frac{(15-32.33)^2}{32.33} + \frac{(38-20.67)^2}{20.67} + \frac{(46-28.67)^2}{28.67} + \frac{(1-18.33)^2}{18.33}$$

$$= 9.29 + 14.53 + 10.48 + 16.38 = 50.68.$$

Table 5.2. *Expected Frequencies (fe) of Nursery School and Grade School Children Who Delayed or Did Not Delay*

Response	Group		
	NS	GS	Totals
Delay	32.33	28.67	61.00
No Delay	20.67	18.33	39.00
Totals	53.00	47.00	100.00

From Table M with 1 df this χ^2 is observed to be highly significant ($<.001$). Therefore, the data indicate that the GS group had a significantly higher proportion of Ss that were able to delay.

The assumptions for the χ^2 test have been clearly stated by Hays:

1. each and every observation is independent of each other observation;
2. each observation qualifies for one and only one cell in the table;
3. sample size N is large (1963, p. 592).

The first assumption of independence is the one which is most often violated. One quick check on independence is to compare the total number of Ss with N, the total number of observations for the contingency table. If N is greater than the number of Ss, then S or Ss are contributing more than one score to a cell (or cells) and the independence criterion has been violated. The third assumption of N size is a somewhat complicated issue. If $N > 20$, then the χ^2 test can be used, provided the *expected* frequency in each of the four cells is $\geqslant 5$. If $N < 20$ or one or more fe's are <5 then Fisher's exact test (see below) should be employed. Even when $N > 20$ and all fe's are $\geqslant 5$, the χ^2 test should always be corrected to provide a better fit between the approximate probabilities obtained from the continuous χ^2 distributions in Table M and the exact probabilities obtained from the true χ^2 distributions which are discrete (Cochran, 1942). This correction, termed Yates' correction for continuity, consists of reducing the *absolute* size of deviations ($fo - fe$) by 0.5. Thus the χ^2 formula with Yates' correction is:

$$\chi_c^2 = \Sigma \frac{(|fo-fe| - 0.5)^2}{fe}.$$

Analyzing Beale's results with this formula, we have:

$$\chi_c^2 = \frac{(\mid 15 - 32.33 \mid - 0.5)^2}{32.33} + \frac{(\mid 38 - 20.67 \mid - 0.5)^2}{20.67} + \frac{(\mid 46 - 28.67 \mid - 0.5)^2}{28.67}$$

$$+ \frac{(\mid 1 - 18.33 \mid - 0.5)^2}{18.33}$$

$$= 8.76 + 13.70 + 9.88 + 15.45 = 47.79.$$

The application of Yates' correction always reduces the χ^2, i.e., $(\chi^2 > \chi_c^2)$, but the difference between the two groups of children remains highly significant. Again, it should be stressed that Yates' correction should always be used with a 2×2 table because the resulting probability value will more closely approximate the exact probability value. Finally, to perform a one-tailed test with 1 *df* the probability levels in Table M should be halved and the table would then be read from right to left as .0005, .0025, .005, .0125, and so on.

Let us now take up an example where N is close to 20. In another part of Beale's experiment 21 children were confronted with the conflict situation when the attractiveness of the less desired toy was higher. The frequencies of children who delayed or did not delay under these conditions in the two groups are shown in Table 5.3. Since N is small and the *fe* for the upper right

Table 5.3.*   *Frequencies of Nursery School and Grade School Children Who Delayed or Did Not Delay When the Valence of the Less Desired Toy Was Increased (Beale, 1956)*

| | Response | | |
Group	Delay	No Delay	Totals
NS	2 (A)	7 (B)	9
GS	10 (C)	2 (D)	12
Totals	12	9	21

*Reprinted by permission of the author from Elizabeth Beale, "A Developmental Analysis of Children's Delay Behavior in a Temptation Type of Conflict Situation," p. 96. Ph.D. dissertation, The University of Kansas, 1956.

cell is < 5, Fisher's exact test is appropriate. Fisher's test, another randomization test, yields an exact one-tail probability for the occurrence of the frequencies in a given 2×2 table *and* for all other more extreme tables having the same marginal totals. In our example, there are two other tables:

1	8
11	1

and

0	9
12	0

. First, the probability of the original table is found by using Fisher's formula:

$$\text{one-tail } p = \frac{(A+B)!(C+D)!(A+C)!(B+D)!}{N!A!B!C!D!}.$$

Substituting the fo's in Table 5.3 for the appropriate symbols we have:

$$\text{one-tail } p = \frac{9!12!12!9!}{21!2!7!10!2!} = .00808.$$

Next, the same formula is applied successively to the two more extreme tables and the three probability values are summed. Fortunately, none of this has to be done for several statisticians (Finney, Latscha, Bennett, & Hsu, 1963) have performed all of the laborious calculations. Thus, we can get the answer to this and other problems directly from Table T. For convenience sake in using Table T, we will reverse A and C and B and D. Then we can enter Table T with $A+B = 12$ and $C+D = 9$. Since $A = 10$, then C must be $\leqslant 3$ for significance. Because $C = 2$ (in the relabelled table), it is significant at the .01 level for a one-tail test (or .02 for a two-tailed test). The one-tailed probability values in Table T are conservatively rounded values, which permits us to say that $C = 2$ is significant at .01 rather than at .025. Thus the data in Table 5.3 indicate that the grade-school Ss were better able to delay in the conflict situation than the nursery-school Ss.

In summary, a 2×2 table for two groups and a dichotomous response is analyzed by a χ^2 test corrected for continuity when $N > 20$ and all expected frequencies are $\geqslant 5$. When neither or both of these conditions can be met, Fisher's exact test is appropriate and this test can be done *sans* calculations by reference to Table T (for extended Tables, see Finney, et al., 1963). The most critical assumption for χ^2 is that of independence. If matched groups are involved, a different test, described later, is required.

Class Frequencies of k Independent Groups

Following our usual organization, we shall now turn to an experimental arrangement in which there are k independent groups. In another section of the Beale study the conflict behavior of nursery, kindergarten, and grade-school Ss was investigated. Table 5.4 displays the frequencies of delay and no delay responses for these three groups. To test the differences in the proportions of delay responses among the three groups, a χ^2 test is performed. The fact that the df for this 2×3 contingency table are greater than 1, i.e., $df = (R-1)(C-1) = (2-1)(3-1) = 2$, removes the necessity for Yates' correction for continuity. Furthermore, the criterion that all fe must be at least 5 is not enforced. In fact, Cochran (1954) has proposed that when

Table 5.4.* Frequencies of Nursery School, Kindergarten, and Grade School Children Who Delayed or Did Not Delay (Beale, 1956)

Response	NS	Group K	GS	Totals
Delay	5	11	21	37
No Delay	14	9	3	26
Totals	19	20	24	63

*Reprinted by permission of the author from Elizabeth Beale, "A Developmental Analysis of Children's Delay Behavior in a Temptation Type of Conflict Situation," p. 95. Ph.D. dissertation, The University of Kansas, 1956.

$df > 1$: (a) 20% of the cells can have fe's less than 5; and (b) that a minimum $fe = 1$ is permissible. From these considerations, it follows that the data in Table 5.4 may be analyzed by the original uncorrected χ^2 formula. The fe values are determined in the same manner as those for a 2×2 table (see Table 5.5). Except for slight rounding errors, the sums of the fe are equal to

Table 5.5. Expected Frequencies (fe) for the Data in Table 5.4

Response	NS	Group K	GS	Totals
Delay	11.16	11.75	14.09	37.00
No Delay	7.84	8.25	9.90	25.99
Totals	19.00	20.00	23.99	62.99

the marginal totals of fo. Applying the χ^2 formula, we have:

$$\chi^2 = \Sigma \frac{(fo - fe)^2}{fe}$$

$$\chi^2 = \frac{(5 - 11.16)^2}{11.16} + \frac{(14 - 7.84)^2}{7.84} + \frac{(11 - 11.75)^2}{11.75} + \frac{(9 - 8.25)^2}{8.25} + \frac{(21 - 14.09)^2}{14.09} +$$

$$\frac{(3 - 9.90)^2}{9.90}$$

$$= 3.40 + 4.84 + .05 + .07 + 3.39 + 4.81 = 16.56.$$

With $df = 2$ the obtained χ^2 is significant (Table M) at less than the .001 level. Where are we now? That's right, Virginia, we're back at the old multiple-comparison problem. The χ^2 informs us that there is a relationship between age and type of response, but partitioning of the χ^2 table is necessary to isolate the difference(s) among the groups.

The same χ^2 technique is applicable when more classes of responses exist. Actually, the conflict responses were classified into three types by Beale. The third type she called interrupted delay. In this kind of behavior the child touched the less desired toy one or more times during the 20-minute delay period but released the toy when reminded of the conditions of the experiment. In other words, the children were able to delay, but they could not keep their grimy little hands off the immediate toy during the wait.

Table 5.6.* *Frequencies of Nursery School, Kindergarten, and Grade School Children Who Delayed, Showed Interrupted Delay, or Did Not Delay (Beale, 1956)*

| | | Group | | |
Response	NS	K	GS	Totals
Delay	5	11	21	37
Interrupted Delay	6	6	0	12
No Delay	14	9	3	26
Totals	25	26	24	75

*Reprinted by permission of the author from Elizabeth Beale, "A Developmental Analysis of Children's Delay Behavior in a Temptation Type of Conflict Situation," p. 96. Ph.D. dissertation, The University of Kansas, 1956.

The results of this portion of the study are displayed in Table 5.6. A χ^2 test of these data using the same uncorrected χ^2 formula, yielded a $\chi^2 = 24.04$ which for $df = 4$, $[(R-1)(C-1) = (3-1)(3-1) = 4]$, is significant at less than the .001 level. Yes, Virginia, you're right again.

Partitions with k Independent Groups

In the early days of the West, investigators after gazing for a spell in rapt astonishment at a significant χ^2, then did their thing—further analyses. Now a big contingency table can always be partitioned into a lot of little contingency tables (e.g., 2×2's). If the investigator pursues this course (it's like running all possible t tests), then he ought to pay a price for his unbridled passion for doing 2×2 tables. That is to say, both the investigator and the scientific community need some kind of protection in the form of significance levels being adjusted for the number of contrasts that are performed. Thus our topic is: How can a contingency table (with $df > 1$) be partitioned with protection being provided for the number of comparisons?

We shall consider two kinds of partitions.[1] The first type, proposed by Ryan (1960), is the analogue of the pairwise tests described in the previous sections. In brief, all possible χ^2 tests are performed between k groups but the required significance level is adjusted depending upon how far apart the groups in question are when they have ordered in terms of increasing proportions. For the two extreme groups, a χ^2 for the $2\alpha/k(k-1)$ level of significance is required. For the comparison between the proportions of the first and $k-1$ groups and between the second and k groups, the required probability level is $2\alpha/k(k-2)$, and so on. Thus Ryan's test is again a variant of the Tukey B test.

Let us try out this technique with the data in Table 5.4. Since $k = 3$ the required probability value for the GS–NS comparison using $\alpha = .05$ is: $2(.05)/3(3-1) = .017$. For the other two comparisons, GS–K and K–NS, it is: $2\alpha/k(k-2) = 2(.05)/3(3-2) = .033$. The χ_c^2 for the extreme groups is 14.15 which is significant at less than the .001 level and therefore exceeds the required .017 level. For the K–NS comparison, χ_c^2 is 2.22 which fails to achieve the required level of .033. The GS–K χ_c^2 is 4.28 which falls between .05 and .025 by Table M and is significant at .033 by the Bliss χ^2 chart in Wilcoxon (1949). Thus the Ryan tests indicate that the GS Ss made a higher proportion of delay responses than both the NS and K Ss but the latter two groups did not differ from one another. One practical problem with Ryan's test is the necessity for extended χ^2 tables to determine whether or not obtained χ^2's are significant at the various unusual required probability values. This problem can be solved by using Bliss's chart for χ^2 (1944) which has been reprinted in Wilcoxon (1949) or by employing a normal deviate test (Table N) for differences in proportions. Ryan (1960) has elected to follow the second approach and described it fully.

A second method for partitioning χ^2 tables is by means of what are termed *orthogonal* or independent comparisons.[2] When a zealous investigator breaks a contingency table into all possible 2×2 tables and calculates the χ^2's for these tables, he will find that the sum of the χ^2's for the components will not equal the total χ^2 value for the original table. With orthogonal comparisons, on the other hand, the χ^2's and df's for the components are additive, i.e., their sums will equal the total χ^2 and df for the whole contingency table. Thus the orthogonal-comparison method serves to reduce the number of

---

1. For some other approaches to this problem see Marascuilo (1966) and Cohen (1967).

2. There are orthogonal-comparison methods that may be used in place of the multiple-comparison methods described in Chapter 3. We have not included these but the interested reader can find out about them in Edwards (1968) and Hays (1963).

contrasts by including only those selected comparisons that are independent of one another.

To exemplify this procedure, which is described in detail by Castellan (1965) and Bresnahan and Shapiro (1966), we will apply it to the Beale data in Table 5.6 for which the overall χ^2 was 24.04 with 4 df. Let us suppose that the investigator's primary interest was in contrasting the no delay + interrupted delay vs delay in the nursery-school + kindergarten children vs the grade school children. To end up with this particular contrast, the rows in Table 5.6 will be rearranged into Table 5.7, a manipulation that has no effect on the total χ^2. Since $df = 4$, the rearranged table can be broken down into four 2 × 2 tables, each with 1 df. These four contrasts are shown in Table 5.8.

Table 5.7.   A Rearrangement of the Row Data in
Table 5.6 for Orthogonal Contrasts

| Response | Group | | | |
	NS	K	GS	Totals
No Delay	14	9	3	26
Interrupted Delay	6	6	0	12
Delay	5	11	21	37
Totals	25	26	24	75

Table 5.8.   Four Orthogonal Contrasts of the Data in Table 5.7

(1)

| Response | Group | | |
	NS	K	Totals
No Delay	14	9	23
Int. Delay	6	6	12
Totals	20	15	35

(2)

| Response | Group | | |
	NS + K	GS	Totals
No Delay	23	3	26
Int. Delay	12	0	12
Totals	35	3	38

(3)

| Response | Group | | |
	NS	K	Totals
No D + Int. D	20	15	35
Delay	5	11	16
Totals	25.	26	51

(4)

| Response | Group | | |
	NS + K	GS	Totals
No D + Int. D	35	3	38
Delay	16	21	37
Totals	51	24	75

The special ways of subdividing contingency tables for various *df* may be found in Castellan (1965) and Bresnahan and Shapiro (1966). The next step is to obtain a χ^2 for each partition using a *special* χ^2 formula:

$$\chi^2 = \Sigma \frac{(fo - fe)^2}{Fe}$$

Where *Fe* is the expected frequency based on the marginal totals from the *original* complete table (in our case Table 5.6). In this particular example, inspection of the four partitions suggests that it might be fruitful to analyze table (4) first. When this is done with the special formula, $\chi^2 = 20.58$ which for 1 *df* is highly significant. Moreover, since the χ^2 for the original table was 24.04 most of the variation is attributable to this comparison. Therefore, it would not be worthwhile analyzing the remaining contrasts for the unaccounted for portion of the total χ^2 is only $24.04 - 20.58 = 3.46$.

Which of the two methods of partitioning a contingency table should be used? The answer would seem to depend upon what questions the research worker is interested in answering. We suspect that most investigators will be concerned with comparing *k* proportions. For this purpose, Ryan's test is better. For more complicated, independent "breaks," the method of orthogonal comparisons would seem preferable. At the very least, both methods have some built-in protection against Type I errors not present in the wild and wooly ways of the past. The Ryan method adjusts the significance levels in terms of the number of comparisons and the method of orthogonal comparisons limits the number of comparisons to specific independent partitions.

Class Frequencies of Two Matched Groups

Our statistical merry-go-round has traveled its circular path, and we are back again at the experimental paradigm of two matched groups. However, in this case the behavioral measure is dichotomous in nature, e.g., pass vs fail, solve vs did not solve, etc. Matching involves the same manipulations as before – either the *N* Ss are tested twice or *N* pairs of Ss, matched on some other variable and randomly assigned to the two treatments, are exposed to a single treatment. The strengths and weaknesses of the two matched group designs are still with us: good matching variables are necessary for enhanced efficiency, carry-over effects can be disastrous, etc. Finally, it should be noted that although the data from such investigations are in the form of frequencies, they cannot be subjected to the usual χ^2 procedure. The reason for this is that the frequencies, coming from matched Ss, violate the fundamental χ^2 assumption of independence.

To illustrate the treatment of dichotomous behavioral data obtained from matched groups, we will look at some research by Snyder (1956) on the "Kohnstamm phenomenon." The Kohnstamm phenomenon, first reported by Salmon (1914) and Kohnstamm (1915), is a post-contraction phenomenon consisting of an involuntary upward movement of the arm following brief voluntary isometric contraction of the arm. If a human S presses the back of his hand vigorously against a wall for 5 to 25 seconds with the arm being kept free of body contact and then moves from the wall and relaxes, the arm "seems to lose weight" and move upward. Snyder investigated the occurrence and personality correlates of this phenomenon with 41 Ss under four conditions of increasing suggestion: Condition I–S naive; II–S informed that something might happen to his arm; III–S informed about the arm rise and given a demonstration; IV–S told the phenomenon was a reflex reaction. The data from Snyder's experiment are shown in Table 5.9. An entry of 1

Table 5.9.*   Kohnstamm Reactivity under Four Instruction Conditions (Snyder, 1956)

Number of Ss		Conditions I	II	III	IV	L_i
11		1	1	1	1	44
1		0	1	1	1	3
5		0	0	1	1	10
4		0	0	0	1	4
20		0	0	0	0	0
41	Gj	11	12	17	21	61

*Reprinted by permission of the author, from Rebecca Snyder, "Personality Characteristics Associated with the Kohnstamm Phenomenon." p. 43. Ph.D. dissertation, The University of Kansas, 1956.

denotes that S exhibited the Kohnstamm phenomenon; 0 denotes that S did not.

The first question we will ask is: Did the proportion of Ss showing the Kohnstamm phenomenon differ under instructions I and IV? Under condition I the proportion is: $11/41 = .27$; and under condition IV it is: $21/41 = .51$. (Alternatively, we could ask: Did a change in Kohnstamm reactivity occur from condition I to IV?) The proportions cannot be evaluated by the regular χ^2 test because they are based upon the same Ss tested twice. The appropriate test here is McNemar's test for correlated proportions (Siegel, 1956). To perform this test it is necessary to assign each S from Table 5.9 to *one and only one cell* of a 2×2 table (Table 5.10). The 11 Ss who displayed the phenomenon under both conditions are tallied in cell B. The 20 Ss who did not respond under either condition are assigned to cell C. The 10 Ss

Table 5.10.   A Four-Fold Table of Changes in
Kohnstamm Reactivity

		Condition IV		
		0	1	Totals
Condition I	1	0 (A)	11 (B)	11
	0	20 (C)	10 (D)	30
Totals		20	21	41

who did not respond under I but did under IV are in cell D. Since no S responded in I but failed in IV, cell A is empty. Note that the total N = 41, which equals the number of Ss. To test the frequencies in Table 5.10 McNemar's formula for χ_c^2 is used:

$$\chi_c^2 = \frac{(|A-D|-1)^2}{A+D}$$

The 1 in the numerator of the formula is Yates' correction for continuity. This correction is again necessary because actual χ^2 values are discrete and they are being evaluated against the continuous χ^2 distributions in Table M. Applying the formula, we have:

$$\chi_c^2 = \frac{(|0-10|-1)^2}{0+10} = 8.1$$

The *df* for this test is 1. From Table M it is apparent that the obtained χ_c^2 is significant at less than the .005 level. Thus the test indicates that a significant difference in the proportion of Kohnstamm responses occurred from condition I to IV or, alternatively, that a significant change in Kohnstamm responses occurred from condition I to IV. The interpretation of this outcome is complicated by the fact that since the Ss were exposed to all four treatments in the same order. The higher proportion of responses under condition IV could represent a cumulative effect of instructions, fatigue, the desire of Ss to go home, etc., rather than to the effects of the condition IV instructions per se. We'll say it again – matched groups designs are tricky and those in which S gets all treatments are the trickiest of all.

It should be pointed out that the McNemar formula only includes the frequencies of the Ss who *change* their response, i.e., cells A and D. The Ss who do not change, i.e., those in cells B and C, do not enter into the calculations. The null hypothesis is that the number of Ss changing in one direction should be equal to those changing in the other or that $A = D$. Accordingly, we are dealing with binomial problem and the table for the Sign test (Table Q) can be used to evaluate the frequencies in A and D. For $N = A + D = 10$ and $r = 0$ the probability is .01. This alternative procedure is, in fact, required when the fe's in A and D are < 5. The fe for this particular type of four-fold table is: $fe = (A + D)/2$. Although McNemar's χ^2 test is simple to perform, we can see no reason for failing to use the Sign test table for all problems, whatever the size of N.

The efficiency of the McNemar test is equivalent to that of the Sign test, discussed above, and it is the highest when $A + D = 6$ (Siegel, 1956). It should be noted further that the test is limited to the case where matching is present and the dependent variable is measured on a dichotomous scale. The most frequent error in its use (by students, of course) is to "beef up" the sample by ingeniously tallying *both* of each S's test scores in the four-fold table. The resulting "N" is impressively large but inflated. Proper use of the test demands that each matched pair must contribute only one tally to one and only one cell.

Class Frequencies of k Matched Groups

Given the Snyder data in Table 5.9 we can ask: Are the proportions of Kohnstamm responses equal for the four conditions? (Or alternatively: Did the proportions change over the conditions?). In actual research the whole table would be analyzed first. We merely selected two conditions in the previous section to demonstrate McNemar's test for two matched groups.

The research question can be answered by Cochran's test (Siegel, 1956) which is a simple extension of McNemar's test to k matched groups. The formula for Cochran's test is:

$$Q = \frac{k(k-1) \sum_{1}^{k} (G_j - \overline{G})^2}{k \sum_{1}^{N} L_i - \sum_{1}^{N} L_i^2},$$

where k = the number of treatments,

G_j = sum of "successes" in the jth treatment,

$\overline{G}$ = mean of G_j,

L_i = sum of "successes" for the ith S.

The mean of G_j is $\overline{G} = 61/4 = 15.25$. Getting the remaining sums from Table 39, we have:[3]

$$Q = \frac{4\,(3)\,[(11-15.25)^2+(12-15.25)^2+(17-15.25)^2+(21-15.25)^2]}{4\,(61)-[176+9+20+4]}$$

$$= \frac{12\,(64.75)}{244-209} = 22.20.$$

The resulting Q is distributed as a χ^2 and assessed with $df = k-1 = 4-1 = 3$. By reference to Table M the Q is found to be significant at less than the .001 level.

At this point a few alert, perceptive, and intelligent students (including Virginia) will mutter: "So what! All the Q shows is that there's an overall difference in the proportions. What we want now is a way of making multiple-comparison tests of the proportions." Yes, alert, perceptive, and intelligent students you are so right! Before developing this problem, however, we must inquire about the efficiency of Cochran's Q. We may summarize the knowledge on this topic succinctly by saying it is nonexistent.

Multiple Comparisons of Class Frequencies with k Matched Groups

An investigator has the choice of two techniques for performing multiple-comparisons of the proportions arising from k matched groups: (a) the Ryan test (1960); and (b) the Multiple-Sign test (Miller, 1966). In the Ryan test the significance levels for McNemar χ^2 tests or Sign tests would be adjusted, in the same manner as before, as a function of how far apart the groups being contrasted are when they have been ordered in terms of in-creasing proportions. With the Multiple-Sign test no calculations beyond counting signs are necessary. One simply checks the number of S_+'s against Miller's table (Table S) for significance. Although we have carried out both of these procedures in Chapter 4 with the Weil et al. data, we will do them again with Snyder's data from Table 5.9.

---

3. The L_i symbol needs clarification. Normally the data for a Cochran Q will be set up according to Ss:

S	I	II	Treatment III	IV	L_i	L_i^2
1	1	1	1	1	4	16
2	1	1	1	1	4	16
$\vdots$	$\vdots$	$\vdots$	$\vdots$	$\vdots$	$\vdots$	$\vdots$
41	0	0	0	0	0	0

Since there are 11 Ss like S1, L_i for these Ss is $11(4) = 44$ and L_i^2 is $11(16) = 176$.

The Ryan test requires a significance level of $2\alpha/k(k-1) = 2(.05)/4(3) = .0083$ for comparing the proportions of the extreme conditions (I and IV) at the .05 level of significance. For the remaining comparisons the critical probability values are: $2\alpha/k(k-2) = 2(.05)/4(2) = .0125$ and $2\alpha/k(k-3) = 2(.05)/4(1) = .025$. In the previous section, the McNemar test of the extreme groups disclosed a $\chi_c^2 = 8.1$. The probability of this χ^2 from the Bliss chart (Wilcoxon, 1949) is .004. Since .004 is less than the required .0083, this contrast is significant. The only other comparison in the Snyder data that is significant is II vs IV; here the $\chi_c^2 = 7.1$ which is significant at .008 and exceeds the required .0125 value. Thus, the application of Ryan's test to the Snyder data indicates that the proportion of Kohnstamm responses is higher for condition IV than for both I and II.

In the case of the Multiple-Sign approach, for IV vs I the $N = 10$ and $S_+ = 10$. This comparison is significant for $k = 4$ and $\alpha = .05$ by Miller's table (Table S). For IV vs II, $N = 9$ and $S_+ = 9$. This comparison is also significant for $k = 4$ and $\alpha = .05$. No other comparisons are found to be different by this procedure. It is clear that these two techniques yield the same indications in this instance. Until more is known about the properties of the two techniques, we are biased in favor of the Multiple-Sign test because even little old ladies wearing straw hats decorated with plastic flowers can be taught to do this test!

By now a few alert, perceptive, and intelligent students (including Virginia wherever you are) are muttering again: "Why do Cochran's Q test for k correlated proportions when we can do a Ryan test or a Multiple-Sign test between the extreme groups?" Why, indeed, alert, perceptive, and intelligent students (including Virginia, wherever you are)! As they say in the space game, why not fire one and see if it can get off the launch pad? Is Cochran's Q a better test? Let's try them out and see.

A Mini-Summary and More Words-To-Live-By

In this Chapter we have described a series of statistical tests for analyzing frequency-type data. The experimental paradigms of: (a) two independent groups; (b) k independent groups; (c) two matched groups; and (d) k matched groups were considered. After (b) and (d) the ever-present multiple-comparison problem was examined. Two techniques of partitioning contingency tables with $df > 1$ were described: Ryan's test of k proportions and the method of orthogonal contrasts. Two techniques of comparing k correlated proportions were described: Ryan's test and the Multiple-Sign test.

If an investigator has numbers should he convert them to frequencies and use the methods of this chapter? For example, the Klein data in Table 3.3 could be converted to frequencies by finding the median of *all* scores and then counting up the frequencies of scores above and below the grand median for each of the six groups. This procedure would yield a 2×6 contingency table that could be analyzed by χ^2. This so-called median test (Siegel, 1956) is most inefficient and therefore not to be recommended. In general, converting numbers to frequencies is inadvisable unless one wants a quick and dirty test. If the quick and dirty test fails to achieve significance, the quick and dirty test user is vulnerable to the criticism that he used a low-power test. However, if the quick and dirty test does work, then the investigator cannot be criticized for using a low-power test.

Chi-square tests are not taken up in Bradley's (1968) extensive analysis of nonparametric techniques. His arguments for this stand (1968, pp. 247 ff.) are worth a careful reading. He concludes by saying: "The article by Lewis and Burke (1949) strongly suggests that chi-square is one of the most misused classical statistics" (1968, p. 249). In the present chapter we have attempted to alert the student to some of these misuses of χ^2 such as: violation of independence, inflating N's, failing to correct for continuity, ignoring too small expected frequencies, using the classical χ^2 test when Fisher's test is appropriate, and using McNemar's χ^2 test when the binominal or the Sign test is called for.

PROBLEMS

1. Forty mothers reported that their infants cried incessantly after being put down for the night. Twenty mothers (randomly selected) were told to pick their infants up and cuddle them. The remaining 20 mothers were told to ignore the crying. In follow-up interviews six months later 15 mothers in the first group and 5 mothers in the second group reported that their infants were still crying at bedtime. Did the percentages of infants crying differ ($p = .05$, two tail) in the two groups six months later?

2. In a problem-solving experiment 20 Ss were divided randomly and equally into two groups. Those in the control group were given the regular instructions. In the experimental group the same instructions were administered except that the experimenter added: "Don't be afraid to try weird solutions." In the control group three Ss solved the problem in 20 minutes and seven Ss did not. In the experimental group eight Ss were successful and two Ss were not. Did the percentages of Ss' solving the task differ significantly in the two groups? Use a two-tail test at the .05 level.

3. Suppose that in the Beale study (1956) the response of interrupted delay was regarded as a form of delay. Accordingly, in Table 5.6 (p. 129) the frequencies for delay and interrupted delay might be pooled to form a

2×3 contingency table. Was there an overall difference ($p = .05$) in the frequencies of delay + interrupted delay vs no delay among the three groups?

4. Make multiple comparisons at the .05 level of the frequencies of delay + interrupted delay vs no delay in problem 3.

5. In developing a creativity test for college freshmen, 46 Ss were tested on two items. Fourteen Ss passed both items 1 and 2. Two Ss passed item 1 but failed item 2. Twenty Ss failed item 1 but passed item 2. Did the percentages of Ss' passing differ ($p = .01$) on the two items?

6. In a further investigation of creativity 18 sets of three Ss per set, matched on intelligence, were tested on three items (i.e., each S was tested on only one item). The Ss in 2 sets failed all three items (FFF). In 4 sets the first two items were failed but the third was passed (FFP). In 11 sets the first item was failed but the other two were passed (FPP). In one set all items were passed (PPP). Did the percentage of those passing vary ($p = .05$) over the items?

CHAPTER SIX

Steps to Inference:
IV. Relationships

... but let me simply say that many of the analyses we have had of the nature-nurture controversy by means of correlational analysis lead me to suggest that correlation is an instrument of the devil. — E. R. Hilgard

The Case of Harvey—Traffic Engineer

Let us get into correlation problems by means of a true case history — only the names have been changed slightly to protect the young and innocent. Harvey is 39 years old. He is married, has an overweight nag of a wife, three kids, 37 (at last count) gerbils, a weird dog named Lester, and an even more overweight bigger nag of a mother-in-law. Harvey hates his mother-in-law and is planning to kill her. However, the details of the plan are not "finalized" (to use one of Harvey's favorite words). Every day Harvey goes by bus (he does not drive a car) from his overcrowded brownstone apartment to his office. He is not an imposing figure. He wears a badly wrinkled six-year-old Brooks Brothers suit and always tops it off with the same tie — it was striped but now it's spotted (chicken soup). Some people think Harvey never takes his tie off. This is only partly true. Although almost bald Harvey always manages to display an impressive crop of dandruff on his suit coat. He suffers from a chronic copious post-nasal drip that leads to incessant nose-blowing and drives his fellow workers out of their gourds. ("If you blow your nose one more time, Harve, I'm going to let you have it.") His wife and mother-in-law also have the sinus thing going, so Harvey's Kleenex bill is fantastic.

All this stuff is superficial because the real action is going on in Harvey's head. Harvey's bag is traffic engineering. Problem: How to get all of the cars, buses, trucks, motor scooters, motorcycles, push carts, etc. home at night in order that they can be ready for tomorrow's return traffic fiasco? Actually, at a deeper level in Harvey's psyche is his real thing — car wrecks. There's nothing like a crumpled fender, spritzing radiator, and a smashed windshield to turn Harvey on. This interest should not be confused with aggression; outside of his mother-in-law Harvey wouldn't hurt a fly.

But enough of this rich clinical background material, let's get to the point. One day while Harvey was studying traffic flow charts, accident data, and mounds of other figures, he stumbled on to something big — the heights of women's skirts above and below the knee for 20 different time periods. When he put the skirt data alongside of the accident (car) data (corrected for the number of cars traveling in the city at those times) the following picture in Table 6.1 emerged. At this point, we'll leave Harvey, his sinus

Table 6.1.   Harvey's Data on Skirt Heights (X) *and Accident Rates* (Y) *for 20 Time Periods*

Time Period	X	Y	XY
1	5[a]	35	175
2	3	33	99
3	2	23	46
4	0	19	0
5	− 1[b]	25	− 25
6	− 3	13	− 39
7	− 4	8	− 32
8	− 5	17	− 85
9	− 6	10	− 60
10	− 8	5	− 40
11	− 7	2	− 14
12	− 5	10	− 50
13	− 4	15	− 60
14	− 4	22	− 88
15	− 2	20	− 40
16	0	23	0
17	1	28	28
18	3	27	81
19	4	30	120
20	5	30	150
Totals	− 26	395	166

[a]Above the Knee
[b]Below the Knee

problem, his mother-in-law, etc. to his analyst and we will worry about Harvey's data.

Linear Relationships—Numbers

If we examine Table 6.1, it looks different from the kinds of data we have encountered before. It resembles the data from two matched groups in that there are two scores, accident rate and skirt height, for each experimental unit, time period. (Frequently in psychology the units are Ss.) However, instead of having two scores from the *same* variable (e.g., two heart-rate scores per S as in Table 3.13) there are scores for two *different* variables. This type of data arrangement is often referred to as *bivariate* data. Since the data appear to be different from any kind we have analyzed before, how should we proceed?

Let us begin as always with some questions: Is there a relationship between skirt height and accident rates? Is it a strong relationship? Is it a direct relationship (as skirts go up, accidents increase) or inverse (as skirts go up, accidents decrease)? Is the relationship between skirt height and accident rate a linear, straight-line one or is it curvilinear? We can get some hints as to the answers to these questions by simply plotting the data in Table 6.1. The scores for skirt height will range from minus on the left to plus on the right along the horizontal X axis, and accident rates increase from bottom to top on the Y axis. Twenty points, one for the X and Y scores for each time period are plotted in Figure 6.1. This type of graph is called a *scatter diagram*. (When there are a large number of Ss, say a hundred or more, it is helpful to group the data for the variables into 10 to 20 classes following the procedure described in Chapter 2.) Study of Figure 6.1 suggests that there is indeed a relationship between skirt height and accidents. Moreover, it is a direct one: as skirt heights go up accidents happen. And the relationship is a linear one — a line of "best fit" passing through the twenty points would be a straight one. "Best fit" means a line that minimizes the errors of prediction. By use of an equation we have drawn a line through the points. Given a skirt height score (X), e.g., one inch below the knee, our predicted accident rate (Y') would be the accident rate score which is opposite to the intersection of the line of best fit or *regression line* and a vertical line extending upward from $X = -1$. Thus our predicted score would be $Y' = 20.5$. Note that the actual Y score for $X = -1$ was 25. The difference between the predicted score and actual score is an error of prediction, i.e., $Y' - Y =$ error. Since some errors would be positive and some negative, the errors are squared and summed. Accordingly, the quantity $\Sigma(Y' - Y)^2$ represent the total squared errors in prediction and $\Sigma(Y' - Y)^2/N$ is the average squared error.

By the use of equations it is possible to place precisely two regression lines through the points in a scatter diagram. One regression line is used to predict *Y* from *X* (see Figure 6.1) and the other line is used to predict *X* from *Y*. These lines meet the criterion of "least squares"; i.e., they are drawn so as to minimize the errors of prediction as these have just been defined. Furthermore, the equations for the two lines, called *regression equations*, permit specific quantitative predictions. In this brief introduction to correlation we are going to deal only superficially with prediction problems, so we will leave these matters for the moment.

One question raised above was: Is it a strong relationship? From Figure 6.1 the answer is yes. In fact, the student should savor Figure 6.1 as he would aged brandy or a fine Churchill Havana cigar, because if he does research

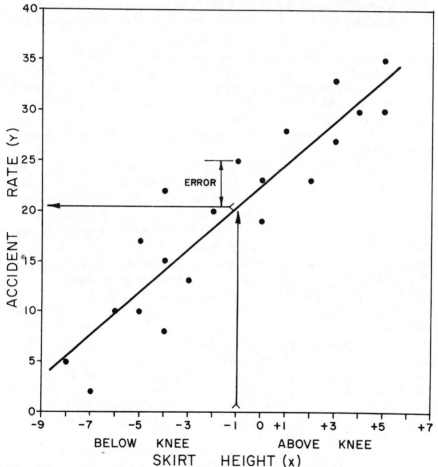

Figure 6.1. A scatter diagram of the data from Table 6.1. The straight line through the points is the regression line for predicting Y from X.

in psychology, he will be unlikely to see data that pretty often! (While Harvey's story is true in every detail, the data in Table 6.1 were made up.) In any event, what is needed is a numerical index in place of an eyeball to tell us: (a) the *direction* of the relationship, i.e., whether it is a direct or an inverse relationship; and (b) the *strength* of the relationship. One index is the Pearson product-moment r. The *correlation coefficient*, r, ranges in gradations from -1.00 to $+1.00$: an $r = -1.00$ signifies a perfect inverse relationship; an $r = +1.00$ indicates a perfect direct relationship; and an $r = 0.00$ denotes no relationship between the two variables. As r increases in size toward either -1.00 or $+1.00$, the strength of the relationship increases. Thus the *sign* of the correlation coefficient is informative as to the *direction* of the relationship and the *magnitude* of r is informative as to the *strength* of the relationship. Incidentally, a negative correlation would be revealed in a scatter diagram like Figure 6.1 by an alignment of points in the opposite direction, i.e., extending from the lower right-hand quadrant to the upper left-hand quadrant. The amount of scatter of the points about the regression line gives an indication of the strength of r. As the scatter decreases, the r becomes larger. An r close to zero, in contrast, appears as a circular or elliptical array of points. In the case of a perfect r, either $+1.00$ or -1.00, there is only one regression line and all points fall on it. Don't look for these in psychology.

Although there are straightforward formulas for finding r, we will approach correlation by means of analysis of variance (Quenouille, 1952). While this presentation may be more difficult to understand, it should demonstrate that correlation is not as unrelated to the earlier topics as it appeared at first glance and we believe that it is a more fruitful method of analyzing data. Let us again think in terms of partitioning total variation. This time, we are interested in the total variation in the Y scores or SS_{T_Y}. As in Chapter 3, SS_{T_Y} is the variation of all of the Y scores about the grand mean of the Y scores. Rather than partition SS_{T_Y} into SS_{B_Y} and SS_{W_Y}, as we did in simple analysis of variance, we will divide SS_{T_Y} into two different additive portions. One portion is the variation ascribable to X. Synonymous phrases to "ascribable to X" are "explainable in terms of X" or "predictable from X." The second portion of the variation is called "unaccountable" variation. In other words, the total variation in Y can be broken into two parts, one part is ascribable to X and the other part is unaccountable or due to unknown causes. This approach serves to raise a new and fundamental question: How much of the variation in Y can be accounted for in terms of X?[1] As the

---

1. This same question can be asked with respect to the statistical techniques covered in Chapter 3. For example, we can ask regarding the Klein data in Table 3.3: How much of the variation in the entry data can be explained in terms of the percentage of reinforcement during training? See Hays (1963) for a full description of this approach.

portion of variation ascribable to X increases, the size of r increases as well as our ability to make accurate predictions.

In order to implement this analysis of variance approach to correlation, a new term, *covariation*, needs to be introduced. As the prefix "co-" implies, we are concerned with the variation of *both* variables. Instead of referring to this quantity as a sum of squares, it is termed a *sum of products*. In terms of a computational formula:

$$SP_{XY} = \Sigma XY - \frac{(\Sigma X)(\Sigma Y)}{N}.$$

If the sum of products is divided by its appropriate *df*, then the resulting variance estimate is called the *covariance*:

$$s_{XY}{}^2 = \frac{SP_{XY}}{df} = \frac{SP_{XY}}{N-1}.$$

More formally, the covariance is "the mean product of the deviations of each variable from their overall means" (Quenouille, 1952, p. 57). Unlike variances which are always positive numbers, covariances can be either positive or negative. A positive covariance denotes a direct relationship between X and Y; a negative covariance signifies an inverse relationship between X and Y. Then why not use the covariance as index of correlation? The reason this is not done is that while a covariance shows the direction of the relationship, it tells nothing about the strength of the relationship. We shall return to this problem shortly.

We are now ready to analyze the data in Table 6.1. The total variation in Y is found by the regular formula:

$$SS_{T_Y} = \Sigma Y^2 - \frac{(\Sigma Y)^2}{N},$$

$$SS_{T_Y} = 9531 - \frac{(395)^2}{20},$$

$$SS_{T_Y} = 9531 - 7801.25 = 1729.75.$$

The total variation in the X scores is:

$$SS_{T_X} = \Sigma X^2 - \frac{(\Sigma X)^2}{N},$$

$$SS_{T_X} = 350 - \frac{(-26)^2}{20},$$

$$SS_{T_X} = 350 - 33.80 = 316.20.$$

The sum of products is:

$$SP_{XY} = \Sigma XY - \frac{(\Sigma X)(\Sigma Y)}{N},$$

$$SP_{XY} = 166 - \frac{(-26)(395)}{20},$$

$$SP_{XY} = 166 + 513.50 = 679.50.$$

Next, it is possible to attain the portion of the total variation in Y which is ascribable to X ($SS_{Y.x}$):

$$SS_{Y.x} = \frac{(SP_{XY})^2}{SS_{T_X}},$$

$$SS_{Y.x} = \frac{(679.50)^2}{316.20},$$

$$SS_{Y.x} = 1460.22.$$

The unaccounted for variation in Y is: $SS_{T_Y} - SS_{Y.x} = 1729.75 - 1460.22 = 269.53$. The df for SS_{T_y} are $N - 1 = 20 - 1 = 19$. The variation ascribable to X has a single df. Therefore, unaccountable variation has $df = N - 2 = 20 - 2 = 18$.

Table 6.2.   Summary Table for a Regression Analysis of Data
in Table 6.1

Source of Variation	SS	df	s^2	F
Ascribable to X	1460.22	1	1460.22	97.54
Unaccounted for (Error)	269.53	18	14.97	
Total	1729.75	19		

It is convenient to put these quantities into a summary table (Table 6.2). In order to learn whether or not a significant portion of the total variation in Y can be accounted for in terms of X, an F test is performed by testing the variance ascribable to X against the unaccounted for variance:

$$F = \frac{s_{Y.x}^2}{s_E^2} = \frac{1460.22}{14.97} = 97.54.$$

The resulting F, which is highly significant ($p < .001$) for $df = 1, 18$ by Table F, shows that a significant portion of the Y variation is accounted for by X.

Or in other words, there is a significant relationship between X and Y.

It may be noted that SP_{XY} is positive. Thus the relationship between X and Y is a direct one. To secure a better index of relationship both variables must be transformed to a common scale. The transformation that is used is called a standard-score transformation. Standard or Z scores for X and Y are:

$$Z_X = \frac{X - M_X}{s_X};$$

$$Z_Y = \frac{Y - M_Y}{s_Y};$$

Standard scores always have a mean of zero and a variance of unity. Instead of performing the Z-score transformation on each score separately, it can be done in one operation. The following formula permits such a determination of r:

$$r = \frac{SP_{XY}/N - 1}{\sqrt{(SS_{T_X}/N - 1)(SS_{T_Y}/N - 1)}},$$

$$r = \frac{679.50/20 - 1}{\sqrt{(316.20/20 - 1)(1729.75/20 - 1)}},$$

$$r = .92.$$

Is this high r significant? One way of testing the significance of r is the F ratio for the regression analysis in Table 6.2; the significant F means a significant correlation between the two variables. A second method of testing r is to look the r up in Table U for number of points, 20. This method yields a comparable answer. The phrase, "The correlation is significant," generally means that the r in question differs significantly from an $r = 0$. It is possible, however, to test the significance of the difference of r from values other than zero (see Edwards, 1950; 1960).

In addition to the information provided about the direction and strength of the relationship, r is also informative as to the percentage of the total variance in Y that is accounted for by X. This information is found by squaring r and multiplying the result by 100%. Since $r^2 = (.92)^2 = .85$, about 85% (100% × .85) of the variance in Y is explainable by X. It should also be mentioned that the correlation coefficient is independent of scale and therefore can be compared to other r's.

Let us return to the prediction problem. The equation for the regression line for predicting Y from X is:

$$Y' - M_Y = b_{YX}(X - M_X).$$

The new term, b_{YX}, is a *regression coefficient*. Actually, it is the *slope* of the line of best fit or a "weight" which enables us to make predictions whose errors will be minimal. From the available information, b_{YX} can be readily obtained:

$$b_{YX} = \frac{SP_{XY}}{SS_{T_X}},$$

$$b_{YX} = \frac{679.50}{316.20} = 2.15.$$

Substituting this value in the regression equation formula, we have:

$$Y' - \frac{395}{20} = 2.15\left[X - \frac{(-26)}{20}\right],$$

$$Y' = 2.15X + 22.55.$$

If we wish to predict an S's Y score in a future sample, we insert his X score in the final simplified regression equation.

A comparable regression equation for predicting X from Y is:

$$X' - M_X = b_{XY}(Y - M_Y).$$

In this instance the regression coefficient is:

$$b_{XY} = \frac{SP_{XY}}{SS_{T_Y}}.$$

Despite the elegance of these correlational methods, their applications to psychological data have so far led to rather disappointing results. Correlations between $-.40$ and $+.40$ are often observed, but data like Harvey's are not easy to come by. Why is this? Do we have the wrong variables or is psychology, as Brunswik (1956) contended, doomed to a fate of probabilistic laws?

Powerful methods like the Pearson product-moment r require that a price be paid in the form of demanding assumptions. To make inferences about *populations*, it is assumed that: (a) linearity exists, and (b) the distribution of the XY points is *bivariate normal*. By (a) is meant that the regression lines are straight lines. The Pearson product-moment r is entirely inappropriate for a curvilinear relationship. By (b) is meant that the points on the scatter diagram pile up so as to form a three-dimensional normal surface (the third dimension is frequency). If the X and Y scores are put into classes, then the Y scores in the X classes should be normally distributed and have equal variances (*homoscedastacity*) and similarly for the X scores in Y classes. A further assumption is that of (c) independence of observations. That is, the

X and Y scores for S1 (in our example, time periods) are uninfluenced by S2's X and Y scores, and so on. It should be noted, however, that correlation and linear regression can be employed as descriptive statistics for the sample in question without making assumption b (cf. Hays, 1963, p. 510).

In summary, the Pearson product-moment r is an index that reveals the direction and strength of the relationship between two variables. Associated with it are regression equations which permit the specific prediction of one variable from the other. Regression analysis enables an investigator to determine how much of the variance in the dependent variable can be ascribed to the independent variable. The essential assumptions for population inferences for the Pearson product-moment r are: (a) linearity of regression; (b) a bivariate normal distribution; and (c) independence of observations among Ss. Finally, mention should be made of the fact that there are elaborate extensions of r to multivariate data. For example, one case is that of k independent variables and a single dependent variable (*multiple correlation and regression*), another case is k independent and k dependent variables (*canonical correlation*), and another case is k variables (*factor analysis*). Fortunately, for both the student and author, none of these extensions will be considered here.

At this point the reader is doubtless suffering from some psychosomatic ailment induced by the previous section. The R is simple — a neat but quick and dirty correlation technique. Quenouille (1952), in an excellent book that was ahead of its time, has just what the doctor ordered: the medial test. To perform this test (a) make a scatter diagram like Figure 6.1. (b) Put a vertical medial line through the points so that half of the points fall to the left of the line and half to the right. (If any points fall on the line, be expansive — throw them out and reduce the N by the number thrown out.) (c) Erect a horizontal medial line, again dividing the points so that half fall above the line and half below. (Repeat the expansiveness for the line-straddlers.) (d) Count the number of points in any quadrant and check for the significance of the relationship for the total number of points, N, in Table V. (If the number of points in two diagonal quadrants is unequal, enter the table for the average number of points for the two quadrants.) If the number of points is significant, there is a significant relationship between the two variables.

Let us apply the medial test to the data in Figure 6.1. When the two medial lines are drawn through the points, there are 9 points in the upper right quadrant. For $N = 20$ this number of points is significant by Table V at the .01 level of significance.

If a correlation coefficient is desired, a simple formula is available:

$$\phi = \frac{2\,(\text{Total points in upper right and lower left quadrants})}{N} - 1.$$

For the present problem:

$$\phi = \frac{2(9+9)}{20} - 1 = +.80.$$

The limits of ϕ are the same as those for r, i.e., -1.00 to $+1.00$. The idea may have occurred to the reader that the scatter diagram might be unnecessary. The number of points in the quadrants could be found by determining the median for each set of scores. This procedure is not advisable, however, because the scatter diagram provides a valuable eyeball check on linearity (which is assumed with the medial coefficient). In fact, it is always a sound tactic in correlational analysis to make a scatter diagram. Besides the information it imparts about linearity, it may suggest that an elaborate analysis of the data with r is not worth the trip.

What are the assumptions for the medial coefficient? There are two: (a) linearity and (b) independence of observations among Ss. If ϕ is used on a nonlinear relation (e.g., U-shaped), it will yield a low value (Quenouille, 1952, p. 45). Regarding the properties of the test, Quenouille has stated: "The method is most useful for a large number of observations, and has an efficiency of 41 per cent for observations following a bivariate normal distribution" (1959, p. 28). The remark on efficiency means that to achieve the same power as an r with $N = 41$, an $N = 100$ would be needed with a ϕ. This statement is true for data which meet three assumptions above for r. We've already seen the quickness of the medial test, the low power efficiency reported by Quenouille is the dirty part. Nevertheless, quick and dirty tests like the medial coefficient have their place. They can be used as preliminary tests to see if a fuller time-consuming numerical analysis is likely to be of value. If data are readily attainable, quick and dirty tests can be employed as the method of analysis as increasing the N can serve to offset their low power efficiency.

Curvilinear Relationships—Numbers

Both the Pearson product-moment r and Quenouille's medial test assume linearity of regression; that is, that the line of best fit is a straight line. How do we know that the linearity assumption is tenable? If linearity does not exist, how do we deal with the data? To explore this problem, let us consider some data from a stimulus generalization investigation by Grice and Saltz (1950). These investigators trained 60 rats to run to a white circle whose area was 20 sq. cm. Following training, the Ss were randomly divided into four groups of 15 Ss and each group was tested with circles whose areas were 20, 32, 50, and 79 sq. cm., respectively. The data in Table 6.3 are the number of responses to the stimuli for each S in 25 test trials. In this case we don't need to make a scatter diagram of the data. Inspection of the means at the bottom of Table 6.3 is sufficient to produce some nervousness about the linearity assumption. The data also raise another question: How can a correlation analysis be done when there does not appear to be bivariate data? Actually, there is bivariate data — one variable is the S's test score and the second is the size of test stimulus that S was exposed to. Therefore, the

Table 6.3.* Number of Responses in 25 Test Trials (Grice and Saltz, 1950)

| | Area of Test Stimulus | | |
20	32	50	79
9	22	8	12
19	13	11	4
10	17	2	1
21	20	3	8
10	8	4	14
18	22	6	14
11	12	10	5
18	8	13	8
23	14	15	4
10	9	10	11
10	8	4	3
10	14	10	5
9	13	4	5
10	16	8	4
8	4	1	0
$M = 13.1$	13.3	7.3	6.5

*Reprinted by permission of the publisher and authors from G. R. Grice and E. Saltz, "The Generalization of an Instrumental Response to Stimuli Varying in the Size Dimension," *Journal of Experimental Psychology*, 40, p. 704. Copyright 1950, American Psychological Association.

question can be asked: Is there a relationship between test stimulus area and number of responses? A further question is: Is the relationship between test stimulus area and the number of responses linear?

To answer these questions a combination of simple analysis of variance and regression analysis will be employed. A general test of the relationship between the two variables is provided by a simple analysis of variance of the numbers of responses for the four groups. If a significant F is observed, then the two variables are related. The total SS for the number of responses, Y, is determined in the usual manner:

$$SS_{T_Y} = \Sigma\Sigma Y^2 - \frac{(\Sigma\Sigma Y)^2}{N},$$

$$SS_{T_Y} = 7961 - \frac{(603)^2}{60},$$

$$SS_{T_Y} = 7961 - 6060.15 = 1900.85.$$

The SS between groups in Y is:

$$SS_{B_Y} = \frac{(\Sigma X_1)^2}{N_1} + \frac{(\Sigma X_2)^2}{N_2} + \cdots + \frac{(\Sigma X_k)^2}{N_k} - \frac{(\Sigma\Sigma X)^2}{N},$$

$$SS_{B_Y} = \frac{(196)^2}{15} + \frac{(200)^2}{15} + \frac{(109)^2}{15} + \frac{(98)^2}{15} - \frac{(603)^2}{60},$$

$$SS_{B_Y} = 6660.07 - 6060.15 = 599.92.$$

By subtraction the $SS_{W_Y} = 1900.85 - 599.92 = 1300.93$. Putting these values in the top of a summary table (Table 6.4), an F test can be carried out. The fact the resulting F is significant at less than the .001 level for $df = 3, 56$ in Table F, indicates that there is a relationship between area of the test

Table 6.4. **Summary Table for Analysis of Variance and Regression Analysis of Response Data**

Source of Variation	SS	df	s^2	F
Between groups	599.92	3	199.97	8.61
Within groups	1300.93	56	23.23	
Total	1900.85	59		
Linear effect of X	494.08	1	494.08	21.27
Nonlinear effect of X	105.84	2	52.92	2.28
Within groups	1300.93	56	23.23	
Total	1900.85	59		

stimulus and number of test responses. But is the relationship a linear one?

To answer this question, an additional analysis must be undertaken. The form of this analysis is to divide the between variation in Table 6.4 into two components: (a) a sum of squares ascribable to the linear effects of X; and (b) a residual sum of squares due to the nonlinear effects of X. The linear component (a) can be found by using the method from the preceding section on correlation. Then the residual (b) can be obtained by subtraction.

Let's tackle (a). Since the stimulus areas are equally spaced on a log scale, we can simplify the calculations by replacing the X scores of 20, 32, 50, and 79 by 1, 2, 3, and 4. Multiplying every Y score in column 1 by $X = 1$, those in column 2 by $X = 2$, and so on, the sum of products can be determined:[2]

$$SP_{XY} = \Sigma\Sigma XY - \frac{(\Sigma\Sigma X)(\Sigma\Sigma Y)}{N},$$

$$SP_{XY} = 1315 - \frac{(150)(603)}{60},$$

$$SP_{XY} = 1315 - (1507.50) = -192.50.$$

The negative SP value confirms what is obvious from an inspection of the data — a negative correlation — as the area of the stimulus increases, the frequency of responses generally decreases.

The sum of squares for X are:

$$SS_{T_X} = \Sigma\Sigma X^2 - \frac{(\Sigma\Sigma X)^2}{N},$$

$$SS_{T_X} = 450 - \frac{(150)^2}{60},$$

$$SS_{T_X} = 450 - 375 = 75.$$

The portion of the total variation in Y due to the linear effects of X is:

$$SS_{Y.X} = \frac{(SP_{XY})^2}{SS_{T_X}},$$

$$SS_{Y.X} = \frac{(-192.50)^2}{75},$$

$$SS_{Y.X} = \frac{37056.25}{75} = 494.08.$$

By subtracting this quantity from SS_{B_Y}, the sum of squares due to the nonlinear effects of X is secured: $599.92 - 494.08 = 105.84$. The SS_{B_Y} has 3 df. Subtracting the 1 df for the variation due to the linear effects of X, leaves 2 df for the nonlinear effects of X. We can now put these values into the lower portion of Table 6.4. Thus the between groups variation in Y has been par-

2. Actually in this case the response sums for the four groups can be multiplied by 1, 2, 3, and 4, respectively.

titioned into two components, a large portion due to the linear effects of X and a small portion due to the nonlinear effects of X. By testing these components with F tests against the within or unaccountable variance, the linear component is found to be significant ($p < .001$), but the nonlinear component is not. Accordingly, the line of best fit through the Grice-Saltz data would be a straight line. Had the nonlinear component proved to be significant, further analysis could be done to determine and test the variation due to X^2 and X^3 and a *curvilinear* regression equation could be found [see Quenouille (1952, Chapter 6); Hays (1963, Chapter 16)].

Although the calculation of r is quite appropriate for the Grice-Saltz data, let us find another index of correlation, the *correlation ratio*. The correlation ratio, *eta*, is mandatory when nonlinearity exists. It is, however, a general index of relationship that can be applied to either linear or nonlinear data. It is readily obtained from the information for the simple analysis of variance in the summary table (top half of Table 6.4):

$$E_{YX} = \sqrt{\frac{SS_{B_Y}}{SS_{T_Y}}}.$$

Applying the values from Table 6.4, we have:

$$E_{YX} = \sqrt{\frac{599.92}{1900.85}},$$

$$E_{YX} = \sqrt{.316} = +.562.$$

Since the square root is always taken as positive, *eta* always ranges from zero to one. The test of significance of *eta* is simply the usual between/within F test as in the top half of Table 6.4. As the F is significant, then *eta* is also.

The concern of this section was with testing for linearity. First, a relationship is determined by performing a simple analysis of variance test. Then the linearity assumption is assessed by partitioning the between SS for the dependent variable Y into two components: (a) that due to the linear effects of X; and (b) that due to the nonlinear effects of X. F tests of these components disclose whether either or both components are significant. When the nonlinear component is significant, further analysis can be performed to determine the nature of the nonlinearity and to develop a curvilinear regression equation for prediction purposes. Such a nonlinear analysis was not carried out. When nonlinearity exists, the appropriate index of correlation is *eta*, the correlation ratio. *Eta*'s range in size from zero to one. When the treatment means are identical, *eta* will be zero. When the means diverge greatly and the observations cluster closely around the means, *eta* will approach unity. The test of significance for *eta* is the *F* from a simple analysis of variance paradigm.

Monotonic Relationships—Ranks

Recently Tukey (1969; Mosteller & Tukey, 1968) has been extolling the virtues of a statistical technique called "the jackknife." "Tukey adopted the name of 'jackknife' for his procedure, since a boy scout's 'jackknife' is symbolic of a rough-and-ready instrument capable of being used in all contingencies and emergencies" (Miller, 1964). The last statistical technique to be taken up is not Tukey's jackknife, but it is a rank correlation technique *Tau* (τ), devised by Kendall (1948), that has some of the versatility of a jack-knife.[3] Being a ranks method, it gets unwieldy with large samples – like a jackknife it's great for whittling sticks but poor for chopping down trees. There is another rank correlation technique, Spearman's *rho*, but it has not been developed as fully as *Tau* and its sampling distribution is "messier." In view of the advantages of *Tau* over *rho*, only the former will be presented.

Kendall describes *Tau* as a "coefficient of disarray." Disarray refers to the number of "moves" that are required to put one ranking (e.g., *Y*) into order when the *X* ranking is in perfect order. Suppose we have the ranks 1, 2, 3, 4, 5 for S1 to S5 for variable *X* and the ranks 1, 3, 4, 2, 5 for the same Ss for variable *Y*. In this instance two moves (interchanging 2 and 4 and then interchanging 2 and 3) would be required to bring *Y* into order. When there is no disarray, e.g., ranks 1, 2, 3, 4, 5 for *X* and 1, 2, 3, 4, 5 for *Y*, *Tau* is +1.00. Where the ranks are 1, 2, 3, 4, 5 for *X* and 5, 4, 3, 2, 1 for *Y*, *Tau* is −1.00. Thus, the magnitude of *Tau* is related to the degree of disarray, and the limits of *Tau* are +1.00 to −1.00.

Let us look at some actual data. Welker (1956) was interested in the relationship between the chronological age of chimpanzees and their exploration of objects. Eight chimps, ranging in age from 10 months to 57 months, were exposed to stimulus situations consisting of one to three objects. In Table 6.5 are presented the sex and ages of the Ss, manipulation scores *M* (reflecting the number of times S touched an object), and *F* (the number of stimulus situations in which S attained a criterion of familiarity by touching an object for 50 out of 60 five-second periods in a five-minute session). Is the age of Ss related to exploratory behavior as measured by manipulation, *M*? To answer this question the scores for each variable are ranked in size from 1 to 8. To calculate *Tau*, we put the scores for one variable in a perfect increasing order and examine the disarray in the other variable. Since age is already in a perfect order we can look at the corresponding ranks

for $M: \begin{matrix} a & b & c & d & e & f & g & h \\ 3 & 2 & 1 & 4 & 5 & 7 & 8 & 6 \end{matrix}$. For each rank separately in succession (a–h) we

3. Would the graduate student who stole my copy of Kendall's *Rank correlation methods* please return it? Wrap it in plain brown paper, mail it, and no questions will be asked.

count the number of ranks to the right that are larger and the number that are smaller. For the first rank, a, there are 5 ranks that are larger than 3 and

Table 6.5.* Exploration Scores and Ranks by Chimpanzees of Different Ages (Welker, 1956)

| S | Sex | Age in Mos. | M | F | Ranks | | | |
					Sex	Age	M	F
1	Male	10	4	2	2	1	3	3
2	Male	11	2	1	2	2	2	1.5
3	Female	13	1	1	6	3	1	1.5
4	Female	26	7	6	6	4	4	6
5	Female	35	29	5	6	5	5	4.5
6	Female	43	57	10	6	6	7	7.5
7	Male	50	60	10	2	7	8	7.5
8	Female	57	41	5	6	8	6	4.5

*Reprinted by permission of the publisher and author from W. I. Welker, "Effects of Age and Experience on Play and Exploration of Young Chimpanzees," *Journal of Comparative and Physiological Psychology*, 49, pp. 224 and 225. Copyright 1956, American Psychological Association.

to the right (4, 5,. 7, 8, 6) and 2 that are smaller (2, 1). The score for a is: $(5-2)$. For b there are 5 ranks larger than 2 and 1 smaller. The score for b is: $(5-1)$. Repeating this process for the remaining ranks, we get the scores:

$$
\begin{array}{ll}
\text{a } (5-2) = 3 & \text{e } (3-0) = \quad 3 \\
\text{b } (5-1) = 4 & \text{f } (1-1) = \quad 0 \\
\text{c } (5-0) = 5 & \text{g } (0-1) = -1 \\
\text{d } (4-0) = \overline{4} & \\
\qquad\qquad 16 \qquad + \qquad\qquad \overline{2} = 18 = S
\end{array}
$$

The sum of these scores from a to h is $S = 18$. To determine whether or not a relationship is present, Table W is entered for $N = 8$. The probability value for $S = 18$ is .016 (one tail) or .032 (two tail). Therefore, a significant direct relationship exists between age and manipulation for young chimps.

The correlation coefficient, *Tau*, is found by use of Kendall's formula:

$$
\tau = \frac{S}{\dfrac{N}{2}(N-1)}.
$$

For the rankings under consideration:

$$
\tau = \frac{18}{\dfrac{8}{2}(7)} = +.64.
$$

When ties are present, things become a little more complicated. (a) Tied observations are assigned midranks. (b) In calculating Kendall's S, adjacent tied ranks contribute zero to S. (c) Two correlation coefficients, τ_a and τ_b, may be calculated. τ_a is the extent of agreement between a ranking and a second ranking for which there is an objective order. For example, an observer could be asked to rank 10 lights in intensity. τ_a would reflect his *accuracy* in attaining the actual intensity of the lights. τ_b is the extent of *agreement* between two rankings when there is no objective order. For example, two personnel managers might rank 10 salesmen on their "friend-liness." There is no objective order of friendliness – only agreement of the two judges can be assessed. The formula for τ_a is the standard formula given above:

$$\tau_a = \frac{S}{\frac{N}{2}(N-1)}.$$

The formula for τ_b, on the other hand, involves corrections in the denominator for the ties in each ranking:

$$\tau_b = \frac{S}{\sqrt{\left[\frac{N}{2}(N-1)\right] - T}\ \sqrt{\left[\frac{N}{2}(N-1)\right] - U}}$$

where

$$T = \tfrac{1}{2}\Sigma t(t-1),$$

$$U = \tfrac{1}{2}\Sigma u(u-1),$$

$$t = \text{no. of tied scores in a set in } X,$$

$$u = \text{no. of tied scores in a set in } Y.$$

Since T and U, the corrections for ties in the two rankings, decrease the size of the denominator in contrast to the uncorrected denominator, τ_b is always larger than τ_a.

We can apply the τ_b formula to the M and F measures of exploration. When M is ordered in terms of increasing ranks, the corresponding ranks for F are: $\begin{matrix} a & b & c & d & e & f & g & h \\ 1.5 & 1.5 & 3 & 6 & 4.5 & 4.5 & 7.5 & 7.5 \end{matrix}$. S then is:

a $(6-0) = 6$	e $(2-0) = 2$
b $(6-0) = 6$	f $(2-0) = 2$
c $(5-0) = 5$	g $(0-0) = 0$
d $(2-2) = 0$	

$$17 \quad + \quad 4 = 21 = S$$

For $N = 8$, from Table U the probability of $S = 21$ is observed to be less than .001 (one-tailed test) or .002 (two-tailed test). The two measures show a high degree of agreement. To demonstrate the correction for ties, τ_b will be found. As there are no tied observations in M, $T = 0$. There are three sets of ties in F: 1, 1; 5, 5; and 10, 10. For each set: $u(u-1) = 2(2-1) = 2$. Thus, the correction U for ties in F is:

$$U = \tfrac{1}{2}\Sigma u(u-1),$$

$$U = \tfrac{1}{2}(2+2+2) = 3.$$

Then τ_b from the formula above is:

$$\tau_b = \frac{21}{\sqrt{\left[\frac{8}{2}(7)-0\right]}\sqrt{\left[\frac{8}{2}(7)-3\right]}},$$

$$\tau_b = \frac{21}{26.46} = +.79.$$

Some indication as to the utility of *Tau* may be shown by another application. Suppose the question were asked: Is manipulatory behavior (M) related to the sex of the S? There were 3 males and 5 females. Using midranks, the sex of the Ss can be ranked as in column 6 of Table 6.5. The 3 males, instead of getting the usual ranks, 1, 2, and 3, are given the midrank of 2. Likewise the 5 females receive the midrank of 6 instead of 4, 5, 6, 7, and 8. (It does not matter whether sex is ordered male-female or female-male; *Tau* will be the same except for its sign.) When we put the ranks for M in an increasing order, the corresponding ranks for sex are: $\begin{array}{cccccccc} a & b & c & d & e & f & g & h \\ 6 & 2 & 2 & 6 & 6 & 6 & 6 & 2. \end{array}$

Then S is:

a	$(0-3) = -3$		e	$(0-1) = -1$	
b	$(4-0) = 4$		f	$(0-1) = -1$	
c	$(4-0) = 4$		g	$(0-1) = -1$	
d	$(0-1) = \underline{-1}$				
	4	$+$		$\underline{-3} = 1 = S$	

With an S this small, there is clearly no relationship between sex and manipulatory behavior. It should be noted that in this example a two-independent groups design was assessed by *Tau*. *Tau* can also be applied to k independent groups in the same way. One word of warning: in calculating S when there are ties in both rankings, both rankings must be attended to because adjacent ties in *either* ranking result in a zero contribution to S.

When samples are small, $N = 4$ to 10, the significance of *Tau* can be found by using Table U. The one-tail probability values based on randomization of ranks for different S and N are exact. When $N > 10$ a normal deviate test yields approximate probability values. The formula for testing the significance of *Tau* when $N > 10$ is:

$$Z = \frac{|S| - 1}{\sigma_s} = \frac{|S| - 1}{\sqrt{\frac{1}{18} [N(N-1)(2N+5)]}}$$

The obtained Z is then evaluated as a normal deviate score in Table N.

Lynch (1968) investigated heart rate in 16 dogs during a classical conditioning study in which the conditioned stimulus (CS) was a tone, shock to the leg

Table 6.6.* *Variability (Standard Deviations) of Heart Rate under Resting and Post-Shock Conditions (Lynch, 1968)*

Dog	Resting Score	Resting Ranks	Post-Shock Score	Post-Shock Ranks
A	21.72	14	10.14	11
B	12.16	4	8.00	5
C	13.17	6	10.34	12
D	16.30	11	7.28	3
E	14.14	8	5.38	1
F	13.78	7	7.41	4
G	11.09	3	8.06	6
H	6.16	1	6.48	2
I	12.49	5	8.30	9
J	20.51	13	12.76	14
K	15.93	10	10.63	13
L	14.89	9	8.24	7.5
M	7.21	2	9.69	10
N	16.82	12	8.24	7.5
O	26.07	15	13.45	15
P	29.47	16	16.18	16

*Reprinted by permission of the publisher and author from J. J. Lynch, *The Psychological Record*, 18, p. 104, 1968.

was the unconditioned stimulus (US), and leg flexion was the response. Lynch's data in the form of the standard deviations of heart rate during resting (when S was first put in the experimental chamber) and post-US (10 seconds following the termination of the CS and US) are shown in Table 6.6. When the two sets of scores are ranked and the ranks for resting heart rate variability are ordered in terms of increasing ranks, S is found to be 51 and *Tau* = .425.

To test the significance of the relationship the Z test is performed:

$$Z = \frac{51-1}{\sqrt{\dfrac{1}{18}[16(15)(37)]}}$$

$$= \frac{50}{22.21} = 2.25.$$

From Table N the two-tail probability of a $Z = 2.25$ is .024. Therefore, a significant but small positive relationship is indicated between the variability of heart rate during resting and after the presentation of the US. When ties are present, the formula for σ_S requires correction (see Kendall for formulas, 1948, p. 43). We did not correct for the single pair of tied observations in the present example because the effect of one such tie is minimal and it would have only slightly increased an already significant Z. Parenthetically, it might be noted that the Z formula provides fairly accurate probability values even for small N values (Kendall, 1948; Wike, 1955).

What assumptions must be fulfilled for *Tau*? There are two: (a) monotonicity; and (b) independence of Ss' scores from one another. Regarding (a), a monotonic relationship is one in which for every increase in X there is an increase in Y, or in which for every increase in X there is a decrease in Y. Linear relationships are monotonic, but there can be others (cf. Hays, 1963, pp. 642 f.). For nonmonotonic relationships, e.g., as X increases, Y first increases and then decreases, Quenouille (1952, pp. 43 f.) has a graphical test.

We have not done full justice to Kendall's *Tau*. It can be applied to a great variety of problems when the data are rankable or in the form of ranks. The interested reader will find that time spent perusing Kendall's thin volume (1948) will be very worthwhile. Finally, it needs to be stressed that not only is Kendall's *Tau* a versatile statistical tool that involves a minimum of assumptions, but it is also a highly efficient statistic. Bradley (1968, p. 285) has reported that its efficiency is about 91 % when contrasted with r under conditions in which the assumptions for r were fulfilled.

A Nonsummary

Inasmuch as superb, crisp summaries have been included throughout this chapter, there is no point in repeating these. Instead, we will close this brief introduction to correlation with a few comments on correlation.

These comments are instigated largely by Tukey's recent remarks (1969) on correlation coefficients as methods of analyzing data. Some of Tukey's points are: (a) correlation coefficients are less likely to be stable over experiments than regression coefficients; (b) they encourage investigators to ignore units of measurement for their variables; and (c) "when we are calculating from data, regression formulas, covariances, and even variance components answer meaningful questions better" (1969, p. 89). Tukey's comments on the greater stability of regression coefficients than correlation coefficients is an interesting one. The writer simply has not had sufficient experience to judge the validity of this assertion. It is certainly true, however, that in psychological research correlation coefficients are not renowned for their stability.

We would, of course, concur completely with Tukey's final comment (c); this was one reason for approaching correlation by means of analysis of variance and regression analysis. In the early days of psychology innumerable correlation coefficients were calculated. There is even a legend to the effect that one graduate student in a large nameless university (located near the place where the sun sets) had to be restrained from doing correlation coefficients by locking up the calculator room. That, however, is only a legend. More currently, emphasis is being placed upon regression analysis, trend analysis, and the like. These approaches, which yield estimates of variance that can be accounted for and more precise information regarding the nature of the relationships, would appear to be more fruitful lines of analysis than merely reporting the *r* between two variables. In Tukey's beautiful prose: "Sweeping things under the rug is the enemy of good data analysis. Often using the correlation coefficient is 'sweeping things under the rug with a vengeance" (1969, p. 89).

Perhaps, some sweeping is going on too when an investigator merely reports the *F* from an analysis of variance test and a subsequent comparison of means. At least with the *F* test, the summary table provides some indications as to the amount of variation attributable to different sources. But the question: How much of the variance in the dependent variable is ascribable to the independent variable? is an important one. We did not include it in our account of analysis of variance in Chapter 3 so the student is advised to consult Hay's excellent book (1963) for remedial treatment.

PROBLEMS

1. Forty undergraduates were tested in a verbal discrimination task. X is the number of errors committed during nine learning trials; Y is the number of words recalled in a subsequent free recall test:

S	X	Y	S	X	Y	S	X	Y	S	X	Y
1	5	8	11	8	5	21	11	9	31	13	2
2	5	10	12	9	10	22	11	6	32	14	5
3	6	11	13	9	9	23	11	4	33	14	2
4	6	10	14	9	7	24	12	8	34	15	6
5	6	8	15	9	5	25	12	7	35	15	4
6	7	10	16	10	9	26	12	5	36	15	1
7	7	8	17	10	8	27	12	3	37	16	2
8	7	7	18	10	7	28	13	8	38	16	1
9	8	10	19	10	5	29	13	6	39	17	2
10	8	9	20	10	3	30	13	3	40	17	1

Plot these data in a scatter diagram using $i = 1$ for both variables. By inspection does the relationship appear to be linear? Does it appear to be a direct or inverse relationship?

2. Can a significant ($p = .01$) portion of the Y variation be accounted for in terms of X?

3. Find r. Is it significant?

4. Determine a regression equation for predicting Y from X.

5. Using the regression equation, find the Y' values for $X = 6$, $X = 11$, and $X = 16$. Plot these three X, Y' values in the scatter diagram in problem 1. Construct a regression line by putting a straight line through these three points.

6. With the regression *line* find Y' for $X = 10$. Check this value by finding Y' for $X = 10$ from the regression *equation*.

7. Construct horizontal and vertical medial lines through the scatter diagram in problem 1 so that (a) 20 points are above the horizontal line and 20 points are below and (b) 20 points are to the right of the vertical line and 20 points to the left. Is there a significant relationship ($p = .01$) between the two variables?

8. Using the points in problem 7, find a medial coefficient.

9. An experimenter tested the speed of escaping from shock with 30 rats. There were five levels (equally spaced) of increasing shock (A – E). In

the table below are presented the speed scores for the six Ss in each shock intensity group:

		Shock Group		
A	B	C	D	E
3	5	6	8	8
3	2	6	9	6
4	3	3	5	4
1	4	5	8	4
2	6	7	6	6
2	4	4	7	5

Make a scatter diagram with Y denoting speed of response, X as shock intensity, and $i = 1$ for both variables. Does the relationship appear to be linear?

10. Is there a significant ($p = .05$) relationship between the two variables? If so, test the relationship for linearity and find an index of relationship, r or E_{YX}, depending upon which is appropriate.

11. From the data in Table 3.25 (p. 90) for Ss 13–24 on Days 1 and 4, determine whether or not there was a significant ($p = .05$, two tail) relationship between performance on the two days. Apply a ranks method and calculate an index of relationship.

CHAPTER SEVEN

Closing Shots

Repetition is the basis for judging variability and significance and confidence. Repetition of results, each significant, is the basis, according to Fisher, of scientific truth. — J. W. Tukey

Testing Statistical Hypotheses vs Confidence Intervals

In the wild days out West when cowboys didn't use spray deodorant or amplified guitars, psychologists often handled their data quite differently than they do today. Lacking the plethora of statistical tests, they were often content to present treatment means and some indices, e.g., standard deviations or probable errors, denoting the variability of their observations. Were these old duffers so crazy? We think not.

In the foregoing portions of the book we have concentrated exclusively upon the testing of statistical hypotheses. We were interested in questions like: Is there a significant difference somewhere among these means (or variances)? What specific means (or variances) differ from one another? Is there a significant relationship between these two variables? And so on. Such questions do not exhaust the procedures of data analysis. The data analysis game isn't finished when the null hypothesis is rejected and treatment means are contrasted. Another crucial question is: How large is the treatment effect that we have observed?

The issue of testing statistical hypotheses vs confidence intervals has been delineated nicely by Miller (1966). In comparing two means, M_1 and M_2, he points out that nine hypotheses can actually be tested: (a) $M_1 = M_2$; (b) $M_1 > 0$, $M_2 = 0$; (c) $M_1 < 0$, $M_2 = 0$; (d) $M_1 = 0$, $M_2 > 0$; (e) $M_1 = 0$, $M_2 < 0$; and so on. Then Miller comments:

In addition to a choice between the nine hypotheses the experimenter may also require some statement as to the size of the nonnull effect. This is the juncture at

164

which tests of significance and confidence intervals part company. For some problems the nonnull effect is worthy of consideration only if the magnitude of the effect is sufficient to produce a scientific, technologic, philosophic, or social change. Mere statistical significance is not enough to warrant its notice; the effect must also be biologically, physically, socially, etc., significant as well. *To answer the question of the apparent magntiude of the effect, the experimenter needs point and interval estimates; tests of significance will not suffice* (1966, p. 4, emphasis added).

Could we perhaps, dispense with tests of statistical hypotheses altogether? Again, Miller has provided a reasonable answer to this question:

> In other situations it may be that any difference from nullity, no matter how small or large, is of importance. If the existence of any nonnull effect will demolish an existing theory or give a clue to understanding some previously unexplained phenomenon, then a test of significance is what is required. . .
>
> There are those who might argue against the existence of either one or both of these situations, but this author is inclined to concede that both can arise (1966, p. 4).

Let us examine two pertinent examples, one hypothetical and the other painfully real. Imagine that a drug researcher creates a new drug designed to produce weight loss in humans. Suppose further that fifty Ss who took the drug for one year, each lost *one* pound; while fifty control Ss, who were exposed to a placebo, neither gained nor lost any weight. In this instance the difference between the means of the two groups would be highly significant, but the small amount of weight loss produced by the new drug would render it useless.

An experiment (Wike & Barrientos, 1958) was designed to compare the generalized secondary reward value of a goal box for rats vs the goal box's simple secondary reward value. The difference was significant in favor of the generalized secondary reinforcer, but Kelleher and Gollub (1962), quite properly, were not impressed. They stated:

> Although the difference between generalized and simple conditioned reinforcers was statistically significant, the absolute value of the difference was only 0.62 trials out of 15. The difference between generalized and simple conditioned reinforcers was slightly greater under water than under food deprivation (0.94 out of 15 trials) . . .
>
> The small order of magnitude of preference for the generalized reinforcer does not allow one to make any extensive generalizations of these results (1962, p. 587).

Thus in polite terms Kelleher and Gollub were saying the observed effects were significant but their magnitudes were piddling.

Both of these examples serve to highlight the importance of the question: What is the magnitude of the effect? Tests of significance and statistically significant differences do not provide an answer to this question. The procedure for determining the magnitude of an effect consists of obtaining estimates of population parameters. By use of the information in a sample it is possible to calculate the limits within which a population value like the mean (μ) is likely to fall. These limits are termed *confidence limits* and the distance between these limits is termed a *confidence interval*. When the variance of the population is unknown, the confidence limits for μ are:

$$M + (t)(s_M) \qquad M - (t)(s_M),$$

where M is the sample mean and s_M is the standard error of the mean. The value of t which is selected by the investigator determines the degree of confidence in the assertion that μ will be contained within the confidence interval. If a t corresponding to the .05 level of significance (two-tail) for the df of $N - 1$ is used, then we will obtain the 95% confidence interval. Edwards says: "When we say we are 95% confident that μ falls within the 95% confidence interval, we are expressing our degree of confidence that, in repeated sampling, such an inference will be correct 95 times in 100" (1968, p. 83). If we wish to be more confident that μ will fall within the confidence interval, then we may employ a larger t value, e.g., a t for .01 or .001. This procedure will, of course, enlarge the confidence limits and increase the size of the confidence interval.

Let us consider some data from Rosenthal (1966, p. 146) on experimenter bias. Five experimenters tested 18–24 Ss with a standardized set of ten photographs. The experimenters were informed that their Ss would give an average rating of about 5 to the photographs. The mean values reported by the five experimenters were: .66, .45, .35, .31, and .25. The M of these scores is .40. What are the 95% confidence limits for μ? Using the formula in Chapter 3, s_M is found to be .07. The t value for the .05 level for 4 $df(N - 1 = 5 - 1 = 4)$ from Table E is 2.776. The confidence limits are: $.40 + (2.776)(.07) = .59$; $.40 - (2.776)(.07) = .21$. In other words, with repetitions of the study we would expect μ to fall between .21 and .59 in 95 out of the 100 instances.

Having obtained these confidence limits, what do we do with them? At this point the judgments of scientists enter the picture. They must decide in terms of the conditions of the experiment, their scientific intuition, other knowledge, etc. whether or not an effect of this magnitude is an "important" one. For example, the pictures employed in Rosenthal's study were selected so that they had a mean rating of zero in his standardization population. The rating scale that the Ss used ranged from -10 (signifying that the person in the picture "has been experiencing extreme failure") to $+10$ ("has been experiencing extreme success"). The critic might decide that the size of the effect, .21 to .59, is small, considering the 20-point rating scale at S's disposal. While the writer, on the basis of other replications and conditions reported by Rosenthal, believes the bias effect to be reliable, he would question its generality because of the ambiguous nature of the task generally investigated in the Rosenthal studies. In this experimental instance and in many cases, psychologists may not agree in their judgments of the importance of an effect. Although confidence limits can be determined reliably, the decisions about the importance of an effect represent value judgments.

Finally, it should be noted that confidence limits procedures are available for many population parameters besides μ. Confidence limits can be found for variances, correlations, differences in means, medians, proportions, etc. In the case of the median, Dixon and Massey (1951, p. 360) have provided a table that permits one to find the 95% and 99% confidence limits after merely ordering the observations in terms of their size. In conclusion, the question about the magnitude of an effect cannot be answered by significance tests. It requires the determination of population parameters by confidence interval procedures and its importance depends upon the judgments of competent specialists.

Multiple-Analysis Revisited

In Chapter 2 and in other places, following the suggestions of Underwood (1957) and Tukey (1962), we advocated the multiple-analysis of data. That is to say, the position was taken that it might be scientifically profitable to analyze the data from an experiment in many different ways. This means fractionating the data in different ways, trying to graph it in various manners, attempting different transformations to bring out simpler relationships, and so on. Tukey (1962) has reported that this tactic is very common in the physical sciences and that it has accelerated scientific progress there.

We also took a radical position regarding the interpretation of the outcomes of a single psychological experiment. We argued that all that results from an experiment are indications, i.e., hypotheses to be verified in later experiments. And further we contended that "facts" or "truth" are established only by subsequent replications. These views are not, however, as radical as they appear at first glance. Tukey says:

> The modern test of significance, before which so many editors of psychological journals are reported to bow down, owes more to R. A. Fisher than to any other man. Yet Sir Ronald's standard of firm knowledge was not one very extremely significant result, but rather the ability to repeatedly get results significant at 5% (1969, p. 85).

Fisher's own words on this matter are:

> In order to assert that a natural phenomenon is experimentally demonstrable we need, not an isolated record, but a reliable method of procedure. In relation to the test of significance, we may say that a phenomenon is experimentally demonstrable when we know how to conduct an experiment which will rarely fail to give us a statistically significant result (1942, pp. 13f.).

In the same vein, Edwards asserts: "It should also be clear that no single experiment can establish the absolute proof of the falsity of a null hypothesis, no matter how improbable the outcome of the experiment under the null hypothesis" (1968, p. 22). This theme is repeated at a later point where Edwards says: ". . . the outcome of any single experiment is necessarily inconclusive" (1968, p. 65). It is apparent that the attitude toward experimental outcomes as providing indications rather than firm conclusions is far from unorthodox. In fact, it is clearly in the Fisher tradition.

Let us now consider a different line of methodological analysis by Meehl (1967) and Lykken (1968). This line of analysis is relevant to our arguments because like multiple-analysis it leads to two of the same implications, *viz*, (a) that the findings of a single investigation must be regarded with considerable caution, and (b) that the replication of findings must be assigned a high priority in research in the behavioral sciences. Meehl's paper contains a carefully-reasoned description of a methodological paradox existing between psychology and physics. Meehl's summary of this paradox is as follows:

> Because physical theorists typically predict numerical values, an improvement in experimental precision reduces the tolerance range and hence increases [theoretical] corrobability. In most psychological research, improved power of a statistical design leads to a prior probability approaching $\frac{1}{2}$ of finding a significant difference in the theoretically predicted direction. Hence the corroboration yielded by "success" is very weak, and becomes weaker with the increased precision. "Statistical significance" plays a logical role in psychology precisely the reverse of its role in physics (1967, p. 103).

While Meehl neatly excised this paradox, he did not see any simple strategies for its resolution.

Lykken (1968) has probed the paradox further. He suggested that there is a noise-level of significance running through psychological research which may be the product of: (a) the positive correlation between "good" psychological and physical variables; (b) experimenter bias; (c) the covariance from common method; and (d) the effects of transitory state factors, like the S's level of anxiety, fatigue, or need to please the researcher, upon experimental variables. Thus an investigator may observe differences in means or correlations among molar psychological variables of about .20 which are nothing more than artifacts of this noise-level. Furthermore, the investigator may, as a consequence of observing such a relationship, erroneously claim support for a theory undergoing test. There may be no necessary connection between the investigator's theory and his "significant" result but the investigator falsely receives an increment in confidence in the validity of his theory.

One obvious implication of the Meehl-Lykken analysis is that the findings of any single study must be viewed with considerable caution. Since they may merely be reflections of the noise-level of significance, they are best regarded as indications rather than facts. Their establishment as facts is dependent upon experimental replications.

Moreover, the validity of a theory is not dependent upon the observation of an isolated significant difference but, to use Lykken's phrase, upon "multiple corroboration." Lykken has asserted: "The conclusion seems inescapable that the only really satisfactory solution to the problem of corroborating such theories is that of *multiple corroboration*, the derivation and testing of a number of separate, quasi-independent predictions" (1968, p. 154). These considerations force a different conception of the science game upon us. Just as there is a stereotype of the scientist as a lonely old kook in a white lab coat running around a laboratory filled with lots of bubbling things and many dials, there is also a stereotype of "the great experiment." The great experiment is a single brilliantly-conceived study that produces a highly significant result that "proves" the theory and demolishes all others. The science game simply does not follow this script. Instead it involves successive investigations to establish facts and the multiple corroboration of theories. (Unfortunately, research also includes many false steps and many disasters; a physicist friend has aptly described research as "a life of self-inflicted punishment"!)

It has been wisely written by the Italian Tourist Bureau that "all roads lead to Roma." In science, however, all roads lead to replication. Accordingly, we shall complete this section with a brief discussion of some techniques of replication. This important topic has been considered in greater detail by Sidman (1960), Rosenthal (1966), and Lykken (1968). Lykken has distinguished between three forms of replication: literal, operational, and constructive. These are described as follows:

> *Literal replication* . . . would involve exact duplication of the first investigator's sampling procedures, experimental conditions, measuring techniques, and methods of analysis . . . In the case of *operational* replications . . . one strives to duplicate exactly just the sampling and experimental procedures given in the first author's report of his research . . . In the quite different process of *constructive replication*, one deliberately avoids imitation of the first author's methods. To obtain an ideal constructive replication, one would provide a competent investigator with *nothing more than* a clear statement of the empirical "fact" which the first author would claim to have established (1968, p. 155f.).

Literal replication consists of the investigator repeating his own investigation. (Sidman (1960) has analyzed this problem thoroughly, particularly with reference to the single-organism research strategy of the Skinner group.) Operational replication entails the repetition of an investigation by another investigator. In general, scientists tend to weight a replication by another investigator more heavily than a replication by the original investigator. Constructive replication can be done either by the original investigator or by other research workers. What is done is to attempt to verify an *observed relationship* in another experiment in which the conditions differ in one or more respects from the original study.[1] For example, suppose it were found that anxiety, as indexed by the Taylor manifest anxiety scale, directly affects behavioral variable *Y*. A constructive replication might consist of demonstrating that anxiety, as manipulated by varying degree of noxious stimulation, affects *Y* in the same manner. In a successful constructive replication not only is the original relationship verified, but also its generality is extended. Constructive replication is thus a powerful research strategy when it is successful. On the other hand, when constructive replication fails, the investigator pays a price for using this powerful tool. He doesn't know whether the original relationship was in error or whether it simply does not hold for the altered conditions of his constructive replication. What mode of replication will be employed by investigators will vary. Some cautious investigators like to be certain that their work will withstand operational replication, and therefore they will be prone to follow the path of literal replication. Others, who like to take giant steps, will prefer the more powerful but risky procedure of constructive replication. Obviously, progress in science requires both of these extreme types of research workers.

In summary, we have stressed again the importance of: (a) multiple-analysis of data; (b) regarding the results of a single psychological investigation as indications rather than as facts; and (c) replication in the establishment of facts. We were also led to the latter two beliefs by the Meehl-Lykken analysis of statistical significance. This latter analysis included an emphasis on multiple corroboration of theories and a consideration of different kinds of replication strategies. Let us complete this section with some thoughtful words from Lykken: "The moral of this story is that the finding of statistical significance is perhaps the least important attribute of a good experiment; it is *never* a sufficient condition for concluding a theory has been corroborated, that a useful fact has been established with reasonable confidence — or that an experimental report ought to be published" (1968, p. 158).

Some Tactics for Research and Data Analysis

Throughout the book various suggestions have been offered for doing research in psychology and analyzing data. In concluding the book we shall summarize some of these suggestions.

---

1. We would argue that what Lykken calls constructive replication is virtually identical to what Sidman (1960) terms *systematic replication*. Lykken (1968, p. 156, fn. 3) has, however, questioned the identity of the two procedures.

Chapter 1

(a) A major purpose of research is to answer questions.

(b) Research can be done without hypotheses.

(c) Instead of worrying about statistical analysis, effort should be directed toward the design and execution of a sound experiment. Statistics can't save a bad experiment.

(d) Pilot experiments may be valuable in providing information prior to launching a full experiment.

Chapter 2

(a) Multiple-analysis, analyzing the data from an experiment in many ways, is advised as a device to determine what's in the data.

(b) The results of a single psychological experiment should be regarded as indications rather than facts.

(c) Facts are the product of experimental replications.

(d) When a number of observations (say 30 or more) are available, histograms or frequency polygons will provide eyeball information regarding the shapes of the distributions, their central tendencies, and variabilities.

(e) The mean and standard deviation (or variance) of a set of scores are preferred indices of central tendency and variability but these indices are distorted greatly by outlying observations.

(f) With extreme observations, the median and percentile ranges are preferred indices of central tendency and variability because they are unaffected by outliers.

(g) Much data in psychology are "spotty," i.e., the distributions straggle too much and often include outliers.

(h) Skewed distributions can sometimes be normalized by transformations. Changes of scale to square roots, logs, and reciprocals may help reduce positive skew and arc-sine transformations may normalize proportions.

(i) Transformations may also be useful to equalize variances and to simplify relationships.

(j) Tests like Dixon's should be applied to detect outliers.

(k) If an experimental treatment consistently produces outliers, they should be retained in the array of scores.

Chapter 3

(a) One-tailed tests of significance should be used only when assessing the results of a replication experiment or when testing a specific directional hypothesis derived from a well-articulated theory.

(b)   Violation of the independence of observations assumption can produce marked errors of inference in t and F tests of means from independent groups.

(c)   Nonindependence of observations results from nonrandom assignment of Ss to treatments, and when repeated observations for the same Ss or data from matched groups are analyzed.

(d)   Not too much attention should be paid to scales of measurement — even counts with a range of 8 to 10 can be handled by t and F tests.[2]

(e)   The older tests for homogeneity of variance, like the F test, F_{max}, Bartlett's test, and Cochran's test, are markedly influenced by nonnormality.

(f)   Box's variance test is a sounder procedure to assess homogeneity of variance than the earlier tests and the untrained eyeball.

(g)   The t and F tests for means appear to be fairly robust, but they may not be the optimal tests when nonnormality and heterogeneity of variance are marked.

(h)   Equal sample sizes should be used to facilitate computations and minimize the effects of nonnormality and heterogeneity of variance.

(i)   The effects of nonnormality and heterogeneity of variance are reduced by increasing sample sizes.

(j)   The Tukey B test appears to be the best technique for making pairwise comparisons of the means for independent groups *after* a significant overall F test.

(k)   Matched groups designs are more efficient than independent groups designs only when the matching variable is substantially and positively correlated with the dependent variable.

(l)   Randomized blocks designs are less tricky to interpret than repeated measurements designs.

(m)   Testing for the treatment effect in a k matched groups design should be done by examining the F's from both the usual and Box's conservative test.

(n)   The Bonferroni t test is recommended for comparing correlated means after a significant F test.

(o)   Whenever comparisons are performed after a significant overall test, procedures incorporating adjustments for the number of comparisons should be used.

(p)   Factorial designs, which result from the crossing of two or more independent variables, are more efficient than independent experiments. Factorial designs provide estimates of main effects and random error based on more df as well as information regarding the interactions of variables.

2. For a sampling investigation on this matter, see Baker, Hardyck, and Petrinovich (1966).

(q) Interactions may be the result of the combination of experimental factors (intrinsic), the consequence of some extraneous variable affecting a treatment group's scores (extrinsic), or a combination of both. Detection of an extraneous factor involves an examination of the procedure of the investigation.

(r) Some interactions can be "made to disappear" by rescaling the dependent variable, e.g., by a log transformation. If an interaction is accepted as "real," its nature should be explored by further tests. We advocated tests of simple main effects and simple interaction effects, followed by appropriate multiple-comparison tests when necessary.

(s) If factorial designs include more than several factors, they require many groups and Ss, they become difficult to carry out, and they may result in higher order interactions that present serious problems of interpretation.

Chapter 4

(a) The Wilcoxon and Kruskal-Wallis tests are efficient procedures for comparing the locations of two and k independent groups, respectively, when the usual parametric assumptions of normality and equal variances are violated to a marked degree or the original data are in the form of ranks.

(b) The Steel test is recommended for making pairwise comparisons of k independent groups after a significant Kruskal-Wallis test.

(c) For the analysis of matched groups, the Sign test and Friedman's test are suggested for two and k groups, respectively.

(d) The Multiple-Sign test is proposed for pairwise comparisons after a significant Friedman's test.

Chapter 5

(a) χ^2 tests are suitable for the comparison of the observed frequencies in different classes.

(b) If $N > 20$, the χ^2 test corrected for continuity can be applied to a 2×2 table when the expected frequencies in each cell are ≥ 5.

(c) If either of these conditions is not fulfilled, then Fisher's exact test should be employed.

(d) For contingency tables with $df > 1$, corrections for continuity do not have to be made and small expected frequencies are relatively unimportant.

(e) Following significant χ^2 tests with $df > 1$, partitions should be made by either Ryan's test or by orthogonal comparisons of frequencies.

(f) Frequencies from two or k matched groups (and dichotomous classes)

can be analyzed by McNemar's test and Cochran's test, respectively.
(g) For comparisons after a significant Cochran's test, the Multiple-Sign test is recommended.

Chapter 6

(a) It is useful to plot bivariate data in a scatter diagram to obtain an eyeball check on the degree and direction of the relationship and its linearity.
(b) The sign of the Pearson product-moment r indicates the direction of the relationship and its size shows the strength of the relationship.
(c) Regression analysis is recommended to determine the amount of variance in the dependent variable accounted for in terms of the independent variable and to test the significance of r. The square of $r \times 100\%$ also indicates the percentage of variance accounted for by the independent variable.
(d) By means of regression equations precise quantitative predictions can be made of one variable from the other.
(e) Linearity of regression is assumed with r.
(f) Quenouille's medial coefficient is recommended as a quick and dirty test for a linear relationship.
(g) Curvilinear relationships may be investigated by a combination of simple analysis of variance and regression analysis.
(h) A curvilinear regression equation may be found for predicting when linearity does not exist.
(i) *Eta* is the appropriate coefficient of correlation when nonlinearity is present.
(j) The significance of *eta* is tested by a simple analysis of variance.
(k) Kendall's *Tau* is an efficient and versatile rank correlation coefficient. It assumes, however, independence of observations and monotonicity.
(l) The restriction of data analysis to correlation coefficients alone is "sweeping things under the rug."

Chapter 7

(a) The question as to the size of an effect cannot be answered by significance tests but necessitates the use of confidence intervals.
(b) Having established the size of an effect, its importance depends upon the value judgements of competent specialists.
(c) (d) (e) are the same as (a) (b) (c) for Chapter 2.
(f) Possibly there is a noise-level of significance running through behavioral research which demands that the findings of single studies be regarded as indications and that replications be regarded as a necessity.

(g) Three forms of replication – literal, operational and constructive – are possible. In literal replication the original investigator repeats his own study. In operational replication another investigator repeats the original study. In constructive replication either the original or another investigator attempts to reproduce a relationship in an experiment which differs from the original experiment.

(h) Constructive replication, when successful, not only replicates a relationship but extends its generality. When constructive replication fails, constructive replication lacks constructiveness.

(i)   Operational replications score more points than literal replications in terms of replicability.

(j)   Theories in psychology are validated by a process of multiple corroboration in which multiple, quasi-independent implications of the theory are tested.

Final Remarks

In closing we would like to leave the reader with an excerpt from "The research man's prayer" (McCleary, 1960): "Help me be SCHIZOPHRENIC to sustain myself by finding hopeful trends in random data." We would advise transferring these words on to a pennant. After those very bad days in the lab, wave your pennant vigorously and smile!

Answers to the Even-Numbered Problems

Chapter 2

2. $M = 17.19$, Mdn $= 13$, Mode $= 7$
4. $s = 11.36$
6. Yes, R for 114 $= .69$, $p < .01$
   No, R for 62 $= .36$, $p > .05$
   To Winsorize the distribution, replace 114 with 62.

Chapter 3

2. No, $t = 2.43$, $df = 22$, $.05 > p > .02$
4. Yes, $F = 5.06$, $df = 3$ and 44, $p < .005$
6. Only $M = 13.00$ is different from $M = 2.58$ (required critical difference $= 9.82$ for this comparison).
8. For Days, $F = 3.18$. By regular F test with $df = 3$ and 33, $p < .05$; by a conservative F test $df = 1$ and 11, $p > .10$. (Hint: What implication does *not* rejecting the null hypothesis have for problem 9?)
10. Training: $\quad\quad F = 2.56$, $df = 1$ and 44, $p > .05$
    Test: $\quad\quad\quad F = 7.62$, $df = 1$ and 44, $p < .01$
    Training $\times$ Test: $\quad F = 5.02$, $df = 1$ and 44, $p < .05$
12. Training $\times$ Test $\times$ Days: $SS = 129.43$

14. Source of Variation   *df*
        Meaningfulness   2
        Within Groups   27
        Trials   9
        Meaningfulness × Trials   18
        Error   243
                                    ———
         Total   299

Apply regular F tests for trials ($df = 9$ and 243) and meaningfulness ×
trials ($df = 18$ and 243) *and* conservative F tests with $df = 1$ and 27 and
$df = 2$ and 27 for trials and meaningfulness × trials, respectively.

16. Source of Variation   *df*
          A 2
          B 3
          C 1
          $A \times B$ 6
          $A \times C$ 2
          $B \times C$ 3
          $A \times B \times C$ 6
        Within Groups   96
                                      ———
         Total   119

Test for the simple main effects of A (or B, depending upon the interest
of the investigator), using s_w^2 as an error term. Compare the M's within
the *significant* simple main effects of A (or B) by Tukey's B test with
$\sqrt{s_w^2}$ as an estimate of s.

Test for the simple interaction effects of $A \times B$ for levels of C (or $A \times C$
for B levels or $B \times C$ for A levels, depending upon the interest of investigator), using s_w^2 as an error term. Partition the *significant* simple interaction effects into simple main effects and test the latter for significance.
Compare the M's within the *significant* simple main effects by Tukey's
B test.

Chapter 4

2. $H = 9.82$, $df = 2$, $p < .01$
4. $N = 12$, $r = 2$, $p = .05$
6. *If* the overall test is significant, then the Multiple-Sign test should be
applied to make pairwise comparisons.

Chapter 5

2. No, from Table T $p = .05$, one tail.

4. Only NS vs GS is significant: $\chi_c^2 = 8.41$, $df = 1$, $p < .01$ (required $p = .017$ for this comparison).
6. $Q = 24.13$, $df = 2$, $p < .001$

Chapter 6

2. Yes, $F = 56.19$, $df = 1$ and 38, $p < .001$.
4. $Y' = -0.68X + 13.43$
6. Y' from regression line $\cong 6.5$. $Y' = 6.63$ from equation.
8. $\phi = -.60$
10. Yes, overall   : $F = 9.33$, $df = 4$ and 25, $p < .001$
     Linear effect of X : $F = 25.86$, $df = 1$ and 25, $p < .001$
     Nonlinear effect of X: $F = 3.83$, $df = 3$ and 25, $p < .025$
     $E_{YX} = .77$

References

Aronson, E. & Carlsmith, J. N. Experimentation in social psychology. In G. Lindzey & E. Aronson (Eds.), *The handbook of social psychology* (2nd ed.). Vol. II. Reading, Mass.: Addison-Wesley, 1968.

Baker, B. O., Hardyck, C. D., & Petrinovich, L. F. Weak measurements vs strong statistics: An empirical critique of S. S. Stevens' proscriptions on statistics. *Educ. Psychol. Msmt.,* 1966, *26,* 291–310.

Bartlett, M. S. Properties of sufficiency and statistical tests. *Proc. Roy. Soc. (London), Ser. A,* 1937, *160,* 268–282.

Beale, Elizabeth A. A developmental analysis of children's delay behavior in a temptation type of conflict situation. Unpublished doctoral dissertation. University of Kansas, 1956.

Bliss, C. I. A chart of the chi-square distribution. *J. Amer. Stat. Assoc.,* 1944, *39,* 246–248.

Boneau, C. A. The effect of violations of assumptions underlying the *t* test. *Psychol. Bull.,* 1960, *57,* 49–64.

Boneau, C. A. A comparison of the power of the *U* and *t* tests. *Psychol. Rev.,* 1962, *69,* 246–256.

Boneau, C. A. & Pennypacker, H. S. Group matching as research strategy: How not to get significant results. *Psychol. Rep.,* 1961, *8,* 143–147.

Box, G. E. P. Non-normality and tests on variances. *Biometrika,* 1953, *40,* 318–335.

Box, G. E. P. Some theorems on quadratic forms applied in the study of analysis of variance problems. *Ann. Math. Stat.,* 1954, *25,* 209–302, 484–498.

Bradley, J. V. *Distribution-free statistical tests.* Englewood Cliffs, N.J.: Prentice-Hall, 1968.

Bresnahan, Jean L. & Shapiro, M. M. A general equation and technique for the exact partitioning of chi-square contingency tables. *Psychol. Bull.,* 1966, *66,* 252–262.

Brunswik, E. *Perception and the representative design of psychological experiments.* Berkeley and Los Angeles: University of California Press, 1956.

Campbell, D. T. & Stanley, J. C. *Experimental and quasi-experimental designs for research.* Chicago: Rand McNally, 1966.

Campbell, N. R. *Symposium: Measurement and its importance for philosophy.* Aristotelian Society, Suppl. Vol. 17. London: Harrison, 1938.

Castellan, N. J., Jr. On the partitioning of contingency tables. *Psychol. Bull.,* 1965, *64*, 330–338.

Cochran, W. G. The distribution of the largest of a set of estimated variances as a fraction of their total. *Ann. Eugenics,* 1941, *11*, 47–52.

Cochran, W. G. The χ^2 correction for continuity. *Iowa State College J. Sci.,* 1942, *16*, 421–436.

Cochran, W. G. Some methods for strengthening the common chi-square tests. *Biometrics,* 1954, *10*, 417–451.

Cohen, J. An alternative to Marascuilo's "Large-sample multiple comparisons" for proportions. *Psychol. Bull.,* 1967, *67*, 199–201.

Dixon, W. J. Processing data for outliers. *Biometrics,* 1953, *9*, 74–89.

Dixon, W. J. & Massey, F. J., Jr. *Introduction to statistical analysis.* New York: McGraw-Hill, 1951.

Dixon, W. J. & Massey, F. J., Jr. *Introduction to statistical analysis.* (2nd ed.) New York: McGraw-Hill, 1957.

Duncan, D. B. Multiple range and multiple *F* tests. *Biometrics,* 1955, *11*, 1–42.

Dunlap, J. W. & Kurtz, A. K. *Handbook of statistical nomographs, tables, and formulas.* New York: World, 1932.

Dunn, Olive, J. Confidence intervals for the means of dependent, normally distributed variables. *J. Amer. Stat. Assoc.,* 1959, *54*, 613–621.

Dunn, Olive J. Multiple comparisons among means. *J. Amer. Stat. Assoc.,* 1961, *56*, 52–64.

Dunn, Olive J. Multiple comparisons using rank sums. *Technometrics,* 1964, *6*, 241–252.

Dwass, M. Some *k*–sample rank-order tests. In I. Olkin, M. Shurye, W. Hoeffding, W. G. Madow, & H. B. Mann (Eds.). *Contributions to probability and statistics* Stanford, Calif.: Stanford University Press, 1960.

Edwards, A. L. *Experimental design in psychological research.* New York: Rinehart, 1950.

Edwards, A. L. *Experimental design in psychological research.* (rev. ed.) New York: Rinehart, 1960.

Edwards, A. L. *Experimental design in psychological research.* (3rd ed.) New York: Holt, Rinehart and Winston, 1968.

Finney, D. J. Table of significance levels for the Fisher-Yates test of significance in 2×2 contingency tables. *Biometrika,* 1948, *35*, 145–156.

Finney, D. J., Latscha, R., Bennett, B. M., & Hsu, P. *Tables for testing significance in a 2×2 contingency table.* London and New York: Cambridge University Press, 1963.

Fisher, R. A. *The design of experiments.* (3rd ed.) Edinburgh: Oliver and Boyd, 1942.

Friedman, M. The use of ranks to avoid the assumption of normality implicit in the analysis of variance. *J. Amer. Stat. Assoc.,* 1937, *32*, 675–701.

Grice, G. R. & Saltz, E. The generalization of an instrumental response to stimuli varying in the size dimension. *J. exp. Psychol.,* 1950, *40*, 702–715.

Guilford, J. P. *Fundamental statistics in psychology and education.* (3rd ed.) New York: McGraw-Hill, 1956.

Harter, H. L., Clemm, D. S., & Guthrie, E. H. The probability integrals of the range and of the studentized range. WADC-TR 58–484, 1959, Vol. 2.

Hartley, H. O. The maximum *F*-ratio as a short-cut test for heterogeneity of variance. *Biometrika,* 1950, *37,* 308–312.

Hays, W. L. *Statistics for psychologists.* New York: Holt, Rinehart and Winston, 1963.

Hilgard, E. R. Discussion of probabilistic functionalism. *Psychol. Rev.,* 1955, *62,* 226–228.

Jones, L. V. Statistical theory and research design. In C. P. Stone & Q. McNemar (Eds.) *Annual review of psychology.* Vol. 6. Stanford, Calif.: Annual Reviews, 1955.

Kelleher, R. T. & Gollub, L. R. A review of positive conditioned reinforcement. *J. exp. Anal. Behav.,* 1962, *5,* 543–597.

Kendall, M. G. *Rank correlation methods.* London: Charles Griffin, 1948.

Kendall, M. G. *Rank correlation methods.* (3rd ed.) London: Charles Griffin, 1962.

Klein, R. M. Intermittent primary reinforcement as a parameter of secondary reinforcement. *J. exp. Psychol.,* 1959, *58,* 423–427.

Kohnstamm, O. Demonstration einer Kataoieartigen Erscheinung beim Gesunden (katatonusversuch). *Neurol. Zentralbi.,* 1915, *34,* 290–291.

Kruskal, W. H. & Wallis, W. A. Use of ranks in one-criterion variance analysis. *J. Amer. Stat. Assoc.,* 1952, *47,* 583–621.

Kruskal, W. H. & Wallis, W. A. Errata. *J. Amer. Stat. Assoc.,* 1953, *48,* 910.

Levinson, D. M. & Sheridan, C. L. Monocular acquisition and interocular transfer of two types of pattern discrimination in hooded rats. *J. comp. physiol. Psychol.,* 1969, *67,* 468–472.

Lewin, K. *A dynamic theory of personality: Selected papers.* New York: McGraw-Hill, 1935.

Lewis, D. & Burke, C. J. The use and misuse of the chi-square test. *Psychol. Bull.,* 1949, *46,* 433–489.

Lindquist, E. F. *Design and analysis of experiments in psychology and education.* Boston: Houghton Mifflin, 1953.

Lykken, D. T. Statistical significance in psychological research. *Psychol. Bull.,* 1968, *70,* 151–159.

Lynch, J. J. Heart rate variability of dogs in classical conditioning. *Psychol. Rec.,* 1968, *18,* 101–106.

Maier, N. R. F., Thurber, J. A., & Janzen, J. C. Studies in creativity: V. The selection process in recall and in problem-solving situations. *Psychol. Rep.,* 1968, *23,* 1003–1022.

Mandler, G. & Kessen, W. *The language of psychology.* New York: Wiley, 1959.

Marascuilo, L. A. Large-sample multiple comparisons. *Psychol. Bull.,* 1966, *65,* 280–290.

MacKinnon, W. J. Table for both the sign test and distribution-free confidence intervals of the median for sample sizes to 1000. *J. Amer. Stat. Assoc.,* 1964, *59,* 935–956.

McCain, G. & Segal, E. M. *The game of science.* Belmont, Calif.: Belmont-Cole, 1969.

McCall, W. A. *How to experiment in education.* New York: Macmillan, 1923.

McCleary, R. A. The research man's prayer. *The Worm Runner's Digest,* 1960, *11.*

Meehl, P. E. Theory-testing in psychology and physics: A methodological paradox. *Philo. Sci.,* 1967, *34,* 103–115.

Miller, R. G., Jr. A trustworthy jacknife. *Ann. Math. Stat.,* 1964, *35,* 1594–1605.

Miller, R. G., Jr. *Simultaneous statistical inference.* New York: McGraw-Hill, 1966.

Miller, R. G., Jr. Jackknifing variances. *Ann. Math. Stat.,* 1968, *39,* 567–582.

Mosteller, F. & Tukey, J. W. Data analysis, including statistics. In G. Lindzey & E. Aronson (Eds.), *The handbook of social psychology*. (2nd ed.) Vol. II. Reading, Mass.: Addison-Wesley, 1968.

Myers, J. L. *Fundamentals of experimental design*. Boston: Allyn and Bacon, 1966.

Nemenyi, P. Distribution-free multiple comparisons. Unpublished doctoral dissertation, Princeton University, 1963.

Norton, D. W. An empirical investigation of some effects of non-normality and heterogeneity on the *F*-distribution. Unpublished doctoral dissertation, State University of Iowa, 1952.

Overstreet, J. D. & Dunham, J. L. Effect of number of values and irrelevant dimensions on dimension selection and associative learning in a multiple-concept problem. *J. exp. Psychol.*, 1969, *79*, 265–268.

Pearson, E. S. & Hartley, H. O. (Eds.) *Biometrika tables for statisticians* (3rd ed.) Vol. I. Cambridge: Cambridge University Press, 1966.

Petrinovich, L. F. & Hardyck, C. D. Error rates for multiple comparison methods: Some evidence concerning the frequency of erroneous conclusions. *Psychol. Bull.*, 1969, *71*, 43–54.

Plutchik, R. *Foundations of experimental research*. New York: Harper & Row, 1968.

Quenouille, M. H. *Introductory statistics*. London: Butterworth-Springer, 1950.

Quenouille, M. H. *Associated measurements*. London: Butterworths, 1952.

Quenouille, M. H. *Rapid statistical calculations*. New York: Hafner, 1959.

The RAND Corporation. *A million random digits*. Glencoe, Ill: The Free Press, 1955.

Reynolds, B. The relationship between the strength of a habit and the degree of drive present during acquisition. *J. exp. Psychol.*, 1949, *39*, 296–305.

Rhyne, A. L. & Steel, R. G. D. A multiple comparisons sign test: All pairs of treatments. *Biometrics*, 1967, *23*, 539–549.

Rosenthal, R. *Experimenter effects in behavioral research*. New York: Appleton-Century-Crofts, 1966.

Ryan, T. A. Multiple comparisons in psychological research. *Psychol. Bull.*, 1959, *56*, 26–47.

Ryan, T. A. Significance tests for multiple comparison of proportions, variances, and other statistics. *Psychol. Bull.*, 1960, *57*, 318–328.

Salmon, A. Nuove osservazioni sui movimenti automatici che si compiono dope gli sforzi muscolari e del loro valore in neuropatholgia. *Atti della Accademia Medico-Fisica Fiorentina*, 1914, *78*–91.

Scheffé, H. A. A method of judging all possible contrasts in the analysis of variance. *Biometrika*, 1953, *40*, 87–104.

Scheffé, H. A. *The analysis of variance*. New York: Wiley, 1959.

Scott, E. D. The effects of reward schedules and drive conditions on secondary reinforcement. Unpublished doctoral dissertation, University of Kansas, 1960.

Sidman, M. *Tactics of scientific research*. New York: Basic Books, 1960.

Sidowski, J. B. (Ed.) *Experimental methods and instrumentation in psychology*. New York: McGraw-Hill, 1966.

Siegel, S. *Nonparametric statistics for the behavioral sciences*. New York: McGraw-Hill, 1956.

Skinner, B. F. A case history in scientific method. *American Psychologist*, 1956, *11*, 221–223.

Snyder, Rebecca. Personality characteristics associated with the Kohnstamm phenomenon. Unpublished doctoral dissertation, University of Kansas, 1956.

Steel, R. G. D. A rank sum test for comparing all pairs of treatments. *Techno-metrics*, 1960, *2*, 197–207.

Steel, R. G. D. Some rank sum multiple comparisons tests. *Biometrics*, 1961, *17*, 539–552.

Stevens, S. S. (Ed.) *Handbook of experimental psychology*. New York: Wiley, 1951.

Student. Errors of routine analysis. *Biometrika*, 1927, *19*, 151–164.

Tukey, J. W. The future of data analysis. *Ann. Math. Stat.*, 1962, *33*, 1–67.

Tukey, J. W. Analyzing data: Sanctification or detective work. *Amer. Psychologist*, 1969, *24*, 83–91.

Underwood, B. J. *Psychological research*. New York: Appleton-Century-Crofts, 1957.

Walker, Helen M. & Lev, J. *Statistical inference*. New York: Holt, 1953.

Wallis, W. A. & Roberts, H. V. *Statistics: A new approach*. Glencoe, Illinois: The Free Press, 1956.

Walsh, J. E. *Handbook of nonparametric statistics*. II: *Results for two and several sample problems*. Princeton, N.J.: D. Van Nostrand, 1965.

Weast, R. C. (Ed.) *Handbook of chemistry and physics* (50th ed.) Cleveland, Ohio: The Chemical Rubber Company, 1969.

Weil, A. T., Zinberg, N. E., & Nelsen, J. M. Clinical and psychological effects of marijuana in man. *Science*, 1968, *162*, 1234–1242.

Welker, W. I. Effects of age and experience on play and exploration of young chimpanzees. *J. comp. physiol. Psychol.*, 1956, *49*, 223–226.

Wike, E. L. A note on significance tests for tau (τ) when N is small. *Psychol. Rep.*, 1955, *1*, 389–391.

Wike, E. L. & Barrientos, G. Secondary reinforcement and multiple-drive reduction. *J. comp. physiol. Psychol.*, 1958, *51*, 640–643.

Wilcoxon, F. Individual comparisons by ranking methods. *Biometric Bull.*, 1945, *1*, 80–82.

Wilcoxon, F. *Some rapid approximate statistical procedures*. New York: American Cyanamid Company, 1949.

Wilcoxon, F., Katti, S. K., & Wilcox, Roberta A. *Critical values and probability levels for the Wilcoxon rank sum test and the Wilcoxon signed rank test*. American Cyanamid Company and the Florida State University, 1963.

Wilcoxon, F. & Wilcox, Roberta A. *Some rapid approximate statistical procedures*. (Rev. ed.) Pearl River, N.Y.: Lederle Laboratories, 1964.

Winer, B. J. *Statistical principles in experimental design*. New York: McGraw-Hill, 1962.

Appendix

Table A: Table of Squares, Square Roots, and Reciprocals of Numbers from 1 to 1000

Table B: Four-Place Logarithms

Table C: Transformation of a Proportion (p) to Radians (ϕ) $[\phi = 2 \arcsin \sqrt{p}]$

Table D: Criteria for Testing Extreme Scores

Table E: Table of t

Table F: Table of F

Table G: Table for F_{max}

Table H: Percentage Points of the Studentized Range, q

Table I: Percentage Points of the Bonferroni t Statistic, $t_{df_E}^{\alpha/2C}$

Table J: Wilcoxon T Values for Unpaired Replicates

Table K: Table of Random Numbers

Table L: Table for Kruskal-Wallis H Test

Table M: Table of Critical Values of Chi-Square

Table N: Table of Z Values in the Normal Distribution

Table O: Percentage Points of the k-Sample Rank Statistics, T'

Table P: Wilcoxon T Values for Paired Replicates

Table Q: Critical r Values for the Sign Test

Table R: Critical χ_r^2 Values for Friedman's Test

Table S: Percentage Points of the k-Sample Sign Statistics S^a

Table T: Table of Critical Values of D (or C) in the Fisher Test

Table U: Table of r for .05 and .01 Level of Significance

Table V: Significance Levels for the Medial Test

Table W: One-Tail Probability of S for Kendall's *Tau*

Table A.* *Table of Squares, Square Roots, and Reciprocals of Numbers from 1 to 1000*

N	N²	√N	1/N	N	N²	√N	1/N
1	1	1.0000	1.000000	41	1681	6.4031	.024390
2	4	1.4142	.500000	42	1764	6.4807	.023810
3	9	1.7321	.333333	43	1849	6.5574	.023256
4	16	2.0000	.250000	44	1936	6.6332	.022727
5	25	2.2361	.200000	45	2025	6.7082	.022222
6	36	2.4495	.166667	46	2116	6.7823	.021739
7	49	2.6458	.142857	47	2209	6.8557	.021277
8	64	2.8284	.125000	48	2304	6.9282	.020833
9	81	3.0000	.111111	49	2401	7.0000	.020408
10	100	3.1623	.100000	50	2500	7.0711	.020000
11	121	3.3166	.090909	51	2601	7.1414	.019608
12	144	3.4641	.083333	52	2704	7.2111	.019231
13	169	3.6056	.076923	53	2809	7.2801	.018868
14	196	3.7417	.071429	54	2916	7.3485	.018519
15	225	3.8730	.066667	55	3025	7.4162	.018182
16	256	4.0000	.062500	56	3136	7.4833	.017857
17	289	4.1231	.058824	57	3249	7.5498	.017544
18	324	4.2426	.055556	58	3364	7.6158	.017241
19	361	4.3589	.052632	59	3481	7.6811	.016949
20	400	4.4721	.050000	60	3600	7.7460	.016667
21	441	4.5826	.047619	61	3721	7.8102	.016393
22	484	4.6904	.045455	62	3844	7.8740	.016129
23	529	4.7958	.043478	63	3969	7.9373	.015873
24	576	4.8990	.041667	64	4096	8.0000	.015625
25	625	5.0000	.040000	65	4225	8.0623	.015385
26	676	5.0990	.038462	66	4356	8.1240	.015152
27	729	5.1962	.037037	67	4489	8.1854	.014925
28	784	5.2915	.035714	68	4624	8.2462	.014706
29	841	5.3852	.034483	69	4761	8.3066	.014493
30	900	5.4772	.033333	70	4900	8.3666	.014286
31	961	5.5678	.032258	71	5041	8.4261	.014085
32	1024	5.6569	.031250	72	5184	8.4853	.013889
33	1089	5.7446	.030303	73	5329	8.5440	.013699
34	1156	5.8310	.029412	74	5476	8.6023	.013514
35	1225	5.9161	.028571	75	5625	8.6603	.013333
36	1296	6.0000	.027778	76	5776	8.7178	.013158
37	1369	6.0828	.027027	77	5929	8.7750	.012987
38	1444	6.1644	.026316	78	6084	8.8318	.012821
39	1521	6.2450	.025641	79	6241	8.8882	.012658
40	1600	6.3246	.025000	80	6400	8.9443	.012500

*Reprinted by permission of the authors from J. W. Dunlap and A. Kurtz, *Handbook of Statistical Nomographs, Tables, and Formulas,* p. 72 81. Copyright 1936, Harcourt, Brace & World. Inc.; and of the author from A. L. Edwards, *Experimental Design in Psychological Research,* pp. 337 349. Copyright 1960, Allen L. Edwards.

Table A — continued

N	N²	√N	1/N	N	N²	√N	1/N
81	6561	9.0000	.012346	121	14641	11.0000	.00826446
82	6724	9.0554	.012195	122	14884	11.0454	.00819672
83	6889	9.1104	.012048	123	15129	11.0905	.00813008
84	7056	9.1652	.011905	124	15376	11.1355	.00806452
85	7225	9.2195	.011765	125	15625	11.1803	.00800000
86	7396	9.2736	.011628	126	15876	11.2250	.00793651
87	7569	9.3274	.011494	127	16129	11.2694	.00787402
88	7744	9.3808	.011364	128	16384	11.3137	.00781250
89	7921	9.4340	.011236	129	16641	11.3578	.00775194
90	8100	9.4868	.011111	130	16900	11.4018	.00769231
91	8281	9.5394	.010989	131	17161	11.4455	.00763359
92	8464	9.5917	.010870	132	17424	11.4891	.00757576
93	8649	9.6437	.010753	133	17689	11.5326	.00751880
94	8836	9.6954	.010638	134	17956	11.5758	.00746269
95	9025	9.7468	.010526	135	18225	11.6190	.00740741
96	9216	9.7980	.010417	136	18496	11.6619	.00735294
97	9409	9.8489	.010309	137	18769	11.7047	.00729927
98	9604	9.8995	.010204	138	19044	11.7473	.00724638
99	9801	9.9499	.010101	139	19321	11.7898	.00719424
100	10000	10.0000	.010000	140	19600	11.8322	.00714286
101	10201	10.0499	.00990099	141	19881	11.8743	.00709220
102	10404	10.0995	.00980392	142	20164	11.9164	.00704225
103	10609	10.1489	.00970874	143	20449	11.9583	.00699301
104	10816	10.1980	.00961538	144	20736	12.0000	.00694444
105	11025	10.2470	.00952381	145	21025	12.0416	.00689655
106	11236	10.2956	.00943396	146	21316	12.0830	.00684932
107	11449	10.3441	.00934579	147	21609	12.1244	.00680272
108	11664	10.3923	.00925926	148	21904	12.1655	.00675676
109	11881	10.4403	.00917431	149	22201	12.2066	.00671141
110	12100	10.4881	.00909091	150	22500	12.2474	.00666667
111	12321	10.5357	.00900901	151	22801	12.2882	.00662252
112	12544	10.5830	.00892857	152	23104	12.3288	.00657895
113	12769	10.6301	.00884956	153	23409	12.3693	.00653595
114	12996	10.6771	.00877193	154	23716	12.4097	.00649351
115	13225	10.7238	.00869565	155	24025	12.4499	.00645161
116	13456	10.7703	.00862069	156	24336	12.4900	.00641026
117	13689	10.8167	.00854701	157	24649	12.5300	.00636943
118	13924	10.8628	.00847458	158	24964	12.5698	.00632911
119	14161	10.9087	.00840336	159	25281	12.6095	.00628931
120	14400	10.9545	.00833333	160	25600	12.6491	.00625000

Table A — continued

N	N²	√N	1/N	N	N²	√N	1/N
161	25921	12.6886	.00621118	201	40401	14.1774	.00497512
162	26244	12.7279	.00617284	202	40804	14.2127	.00495050
163	26569	12.7671	.00613497	203	41209	14.2478	.00492611
164	26896	12.8062	.00609756	204	41616	14.2829	.00490196
165	27225	12.8452	.00606061	205	42025	14.3178	.00487805
166	27556	12.8841	.00602410	206	42436	14.3527	.00485437
167	27889	12.9228	.00598802	207	42849	14.3875	.00483092
168	28224	12.9615	.00595238	208	43264	14.4222	.00480769
169	28561	13.0000	.00591716	209	43681	14.4568	.00478469
170	28900	13.0384	.00588235	210	44100	14.4914	.00476190
171	29241	13.0767	.00584795	211	44521	14.5258	.00473934
172	29584	13.1149	.00581395	212	44944	14.5602	.00471698
173	29929	13.1529	.00578035	213	45369	14.5945	.00469484
174	30276	13.1909	.00574713	214	45796	14.6287	.00467290
175	30625	13.2288	.00571429	215	46225	14.6629	.00465116
176	30976	13.2665	.00568182	216	46656	14.6969	.00462963
177	31329	13.3041	.00564972	217	47089	14.7309	.00460829
178	31684	13.3417	.00561798	218	47524	14.7648	.00458716
179	32041	13.3791	.00558659	219	47961	14.7986	.00456621
180	32400	13.4164	.00555556	220	48400	14.8324	.00454545
181	32761	13.4536	.00552486	221	48841	14.8661	.00452489
182	33124	13.4907	.00549451	222	49284	14.8997	.00450450
183	33489	13.5277	.00546448	223	49729	14.9332	.00448430
184	33856	13.5647	.00543478	224	50176	14.9666	.00446429
185	34225	13.6015	.00540541	225	50625	15.0000	.00444444
186	34596	13.6382	.00537634	226	51076	15.0333	.00442478
187	34969	13.6748	.00534759	227	51529	15.0665	.00440529
188	35344	13.7113	.00531915	228	51984	15.0997	.00438596
189	35721	13.7477	.00529101	229	52441	15.1327	.00436681
190	36100	13.7840	.00526316	230	52900	15.1658	.00434783
191	36481	13.8203	.00523560	231	53361	15.1987	.00432900
192	36864	13.8564	.00520833	232	53824	15.2315	.00431034
193	37249	13.8924	.00518135	233	54289	15.2643	.00429185
194	37636	13.9284	.00515464	234	54756	15.2971	.00427350
195	38025	13.9642	.00512821	235	55225	15.3297	.00425532
196	38416	14.0000	.00510204	236	55696	15.3623	.00423729
197	38809	14.0357	.00507614	237	56169	15.3948	.00421941
198	39204	14.0712	.00505051	238	56644	15.4272	.00420168
199	39601	14.1067	.00502513	239	57121	15.4596	.00418410
200	40000	14.1421	.00500000	240	57600	15.4919	.00416667

Table A — continued

N	N²	√N	1/N	N	N²	√N	1/N
241	58081	15.5242	.00414938	281	78961	16.7631	.00355872
242	58564	15.5563	.00413223	282	79524	16.7929	.00354610
243	59049	15.5885	.00411523	283	80089	16.8226	.00353357
244	59536	15.6205	.00409836	284	80656	16.8523	.00352113
245	60025	15.6525	.00408163	285	81225	16.8819	.00350877
246	60516	15.6844	.00406504	286	81796	16.9115	.00349650
247	61009	15.7162	.00404858	287	82369	16.9411	.00348432
248	61504	15.7480	.00403226	288	82944	16.9706	.00347222
249	62001	15.7797	.00401606	289	83521	17.0000	.00346021
250	62500	15.8114	.00400000	290	84100	17 0294	.00344828
251	63001	15.8430	.00398406	291	84681	17.0587	.00343643
252	63504	15.8745	.00396825	292	85264	17.0880	.00342466
253	64009	15.9060	.00395257	293	85849	17.1172	.00341297
254	64516	15.9374	.00393701	294	86436	17.1464	.00340136
255	65025	15.9687	.00392157	295	87025	17.1756	.00338983
256	65536	16.0000	.00390625	296	87616	17.2047	.00337838
257	66049	16.0312	.00389105	297	88209	17.2337	.00336700
258	66564	16.0624	.00387597	298	88804	17.2627	.00335570
259	67081	16.0935	.00386100	299	89401	17.2916	.00334448
260	67600	16.1245	.00384615	300	90000	17.3205	.00333333
261	68121	16.1555	.00383142	301	90601	17.3494	.00332226
262	68644	16.1864	.00381679	302	91204	17.3781	.00331126
263	69169	16.2173	.00380228	303	91809	17.4069	.00330033
264	69696	16.2481	.00378788	304	92416	17.4356	.00328947
265	70225	16.2788	.00377358	305	93025	17.4642	.00327869
266	70756	16.3095	.00375940	306	93636	17.4929	.00326797
267	71289	16.3401	.00374532	307	94249	17.5214	.00325733
268	71824	16.3707	.00373134	308	94864	17.5499	.00324675
269	72361	16.4012	.00371747	309	95481	17.5784	.00323625
270	72900	16.4317	.00370370	310	96100	17.6068	.00322581
271	73441	16.4621	.00369004	311	96721	17.6352	.00321543
272	73984	16.4924	.00367647	312	97344	17.6635	.00320513
273	74529	16.5227	.00366300	313	97969	17.6918	.00319489
274	75076	16.5529	.00364964	314	98596	17.7200	.00318471
275	75625	16.5831	.00363636	315	99225	17 7482	.00317460
276	76176	16.6132	.00362319	316	99856	17.7764	.00316456
277	76729	16.6433	.00361011	317	100489	17.8045	.00315457
278	77284	16.6733	.00359712	318	101124	17.8326	.00314465
279	77841	16.7033	.00358423	319	101761	17.8606	.00313480
280	78400	16.7332	.00357143	320	102400	17.8885	.00312500

Table A — continued

N	N²	$\sqrt{N}$	1/N	N	N²	$\sqrt{N}$	1/N
321	103041	17.9165	.00311526	361	130321	19.0000	.00277008
322	103684	17.9444	.00310559	362	131044	19.0263	.00276243
323	104329	17.9722	.00309598	363	131769	19.0526	.00275482
324	104976	18.0000	.00308642	364	132496	19.0788	.00274725
325	105625	18.0278	.00307692	365	133225	19.1050	.00273973
326	106276	18.0555	.00306748	366	133956	19.1311	.00273224
327	106929	18.0831	.00305810	367	134689	19.1572	.00272480
328	107584	18.1108	.00304878	368	135424	19.1833	.00271739
329	108241	18.1384	.00303951	369	136161	19.2094	.00271003
330	108900	18.1659	.00303030	370	136900	19.2354	.00270270
331	109561	18.1934	.00302115	371	137641	19.2614	.00269542
332	110224	18.2209	.00301205	372	138384	19.2873	.00268817
333	110889	18.2483	.00300300	373	139129	19.3132	.00268097
334	111556	18.2757	.00299401	374	139876	19.3391	.00267380
335	112225	18.3030	.00298507	375	140625	19.3649	.00266667
336	112896	18.3303	.00297619	376	141376	19.3907	.00265957
337	113569	18.3576	.00296736	377	142129	19.4165	.00265252
338	114244	18.3848	.00295858	378	142884	19.4422	.00264550
339	114921	18.4120	.00294985	379	143641	19.4679	.00263852
340	115600	18.4391	.00294118	380	144400	19.4936	.00263158
341	116281	18.4662	.00293255	381	145161	19.5192	.00262467
342	116964	18.4932	.00292398	382	145924	19.5448	.00261780
343	117649	18.5203	.00291545	383	146689	19.5704	.00261097
344	118336	18.5472	.00290698	384	147456	19.5959	.00260417
345	119025	18.5742	.00289855	385	148225	19.6214	.00259740
346	119716	18.6011	.00289017	386	148996	19.6469	.00259067
347	120409	18.6279	.00288184	387	149769	19.6723	.00258398
348	121104	18.6548	.00287356	388	150544	19.6977	.00257732
349	121801	18.6815	.00286533	389	151321	19.7231	.00257069
350	122500	18.7083	.00285714	390	152100	19.7484	.00256410
351	123201	18.7350	.00284900	391	152881	19.7737	.00255754
352	123904	18.7617	.00284091	392	153664	19.7990	.00255102
353	124609	18.7883	.00283286	393	154449	19.8242	.00254453
354	125316	18.8149	.00282486	394	155236	19.8494	.00253807
355	126025	18.8414	.00281690	395	156025	19.8746	.00253165
356	126736	18.8680	.00280899	396	156816	19.8997	.00252525
357	127449	18.8944	.00280112	397	157609	19.9249	.00251889
358	128164	18.9209	.00279330	398	158404	19.9499	.00251256
359	128881	18.9473	.00278552	399	159201	19.9750	.00250627
360	129600	18.9737	.00277778	400	160000	20.0000	.00250000

Table A — continued

N	N^2	$\sqrt{N}$	$1/N$	N	N^2	$\sqrt{N}$	$1/N$
401	160801	20.0250	.00249377	441	194481	21.0000	.00226757
402	161604	20.0499	.00248756	442	195364	21.0238	.00226244
403	162409	20.0749	.00248139	443	196249	21.0476	.00225734
404	163216	20.0998	.00247525	444	197136	21.0713	.00225225
405	164025	20.1246	.00246914	445	198025	21.0950	.00224719
406	164836	20.1494	.00246305	446	198916	21.1187	.00224215
407	165649	20.1742	.00245700	447	199809	21.1424	.00223714
408	166464	20.1990	.00245098	448	200704	21.1660	.00223214
409	167281	20.2237	.00244499	449	201601	21.1896	.00222717
410	168100	20.2485	.00243902	450	202500	21.2132	.00222222
411	168921	20.2731	.00243309	451	203401	21.2368	.00221729
412	169744	20.2978	.00242718	452	204304	21.2603	.00221239
413	170569	20.3224	.00242131	453	205209	21.2838	.00220751
414	171396	20.3470	.00241546	454	206116	21.3073	.00220264
415	172225	20.3715	.00240964	455	207025	21.3307	.00219780
416	173056	20.3961	.00240385	456	207936	21.3542	.00219298
417	173889	20.4206	.00239808	457	208849	21.3776	.00218818
418	174724	20.4450	.00239234	458	209764	21.4009	.00218341
419	175561	20.4695	.00238663	459	210681	21.4243	.00217865
420	176400	20.4939	.00238095	460	211600	21.4476	.00217391
421	177241	20.5183	.00237530	461	212521	21.4709	.00216920
422	178084	20.5426	.00236967	462	213444	21.4942	.00216450
423	178929	20.5670	.00236407	463	214369	21.5174	.00215983
424	179776	20.5913	.00235849	464	215296	21.5407	.00215517
425	180625	20.6155	.00235294	465	216225	21.5639	.00215054
426	181476	20.6398	.00234742	466	217156	21.5870	.00214592
427	182329	20.6640	.00234192	467	218089	21.6102	.00214133
428	183184	20.6882	.00233645	468	219024	21.6333	.00213675
429	184041	20.7123	.00233100	469	219961	21.6564	.00213220
430	184900	20.7364	.00232558	470	220900	21.6795	.00212766
431	185761	20.7605	.00232019	471	221841	21.7025	.00212314
432	186624	20.7846	.00231481	472	222784	21.7256	.00211864
433	187489	20.8087	.00230947	473	223729	21.7486	.00211416
434	188356	20.8327	.00230415	474	224676	21.7715	.00210970
435	189225	20.8567	.00229885	475	225625	21.7945	.00210526
436	190096	20.8806	.00229358	476	226576	21.8174	.00210084
437	190969	20.9045	.00228833	477	227529	21.8403	.00209644
438	191844	20.9284	.00228311	478	228484	21.8632	.00209205
439	192721	20.9523	.00227790	479	229441	21.8861	.00208768
440	193600	20.9762	.00227273	480	230400	21.9089	.00208333

Table A — continued

N	N²	√N̄	1/N	N	N²	√N̄	1/N
481	231361	21.9317	.00207900	521	271441	22.8254	.00191939
482	232324	21.9545	.00207469	522	272484	22.8473	.00191571
483	233289	21.9773	.00207039	523	273529	22.8692	.00191205
484	234256	22.0000	.00206612	524	274576	22.8910	.00190840
485	235225	22.0227	.00206186	525	275625	22.9129	.00190476
486	236196	22.0454	.00205761	526	276676	22.9347	.00190114
487	237169	22.0681	.00205339	527	277729	22.9565	.00189753
488	238144	22.0907	.00204918	528	278784	22.9783	.00189394
489	239121	22.1133	.00204499	529	279841	23.0000	.00189036
490	240100	22.1359	.00204082	530	280900	23.0217	.00188679
491	241081	22.1585	.00203666	531	281961	23.0434	.00188324
492	242064	22.1811	.00203252	532	283024	23.0651	.00187970
493	243049	22.2036	.00202840	533	284089	23.0868	.00187617
494	244036	22.2261	.00202429	534	285156	23.1084	.00187266
495	245025	22.2486	.00202020	535	286225	23.1301	.00186916
496	246016	22.2711	.00201613	536	287296	23.1517	.00186567
497	247009	22.2935	.00201207	537	288369	23.1733	.00186220
498	248004	22.3159	.00200803	538	289444	23.1948	.00185874
499	249001	22.3383	.00200401	539	290521	23.2164	.00185529
500	250000	22.3607	.00200000	540	291600	23.2379	.00185185
501	251001	22.3830	.00199601	541	292681	23.2594	.00184843
502	252004	22.4054	.00199203	542	293764	23.2809	.00184502
503	253009	22.4277	.00198807	543	294849	23.3024	.00184162
504	254016	22.4499	.00198413	544	295936	23.3238	.00183824
505	255025	22.4722	.00198020	545	297025	23.3452	.00183486
506	256036	22.4944	.00197628	546	298116	23.3666	.00183150
507	257049	22.5167	.00197239	547	299209	23.3880	.00182815
508	258064	22.5389	.00196850	548	300304	23.4094	.00182482
509	259081	22.5610	.00196464	549	301401	23.4307	.00182149
510	260100	22.5832	.00196078	550	302500	23.4521	.00181818
511	261121	22.6053	.00195695	551	303601	23.4734	.00181488
512	262144	22.6274	.00195312	552	304704	23.4947	.00181159
513	263169	22.6495	.00194932	553	305809	23.5160	.00180832
514	264196	22.6716	.00194553	554	306916	23.5372	.00180505
515	265225	22.6936	.00194175	555	308025	23.5584	.00180180
516	266256	22.7156	.00193798	556	309136	23.5797	.00179856
517	267289	22.7376	.00193424	557	310249	23.6008	.00179533
518	268324	22.7596	.00193050	558	311364	23.6220	.00179211
519	269361	22.7816	.00192678	559	312481	23.6432	.00178891
520	270400	22.8035	.00192308	560	313600	23.6643	.00178571

Table A — continued

N	N²	$\sqrt{N}$	1/N	N	N²	$\sqrt{N}$	1/N
561	314721	23.6854	.00178253	601	361201	24.5153	.00166389
562	315844	23.7065	.00177936	602	362404	24.5357	.00166113
563	316969	23.7276	.00177620	603	363609	24.5561	.00165837
564	318096	23.7487	.00177305	604	364816	24.5764	.00165563
565	319225	23.7697	.00176991	605	366025	24.5967	.00165289
566	320356	23.7908	.00176678	606	367236	24.6171	.00165017
567	321489	23.8118	.00176367	607	368449	24.6374	.00164745
568	322624	23.8328	.00176056	608	369664	24.6577	.00164474
569	323761	23.8537	.00175747	609	370881	24.6779	.00164204
570	324900	23.8747	.00175439	610	372100	24.6982	.00163934
571	326041	23.8956	.00175131	611	373321	24.7184	.00163666
572	327184	23.9165	.00174825	612	374544	24.7386	.00163399
573	328329	23.9374	.00174520	613	375769	24.7588	.00163132
574	329476	23.9583	.00174216	614	376996	24.7790	.00162866
575	330625	23.9792	.00173913	615	378225	24.7992	.00162602
576	331776	24.0000	.00173611	616	379456	24.8193	.00162338
577	332929	24.0208	.00173310	617	380689	24.8395	.00162075
578	334084	24.0416	.00173010	618	381924	24.8596	.00161812
579	335241	24.0624	.00172712	619	383161	24.8797	.00161551
580	336400	24.0832	.00172414	620	384400	24.8998	.00161290
581	337561	24.1039	.00172117	621	385641	24.9199	.00161031
582	338724	24.1247	.00171821	622	386884	24.9399	.00160772
583	339889	24.1454	.00171527	623	388129	24.9600	.00160514
584	341056	24.1661	.00171233	624	389376	24.9800	.00160256
585	342225	24.1868	.00170940	625	390625	25.0000	.00160000
586	343396	24.2074	.00170648	626	391876	25.0200	.00159744
587	344569	24.2281	.00170358	627	393129	25.0400	.00159490
588	345744	24.2487	.00170068	628	394384	25.0599	.00159236
589	346921	24.2693	.00169779	629	395641	25.0799	.00158983
590	348100	24.2899	.00169492	630	396900	25.0998	.00158730
591	349281	24.3105	.00169205	631	398161	25.1197	.00158479
592	350464	24.3311	.00168919	632	399424	25.1396	.00158228
593	351649	24.3516	.00168634	633	400689	25.1595	.00157978
594	352836	24.3721	.00168350	634	401956	25.1794	.00157729
595	354025	24.3926	.00168067	635	403225	25.1992	.00157480
596	355216	24.4131	.00167785	636	404496	25.2190	.00157233
597	356409	24.4336	.00167504	637	405769	25.2389	.00156986
598	357604	24.4540	.00167224	638	407044	25.2587	.00156740
599	358801	24.4745	.00166945	639	408321	25.2784	.00156495
600	360000	24.4949	.00166667	640	409600	25.2982	.00156250

Table A — continued

N	N²	√N	1/N	N	N²	√N	1/N
641	410881	25.3180	.00156006	681	463761	26.0960	.00146843
642	412164	25.3377	.00155763	682	465124	26.1151	.00146628
643	413449	25.3574	.00155521	683	466489	26.1343	.00146413
644	414736	25.3772	.00155280	684	467856	26.1534	.00146199
645	416025	25.3969	.00155039	685	469225	26.1725	.00145985
646	417316	25.4165	.00154799	686	470596	26.1916	.00145773
647	418609	25.4362	.00154560	687	471969	26.2107	.00145560
648	419904	25.4558	.00154321	688	473344	26.2298	.00145349
649	421201	25.4755	.00154083	689	474721	26.2488	.00145138
650	422500	25.4951	.00153846	690	476100	26.2679	.00144928
651	423801	25.5147	.00153610	691	477481	26.2869	.00144718
652	425104	25.5343	.00153374	692	478864	26.3059	.00144509
653	426409	25.5539	.00153139	693	480249	26.3249	.00144300
654	427716	25.5734	.00152905	694	481636	26.3439	.00144092
655	429025	25.5930	.00152672	695	483025	26.3629	.00143885
656	430336	25.6125	.00152439	696	484416	26.3818	.00143678
657	431649	25.6320	.00152207	697	485809	26.4008	.00143472
658	432964	25.6515	.00151976	698	487204	26.4197	.00143266
659	434281	25.6710	.00151745	699	488601	26.4386	.00143062
660	435600	25.6905	.00151515	700	490000	26.4575	.00142857
661	436921	25.7099	.00151286	701	491401	26.4764	.00142653
662	438244	25.7294	.00151057	702	492804	26.4953	.00142450
663	439569	25.7488	.00150830	703	494209	26.5141	.00142248
664	440896	25.7682	.00150602	704	495616	26.5330	.00142045
665	442225	25.7876	.00150376	705	497025	26.5518	.00141844
666	443556	25.8070	.00150150	706	498436	26.5707	.00141643
667	444889	25.8263	.00149925	707	499849	26.5895	.00141443
668	446224	25.8457	.00149701	708	501264	26.6083	.00141243
669	447561	25.8650	.00149477	709	502681	26.6271	.00141044
670	448900	25.8844	.00149254	710	504100	26.6458	.00140845
671	450241	25.9037	.00149031	711	505521	26.6646	.00140647
672	451584	25.9230	.00148810	712	506944	26.6833	.00140449
673	452929	25.9422	.00148588	713	508369	26.7021	.00140252
674	454276	25.9615	.00148368	714	509796	26.7208	.00140056
675	455625	25.9808	.00148148	715	511225	26.7395	.00139860
676	456976	26.0000	.00147929	716	512656	26.7582	.00139665
677	458329	26.0192	.00147710	717	514089	26.7769	.00139470
678	459684	26.0384	.00147493	718	515524	26.7955	.00139276
679	461041	26.0576	.00147275	719	516961	26.8142	.00139082
680	462400	26.0768	.00147059	720	518400	26.8328	.00138889

Table A — continued

N	N²	$\sqrt{N}$	1/N	N	N²	$\sqrt{N}$	1/N
721	519841	26.8514	.00138696	761	579121	27.5862	.00131406
722	521284	26.8701	.00138504	762	580644	27.6043	.00131234
723	522729	26.8887	.00138313	763	582169	27.6225	.00131062
724	524176	26.9072	.00138122	764	583696	27.6405	.00130890
725	525625	26.9258	.00137931	765	585225	27.6586	.00130719
726	527076	26.9444	.00137741	766	586756	27.6767	.00130548
727	528529	26.9629	.00137552	767	588289	27.6948	.00130378
728	529984	26.9815	.00137363	768	589824	27.7128	.00130208
729	531441	27.0000	.00137174	769	591361	27.7308	.00130039
730	532900	27.0185	.00136986	770	592900	27.7489	.00129870
731	534361	27.0370	.00136799	771	594441	27.7669	.00129702
732	535824	27.0555	.00136612	772	595984	27.7849	.00129534
733	537289	27.0740	.00136426	773	597529	27.8029	.00129366
734	538756	27.0924	.00136240	774	599076	27.8209	.00129199
735	540225	27.1109	.00136054	775	600625	27.8388	.00129032
736	541696	27.1293	.00135870	776	602176	27.8568	.00128866
737	543169	27.1477	.00135685	777	603729	27.8747	.00128700
738	544644	27.1662	.00135501	778	605284	27.8927	.00128535
739	546121	27.1846	.00135318	779	606841	27.9106	.00128370
740	547600	27.2029	.00135135	780	608400	27.9285	.00128205
741	549081	27.2213	.00134953	781	609961	27.9464	.00128041
742	550564	27.2397	.00134771	782	611524	27.9643	.00127877
743	552049	27.2580	.00134590	783	613089	27.9821	.00127714
744	553536	27.2764	.00134409	784	614656	28.0000	.00127551
745	555025	27.2947	.00134228	785	616225	28.0179	.00127389
746	556516	27.3130	.00134048	786	617796	28.0357	.00127226
747	558009	27.3313	.00133869	787	619369	28.0535	.00127065
748	559504	27.3496	.00133690	788	620944	28.0713	.00126904
749	561001	27.3679	.00133511	789	622521	28.0891	.00126743
750	562500	27.3861	.00133333	790	624100	28.1069	.00126582
751	564001	27.4044	.00133156	791	625681	28.1247	.00126422
752	565504	27.4226	.00132979	792	627264	28.1425	.00126263
753	567009	27.4408	.00132802	793	628849	28.1603	.00126103
754	568516	27.4591	.00132626	794	630436	28.1780	.00125945
755	570025	27.4773	.00132450	795	632025	28.1957	.00125786
756	571536	27.4955	.00132275	796	633616	28.2135	.00125628
757	573049	27.5136	.00132100	797	635209	28.2312	.00125471
758	574564	27.5318	.00131926	798	636804	28.2489	.00125313
759	576081	27.5500	.00131752	799	638401	28.2666	.00125156
760	577600	27.5681	.00131579	800	640000	28.2843	.00125000

Table A — continued

N	N²	√N̄	1/N	N	N²	√N̄	1/N
801	641601	28.3019	.00124844	841	707281	29.0000	.00118906
802	643204	28.3196	.00124688	842	708964	29.0172	.00118765
803	644809	28.3373	.00124533	843	710649	29.0345	.00118624
804	646416	28.3549	.00124378	844	712336	29.0517	.00118483
805	648025	28.3725	.00124224	845	714025	29.0689	.00118343
806	649636	28.3901	.00124069	846	715716	29.0861	.00118203
807	651249	28.4077	.00123916	847	717409	29.1033	.00118064
808	652864	28.4253	.00123762	848	719104	29.1204	.00117925
809	654481	28.4429	.00123609	849	720801	29.1376	.00117786
810	656100	28.4605	.00123457	850	722500	29.1548	.00117647
811	657721	28.4781	.00123305	851	724201	29.1719	.00117509
812	659344	28.4956	.00123153	852	725904	29.1890	.00117371
813	660969	28.5132	.00123001	853	727609	29.2062	.00117233
814	662596	28.5307	.00122850	854	729316	29.2233	.00117096
815	664225	28.5482	.00122699	855	731025	29.2404	.00116959
816	665856	28.5657	.00122549	856	732736	29.2575	.00116822
817	667489	28.5832	.00122399	857	734449	29.2746	.00116686
818	669124	28.6007	.00122249	858	736164	29.2916	.00116550
819	670761	28.6182	.00122100	859	737881	29.3087	.00116414
820	672400	28.6356	.00121951	860	739600	29.3258	.00116279
821	674041	28.6531	.00121803	861	741321	29.3428	.00116144
822	675684	28.6705	.00121655	862	743044	29.3598	.00116009
823	677329	28.6880	.00121507	863	744769	29.3769	.00115875
824	678976	28.7054	.00121359	864	746496	29.3939	.00115741
825	680625	28.7228	.00121212	865	748225	29.4109	.00115607
826	682276	28.7402	.00121065	866	749956	29.4279	.00115473
827	683929	28.7576	.00120919	867	751689	29.4449	.00115340
828	685584	28.7750	.00120773	868	753424	29.4618	.00115207
829	687241	28.7924	.00120627	869	755161	29.4788	.00115075
830	688900	28.8097	.00120482	870	756900	29.4958	.00114943
831	690561	28.8271	.00120337	871	758641	29.5127	.00114811
832	692224	28.8444	.00120192	872	760384	29.5296	.00114679
833	693889	28.8617	.00120048	873	762129	29.5466	.00114548
834	695556	28.8791	.00119904	874	763876	29.5635	.00114416
835	697225	28.8964	.00119760	875	765625	29.5804	.00114286
836	698896	28.9137	.00119617	876	767376	29.5973	.00114155
837	700569	28.9310	.00119474	877	769129	29.6142	.00114025
838	702244	28.9482	.00119332	878	770884	29.6311	.00113895
839	703921	28.9655	.00119190	879	772641	29.6479	.00113766
840	705600	28.9828	.00119048	880	774400	29.6648	.00113636

Table A — continued

N	N²	√N	1/N	N	N²	√N	1/N
881	776161	29.6816	.00113507	921	848241	30.3480	.00108578
882	777924	29.6985	.00113379	922	850084	30.3645	.00108460
883	779689	29.7153	.00113250	923	851929	30.3809	.00108342
884	781456	29.7321	.00113122	924	853776	30.3974	.00108225
885	783225	29.7489	.00112994	925	855625	30.4138	.00108108
886	784996	29.7658	.00112867	926	857476	30.4302	.00107991
887	786769	29.7825	.00112740	927	859329	30.4467	.00107875
888	788544	29.7993	.00112613	928	861184	30.4631	.00107759
889	790321	29.8161	.00112486	929	863041	30.4795	.00107643
890	792100	29.8329	.00112360	930	864900	30.4959	.00107527
891	793881	29.8496	.00112233	931	866761	30.5123	.00107411
892	795664	29.8664	.00112108	932	868624	30.5287	.00107296
893	797449	29.8831	.00111982	933	870489	30.5450	.00107181
894	799236	29.8998	.00111857	934	872356	30.5614	.00107066
895	801025	29.9166	.00111732	935	874225	30.5778	.00106952
896	802816	29.9333	.00111607	936	876096	30.5941	.00106838
897	804609	29.9500	.00111483	937	877969	30.6105	.00106724
898	806404	29.9666	.00111359	938	879844	30.6268	.00106610
899	808201	29.9833	.00111235	939	881721	30.6431	.00106496
900	810000	30.0000	.00111111	940	883600	30.6594	.00106383
901	811801	30.0167	.00110988	941	885481	30.6757	.00106270
902	813604	30.0333	.00110865	942	887364	30.6920	.00106157
903	815409	30.0500	.00110742	943	889249	30.7083	.00106045
904	817216	30.0666	.00110619	944	891136	30.7246	.00105932
905	819025	30.0832	.00110497	945	893025	30.7409	.00105820
906	820836	30.0998	.00110375	946	894916	30.7571	.00105708
907	822649	30.1164	.00110254	947	896809	30.7734	.00105597
908	824464	30.1330	.00110132	948	898704	30.7896	.00105485
909	826281	30.1496	.00110011	949	900601	30.8058	.00105374
910	828100	30.1662	.00109890	950	902500	30.8221	.00105263
911	829921	30.1828	.00109769	951	904401	30.8383	.00105152
912	831744	30.1993	.00109649	952	906304	30.8545	.00105042
913	833569	30.2159	.00109529	953	908209	30.8707	.00104932
914	835396	30.2324	.00109409	954	910116	30.8869	.00104822
915	837225	30.2490	.00109290	955	912025	30.9031	.00104712
916	839056	30.2655	.00109170	956	913936	30.9192	.00104603
917	840889	30.2820	.00109051	957	915849	30.9354	.00104493
918	842724	30.2985	.00108932	958	917764	30.9516	.00104384
919	844561	30.3150	.00108814	959	919681	30.9677	.00104275
920	846400	30.3315	.00108696	960	921600	30.9839	.00104167

Table A — continued

N	N²	$\sqrt{N}$	1/N	N	N²	$\sqrt{N}$	1/N
961	923521	31.0000	.00104058	981	962361	31.3209	.00101937
962	925444	31.0161	.00103950	982	964324	31.3369	.00101833
963	927369	31.0322	.00103842	983	966289	31.3528	.00101729
964	929296	31.0483	.00103734	984	968256	31.3688	.00101626
965	931225	31.0644	.00103627	985	970225	31.3847	.00101523
966	933156	31.0805	.00103520	986	972196	31.4006	.00101420
967	935089	31.0966	.00103413	987	974169	31.4166	.00101317
968	937024	31.1127	.00103306	988	976144	31.4325	.00101215
969	938961	31.1288	.00103199	989	978121	31.4484	.00101112
970	940900	31.1448	.00103093	990	980100	31.4643	.00101010
971	942841	31.1609	.00102987	991	982081	31.4802	.00100908
972	944784	31.1769	.00102881	992	984064	31.4960	.00100806
973	946729	31.1929	.00102775	993	986049	31.5119	.00100705
974	948676	31.2090	.00102669	994	988036	31.5278	.00100604
975	950625	31.2250	.00102564	995	990025	31.5436	.00100503
976	952576	31.2410	.00102459	996	992016	31.5595	.00100402
977	954529	31.2570	.00102354	997	994009	31.5753	.00100301
978	956484	31.2730	.00102249	998	996004	31.5911	.00100200
979	958441	31.2890	.00102145	999	998001	31.6070	.00100100
980	960400	31.3050	.00102041	1000	1000000	31.6228	.00100000

Table B.*   Four-Place Logarithms
Four-place mantissas of common logarithms

N	0	1	2	3	4	5	6	7	8	9	Proportional Parts 1 2 3 4 5 6 7 8 9
10	0000	0043	0086	0128	0170	0212	0253	0294	0334	0374	†4 8 12 17 21 25 29 33 37
11	0414	0453	0492	0531	0569	0607	0645	0682	0719	0755	4 8 11 15 19 23 26 30 34
12	0792	0828	0864	0899	0934	0969	1004	1038	1072	1106	3 7 10 14 17 21 24 28 31
13	1139	1173	1206	1239	1271	1303	1335	1367	1399	1430	3 6 10 13 16 19 23 26 29
14	1461	1492	1523	1553	1584	1614	1644	1673	1703	1732	3 6 9 12 15 18 21 24 27
15	1761	1790	1818	1847	1875	1903	1931	1959	1987	2014	†3 6 8 11 14 17 20 22 25
16	2041	2068	2095	2122	2148	2175	2201	2227	2253	2279	3 5 8 11 13 16 18 21 24
17	2304	2330	2355	2380	2405	2430	2455	2480	2504	2529	2 5 7 10 12 15 17 20 22
18	2553	2577	2601	2625	2648	2672	2695	2718	2742	2765	2 5 7 9 12 14 16 19 21
19	2788	2810	2833	2856	2878	2900	2923	2945	2967	2989	2 4 7 9 11 13 16 18 20
20	3010	3032	3054	3075	3096	3118	3139	3160	3181	3201	2 4 6 8 11 13 15 17 19
21	3222	3243	3263	3284	3304	3324	3345	3365	3385	3404	2 4 6 8 10 12 14 16 18
22	3424	3444	3464	3483	3502	3522	3541	3560	3579	3598	2 4 6 8 10 12 14 15 17
23	3617	3636	3655	3674	3692	3711	3729	3747	3766	3784	2 4 6 7 9 11 13 15 17
24	3802	3820	3838	3856	3874	3892	3909	3927	3945	3962	2 4 5 7 9 11 12 14 16
25	3979	3997	4014	4031	4048	4065	4082	4099	4116	4133	2 3 5 7 9 10 12 14 15
26	4150	4166	4183	4200	4216	4232	4249	4265	4281	4298	2 3 5 7 8 10 11 13 15
27	4314	4330	4346	4362	4378	4393	4409	4425	4440	4456	2 3 5 6 8 9 11 13 14
28	4472	4487	4502	4518	4533	4548	4564	4579	4594	4609	2 3 5 6 8 9 11 12 14
29	4624	4639	4654	4669	4683	4698	4713	4728	4742	4757	1 3 4 6 7 9 10 12 13
30	4771	4786	4800	4814	4829	4843	4857	4871	4886	4900	1 3 4 6 7 9 10 11 13
31	4914	4928	4942	4955	4969	4983	4997	5011	5024	5038	1 3 4 6 7 8 10 11 12
32	5051	5065	5079	5092	5105	5119	5132	5145	5159	5172	1 3 4 5 7 8 9 11 12
33	5185	5198	5211	5224	5237	5250	5263	5276	5289	5302	1 3 4 5 6 8 9 10 12
34	5315	5328	5340	5353	5366	5378	5391	5403	5416	5428	1 3 4 5 6 8 9 10 11
35	5441	5453	5465	5478	5490	5502	5514	5527	5539	5551	1 2 4 5 6 7 9 10 11
36	5563	5575	5587	5599	5611	5623	5635	5647	5658	5670	1 2 4 5 6 7 8 10 11
37	5682	5694	5705	5717	5729	5740	5752	5763	5775	5786	1 2 3 5 6 7 8 9 10
38	5798	5809	5821	5832	5843	5855	5866	5877	5888	5899	1 2 3 5 6 7 8 9 10
39	5911	5922	5933	5944	5955	5966	5977	5988	5999	6010	1 2 3 4 5 7 8 9 10
40	6021	6031	6042	6053	6064	6075	6085	6096	6107	6117	1 2 3 4 5 6 8 9 10
41	6128	6138	6149	6160	6170	6180	6191	6201	6212	6222	1 2 3 4 5 6 7 8 9
42	6232	6243	6253	6263	6274	6284	6294	6304	6314	6325	1 2 3 4 5 6 7 8 9
43	6335	6345	6355	6365	6375	6385	6395	6405	6415	6425	1 2 3 4 5 6 7 8 9
44	6435	6444	6454	6464	6474	6484	6493	6503	6513	6522	1 2 3 4 5 6 7 8 9
45	6532	6542	6551	6561	6571	6580	6590	6599	6609	6618	1 2 3 4 5 6 7 8 9
46	6628	6637	6646	6656	6665	6675	6684	6693	6702	6712	1 2 3 4 5 6 7 7 8
47	6721	6730	6739	6749	6758	6767	6776	6785	6794	6803	1 2 3 4 5 5 6 7 8
48	6812	6821	6830	6839	6848	6857	6866	6875	6884	6893	1 2 3 4 4 5 6 7 8
49	6902	6911	6920	6928	6937	6946	6955	6964	6972	6981	1 2 3 4 4 5 6 7 8
50	6990	6998	7007	7016	7024	7033	7042	7050	7059	7067	1 2 3 3 4 5 6 7 8
51	7076	7084	7093	7101	7110	7118	7126	7135	7143	7152	1 2 3 3 4 5 6 7 8
52	7160	7168	7177	7185	7193	7202	7210	7218	7226	7235	1 2 2 3 4 5 6 7 7
53	7243	7251	7259	7267	7275	7284	7292	7300	7308	7316	1 2 2 3 4 5 6 6 7
54	7324	7332	7340	7348	7356	7364	7372	7380	7388	7396	1 2 2 3 4 5 6 6 7
N	0	1	2	3	4	5	6	7	8	9	1 2 3 4 5 6 7 8 9

† Interpolation in this section of the table is inaccurate.

*Reprinted by permission of the publisher from R. C. Weast, ed., *Handbook of Chemistry and Physics.* 50th ed., pp. A7–A10. Copyright 1969. The Chemical Rubber Company.

Table B. Four-Place Logarithms – continued

N	0	1	2	3	4	5	6	7	8	9	1	2	3	4	5	6	7	8	9
														Proportional Parts					
55	7404	7412	7419	7427	7435	7443	7451	7459	7466	7474	1	2	2	3	4	5	5	6	7
56	7482	7490	7497	7505	7513	7520	7528	7536	7543	7551	1	2	2	3	4	5	5	6	7
57	7559	7566	7574	7582	7589	7597	7604	7612	7619	7627	1	2	2	3	4	5	5	6	7
58	7634	7642	7649	7657	7664	7672	7679	7686	7694	7701	1	1	2	3	4	4	5	6	7
59	7709	7716	7723	7731	7738	7745	7752	7760	7767	7774	1	1	2	3	4	4	5	6	7
60	7782	7789	7796	7803	7810	7818	7825	7832	7839	7846	1	1	2	3	4	4	5	6	6
61	7853	7860	7868	7875	7882	7889	7896	7903	7910	7917	1	1	2	3	4	4	5	6	6
62	7924	7931	7938	7945	7952	7959	7966	7973	7980	7987	1	1	2	3	3	4	5	6	6
63	7993	8000	8007	8014	8021	8028	8035	8041	8048	8055	1	1	2	3	3	4	5	5	6
64	8062	8069	8075	8082	8089	8096	8102	8109	8116	8122	1	1	2	3	3	4	5	5	6
65	8129	8136	8142	8149	8156	8162	8169	8176	8182	8189	1	1	2	3	3	4	5	5	6
66	8195	8202	8209	8215	8222	8228	8235	8241	8248	8254	1	1	2	3	3	4	5	5	6
67	8261	8267	8274	8280	8287	8293	8299	8306	8312	8319	1	1	2	3	3	4	5	5	6
68	8325	8331	8338	8344	8351	8357	8363	8370	8376	8382	1	1	2	3	3	4	4	5	6
69	8388	8395	8401	8407	8414	8420	8426	8432	8439	8445	1	1	2	2	3	4	4	5	6
70	8451	8457	8463	8470	8476	8482	8488	8494	8500	8506	1	1	2	2	3	4	4	5	6
71	8513	8519	8525	8531	8537	8543	8549	8555	8561	8567	1	1	2	2	3	4	4	5	5
72	8573	8579	8585	8591	8597	8603	8609	8615	8621	8627	1	1	2	2	3	4	4	5	5
73	8633	8639	8645	8651	8657	8663	8669	8675	8681	8686	1	1	2	2	3	4	4	5	5
74	8692	8698	8704	8710	8716	8722	8727	8733	8739	8745	1	1	2	2	3	4	4	5	5
75	8751	8756	8762	8768	8774	8779	8785	8791	8797	8802	1	1	2	2	3	3	4	5	5
76	8808	8814	8820	8825	8831	8837	8842	8848	8854	8859	1	1	2	2	3	3	4	5	5
77	8865	8871	8876	8882	8887	8893	8899	8904	8910	8915	1	1	2	2	3	3	4	4	5
78	8921	8927	8932	8938	8943	8949	8954	8960	8965	8971	1	1	2	2	3	3	4	4	5
79	8976	8982	8987	8993	8998	9004	9009	9015	9020	9025	1	1	2	2	3	3	4	4	5
80	9031	9036	9042	9047	9053	9058	9063	9069	9074	9079	1	1	2	2	3	3	4	4	5
81	9085	9090	9096	9101	9106	9112	9117	9122	9128	9133	1	1	2	2	3	3	4	4	5
82	9138	9143	9149	9154	9159	9165	9170	9175	9180	9186	1	1	2	2	3	3	4	4	5
83	9191	9196	9201	9206	9212	9217	9222	9227	9232	9238	1	1	2	2	3	3	4	4	5
84	9243	9248	9253	9258	9263	9269	9274	9279	9284	9289	1	1	2	2	3	3	4	4	5
85	9294	9299	9304	9309	9315	9320	9325	9330	9335	9340	1	1	2	2	3	3	4	4	5
86	9345	9350	9355	9360	9365	9370	9375	9380	9385	9390	1	1	2	2	3	3	4	4	5
87	9395	9400	9405	9410	9415	9420	9425	9430	9435	9440	0	1	1	2	2	3	3	4	4
88	9445	9450	9455	9460	9465	9460	9474	9479	9484	9489	0	1	1	2	2	3	3	4	4
89	9494	9499	9504	9509	9513	9518	9523	9528	9533	9538	0	1	1	2	2	3	3	4	4
90	9542	9547	9552	9557	9562	9566	9571	9576	9581	9586	0	1	1	2	2	3	3	4	4
91	9590	9595	9600	9605	9609	9614	9619	9624	9628	9633	0	1	1	2	2	3	3	4	4
92	9638	9643	9647	9652	9657	9661	9666	9671	9675	9680	0	1	1	2	2	3	3	4	4
93	9685	9689	9694	9699	9703	9708	9713	9717	9722	9727	0	1	1	2	2	3	3	4	4
94	9731	9736	9741	9745	9750	9754	9759	9763	9768	9773	0	1	1	2	2	3	3	4	4
95	9777	9782	9786	9791	9795	9800	9805	9809	9814	9818	0	1	1	2	2	3	3	4	4
96	9823	9827	9832	9836	9841	9845	9850	9854	9859	9863	0	1	1	2	2	3	3	4	4
97	9868	9872	9877	9881	9886	9890	9894	9899	9903	9908	0	1	1	2	2	3	3	4	4
98	9912	9917	9921	9926	9930	9934	9939	9943	9948	9952	0	1	1	2	2	3	3	4	4
99	9956	9961	9965	9969	9974	9978	9983	9987	9991	9996	0	1	1	2	2	3	3	3	4
N	0	1	2	3	4	5	6	7	8	9	1	2	3	4	5	6	7	8	9

Table C.*   Transformation of a Proportion p to Radians (ϕ)
$$[\phi = 2 \arcsin \sqrt{p}]$$

p	ϕ	p	ϕ	p	ϕ	p	ϕ	p	ϕ
.001	.0633	.041	.4078	.36	1.2870	.76	2.1177	.971	2.7993
.002	.0895	.042	.4128	.37	1.3078	.77	2.1412	.972	2.8053
.003	.1096	.043	.4178	.38	1.3284	.78	2.1652	.973	2.8115
.004	.1266	.044	.4227	.39	1.3490	.79	2.1895	.974	2.8177
.005	.1415	.045	.4275	.40	1.3694	.80	2.2143	.975	2.8240
.006	.1551	.046	.4323	.41	1.3898	.81	2.2395	.976	2.8305
.007	.1675	.047	.4371	.42	1.4101	.82	2.2653	.977	2.8371
.008	.1791	.048	.4418	.43	1.4303	.83	2.2916	.978	2.8438
.009	.1900	.049	.4464	.44	1.4505	.84	2.3186	.979	2.8507
.010	.2003	.050	.4510	.45	1.4706	.85	2.3462	.980	2.8578
.011	.2101	.06	.4949	.46	1.4907	.86	2.3746	.981	2.8650
.012	.2195	.07	.5355	.47	1.5108	.87	2.4039	.982	2.8725
.013	.2285	.08	.5735	.48	1.5308	.88	2.4341	.983	2.8801
.014	.2372	.09	.6094	.49	1.5508	.89	2.4655	.984	2.8879
.015	.2456	.10	.6435	.50	1.5708	.90	2.4981	.985	2.8960
.016	.2537	.11	.6761	.51	1.5908	.91	2.5322	.986	2.9044
.017	.2615	.12	.7075	.52	1.6108	.92	2.5681	.987	2.9131
.018	.2691	.13	.7377	.53	1.6308	.93	2.6062	.988	2.9221
.019	.2766	.14	.7670	.54	1.6509	.94	2.6467	.989	2.9315
.020	.2838	.15	.7954	.55	1.6710	.95	2.6906	.990	2.9413
.021	.2909	.16	.8230	.56	1.6911	.951	2.6952	.991	2.9516
.022	.2978	.17	.8500	.57	1.7113	.952	2.6998	.992	2.9625
.023	.3045	.18	.8763	.58	1.7315	.953	2.7045	.993	2.9741
.024	.3111	.19	.9021	.59	1.7518	.954	2.7093	.994	2.9865
.025	.3176	.20	.9273	.60	1.7722	.955	2.7141	.995	3.0001
.026	.3239	.21	.9521	.61	1.7926	.956	2.7189	.996	3.0150
.027	.3301	.22	.9764	.62	1.8132	.957	2.7238	.997	3.0320
.028	.3363	.23	1.0004	.63	1.8338	.958	2.7288	.998	3.0521
.029	.3423	.24	1.0239	.64	1.8546	.959	2.7338	.999	3.0783
.030	.3482	.25	1.0472	.65	1.8755	.960	2.7389		
.031	.3540	.26	1.0701	.66	1.8965	.961	2.7440		
.032	.3597	.27	1.0928	.67	1.9177	.962	2.7492		
.033	.3654	.28	1.1152	.68	1.9391	.963	2.7545		
.034	.3709	.29	1.1374	.69	1.9606	.964	2.7598		
.035	.3764	.30	1.1593	.70	1.9823	.965	2.7652		
.036	.3818	.31	1.1810	.71	2.0042	.966	2.7707		
.037	.3871	.32	1.2025	.72	2.0264	.967	2.7762		
.038	.3924	.33	1.2239	.73	2.0488	.968	2.7819		
.039	.3976	.34	1.2451	.74	2.0715	.969	2.7876		
.040	.4027	.35	1.2661	.75	2.0944	.970	2.7934		

*Reprinted, with a change in notation, by permission of the publisher from B. J. Winer, *Statistical Principles in Experimental Design*, p. 650. Copyright 1962, McGraw-Hill Book Company.

Table D.* Criteria for Testing Extreme Scores

Statistic	Number of scores, k	Critical values	
		$\alpha = 5\%$	$\alpha = 1\%$
$R = \dfrac{X_2 - X_1}{X_k - X_1}$	3	.941	.988
	4	.765	.889
	5	.642	.780
	6	.560	.698
	7	.507	.637
$R = \dfrac{X_2 - X_1}{X_{k-1} - X_1}$	8	.554	.683
	9	.512	.635
	10	.477	.597
$R = \dfrac{X_3 - X_1}{X_{k-1} - X_1}$	11	.576	.679
	12	.546	.642
	13	.521	.615
$R = \dfrac{X_3 - X_1}{X_{k-2} - X_1}$	14	.546	.641
	15	.525	.616
	16	.507	.595
	17	.490	.577
	18	.475	.561
	19	.462	.547
	20	.450	.535
	21	.440	.524
	22	.430	.514
	23	.421	.505
	24	.413	.497
	25	.406	.489
	26	.399	.486
	27	.393	.475
	28	.387	.469
	29	.381	.463
	30	.376	.457

*Reprinted, with changes in notation, by permission of the publisher and author from W. J. Dixon, "Processing Data for Outliers," *Biometrics*, 9, p. 89, 1953.

Table E.   *Table of t. Percentage points of the t-distribution*

df	p = 0.4 / 2p = 0.8	0.25 / 0.5	0.1 / 0.2	0.05 / 0.1	0.025 / 0.05	0.01 / 0.02	0.005 / 0.01	0.0025 / 0.005	0.001 / 0.002	0.0005 / 0.001
1	0.325	1.000	3.078	6.314	12.706	31.821	63.657	127.32	318.31	636.62
2	.289	0.816	1.886	2.920	4.303	6.965	9.925	14.089	22.327	31.598
3	.277	.765	1.638	2.353	3.182	4.541	5.841	7.453	10.214	12.924
4	.271	.741	1.533	2.132	2.776	3.747	4.604	5.598	7.173	8.610
5	0.267	.727	1.476	2.015	2.571	3.365	4.032	4.773	5.893	6.869
6	.265	.718	1.440	1.943	2.447	3.143	3.707	4.317	5.208	5.959
7	.263	.711	1.415	1.895	2.365	2.998	3.499	4.029	4.785	5.408
8	.262	.706	1.397	1.860	2.306	2.896	3.355	3.833	4.501	5.041
9	.261	.703	1.383	1.833	2.262	2.821	3.250	3.690	4.297	4.781
10	0.260	0.700	1.372	1.812	2.228	2.764	3.169	3.581	4.144	4.587
11	.260	.697	1.363	1.796	2.201	2.718	3.106	3.497	4.025	4.437
12	.259	.695	1.356	1.782	2.179	2.681	3.055	3.428	3.930	4.318
13	.259	.694	1.350	1.771	2.160	2.650	3.012	3.372	3.852	4.221
14	.258	.692	1.345	1.761	2.145	2.624	2.977	3.326	3.787	4.140
15	0.258	0.691	1.341	1.753	2.131	2.602	2.947	3.286	3.733	4.073
16	.258	.690	1.337	1.746	2.120	2.583	2.921	3.252	3.686	4.015
17	.257	.689	1.333	1.740	2.110	2.567	2.898	3.222	3.646	3.965
18	.257	.688	1.330	1.734	2.101	2.552	2.878	3.197	3.610	3.922
19	.257	.688	1.328	1.729	2.093	2.539	2.861	3.174	3.579	3.883
20	0.257	0.687	1.325	1.725	2.086	2.528	2.845	3.153	3.552	3.850
21	.257	.686	1.323	1.721	2.080	2.518	2.831	3.135	3.527	3.819
22	.256	.686	1.321	1.717	2.074	2.508	2.819	3.119	3.505	3.792
23	.256	.685	1.319	1.714	2.069	2.500	2.807	3.104	3.485	3.767
24	.256	.685	1.318	1.711	2.064	2.492	2.797	3.091	3.467	3.745
25	0.256	0.684	1.316	1.708	2.060	2.485	2.787	3.078	3.450	3.725
26	.256	.684	1.315	1.706	2.056	2.479	2.779	3.067	3.435	3.707
27	.256	.684	1.314	1.703	2.052	2.473	2.771	3.057	3.421	3.690
28	.256	.683	1.313	1.701	2.048	2.467	2.763	3.047	3.408	3.674
29	.256	.683	1.311	1.699	2.045	2.462	2.756	3.038	3.396	3.659
30	0.256	0.683	1.310	1.697	2.042	2.457	2.750	3.030	3.385	3.646
40	.255	.681	1.303	1.684	2.021	2.423	2.704	2.971	3.307	3.551
60	.254	.679	1.296	1.671	2.000	2.390	2.660	2.915	3.232	3.460
120	.254	.677	1.289	1.658	1.980	2.358	2.617	2.860	3.160	3.373
∞	.253	.674	1.282	1.645	1.960	2.326	2.576	2.807	3.090	3.291

p is the upper-tail area of the distribution for *df* degrees of freedom, appropriate for use in a single-tail test. For a two-tail test, 2p must be used.

*Reprinted, with changes in notation, by permission of the publisher from E. S. Pearson and H. O. Hartley, Biometrika Tables for Statisticians, Volume 1, p. 146. Copyright 1966. Biometrika.

Table F.*   Table of F
Upper .10 points

df_1 \ df_2	1	2	3	4	5	6	7	8	9	10	12	15	20	24	30	40	60	120	∞
1	39·86	49·50	53·59	55·83	57·24	58·20	58·91	59·44	59·86	60·19	60·71	61·22	61·74	62·00	62·26	62·53	62·79	63·06	63·33
2	8·53	9·00	9·16	9·24	9·29	9·33	9·35	9·37	9·38	9·39	9·41	9·42	9·44	9·45	9·46	9·47	9·47	9·48	9·49
3	5·54	5·46	5·39	5·34	5·31	5·28	5·27	5·25	5·24	5·23	5·22	5·20	5·18	5·18	5·17	5·16	5·15	5·14	5·13
4	4·54	4·32	4·19	4·11	4·05	4·01	3·98	3·95	3·94	3·92	3·90	3·87	3·84	3·83	3·82	3·80	3·79	3·78	3·76
5	4·06	3·78	3·62	3·52	3·45	3·40	3·37	3·34	3·32	3·30	3·27	3·24	3·21	3·19	3·17	3·16	3·14	3·12	3·10
6	3·78	3·46	3·29	3·18	3·11	3·05	3·01	2·98	2·96	2·94	2·90	2·87	2·84	2·82	2·80	2·78	2·76	2·74	2·72
7	3·59	3·26	3·07	2·96	2·88	2·83	2·78	2·75	2·72	2·70	2·67	2·63	2·59	2·58	2·56	2·54	2·51	2·49	2·47
8	3·46	3·11	2·92	2·81	2·73	2·67	2·62	2·59	2·56	2·54	2·50	2·46	2·42	2·40	2·38	2·36	2·34	2·32	2·29
9	3·36	3·01	2·81	2·69	2·61	2·55	2·51	2·47	2·44	2·42	2·38	2·34	2·30	2·28	2·25	2·23	2·21	2·18	2·16
10	3·29	2·92	2·73	2·61	2·52	2·46	2·41	2·38	2·35	2·32	2·28	2·24	2·20	2·18	2·16	2·13	2·11	2·08	2·06
11	3·23	2·86	2·66	2·54	2·45	2·39	2·34	2·30	2·27	2·25	2·21	2·17	2·12	2·10	2·08	2·05	2·03	2·00	1·97
12	3·18	2·81	2·61	2·48	2·39	2·33	2·28	2·24	2·21	2·19	2·15	2·10	2·06	2·04	2·01	1·99	1·96	1·93	1·90
13	3·14	2·76	2·56	2·43	2·35	2·28	2·23	2·20	2·16	2·14	2·10	2·05	2·01	1·98	1·96	1·93	1·90	1·88	1·85
14	3·10	2·73	2·52	2·39	2·31	2·24	2·19	2·15	2·12	2·10	2·05	2·01	1·96	1·94	1·91	1·89	1·86	1·83	1·80
15	3·07	2·70	2·49	2·36	2·27	2·21	2·16	2·12	2·09	2·06	2·02	1·97	1·92	1·90	1·87	1·85	1·82	1·79	1·76
16	3·05	2·67	2·46	2·33	2·24	2·18	2·13	2·09	2·06	2·03	1·99	1·94	1·89	1·87	1·84	1·81	1·78	1·75	1·72
17	3·03	2·64	2·44	2·31	2·22	2·15	2·10	2·06	2·03	2·00	1·96	1·91	1·86	1·84	1·81	1·78	1·75	1·72	1·69
18	3·01	2·62	2·42	2·29	2·20	2·13	2·08	2·04	2·00	1·98	1·93	1·89	1·84	1·81	1·78	1·75	1·72	1·69	1·66
19	2·99	2·61	2·40	2·27	2·18	2·11	2·06	2·02	1·98	1·96	1·91	1·86	1·81	1·79	1·76	1·73	1·70	1·67	1·63
20	2·97	2·59	2·38	2·25	2·16	2·09	2·04	2·00	1·96	1·94	1·89	1·84	1·79	1·77	1·74	1·71	1·68	1·64	1·61
21	2·96	2·57	2·36	2·23	2·14	2·08	2·02	1·98	1·95	1·92	1·87	1·83	1·78	1·75	1·72	1·69	1·66	1·62	1·59
22	2·95	2·56	2·35	2·22	2·13	2·06	2·01	1·97	1·93	1·90	1·86	1·81	1·76	1·73	1·70	1·67	1·64	1·60	1·57
23	2·94	2·55	2·34	2·21	2·11	2·05	1·99	1·95	1·92	1·89	1·84	1·80	1·74	1·72	1·69	1·66	1·62	1·59	1·55
24	2·93	2·54	2·33	2·19	2·10	2·04	1·98	1·94	1·91	1·88	1·83	1·78	1·73	1·70	1·67	1·64	1·61	1·57	1·53
25	2·92	2·53	2·32	2·18	2·09	2·02	1·97	1·93	1·89	1·87	1·82	1·77	1·72	1·69	1·66	1·63	1·59	1·56	1·52
26	2·91	2·52	2·31	2·17	2·08	2·01	1·96	1·92	1·88	1·86	1·81	1·76	1·71	1·68	1·65	1·61	1·58	1·54	1·50
27	2·90	2·51	2·30	2·17	2·07	2·00	1·95	1·91	1·87	1·85	1·80	1·75	1·70	1·67	1·64	1·60	1·57	1·53	1·49
28	2·89	2·50	2·29	2·16	2·06	2·00	1·94	1·90	1·87	1·84	1·79	1·74	1·69	1·66	1·63	1·59	1·56	1·52	1·48
29	2·89	2·50	2·28	2·15	2·06	1·99	1·93	1·89	1·86	1·83	1·78	1·73	1·68	1·65	1·62	1·58	1·55	1·51	1·47
30	2·88	2·49	2·28	2·14	2·05	1·98	1·93	1·88	1·85	1·82	1·77	1·72	1·67	1·64	1·61	1·57	1·54	1·50	1·46
40	2·84	2·44	2·23	2·09	2·00	1·93	1·87	1·83	1·79	1·76	1·71	1·66	1·61	1·57	1·54	1·51	1·47	1·42	1·38
60	2·79	2·39	2·18	2·04	1·95	1·87	1·82	1·77	1·74	1·71	1·66	1·60	1·54	1·51	1·48	1·44	1·40	1·35	1·29
120	2·75	2·35	2·13	1·99	1·90	1·82	1·77	1·72	1·68	1·65	1·60	1·55	1·48	1·45	1·41	1·37	1·32	1·26	1·19
∞	2·71	2·30	2·08	1·94	1·85	1·77	1·72	1·67	1·63	1·60	1·55	1·49	1·42	1·38	1·34	1·30	1·24	1·17	1·00

*Reprinted, with changes in notation, by permission of the publisher from E. S. Pearson and H. O. Hartley, *Biometrika Tables for Statisticians*, Volume I, pp. 170–175. Copyright 1966, Biometrika.

Table F. Table of F — continued
Upper .05 points

df_2 \ df_1	1	2	3	4	5	6	7	8	9	10	12	15	20	24	30	40	60	120	∞
1	161·4	199·5	215·7	224·6	230·2	234·0	236·8	238·9	240·5	241·9	243·9	245·9	248·0	249·1	250·1	251·1	252·2	253·3	254·3
2	18·51	19·00	19·16	19·25	19·30	19·33	19·35	19·37	19·38	19·40	19·41	19·43	19·45	19·45	19·46	19·47	19·48	19·49	19·50
3	10·13	9·55	9·28	9·12	9·01	8·94	8·89	8·85	8·81	8·79	8·74	8·70	8·66	8·64	8·62	8·59	8·57	8·55	8·53
4	7·71	6·94	6·59	6·39	6·26	6·16	6·09	6·04	6·00	5·96	5·91	5·86	5·80	5·77	5·75	5·72	5·69	5·66	5·63
5	6·61	5·79	5·41	5·19	5·05	4·95	4·88	4·82	4·77	4·74	4·68	4·62	4·56	4·53	4·50	4·46	4·43	4·40	4·36
6	5·99	5·14	4·76	4·53	4·39	4·28	4·21	4·15	4·10	4·06	4·00	3·94	3·87	3·84	3·81	3·77	3·74	3·70	3·67
7	5·59	4·74	4·35	4·12	3·97	3·87	3·79	3·73	3·68	3·64	3·57	3·51	3·44	3·41	3·38	3·34	3·30	3·27	3·23
8	5·32	4·46	4·07	3·84	3·69	3·58	3·50	3·44	3·39	3·35	3·28	3·22	3·15	3·12	3·08	3·04	3·01	2·97	2·93
9	5·12	4·26	3·86	3·63	3·48	3·37	3·29	3·23	3·18	3·14	3·07	3·01	2·94	2·90	2·86	2·83	2·79	2·75	2·71
10	4·96	4·10	3·71	3·48	3·33	3·22	3·14	3·07	3·02	2·98	2·91	2·85	2·77	2·74	2·70	2·66	2·62	2·58	2·54
11	4·84	3·98	3·59	3·36	3·20	3·09	3·01	2·95	2·90	2·85	2·79	2·72	2·65	2·61	2·57	2·53	2·49	2·45	2·40
12	4·75	3·89	3·49	3·26	3·11	3·00	2·91	2·85	2·80	2·75	2·69	2·62	2·54	2·51	2·47	2·43	2·38	2·34	2·30
13	4·67	3·81	3·41	3·18	3·03	2·92	2·83	2·77	2·71	2·67	2·60	2·53	2·46	2·42	2·38	2·34	2·30	2·25	2·21
14	4·60	3·74	3·34	3·11	2·96	2·85	2·76	2·70	2·65	2·60	2·53	2·46	2·39	2·35	2·31	2·27	2·22	2·18	2·13
15	4·54	3·68	3·29	3·06	2·90	2·79	2·71	2·64	2·59	2·54	2·48	2·40	2·33	2·29	2·25	2·20	2·16	2·11	2·07
16	4·49	3·63	3·24	3·01	2·85	2·74	2·66	2·59	2·54	2·49	2·42	2·35	2·28	2·24	2·19	2·15	2·11	2·06	2·01
17	4·45	3·59	3·20	2·96	2·81	2·70	2·61	2·55	2·49	2·45	2·38	2·31	2·23	2·19	2·15	2·10	2·06	2·01	1·96
18	4·41	3·55	3·16	2·93	2·77	2·66	2·58	2·51	2·46	2·41	2·34	2·27	2·19	2·15	2·11	2·06	2·02	1·97	1·92
19	4·38	3·52	3·13	2·90	2·74	2·63	2·54	2·48	2·42	2·38	2·31	2·23	2·16	2·11	2·07	2·03	1·98	1·93	1·88
20	4·35	3·49	3·10	2·87	2·71	2·60	2·51	2·45	2·39	2·35	2·28	2·20	2·12	2·08	2·04	1·99	1·95	1·90	1·84
21	4·32	3·47	3·07	2·84	2·68	2·57	2·49	2·42	2·37	2·32	2·25	2·18	2·10	2·05	2·01	1·96	1·92	1·87	1·81
22	4·30	3·44	3·05	2·82	2·66	2·55	2·46	2·40	2·34	2·30	2·23	2·15	2·07	2·03	1·98	1·94	1·89	1·84	1·78
23	4·28	3·42	3·03	2·80	2·64	2·53	2·44	2·37	2·32	2·27	2·20	2·13	2·05	2·01	1·96	1·91	1·86	1·81	1·76
24	4·26	3·40	3·01	2·78	2·62	2·51	2·42	2·36	2·30	2·25	2·18	2·11	2·03	1·98	1·94	1·89	1·84	1·79	1·73
25	4·24	3·39	2·99	2·76	2·60	2·49	2·40	2·34	2·28	2·24	2·16	2·09	2·01	1·96	1·92	1·87	1·82	1·77	1·71
26	4·23	3·37	2·98	2·74	2·59	2·47	2·39	2·32	2·27	2·22	2·15	2·07	1·99	1·95	1·90	1·85	1·80	1·75	1·69
27	4·21	3·35	2·96	2·73	2·57	2·46	2·37	2·31	2·25	2·20	2·13	2·06	1·97	1·93	1·88	1·84	1·79	1·73	1·67
28	4·20	3·34	2·95	2·71	2·56	2·45	2·36	2·29	2·24	2·19	2·12	2·04	1·96	1·91	1·87	1·82	1·77	1·71	1·65
29	4·18	3·33	2·93	2·70	2·55	2·43	2·35	2·28	2·22	2·18	2·10	2·03	1·94	1·90	1·85	1·81	1·75	1·70	1·64
30	4·17	3·32	2·92	2·69	2·53	2·42	2·33	2·27	2·21	2·16	2·09	2·01	1·93	1·89	1·84	1·79	1·74	1·68	1·62
40	4·08	3·23	2·84	2·61	2·45	2·34	2·25	2·18	2·12	2·08	2·00	1·92	1·84	1·79	1·74	1·69	1·64	1·58	1·51
60	4·00	3·15	2·76	2·53	2·37	2·25	2·17	2·10	2·04	1·99	1·92	1·84	1·75	1·70	1·65	1·59	1·53	1·47	1·39
120	3·92	3·07	2·68	2·45	2·29	2·17	2·09	2·02	1·96	1·91	1·83	1·75	1·66	1·61	1·55	1·50	1·43	1·35	1·25
∞	3·84	3·00	2·60	2·37	2·21	2·10	2·01	1·94	1·88	1·83	1·75	1·67	1·57	1·52	1·46	1·39	1·32	1·22	1·00

Table F. Table of F — continued
Upper .025 points

df_1 / df_2	1	2	3	4	5	6	7	8	9	10	12	15	20	24	30	40	60	120	∞
1	647·8	799·5	864·2	899·6	921·8	937·1	948·2	956·7	963·3	968·6	976·7	984·9	993·1	997·2	1001	1006	1010	1014	1018
2	38·51	39·00	39·17	39·25	39·30	39·33	39·36	39·37	39·39	39·40	39·41	39·43	39·45	39·46	39·46	39·47	39·48	39·49	39·50
3	17·44	16·04	15·44	15·10	14·88	14·73	14·62	14·54	14·47	14·42	14·34	14·25	14·17	14·12	14·08	14·04	13·99	13·95	13·90
4	12·22	10·65	9·98	9·60	9·36	9·20	9·07	8·98	8·90	8·84	8·75	8·66	8·56	8·51	8·46	8·41	8·36	8·31	8·26
5	10·01	8·43	7·76	7·39	7·15	6·98	6·85	6·76	6·68	6·62	6·52	6·43	6·33	6·28	6·23	6·18	6·12	6·07	6·02
6	8·81	7·26	6·60	6·23	5·99	5·82	5·70	5·60	5·52	5·46	5·37	5·27	5·17	5·12	5·07	5·01	4·96	4·90	4·85
7	8·07	6·54	5·89	5·52	5·29	5·12	4·99	4·90	4·82	4·76	4·67	4·57	4·47	4·42	4·36	4·31	4·25	4·20	4·14
8	7·57	6·06	5·42	5·05	4·82	4·65	4·53	4·43	4·36	4·30	4·20	4·10	4·00	3·95	3·89	3·84	3·78	3·73	3·67
9	7·21	5·71	5·08	4·72	4·48	4·32	4·20	4·10	4·03	3·96	3·87	3·77	3·67	3·61	3·56	3·51	3·45	3·39	3·33
10	6·94	5·46	4·83	4·47	4·24	4·07	3·95	3·85	3·78	3·72	3·62	3·52	3·42	3·37	3·31	3·26	3·20	3·14	3·08
11	6·72	5·26	4·63	4·28	4·04	3·88	3·76	3·66	3·59	3·53	3·43	3·33	3·23	3·17	3·12	3·06	3·00	2·94	2·88
12	6·55	5·10	4·47	4·12	3·89	3·73	3·61	3·51	3·44	3·37	3·28	3·18	3·07	3·02	2·96	2·91	2·85	2·79	2·72
13	6·41	4·97	4·35	4·00	3·77	3·60	3·48	3·39	3·31	3·25	3·15	3·05	2·95	2·89	2·84	2·78	2·72	2·66	2·60
14	6·30	4·86	4·24	3·89	3·66	3·50	3·38	3·29	3·21	3·15	3·05	2·95	2·84	2·79	2·73	2·67	2·61	2·55	2·49
15	6·20	4·77	4·15	3·80	3·58	3·41	3·29	3·20	3·12	3·06	2·96	2·86	2·76	2·70	2·64	2·59	2·52	2·46	2·40
16	6·12	4·69	4·08	3·73	3·50	3·34	3·22	3·12	3·05	2·99	2·89	2·79	2·68	2·63	2·57	2·51	2·45	2·38	2·32
17	6·04	4·62	4·01	3·66	3·44	3·28	3·16	3·06	2·98	2·92	2·82	2·72	2·62	2·56	2·50	2·44	2·38	2·32	2·25
18	5·98	4·56	3·95	3·61	3·38	3·22	3·10	3·01	2·93	2·87	2·77	2·67	2·56	2·50	2·44	2·38	2·32	2·26	2·19
19	5·92	4·51	3·90	3·56	3·33	3·17	3·05	2·96	2·88	2·82	2·72	2·62	2·51	2·45	2·39	2·33	2·27	2·20	2·13
20	5·87	4·46	3·86	3·51	3·29	3·13	3·01	2·91	2·84	2·77	2·68	2·57	2·46	2·41	2·35	2·29	2·22	2·16	2·09
21	5·83	4·42	3·82	3·48	3·25	3·09	2·97	2·87	2·80	2·73	2·64	2·53	2·42	2·37	2·31	2·25	2·18	2·11	2·04
22	5·79	4·38	3·78	3·44	3·22	3·05	2·93	2·84	2·76	2·70	2·60	2·50	2·39	2·33	2·27	2·21	2·14	2·08	2·00
23	5·75	4·35	3·75	3·41	3·18	3·02	2·90	2·81	2·73	2·67	2·57	2·47	2·36	2·30	2·24	2·18	2·11	2·04	1·97
24	5·72	4·32	3·72	3·38	3·15	2·99	2·87	2·78	2·70	2·64	2·54	2·44	2·33	2·27	2·21	2·15	2·08	2·01	1·94
25	5·69	4·29	3·69	3·35	3·13	2·97	2·85	2·75	2·68	2·61	2·51	2·41	2·30	2·24	2·18	2·12	2·05	1·98	1·91
26	5·66	4·27	3·67	3·33	3·10	2·94	2·82	2·73	2·65	2·59	2·49	2·39	2·28	2·22	2·16	2·09	2·03	1·95	1·88
27	5·63	4·24	3·65	3·31	3·08	2·92	2·80	2·71	2·63	2·57	2·47	2·36	2·25	2·19	2·13	2·07	2·00	1·93	1·85
28	5·61	4·22	3·63	3·29	3·06	2·90	2·78	2·69	2·61	2·55	2·45	2·34	2·23	2·17	2·11	2·05	1·98	1·91	1·83
29	5·59	4·20	3·61	3·27	3·04	2·88	2·76	2·67	2·59	2·53	2·43	2·32	2·21	2·15	2·09	2·03	1·96	1·89	1·81
30	5·57	4·18	3·59	3·25	3·03	2·87	2·75	2·65	2·57	2·51	2·41	2·31	2·20	2·14	2·07	2·01	1·94	1·87	1·79
40	5·42	4·05	3·46	3·13	2·90	2·74	2·62	2·53	2·45	2·39	2·29	2·18	2·07	2·01	1·94	1·88	1·80	1·72	1·64
60	5·29	3·93	3·34	3·01	2·79	2·63	2·51	2·41	2·33	2·27	2·17	2·06	1·94	1·88	1·82	1·74	1·67	1·58	1·48
120	5·15	3·80	3·23	2·89	2·67	2·52	2·39	2·30	2·22	2·16	2·05	1·94	1·82	1·76	1·69	1·61	1·53	1·43	1·31
∞	5·02	3·69	3·12	2·79	2·57	2·41	2·29	2·19	2·11	2·05	1·94	1·83	1·71	1·64	1·57	1·48	1·39	1·27	1·00

Table F. Table of F — continued
Upper .01 points

df_2 \ df_1	1	2	3	4	5	6	7	8	9	10	12	15	20	24	30	40	60	120	∞
1	4052	4999.5	5403	5625	5764	5859	5928	5981	6022	6056	6106	6157	6209	6235	6261	6287	6313	6339	6366
2	98.50	99.00	99.17	99.25	99.30	99.33	99.36	99.37	99.39	99.40	99.42	99.43	99.45	99.46	99.47	99.47	99.48	99.49	99.50
3	34.12	30.82	29.46	28.71	28.24	27.91	27.67	27.49	27.35	27.23	27.05	26.87	26.69	26.60	26.50	26.41	26.32	26.22	26.13
4	21.20	18.00	16.69	15.98	15.52	15.21	14.98	14.80	14.66	14.55	14.37	14.20	14.02	13.93	13.84	13.75	13.65	13.56	13.46
5	16.26	13.27	12.06	11.39	10.97	10.67	10.46	10.29	10.16	10.05	9.89	9.72	9.55	9.47	9.38	9.29	9.20	9.11	9.02
6	13.75	10.92	9.78	9.15	8.75	8.47	8.26	8.10	7.98	7.87	7.72	7.56	7.40	7.31	7.23	7.14	7.06	6.97	6.88
7	12.25	9.55	8.45	7.85	7.46	7.19	6.99	6.84	6.72	6.62	6.47	6.31	6.16	6.07	5.99	5.91	5.82	5.74	5.65
8	11.26	8.65	7.59	7.01	6.63	6.37	6.18	6.03	5.91	5.81	5.67	5.52	5.36	5.28	5.20	5.12	5.03	4.95	4.86
9	10.56	8.02	6.99	6.42	6.06	5.80	5.61	5.47	5.35	5.26	5.11	4.96	4.81	4.73	4.65	4.57	4.48	4.40	4.31
10	10.04	7.56	6.55	5.99	5.64	5.39	5.20	5.06	4.94	4.85	4.71	4.56	4.41	4.33	4.25	4.17	4.08	4.00	3.91
11	9.65	7.21	6.22	5.67	5.32	5.07	4.89	4.74	4.63	4.54	4.40	4.25	4.10	4.02	3.94	3.86	3.78	3.69	3.60
12	9.33	6.93	5.95	5.41	5.06	4.82	4.64	4.50	4.39	4.30	4.16	4.01	3.86	3.78	3.70	3.62	3.54	3.45	3.36
13	9.07	6.70	5.74	5.21	4.86	4.62	4.44	4.30	4.19	4.10	3.96	3.82	3.66	3.59	3.51	3.43	3.34	3.25	3.17
14	8.86	6.51	5.56	5.04	4.69	4.46	4.28	4.14	4.03	3.94	3.80	3.66	3.51	3.43	3.35	3.27	3.18	3.09	3.00
15	8.68	6.36	5.42	4.89	4.56	4.32	4.14	4.00	3.89	3.80	3.67	3.52	3.37	3.29	3.21	3.13	3.05	2.96	2.87
16	8.53	6.23	5.29	4.77	4.44	4.20	4.03	3.89	3.78	3.69	3.55	3.41	3.26	3.18	3.10	3.02	2.93	2.84	2.75
17	8.40	6.11	5.18	4.67	4.34	4.10	3.93	3.79	3.68	3.59	3.46	3.31	3.16	3.08	3.00	2.92	2.83	2.75	2.65
18	8.29	6.01	5.09	4.58	4.25	4.01	3.84	3.71	3.60	3.51	3.37	3.23	3.08	3.00	2.92	2.84	2.75	2.66	2.57
19	8.18	5.93	5.01	4.50	4.17	3.94	3.77	3.63	3.52	3.43	3.30	3.15	3.00	2.92	2.84	2.76	2.67	2.58	2.49
20	8.10	5.85	4.94	4.43	4.10	3.87	3.70	3.56	3.46	3.37	3.23	3.09	2.94	2.86	2.78	2.69	2.61	2.52	2.42
21	8.02	5.78	4.87	4.37	4.04	3.81	3.64	3.51	3.40	3.31	3.17	3.03	2.88	2.80	2.72	2.64	2.55	2.46	2.36
22	7.95	5.72	4.82	4.31	3.99	3.76	3.59	3.45	3.35	3.26	3.12	2.98	2.83	2.75	2.67	2.58	2.50	2.40	2.31
23	7.88	5.66	4.76	4.26	3.94	3.71	3.54	3.41	3.30	3.21	3.07	2.93	2.78	2.70	2.62	2.54	2.45	2.35	2.26
24	7.82	5.61	4.72	4.22	3.90	3.67	3.50	3.36	3.26	3.17	3.03	2.89	2.74	2.66	2.58	2.49	2.40	2.31	2.21
25	7.77	5.57	4.68	4.18	3.85	3.63	3.46	3.32	3.22	3.13	2.99	2.85	2.70	2.62	2.54	2.45	2.36	2.27	2.17
26	7.72	5.53	4.64	4.14	3.82	3.59	3.42	3.29	3.18	3.09	2.96	2.81	2.66	2.58	2.50	2.42	2.33	2.23	2.13
27	7.68	5.49	4.60	4.11	3.78	3.56	3.39	3.26	3.15	3.06	2.93	2.78	2.63	2.55	2.47	2.38	2.29	2.20	2.10
28	7.64	5.45	4.57	4.07	3.75	3.53	3.36	3.23	3.12	3.03	2.90	2.75	2.60	2.52	2.44	2.35	2.26	2.17	2.06
29	7.60	5.42	4.54	4.04	3.73	3.50	3.33	3.20	3.09	3.00	2.87	2.73	2.57	2.49	2.41	2.33	2.23	2.14	2.03
30	7.56	5.39	4.51	4.02	3.70	3.47	3.30	3.17	3.07	2.98	2.84	2.70	2.55	2.47	2.39	2.30	2.21	2.11	2.01
40	7.31	5.18	4.31	3.83	3.51	3.29	3.12	2.99	2.89	2.80	2.66	2.52	2.37	2.29	2.20	2.11	2.02	1.92	1.80
60	7.08	4.98	4.13	3.65	3.34	3.12	2.95	2.82	2.72	2.63	2.50	2.35	2.20	2.12	2.03	1.94	1.84	1.73	1.60
120	6.85	4.79	3.95	3.48	3.17	2.96	2.79	2.66	2.56	2.47	2.34	2.19	2.03	1.95	1.86	1.76	1.66	1.53	1.38
∞	6.63	4.61	3.78	3.32	3.02	2.80	2.64	2.51	2.41	2.32	2.18	2.04	1.88	1.79	1.70	1.59	1.47	1.32	1.00

Table F. Table of F – continued
Upper .005 points

df_2 \ df_1	1	2	3	4	5	6	7	8	9	10	12	15	20	24	30	40	60	120	∞
1	16211	20000	21615	22500	23056	23437	23715	23925	24091	24224	24426	24630	24836	24940	25044	25148	25253	25359	25465
2	198.5	199.0	199.2	199.2	199.3	199.3	199.4	199.4	199.4	199.4	199.4	199.4	199.4	199.5	199.5	199.5	199.5	199.5	199.5
3	55.55	49.80	47.47	46.19	45.39	44.84	44.43	44.13	43.88	43.69	43.39	43.08	42.78	42.62	42.47	42.31	42.15	41.99	41.83
4	31.33	26.28	24.26	23.15	22.46	21.97	21.62	21.35	21.14	20.97	20.70	20.44	20.17	20.03	19.89	19.75	19.61	19.47	19.32
5	22.78	18.31	16.53	15.56	14.94	14.51	14.20	13.96	13.77	13.62	13.38	13.15	12.90	12.78	12.66	12.53	12.40	12.27	12.14
6	18.63	14.54	12.92	12.03	11.46	11.07	10.79	10.57	10.39	10.25	10.03	9.81	9.59	9.47	9.36	9.24	9.12	9.00	8.88
7	16.24	12.40	10.88	10.05	9.52	9.16	8.89	8.68	8.51	8.38	8.18	7.97	7.75	7.65	7.53	7.42	7.31	7.19	7.08
8	14.69	11.04	9.60	8.81	8.30	7.95	7.69	7.50	7.34	7.21	7.01	6.81	6.61	6.50	6.40	6.29	6.18	6.06	5.95
9	13.61	10.11	8.72	7.96	7.47	7.13	6.88	6.69	6.54	6.42	6.23	6.03	5.83	5.73	5.62	5.52	5.41	5.30	5.19
10	12.83	9.43	8.08	7.34	6.87	6.54	6.30	6.12	5.97	5.85	5.66	5.47	5.27	5.17	5.07	4.97	4.86	4.75	4.64
11	12.23	8.91	7.60	6.88	6.42	6.10	5.86	5.68	5.54	5.42	5.24	5.05	4.86	4.76	4.65	4.55	4.44	4.34	4.23
12	11.75	8.51	7.23	6.52	6.07	5.76	5.52	5.35	5.20	5.09	4.91	4.72	4.53	4.43	4.33	4.23	4.12	4.01	3.90
13	11.37	8.19	6.93	6.23	5.79	5.48	5.25	5.08	4.94	4.82	4.64	4.46	4.27	4.17	4.07	3.97	3.87	3.76	3.65
14	11.06	7.92	6.68	6.00	5.56	5.26	5.03	4.86	4.72	4.60	4.43	4.25	4.06	3.96	3.86	3.76	3.66	3.55	3.44
15	10.80	7.70	6.48	5.80	5.37	5.07	4.85	4.67	4.54	4.42	4.25	4.07	3.88	3.79	3.69	3.58	3.48	3.37	3.26
16	10.58	7.51	6.30	5.64	5.21	4.91	4.69	4.52	4.38	4.27	4.10	3.92	3.73	3.64	3.54	3.44	3.33	3.22	3.11
17	10.38	7.35	6.16	5.50	5.07	4.78	4.56	4.39	4.25	4.14	3.97	3.79	3.61	3.51	3.41	3.31	3.21	3.10	2.98
18	10.22	7.21	6.03	5.37	4.96	4.66	4.44	4.28	4.14	4.03	3.86	3.68	3.50	3.40	3.30	3.20	3.10	2.99	2.87
19	10.07	7.09	5.92	5.27	4.85	4.56	4.34	4.18	4.04	3.93	3.76	3.59	3.40	3.31	3.21	3.11	3.00	2.89	2.78
20	9.94	6.99	5.82	5.17	4.76	4.47	4.26	4.09	3.96	3.85	3.68	3.50	3.32	3.22	3.12	3.02	2.92	2.81	2.69
21	9.83	6.89	5.73	5.09	4.68	4.39	4.18	4.01	3.88	3.77	3.60	3.43	3.24	3.15	3.05	2.95	2.84	2.73	2.61
22	9.73	6.81	5.65	5.02	4.61	4.32	4.11	3.94	3.81	3.70	3.54	3.36	3.18	3.08	2.98	2.88	2.77	2.66	2.55
23	9.63	6.73	5.58	4.95	4.54	4.26	4.05	3.88	3.75	3.64	3.47	3.30	3.12	3.02	2.92	2.82	2.71	2.60	2.48
24	9.55	6.66	5.52	4.89	4.49	4.20	3.99	3.83	3.69	3.59	3.42	3.25	3.06	2.97	2.87	2.77	2.66	2.55	2.43
25	9.48	6.60	5.46	4.84	4.43	4.15	3.94	3.78	3.64	3.54	3.37	3.20	3.01	2.92	2.82	2.72	2.61	2.50	2.38
26	9.41	6.54	5.41	4.79	4.38	4.10	3.89	3.73	3.60	3.49	3.33	3.15	2.97	2.87	2.77	2.67	2.56	2.45	2.33
27	9.34	6.49	5.36	4.74	4.34	4.06	3.85	3.69	3.56	3.45	3.28	3.11	2.93	2.83	2.73	2.63	2.52	2.41	2.29
28	9.28	6.44	5.32	4.70	4.30	4.02	3.81	3.65	3.52	3.41	3.25	3.07	2.89	2.79	2.69	2.59	2.48	2.37	2.25
29	9.23	6.40	5.28	4.66	4.26	3.98	3.77	3.61	3.48	3.38	3.21	3.04	2.86	2.76	2.66	2.56	2.45	2.33	2.21
30	9.18	6.35	5.24	4.62	4.23	3.95	3.74	3.58	3.45	3.34	3.18	3.01	2.82	2.73	2.63	2.52	2.42	2.30	2.18
40	8.83	6.07	4.98	4.37	3.99	3.71	3.51	3.35	3.22	3.12	2.95	2.78	2.60	2.50	2.40	2.30	2.18	2.06	1.93
60	8.49	5.79	4.73	4.14	3.76	3.49	3.29	3.13	3.01	2.90	2.74	2.57	2.39	2.29	2.19	2.08	1.96	1.83	1.69
120	8.18	5.54	4.50	3.92	3.55	3.28	3.09	2.93	2.81	2.71	2.54	2.37	2.19	2.09	1.98	1.87	1.75	1.61	1.43
∞	7.88	5.30	4.28	3.72	3.35	3.09	2.90	2.74	2.62	2.52	2.36	2.19	2.00	1.90	1.79	1.67	1.53	1.36	1.00

Table F. Table of F—continued
Upper .001 points

df_2 \ df_1	1	2	3	4	5	6	7	8	9	10	12	15	20	24	30	40	60	120	∞
1	4053*	5000*	5404*	5625*	5764*	5859*	5929*	5981*	6023*	6056*	6107*	6158*	6209*	6235*	6261*	6287*	6313*	6340*	6366*
2	998.5	999.0	999.2	999.2	999.3	999.3	999.4	999.4	999.4	999.4	999.4	999.4	999.4	999.5	999.5	999.5	999.5	999.5	999.5
3	167.0	148.5	141.1	137.1	134.6	132.8	131.6	130.6	129.9	129.2	128.3	127.4	126.4	125.9	125.4	125.0	124.5	124.0	123.5
4	74.14	61.25	56.18	53.44	51.71	50.53	49.66	49.00	48.47	48.05	47.41	46.76	46.10	45.77	45.43	45.09	44.75	44.40	44.05
5	47.18	37.12	33.20	31.09	29.75	28.84	28.16	27.64	27.24	26.92	26.42	25.91	25.39	25.14	24.87	24.60	24.33	24.06	23.79
6	35.51	27.00	23.70	21.92	20.81	20.03	19.46	19.03	18.69	18.41	17.99	17.56	17.12	16.89	16.67	16.44	16.21	15.99	15.75
7	29.25	21.69	18.77	17.19	16.21	15.52	15.02	14.63	14.33	14.08	13.71	13.32	12.93	12.73	12.53	12.33	12.12	11.91	11.70
8	25.42	18.49	15.83	14.39	13.49	12.86	12.40	12.04	11.77	11.54	11.19	10.84	10.48	10.30	10.11	9.92	9.73	9.53	9.33
9	22.86	16.39	13.90	12.56	11.71	11.13	10.70	10.37	10.11	9.89	9.57	9.24	8.90	8.72	8.55	8.37	8.19	8.00	7.81
10	21.04	14.91	12.55	11.28	10.48	9.92	9.52	9.20	8.96	8.75	8.45	8.13	7.80	7.64	7.47	7.30	7.12	6.94	6.76
11	19.69	13.81	11.56	10.35	9.58	9.05	8.66	8.35	8.12	7.92	7.63	7.32	7.01	6.85	6.68	6.52	6.35	6.17	6.00
12	18.64	12.97	10.80	9.63	8.89	8.38	8.00	7.71	7.48	7.29	7.00	6.71	6.40	6.25	6.09	5.93	5.76	5.59	5.42
13	17.81	12.31	10.21	9.07	8.35	7.86	7.49	7.21	6.98	6.80	6.52	6.23	5.93	5.78	5.63	5.47	5.30	5.14	4.97
14	17.14	11.78	9.73	8.62	7.92	7.43	7.08	6.80	6.58	6.40	6.13	5.85	5.56	5.41	5.25	5.10	4.94	4.77	4.60
15	16.59	11.34	9.34	8.25	7.57	7.09	6.74	6.47	6.26	6.08	5.81	5.54	5.25	5.10	4.95	4.80	4.64	4.47	4.31
16	16.12	10.97	9.00	7.94	7.27	6.81	6.46	6.19	5.98	5.81	5.55	5.27	4.99	4.85	4.70	4.54	4.39	4.23	4.06
17	15.72	10.66	8.73	7.68	7.02	6.56	6.22	5.96	5.75	5.58	5.32	5.05	4.78	4.63	4.48	4.33	4.18	4.02	3.85
18	15.38	10.39	8.49	7.46	6.81	6.35	6.02	5.76	5.56	5.39	5.13	4.87	4.59	4.45	4.30	4.15	4.00	3.84	3.67
19	15.08	10.16	8.28	7.26	6.62	6.18	5.85	5.59	5.39	5.22	4.97	4.70	4.43	4.29	4.14	3.99	3.84	3.68	3.51
20	14.82	9.95	8.10	7.10	6.46	6.02	5.69	5.44	5.24	5.08	4.82	4.56	4.29	4.15	4.00	3.86	3.70	3.54	3.38
21	14.59	9.77	7.94	6.95	6.32	5.88	5.56	5.31	5.11	4.95	4.70	4.44	4.17	4.03	3.88	3.74	3.58	3.42	3.26
22	14.38	9.61	7.80	6.81	6.19	5.76	5.44	5.19	4.99	4.83	4.58	4.33	4.06	3.92	3.78	3.63	3.48	3.32	3.15
23	14.19	9.47	7.67	6.69	6.08	5.65	5.33	5.09	4.89	4.73	4.48	4.23	3.96	3.82	3.68	3.53	3.38	3.22	3.05
24	14.03	9.34	7.55	6.59	5.98	5.55	5.23	4.99	4.80	4.64	4.39	4.14	3.87	3.74	3.59	3.45	3.29	3.14	2.97
25	13.88	9.22	7.45	6.49	5.88	5.46	5.15	4.91	4.71	4.56	4.31	4.06	3.79	3.66	3.52	3.37	3.22	3.06	2.89
26	13.74	9.12	7.36	6.41	5.80	5.38	5.07	4.83	4.64	4.48	4.24	3.99	3.72	3.59	3.44	3.30	3.15	2.99	2.82
27	13.61	9.02	7.27	6.33	5.73	5.31	5.00	4.76	4.57	4.41	4.17	3.92	3.66	3.52	3.38	3.23	3.08	2.92	2.75
28	13.50	8.93	7.19	6.25	5.66	5.24	4.93	4.69	4.50	4.35	4.11	3.86	3.60	3.46	3.32	3.18	3.02	2.86	2.69
29	13.39	8.85	7.12	6.19	5.59	5.18	4.87	4.64	4.45	4.29	4.05	3.80	3.54	3.41	3.27	3.12	2.97	2.81	2.64
30	13.29	8.77	7.05	6.12	5.53	5.12	4.82	4.58	4.39	4.24	4.00	3.75	3.49	3.36	3.22	3.07	2.92	2.76	2.59
40	12.61	8.25	6.60	5.70	5.13	4.73	4.44	4.21	4.02	3.87	3.64	3.40	3.15	3.01	2.87	2.73	2.57	2.41	2.23
60	11.97	7.76	6.17	5.31	4.76	4.37	4.09	3.87	3.69	3.54	3.31	3.08	2.83	2.69	2.55	2.41	2.25	2.08	1.89
120	11.38	7.32	5.79	4.95	4.42	4.04	3.77	3.55	3.38	3.24	3.02	2.78	2.53	2.40	2.26	2.11	1.95	1.76	1.54
∞	10.83	6.91	5.42	4.62	4.10	3.74	3.47	3.27	3.10	2.96	2.74	2.51	2.27	2.13	1.99	1.84	1.66	1.45	1.00

* Multiply these entries by 100.

Table G.*   *Table for* F_{max} *Percentage points of the ratio,*
$$s^2_{max}/s^2_{min}$$
Upper .05 points

df \ k	2	3	4	5	6	7	8	9	10	11	12
2	39·0	87·5	142	202	266	333	403	475	550	626	704
3	15·4	27·8	39·2	50·7	62·0	72·9	83·5	93·9	104	114	124
4	9·60	15·5	20·6	25·2	29·5	33·6	37·5	41·1	44·6	48·0	51·4
5	7·15	10·8	13·7	16·3	18·7	20·8	22·9	24·7	26·5	28·2	29·9
6	5·82	8·38	10·4	12·1	13·7	15·0	16·3	17·5	18·6	19·7	20·7
7	4·99	6·94	8·44	9·70	10·8	11·8	12·7	13·5	14·3	15·1	15·8
8	4·43	6·00	7·18	8·12	9·03	9·78	10·5	11·1	11·7	12·2	12·7
9	4·03	5·34	6·31	7·11	7·80	8·41	8·95	9·45	9·91	10·3	10·7
10	3·72	4·85	5·67	6·34	6·92	7·42	7·87	8·28	8·66	9·01	9·34
12	3·28	4·16	4·79	5·30	5·72	6·09	6·42	6·72	7·00	7·25	7·48
15	2·86	3·54	4·01	4·37	4·68	4·95	5·19	5·40	5·59	5·77	5·93
20	2·46	2·95	3·29	3·54	3·76	3·94	4·10	4·24	4·37	4·49	4·59
30	2·07	2·40	2·61	2·78	2·91	3·02	3·12	3·21	3·29	3·36	3·39
60	1·67	1·85	1·96	2·04	2·11	2·17	2·22	2·26	2·30	2·33	2·36
∞	1·00	1·00	1·00	1·00	1·00	1·00	1·00	1·00	1·00	1·00	1·00

Upper .01 points

df \ k	2	3	4	5	6	7	8	9	10	11	12
2	199	448	729	1036	1362	1705	2063	2432	2813	3204	3605
3	47·5	85	120	151	184	21(6)	24(9)	28(1)	31(0)	33(7)	36(1)
4	23·2	37	49	59	69	79	89	97	106	113	120
5	14·9	22	28	33	38	42	46	50	54	57	60
6	11·1	15·5	19·1	22	25	27	30	32	34	36	37
7	8·89	12·1	14·5	16·5	18·4	20	22	23	24	26	27
8	7·50	9·9	11·7	13·2	14·5	15·8	16·9	17·9	18·9	19·8	21
9	6·54	8·5	9·9	11·1	12·1	13·1	13·9	14·7	15·3	16·0	16·6
10	5·85	7·4	8·6	9·6	10·4	11·1	11·8	12·4	12·9	13·4	13·9
12	4·91	6·1	6·9	7·6	8·2	8·7	9·1	9·5	9·9	10·2	10·6
15	4·07	4·9	5·5	6·0	6·4	6·7	7·1	7·3	7·5	7·8	8·0
20	3·32	3·8	4·3	4·6	4·9	5·1	5·3	5·5	5·6	5·8	5·9
30	2·63	3·0	3·3	3·4	3·6	3·7	3·8	3·9	4·0	4·1	4·2
60	1·96	2·2	2·3	2·4	2·4	2·5	2·5	2·6	2·6	2·7	2·7
∞	1·00	1·0	1·0	1·0	1·0	1·0	1·0	1·0	1·0	1·0	1·0

s^2_{max} is the largest and s^2_{min} the smallest in a set of k independent mean squares, each based on df degrees of freedom. Values in the column $k = 2$ and in the rows $df = 2$ and ∞ are exact. Elsewhere the third digit may be in error by a few units for the 5% points and several units for the 1% points. The third digit figures in brackets for $df = 3$ are the most uncertain.

*Reprinted, with changes in notation, by permission of the publisher from E. S. Pearson and H. O. Hartley, *Biometrika Tables for Statisticians*, Volume 1, p. 202. Copyright 1966, Biometrika.

Table H.* Percentage Points of the Studentized Range, q

df	$1-\alpha$	2	3	4	5	6	7	8	9	10	11	12	13	14	15
							r = number of steps between ordered means								
1	.95	18.0	27.0	32.8	37.1	40.4	43.1	45.4	47.4	49.1	50.6	52.0	53.2	54.3	55.4
	.99	90.0	135	164	186	202	216	227	237	246	253	260	266	272	277
2	.95	6.09	8.3	9.8	10.9	11.7	12.4	13.0	13.5	14.0	14.4	14.7	15.1	15.4	15.7
	.99	14.0	19.0	22.3	24.7	26.6	28.2	29.5	30.7	31.7	32.6	33.4	34.1	34.8	35.4
3	.95	4.50	5.91	6.82	7.50	8.04	8.48	8.85	9.18	9.46	9.72	9.95	10.2	10.4	10.5
	.99	8.26	10.6	12.2	13.3	14.2	15.0	15.6	16.2	16.7	17.1	17.5	17.9	18.2	18.5
4	.95	3.93	5.04	5.76	6.29	6.71	7.05	7.35	7.60	7.83	8.03	8.21	8.37	8.52	8.66
	.99	6.51	8.12	9.17	9.96	10.6	11.1	11.5	11.9	12.3	12.6	12.8	13.1	13.3	13.5
5	.95	3.64	4.60	5.22	5.67	6.03	6.33	6.58	6.80	6.99	7.17	7.32	7.47	7.60	7.72
	.99	5.70	6.97	7.80	8.42	8.91	9.32	9.67	9.97	10.2	10.5	10.7	10.9	11.1	11.2
6	.95	3.46	4.34	4.90	5.31	5.63	5.89	6.12	6.32	6.49	6.65	6.79	6.92	7.03	7.14
	.99	5.24	6.33	7.03	7.56	7.97	8.32	8.61	8.87	9.10	9.30	9.49	9.65	9.81	9.95
7	.95	3.34	4.16	4.69	5.06	5.36	5.61	5.82	6.00	6.16	6.30	6.43	6.55	6.66	6.76
	.99	4.95	5.92	6.54	7.01	7.37	7.68	7.94	8.17	8.37	8.55	8.71	8.86	9.00	9.12
8	.95	3.26	4.04	4.53	4.89	5.17	5.40	5.60	5.77	5.92	6.05	6.18	6.29	6.39	6.48
	.99	4.74	5.63	6.20	6.63	6.96	7.24	7.47	7.68	7.87	8.03	8.18	8.31	8.44	8.55
9	.95	3.20	3.95	4.42	4.76	5.02	5.24	5.43	5.60	5.74	5.87	5.98	6.09	6.19	6.28
	.99	4.60	5.43	5.96	6.35	6.66	6.91	7.13	7.32	7.49	7.65	7.78	7.91	8.03	8.13
10	.95	3.15	3.88	4.33	4.65	4.91	5.12	5.30	5.46	5.60	5.72	5.83	5.93	6.03	6.11
	.99	4.48	5.27	5.77	6.14	6.43	6.67	6.87	7.05	7.21	7.36	7.48	7.60	7.71	7.81
11	.95	3.11	3.82	4.26	4.57	4.82	5.03	5.20	5.35	5.49	5.61	5.71	5.81	5.90	5.99
	.99	4.39	5.14	5.62	5.97	6.25	6.48	6.67	6.84	6.99	7.13	7.26	7.36	7.46	7.56

12	.95	3.08	3.77	4.20	4.51	4.75	4.95	5.12	5.27	5.40	5.51	5.62	5.71	5.80	5.88
	.99	4.32	5.04	5.50	5.84	6.10	6.32	6.51	6.67	6.81	6.94	7.06	7.17	7.26	7.36
13	.95	3.06	3.73	4.15	4.45	4.69	4.88	5.05	5.19	5.32	5.43	5.53	5.63	5.71	5.79
	.99	4.26	4.96	5.40	5.73	5.98	6.19	6.37	6.53	6.67	6.79	6.90	7.01	7.10	7.19
14	.95	3.03	3.70	4.11	4.41	4.64	4.83	4.99	5.13	5.25	5.36	5.46	5.55	5.64	5.72
	.99	4.21	4.89	5.32	5.63	5.88	6.08	6.26	6.41	6.54	6.66	6.77	6.87	6.96	7.05
16	.95	3.00	3.65	4.05	4.33	4.56	4.74	4.90	5.03	5.15	5.26	5.35	5.44	5.52	5.59
	.99	4.13	4.78	5.19	5.49	5.72	5.92	6.08	6.22	6.35	6.46	6.56	6.66	6.74	6.82
18	.95	2.97	3.61	4.00	4.28	4.49	4.67	4.82	4.96	5.07	5.17	5.27	5.35	5.43	5.50
	.99	4.07	4.70	5.09	5.38	5.60	5.79	5.94	6.08	6.20	6.31	6.41	6.50	6.58	6.65
20	.95	2.95	3.58	3.96	4.23	4.45	4.62	4.77	4.90	5.01	5.11	5.20	5.28	5.36	5.43
	.99	4.02	4.64	5.02	5.29	5.51	5.69	5.84	5.97	6.09	6.19	6.29	6.37	6.45	6.52
24	.95	2.92	3.53	3.90	4.17	4.37	4.54	4.68	4.81	4.92	5.01	5.10	5.18	5.25	5.32
	.99	3.96	4.54	4.91	5.17	5.37	5.54	5.69	5.81	5.92	6.02	6.11	6.19	6.26	6.33
30	.95	2.89	3.49	3.84	4.10	4.30	4.46	4.60	4.72	4.83	4.92	5.00	5.08	5.15	5.21
	.99	3.89	4.45	4.80	5.05	5.24	5.40	5.54	5.56	5.76	5.85	5.93	6.01	6.08	6.14
40	.95	2.86	3.44	3.79	4.04	4.23	4.39	4.52	4.63	4.74	4.82	4.91	4.98	5.05	5.11
	.99	3.82	4.37	4.70	4.93	5.11	5.27	5.39	5.50	5.60	5.69	5.77	5.84	5.90	5.96
60	.95	2.83	3.40	3.74	3.98	4.16	4.31	4.44	4.55	4.65	4.73	4.81	4.88	4.94	5.00
	.99	3.76	4.28	4.60	4.82	4.99	5.13	5.25	5.36	5.45	5.53	5.60	5.67	5.73	5.79
120	.95	2.80	3.36	3.69	3.92	4.10	4.24	4.36	4.48	4.56	4.64	4.72	4.78	4.84	4.90
	.99	3.70	4.20	4.50	4.71	4.87	5.01	5.12	5.21	5.30	5.38	5.44	5.51	5.56	5.61
∞	.95	2.77	3.31	3.63	3.86	4.03	4.17	4.29	4.39	4.47	4.55	4.62	4.68	4.74	4.80
	.99	3.64	4.12	4.40	4.60	4.76	4.88	4.99	5.08	5.16	5.23	5.29	5.35	5.40	5.45

*Reprinted, with a change in notation, by permission of the author, H. Leon Harter et. al., from *The Probability Integrals of the Range and of the Studentized Range*, WADC Tech. Rep. 58–484, Vol. 2, 1959.

Table I.*   *Percentage Points of the Bonferroni* t *Statistic* $t^{\alpha/2C}_{df_E}$

α = .05

df/C	2	3	4	5	6	7	8	9	10	15	20	25	30	35	40	45	50
5	3.17	3.54	3.81	4.04	4.22	4.38	4.53	4.66	4.78	5.25	5.60	5.89	6.15	6.36	6.56	6.70	6.86
7	2.84	3.13	3.34	3.50	3.64	3.76	3.86	3.95	4.03	4.36	4.59	4.78	4.95	5.09	5.21	5.31	5.40
10	2.64	2.87	3.04	3.17	3.28	3.37	3.45	3.52	3.58	3.83	4.01	4.15	4.27	4.37	4.45	4.53	4.59
12	2.56	2.78	2.94	3.06	3.15	3.24	3.31	3.37	3.43	3.65	3.80	3.93	4.04	4.13	4.20	4.26	4.32
15	2.49	2.69	2.84	2.95	3.04	3.11	3.18	3.24	3.29	3.48	3.62	3.74	3.82	3.90	3.97	4.02	4.07
20	2.42	2.61	2.75	2.85	2.93	3.00	3.06	3.11	3.16	3.33	3.46	3.55	3.63	3.70	3.76	3.80	3.85
24	2.39	2.58	2.70	2.80	2.88	2.94	3.00	3.05	3.09	3.26	3.38	3.47	3.54	3.61	3.66	3.70	3.74
30	2.36	2.54	2.66	2.75	2.83	2.89	2.94	2.99	3.03	3.19	3.30	3.39	3.46	3.52	3.57	3.61	3.65
40	2.33	2.50	2.62	2.71	2.78	2.84	2.89	2.93	2.97	3.12	3.23	3.31	3.38	3.43	3.48	3.51	3.55
60	2.30	2.47	2.58	2.66	2.73	2.79	2.84	2.88	2.92	3.06	3.16	3.24	3.30	3.34	3.39	3.42	3.46
120	2.27	2.43	2.54	2.62	2.68	2.74	2.79	2.83	2.86	2.99	3.09	3.16	3.22	3.27	3.31	3.34	3.37
∞	2.24	2.39	2.50	2.58	2.64	2.69	2.74	2.77	2.81	2.94	3.02	3.09	3.15	3.19	3.23	3.26	3.29

α = .01

df/C	2	3	4	5	6	7	8	9	10	15	20	25	30	35	40	45	50
5	4.78	5.25	5.60	5.89	6.15	6.36	6.56	6.70	6.86	7.51	8.00	8.37	8.68	8.95	9.19	9.41	9.68
7	4.03	4.36	4.59	4.78	4.95	5.09	5.21	5.31	5.40	5.79	6.08	6.30	6.49	6.67	6.83	6.93	7.06
10	3.58	3.83	4.01	4.15	4.27	4.37	4.45	4.53	4.59	4.86	5.06	5.20	5.33	5.44	5.52	5.60	5.70
12	3.43	3.65	3.80	3.93	4.04	4.13	4.20	4.26	4.32	4.56	4.73	4.86	4.95	5.04	5.12	5.20	5.27
15	3.29	3.48	3.62	3.74	3.82	3.90	3.97	4.02	4.07	4.29	4.42	4.53	4.61	4.71	4.78	4.84	4.90
20	3.16	3.33	3.46	3.55	3.63	3.70	3.76	3.80	3.85	4.03	4.15	4.25	4.33	4.39	4.46	4.5†‡	4.5†
24	3.09	3.26	3.38	3.47	3.54	3.61	3.66	3.70	3.74	3.91	4.04	4.1†	4.2†	4.3†	4.3†	4.3†	4.4†
30	3.03	3.19	3.30	3.39	3.46	3.52	3.57	3.61	3.65	3.80	3.90	3.98	4.13	4.26	4.1†	4.2†	4.2†
40	2.97	3.12	3.23	3.31	3.38	3.43	3.48	3.51	3.55	3.70	3.79	3.88	3.93	3.97	4.01	4.1†	4.1†
60	2.92	3.06	3.16	3.24	3.30	3.34	3.39	3.42	3.46	3.59	3.69	3.76	3.81	3.84	3.89	3.93	3.97
120	2.86	2.99	3.09	3.16	3.22	3.27	3.31	3.34	3.37	3.50	3.58	3.64	3.69	3.73	3.77	3.80	3.83
∞	2.81	2.94	3.02	3.09	3.15	3.19	3.23	3.26	3.29	3.40	3.48	3.54	3.59	3.63	3.66	3.69	3.72

† Obtained by graphical interpolation.

*Reprinted, with changes in notation, by permission of the publisher and author from O. J. Dunn, "Multiple Comparisons Among Means," *Journal of the American Statistical Association*, 56, p. 55, 1961; and from R. G. Miller, Jr., *Simultaneous Statistical Inference*, p. 238. Copyright 1966, McGraw-Hill Book Company.

Table J.*   Wilcoxon T *Values for Unpaired Replicates*

Probabilities of chance occurrence of a rank total equal to or less than T with N replicates per group. T is given in the body of the table to the nearest whole number.

N	.025 (one tail) .05 (two tail)	.01 .02	.005 .01
5	18	16	15
6	26	24	23
7	37	34	33
8	49	46	44
9	63	59	57
10	79	74	71
11	96	91	88
12	116	110	106
13	137	130	126
14	160	152	148
15	185	177	171
16	212	202	196
17	240	230	223
18	271	260	252
19	303	291	283
20	337	324	316

*Reprinted, with author's corrections, by permission of the publisher from F. Wilcoxon, *Some Rapid Approximate Statistical Procedures*, p. 14. Copyright 1949, American Cyanamid Company.

Table K.*   Table of Random Numbers

```
10 09 73 25 33   76 52 01 35 86   34 67 35 48 76   80 95 90 91 17   39 29 27 49 45
37 54 20 48 05   64 89 47 42 96   24 80 52 40 37   20 63 61 04 02   00 82 29 16 65
08 42 26 89 53   19 64 50 93 03   23 20 90 25 60   15 95 33 47 64   35 08 03 36 06
99 01 90 25 29   09 37 67 07 15   38 31 13 11 65   88 67 67 43 97   04 43 62 76 59
12 80 79 99 70   80 15 73 61 47   64 03 23 66 53   98 95 11 68 77   12 17 17 68 33

66 06 57 47 17   34 07 27 68 50   36 69 73 61 70   65 81 33 98 85   11 19 92 91 70
31 06 01 08 05   45 57 18 24 06   35 30 34 26 14   86 79 90 74 39   23 40 30 97 32
85 26 97 76 02   02 05 16 56 92   68 66 57 48 18   73 05 38 52 47   18 62 38 85 79
63 57 33 21 35   05 32 54 70 48   90 55 35 75 48   28 46 82 87 09   83 49 12 56 24
73 79 64 57 53   03 52 96 47 78   35 80 83 42 82   60 93 52 03 44   35 27 38 84 35

98 52 01 77 67   14 90 56 86 07   22 10 94 05 58   60 97 09 34 33   50 50 07 39 98
11 80 50 54 31   39 80 82 77 32   50 72 56 82 48   29 40 52 42 01   52 77 56 78 51
83 45 29 96 34   06 28 89 80 83   13 74 67 00 78   18 47 54 06 10   68 71 17 78 17
88 68 54 02 00   86 50 75 84 01   36 76 66 79 51   90 36 47 64 93   29 60 91 10 62
99 59 46 73 48   87 51 76 49 69   91 82 60 89 28   93 78 56 13 68   23 47 83 41 13

65 48 11 76 74   17 46 85 09 50   58 04 77 69 74   73 03 95 71 86   40 21 81 65 44
80 12 43 56 35   17 72 70 80 15   45 31 82 23 74   21 11 57 82 53   14 38 55 37 63
74 35 09 98 17   77 40 27 72 14   43 23 60 02 10   45 52 16 42 37   96 28 60 26 55
69 91 62 68 03   66 25 22 91 48   36 93 68 72 03   76 62 11 39 90   94 40 05 64 18
09 89 32 05 05   14 22 56 85 14   46 42 75 67 88   96 29 77 88 22   54 38 21 45 98

91 49 91 45 23   68 47 92 76 86   46 16 28 35 54   94 75 08 99 23   37 08 92 00 48
80 33 69 45 98   26 94 03 68 58   70 29 73 41 35   53 14 03 33 40   42 05 08 23 41
44 10 48 19 49   85 15 74 79 54   32 97 92 65 75   57 60 04 08 81   22 22 20 64 13
12 55 07 37 42   11 10 00 20 40   12 86 07 46 97   96 64 48 94 39   28 70 72 58 15
63 60 64 93 29   16 50 53 44 84   40 21 95 25 63   43 65 17 70 82   07 20 73 17 90

61 19 69 04 46   26 45 74 77 74   51 92 43 37 29   65 39 45 95 93   42 58 26 05 27
15 47 44 52 66   95 27 07 99 53   59 36 78 38 48   82 39 61 01 18   33 21 15 94 66
94 55 72 85 73   67 89 75 43 87   54 62 24 44 31   91 19 04 25 92   92 92 74 59 73
42 48 11 62 13   97 34 40 87 21   16 86 84 87 67   03 07 11 20 59   25 70 14 66 70
23 52 37 83 17   73 20 88 98 37   68 93 59 14 16   26 25 22 96 63   05 52 28 25 62

04 49 35 24 94   75 24 63 38 24   45 86 25 10 25   61 96 27 93 35   65 33 71 24 72
00 54 99 76 54   64 05 18 81 59   96 11 96 38 96   54 69 28 23 91   23 28 72 95 29
35 96 31 53 07   26 89 80 93 54   33 35 13 54 62   77 97 45 00 24   90 10 33 93 33
59 80 80 83 91   45 42 72 68 42   83 60 94 97 00   13 02 12 48 92   78 56 52 01 06
46 05 88 52 36   01 39 09 22 86   77 28 14 40 77   93 91 08 36 47   70 61 74 29 41

32 17 90 05 97   87 37 92 52 41   05 56 70 70 07   86 74 31 71 57   85 39 41 18 38
69 23 46 14 06   20 11 74 52 04   15 95 66 00 00   18 74 39 24 23   97 11 89 63 38
19 56 54 14 30   01 75 87 53 79   40 41 92 15 85   66 67 43 68 06   84 96 28 52 07
45 15 51 49 38   19 47 60 72 46   43 66 79 45 43   59 04 79 00 33   20 82 66 95 41
94 86 43 19 94   36 16 81 08 51   34 88 88 15 53   01 54 03 54 56   05 01 45 11 76
```

*Reprinted by permission of the publisher from *A Million Random Digits*, pp. 1–3. Copyright 1955, The Rand Corporation.

Table K.   Table of Random Numbers — continued

```
98 08 62 48 26    45 24 02 84 04    44 99 90 88 96    39 09 47 34 07    35 44 13 18 80
33 18 51 62 32    41 94 15 09 49    89 43 54 85 81    88 69 54 19 94    37 54 87 30 43
80 95 10 04 06    96 38 27 07 74    20 15 12 33 87    25 01 62 52 98    94 62 46 11 71
79 75 24 91 40    71 96 12 82 96    69 86 10 25 91    74 85 22 05 39    00 38 75 95 79
18 63 33 25 37    98 14 50 65 71    31 01 02 46 74    05 45 56 14 27    77 93 89 19 36

74 02 94 39 02    77 55 73 22 70    97 79 01 71 19    52 52 75 80 21    80 81 45 17 48
54 17 84 56 11    80 99 33 71 43    05 33 51 29 69    56 12 71 92 55    36 04 09 03 24
11 66 44 98 83    52 07 98 48 27    59 38 17 15 39    09 97 33 34 40    88 46 12 33 56
48 32 47 79 28    31 24 96 47 10    02 29 53 68 70    32 30 75 75 46    15 02 00 99 94
69 07 49 41 38    87 63 79 19 76    35 58 40 44 01    10 51 82 16 15    01 84 87 69 38

09 18 82 00 97    32 82 53 95 27    04 22 08 63 04    83 38 98 73 74    64 27 85 80 44
90 04 58 54 97    51 98 15 06 54    94 93 88 19 97    91 87 07 61 50    68 47 66 46 59
73 18 95 02 07    47 67 72 52 69    62 29 06 44 64    27 12 46 70 18    41 36 18 27 60
75 76 87 64 90    20 97 18 17 49    90 42 91 22 72    95 37 50 58 71    93 82 34 31 78
54 01 64 40 56    66 28 13 10 03    00 68 22 73 98    20 71 45 32 95    07 70 61 78 13

08 35 86 99 10    78 54 24 27 85    13 66 15 88 73    04 61 89 75 53    31 22 30 84 20
28 30 60 32 64    81 33 31 05 91    40 51 00 78 93    32 60 46 04 75    94 11 90 18 40
53 84 08 62 33    81 59 41 36 28    51 21 59 02 90    28 46 66 87 95    77 76 22 07 91
91 75 75 37 41    61 61 36 22 69    50 26 39 02 12    55 78 17 65 14    83 48 34 70 55
89 41 59 26 94    00 39 75 83 91    12 60 71 76 46    48 94 97 23 06    94 54 13 74 08

77 51 30 38 20    86 83 42 99 01    68 41 48 27 74    51 90 81 39 80    72 89 35 55 07
19 50 23 71 74    69 97 92 02 88    55 21 02 97 73    74 28 77 52 51    65 34 46 74 15
21 81 85 93 13    93 27 88 17 57    05 68 67 31 56    07 08 28 50 46    31 85 33 84 52
51 47 46 64 99    68 10 72 36 21    94 04 99 13 45    42 83 60 91 91    08 00 74 54 49
99 55 96 83 31    62 53 52 41 70    69 77 71 28 30    74 81 97 81 42    43 86 07 28 34

33 71 34 80 07    93 58 47 28 69    51 92 66 47 21    58 30 32 98 22    93 17 49 39 72
85 27 48 68 93    11 30 32 92 70    28 83 43 41 37    73 51 59 04 00    71 14 84 36 43
84 13 38 96 40    44 03 55 21 66    73 85 27 00 91    61 22 26 05 61    62 32 71 84 23
56 73 21 62 34    17 39 59 61 31    10 12 39 16 22    85 49 65 75 60    81 60 41 88 80
65 13 85 68 06    87 64 88 52 61    34 31 36 58 61    45 87 52 10 69    85 64 44 72 77

38 00 10 21 76    81 71 91 17 11    71 60 29 29 37    74 21 96 40 49    65 58 44 96 98
37 40 29 63 97    01 30 47 75 86    56 27 11 00 86    47 32 46 26 05    40 03 03 74 38
97 12 54 03 48    87 08 33 14 17    21 81 53 92 50    75 23 76 20 47    15 50 12 95 78
21 82 64 11 34    47 14 33 40 72    64 63 88 59 02    49 13 90 64 41    03 85 65 45 52
73 13 54 27 42    95 71 90 90 35    85 79 47 42 96    08 78 98 81 56    64 69 11 92 02

07 63 87 79 29    03 06 11 80 72    96 20 74 41 56    23 82 19 95 38    04 71 36 69 94
60 52 88 34 41    07 95 41 98 14    59 17 52 06 95    05 53 35 21 39    61 21 20 64 55
83 59 63 56 55    06 95 89 29 83    05 12 80 97 19    77 43 35 37 83    92 30 15 04 98
10 85 06 27 46    99 59 91 05 07    13 49 90 63 19    53 07 57 18 39    06 41 01 93 62
39 82 09 89 52    43 62 26 31 47    64 42 18 08 14    43 80 00 93 51    31 02 47 31 67
```

Table K. Table of Random Numbers — continued

59 58 00 64 78	75 56 97 88 00	88 83 55 44 86	23 76 80 61 56	04 11 10 84 08
38 50 80 73 41	23 79 34 87 63	90 82 29 70 22	17 71 90 42 07	95 95 44 99 53
30 69 27 06 68	94 68 81 61 27	56 19 68 00 91	82 06 76 34 00	05 46 26 92 00
65 44 39 56 59	18 28 82 74 37	49 63 22 40 41	08 33 76 56 76	96 29 99 08 36
27 26 75 02 64	13 19 27 22 94	07 47 74 46 06	17 98 54 89 11	97 34 13 03 58
91 30 70 69 91	19 07 22 42 10	36 69 95 37 28	28 82 53 57 93	28 97 66 62 52
68 43 49 46 88	84 47 31 36 22	62 12 69 84 08	12 84 38 25 90	09 81 59 31 46
48 90 81 58 77	54 74 52 45 91	35 70 00 47 54	83 82 45 26 92	54 13 05 51 60
06 91 34 51 97	42 67 27 86 01	11 88 30 95 28	63 01 19 89 01	14 97 44 03 44
10 45 51 60 19	14 21 03 37 12	91 34 23 78 21	88 32 58 08 51	43 66 77 08 83
12 88 39 73 43	65 02 76 11 84	04 28 50 13 92	17 97 41 50 77	90 71 22 67 69
21 77 83 09 76	38 80 73 69 61	31 64 94 20 96	63 28 10 20 23	08 81 64 74 49
19 52 35 95 15	65 12 25 96 59	86 28 36 82 58	69 57 21 37 98	16 43 59 15 29
67 24 55 26 70	35 58 31 65 63	79 24 68 66 86	76 46 33 42 22	26 65 59 08 02
60 58 44 73 77	07 50 03 79 92	45 13 42 65 29	26 76 08 36 37	41 32 64 43 44
53 85 34 13 77	36 06 69 48 50	58 83 87 38 59	49 36 47 33 31	96 24 04 36 42
24 63 73 87 36	74 38 48 93 42	52 62 30 79 92	12 36 91 86 01	03 74 28 38 73
83 08 01 24 51	38 99 22 28 15	07 75 95 17 77	97 37 72 75 85	51 97 23 78 67
16 44 42 43 34	36 15 19 90 73	27 49 37 09 39	85 13 03 25 52	54 84 65 47 59
60 79 01 81 57	57 17 86 57 62	11 16 17 85 76	45 81 95 29 79	65 13 00 48 60
03 99 11 04 61	93 71 61 68 94	66 08 32 46 53	84 60 95 82 32	88 61 81 91 61
38 55 59 55 54	32 88 65 97 80	08 35 56 08 60	29 73 54 77 62	71 29 92 38 53
17 54 67 37 04	92 05 24 62 15	55 12 12 92 81	59 07 60 79 36	27 95 45 89 09
32 64 35 28 61	95 81 90 68 31	00 91 19 89 36	76 35 59 37 79	80 86 30 05 14
69 57 26 87 77	39 51 03 59 05	14 06 04 06 19	29 54 96 96 16	33 56 46 07 80
24 12 26 65 91	27 69 90 64 94	14 84 54 66 72	61 95 87 71 00	90 89 97 57 54
61 19 63 02 31	92 96 26 17 73	41 83 95 53 82	17 26 77 09 43	78 03 87 02 67
30 53 22 17 04	10 27 41 22 02	39 68 52 33 09	10 06 16 88 29	55 98 66 64 85
03 78 89 75 99	75 86 72 07 17	74 41 65 31 66	35 20 83 33 74	87 53 90 88 23
48 22 86 33 79	85 78 34 76 19	53 15 26 74 33	35 66 35 29 72	16 81 86 03 11
60 36 59 46 53	35 07 53 39 49	42 61 42 92 97	01 91 82 83 16	98 95 37 32 31
83 79 94 24 02	56 62 33 44 42	34 99 44 13 74	70 07 11 47 36	09 95 81 80 65
32 96 00 74 05	36 40 98 32 32	99 38 54 16 00	11 13 30 75 86	15 91 70 62 53
19 32 25 38 45	57 62 05 26 06	66 49 76 86 46	78 13 86 65 59	19 64 09 94 13
11 22 09 47 47	07 39 93 74 08	48 50 92 39 29	27 48 24 54 76	85 24 43 51 59
31 75 15 72 60	68 98 00 53 39	15 47 04 83 55	88 65 12 25 96	03 15 21 92 21
88 49 29 93 82	14 45 40 45 04	20 09 49 89 77	74 84 39 34 13	22 10 97 85 08
30 93 44 77 44	07 48 18 38 28	73 78 80 65 33	28 59 72 04 05	94 20 52 03 80
22 88 84 88 93	27 49 99 87 48	60 53 04 51 28	74 02 28 46 17	82 03 71 02 68
78 21 21 69 93	35 90 29 13 86	44 37 21 54 86	65 74 11 40 14	87 48 13 72 20

Table K.   Table of Random Numbers — concluded

```
41 84 98 45 47    46 85 05 23 26    34 67 75 83 00    74 91 06 43 45    19 32 58 15 49
46 35 23 30 49    69 24 89 34 60    45 30 50 75 21    61 31 83 18 55    14 41 37 09 51
11 08 79 62 94    14 01 33 17 92    59 74 76 72 77    76 50 33 45 13    39 66 37 75 44
52 70 10 83 37    56 30 38 73 15    16 52 06 96 76    11 65 49 98 93    02 18 16 81 61
57 27 53 68 98    81 30 44 85 85    68 65 22 73 76    92 85 25 58 66    88 44 80 35 84

20 85 77 31 56    70 28 42 43 26    79 37 59 52 20    01 15 96 32 67    10 62 24 83 91
15 63 38 49 24    90 41 59 36 14    33 52 12 66 65    55 82 34 76 41    86 22 53 17 04
92 69 44 82 97    39 90 40 21 15    59 58 94 90 67    66 82 14 15 75    49 76 70 40 37
77 61 31 90 19    88 15 20 00 80    20 55 49 14 09    96 27 74 82 57    50 81 69 76 16
38 68 83 24 86    45 13 46 35 45    59 40 47 20 59    43 94 75 16 80    43 85 25 96 93

25 16 30 18 89    70 01 41 50 21    41 29 06 73 12    71 85 71 59 57    68 97 11 14 03
65 25 10 76 29    37 23 93 32 95    05 87 00 11 19    92 78 42 63 40    18 47 76 56 22
36 81 54 36 25    18 63 73 75 09    82 44 49 90 05    04 92 17 37 01    14 70 79 39 97
64 39 71 16 92    05 32 78 21 62    20 24 78 17 59    45 19 72 53 32    83 74 52 25 67
04 51 52 56 24    95 09 66 79 46    48 46 08 55 58    15 19 11 87 82    16 93 03 33 61

83 76 16 08 73    43 25 38 41 45    60 83 32 59 83    01 29 14 13 49    20 36 80 71 26
14 38 70 63 45    80 85 40 92 79    43 52 90 63 18    38 38 47 47 61    41 19 63 74 80
51 32 19 22 46    80 08 87 70 74    88 72 25 67 36    66 16 44 94 31    66 91 93 16 78
72 47 20 00 08    80 89 01 80 02    94 81 33 19 00    54 15 58 34 36    35 35 25 41 31
05 46 65 53 06    93 12 81 84 64    74 45 79 05 61    72 84 81 18 34    79 98 26 84 16

39 52 87 24 84    82 47 42 55 93    48 54 53 52 47    18 61 91 36 74    18 61 11 92 41
81 61 61 87 11    53 34 24 42 76    75 12 21 17 24    74 62 77 37 07    58 31 91 59 97
07 58 61 61 20    82 64 12 28 20    92 90 41 31 41    32 39 21 97 63    61 19 96 79 40
90 76 70 42 35    13 57 41 72 00    69 90 26 37 42    78 46 42 25 01    18 62 79 08 72
40 18 82 81 93    29 59 38 86 27    94 97 21 15 98    62 09 53 67 87    00 44 15 89 97

34 41 48 21 57    86 88 75 50 87    19 15 20 00 23    12 30 28 07 83    32 62 46 86 91
63 43 97 53 63    44 98 91 68 22    36 02 40 09 67    76 37 84 16 05    65 96 17 34 88
67 04 90 90 70    93 39 94 55 47    94 45 87 42 84    05 04 14 98 07    20 28 83 40 60
79 49 50 41 46    52 16 29 02 86    54 15 83 42 43    46 97 83 54 82    59 36 29 59 38
91 70 43 05 52    04 73 72 10 31    75 05 19 30 29    47 66 56 43 82    99 78 29 34 78
```

Table L.*   Table for the Kruskal-Wallis H Test

N₁	N₂	N₃	H	p	N₁	N₂	N₃	H	p
2	1	1	2.7000	.500	4	3	2	6.4444	.008
								6.3000	.011
2	2	1	3.6000	.200				5.4444	.046
								5.4000	.051
2	2	2	4.5714	.067				4.5111	.098
			3.7143	.200				4.4444	.102
3	1	1	3.2000	.300	4	3	3	6.7455	.010
3	2	1	4.2857	.100				6.7091	.013
			3.8571	.133				5.7909	.046
								5.7273	.050
3	2	2	5.3572	.029				4.7091	.092
			4.7143	.048				4.7000	.101
			4.5000	.067					
			4.4643	.105	4	4	1	6.6667	.010
								6.1667	.022
3	3	1	5.1429	.043				4.9667	.048
			4.5714	.100				4.8667	.054
			4.0000	.129				4.1667	.082
								4.0667	.102
3	3	2	6.2500	.011					
			5.3611	.032	4	4	2	7.0364	.006
			5.1389	.061				6.8727	.011
			4.5556	.100				5.4545	.046
			4.2500	.121				5.2364	.052
								4.5545	.098
3	3	3	7.2000	.004				4.4455	.103
			6.4889	.011					
			5.6889	.029	4	4	3	7.1439	.010
			5.6000	.050				7.1364	.011
			5.0667	.086				5.5985	.049
			4.6222	.100				5.5758	.051
								4.5455	.099
4	1	1	3.5714	.200				4.4773	.102
4	2	1	4.8214	.057					
			4.5000	.076	4	4	4	7.6538	.008
			4.0179	.114				7.5385	.011
								5.6923	.049
4	2	2	6.0000	.014				5.6538	.054
			5.3333	.033				4.6539	.097
			5.1250	.052				4.5001	.104
			4.4583	.100					
			4.1667	.105	5	1	1	3.8571	.143
4	3	1	5.8333	.021	5	2	1	5.2500	.036
			5.2083	.050				5.0000	.048
			5.0000	.057				4.4500	.071
			4.0556	.093				4.2000	.095
			3.8889	.129				4.0500	.119

Table L. Table for the Kruskal-Wallis H Test—concluded

N_1	N_2	N_3	H	p	N_1	N_2	N_3	H	p
5	2	2	6.5333	.008				5.6308	.050
			6.1333	.013				4.5487	.099
			5.1600	.034				4.5231	.103
			5.0400	.056	5	4	4	7.7604	.009
			4.3733	.090				7.7440	.011
			4.2933	.122				5.6571	.049
5	3	1	6.4000	.012				5.6176	.050
			4.9600	.048				4.6187	.100
			4.8711	.052				4.5527	.102
			4.0178	.095	5	5	1	7.3091	.009
			3.8400	.123				6.8364	.011
5	3	2	6.9091	.009				5.1273	.046
			6.8218	.010				4.9091	.053
			5.2509	.049				4.1091	.086
			5.1055	.052				4.0364	.105
			4.6509	.091	5	5	2	7.3385	.010
			4.4945	.101				7.2692	.010
5	3	3	7.0788	.009				5.3385	.047
			6.9818	.011				5.2462	.051
			5.6485	.049				4.6231	.097
			5.5152	.051				4.5077	.100
			4.5333	.097	5	5	3	7.5780	.010
			4.4121	.109				7.5429	.010
5	4	1	6.9545	.008				5.7055	.046
			6.8400	.011				5.6264	.051
			4.9855	.044				4.5451	.100
			4.8600	.056				4.5363	.102
			3.9873	.098	5	5	4	7.8229	.010
			3.9600	.102				7.7914	.010
5	4	2	7.2045	.009				5.6657	.049
			7.1182	.010				5.6429	.050
			5.2727	.049				4.5229	.099
			5.2682	.050				4.5200	.101
			4.5409	.098	5	5	5	8.0000	.009
			4.5182	.101				7.9800	.010
5	4	3	7.4449	.010				5.7800	.049
			7.3949	.011				5.6600	.051
			5.6564	.049				4.5600	.100
								4.5000	.102

*Reprinted by permission of the publisher and authors from W. H. Kruskal and W. A. Wallis, "Use of Ranks in One Criterion Variance Analysis," 447, pp. 614–617 and "Errata," 48, p. 910, *Journal of the American Statistical Association*, 1952, 1953; and from S. Siegel, *Nonparametric Statistics*, pp. 278–279. Copyright 1956, McGraw-Hill Book Company.

Table M.*   Table of Critical Values of Chi-Square

p / df	0·250	0·100	0·050	0·025	0·010	0·005	0·001
1	1·32330	2·70554	3·84146	5·02389	6·63490	7·87944	10·828
2	2·77259	4·60517	5·99146	7·37776	9·21034	10·5966	13·816
3	4·10834	6·25139	7·81473	9·34840	11·3449	12·8382	16·266
4	5·38527	7·77944	9·48773	11·1433	13·2767	14·8603	18·467
5	6·62568	9·23636	11·0705	12·8325	15·0863	16·7496	20·515
6	7·84080	10·6446	12·5916	14·4494	16·8119	18·5476	22·458
7	9·03715	12·0170	14·0671	16·0128	18·4753	20·2777	24·322
8	10·2189	13·3616	15·5073	17·5345	20·0902	21·9550	26·125
9	11·3888	14·6837	16·9190	19·0228	21·6660	23·5894	27·877
10	12·5489	15·9872	18·3070	20·4832	23·2093	25·1882	29·588
11	13·7007	17·2750	19·6751	21·9200	24·7250	26·7568	31·264
12	14·8454	18·5493	21·0261	23·3367	26·2170	28·2995	32·909
13	15·9839	19·8119	22·3620	24·7356	27·6882	29·8195	34·528
14	17·1169	21·0641	23·6848	26·1189	29·1412	31·3194	36·123
15	18·2451	22·3071	24·9958	27·4884	30·5779	32·8013	37·697
16	19·3689	23·5418	26·2962	28·8454	31·9999	34·2672	39·252
17	20·4887	24·7690	27·5871	30·1910	33·4087	35·7185	40·790
18	21·6049	25·9894	28·8693	31·5264	34·8053	37·1565	42·312
19	22·7178	27·2036	30·1435	32·8523	36·1909	38·5823	43·820
20	23·8277	28·4120	31·4104	34·1696	37·5662	39·9968	45·315
21	24·9348	29·6151	32·6706	35·4789	38·9322	41·4011	46·797
22	26·0393	30·8133	33·9244	36·7807	40·2894	42·7957	48·268
23	27·1413	32·0069	35·1725	38·0756	41·6384	44·1813	49·728
24	28·2412	33·1962	36·4150	39·3641	42·9798	45·5585	51·179
25	29·3389	34·3816	37·6525	40·6465	44·3141	46·9279	52·618
26	30·4346	35·5632	38·8851	41·9232	45·6417	48·2899	54·052
27	31·5284	36·7412	40·1133	43·1945	46·9629	49·6449	55·476
28	32·6205	37·9159	41·3371	44·4608	48·2782	50·9934	56·892
29	33·7109	39·08'5	42·5570	45·7223	49·5879	52·3356	58·301
30	34·7997	40·2560	43·7730	46·9792	50·8922	53·6720	59·703
40	45·6160	51·8051	55·7585	59·3417	63·6907	66·7660	73·402
50	56·3336	63·1671	67·5048	71·4202	76·1539	79·4900	86·661
60	66·9815	74·3970	79·0819	83·2977	88·3794	91·9517	99·607

Table N.* Table of Z Values in the Normal Distribution

Z	0	1	2	3	4	5	6	7	8	9
0.0	.5000	.4960	.4920	.4880	.4840	.4801	.4761	.4721	.4681	.4641
0.1	.4602	.4562	.4522	.4483	.4443	.4404	.4364	.4325	.4286	.4247
0.2	.4207	.4168	.4129	.4090	.4052	.4013	.3974	.3936	.3897	.3859
0.3	.3821	.3783	.3745	.3707	.3669	.3632	.3594	.3557	.3520	.3483
0.4	.3446	.3409	.3372	.3336	.3300	.3264	.3228	.3192	.3156	.3121
0.5	.3085	.3050	.3015	.2981	.2946	.2912	.2877	.2843	.2810	.2776
0.6	.2743	.2709	.2676	.2643	.2611	.2578	.2546	.2514	.2483	.2451
0.7	.2420	.2389	.2358	.2327	.2296	.2266	.2236	.2206	.2177	.2148
0.8	.2119	.2090	.2061	.2033	.2005	.1977	.1949	.1922	.1894	.1867
0.9	.1841	.1814	.1788	.1762	.1736	.1711	.1685	.1660	.1635	.1611
1.0	.1587	.1562	.1539	.1515	.1492	.1469	.1446	.1423	.1401	.1379
1.1	.1357	.1335	.1314	.1292	.1271	.1251	.1230	.1210	.1190	.1170
1.2	.1151	.1131	.1112	.1093	.1075	.1056	.1038	.1020	.1003	.0985
1.3	.0968	.0951	.0934	.0918	.0901	.0885	.0869	.0853	.0838	.0823
1.4	.0808	.0793	.0778	.0764	.0749	.0735	.0721	.0708	.0694	.0681
1.5	.0668	.0655	.0643	.0630	.0618	.0606	.0594	.0582	.0571	.0559
1.6	.0548	.0537	.0526	.0516	.0505	.0495	.0485	.0475	.0465	.0455
1.7	.0446	.0436	.0427	.0418	.0409	.0401	.0392	.0384	.0375	.0367
1.8	.0359	.0351	.0344	.0336	.0329	.0322	.0314	.0307	.0301	.0294
1.9	.0287	.0281	.0274	.0268	.0262	.0256	.0250	.0244	.0239	.0233
2.0	.0228	.0222	.0217	.0212	.0207	.0202	.0197	.0192	.0188	.0183
2.1	.0179	.0174	.0170	.0166	.0162	.0158	.0154	.0150	.0146	.0143
2.2	.0139	.0136	.0132	.0129	.0125	.0122	.0119	.0116	.0113	.0110
2.3	.0107	.0104	.0102	.0099	.0096	.0094	.0091	.0089	.0087	.0084
2.4	.0082	.0080	.0078	.0075	.0073	.0071	.0069	.0068	.0066	.0064
2.5	.0062	.0060	.0059	.0057	.0055	.0054	.0052	.0051	.0049	.0048
2.6	.0047	.0045	.0044	.0043	.0041	.0040	.0039	.0038	.0037	.0036
2.7	.0035	.0034	.0033	.0032	.0031	.0030	.0029	.0028	.0027	.0026
2.8	.0026	.0025	.0024	.0023	.0023	.0022	.0021	.0021	.0020	.0019
2.9	.0019	.0018	.0018	.0017	.0016	.0016	.0015	.0015	.0014	.0014
3.0	.0013	.0013	.0013	.0012	.0012	.0011	.0011	.0011	.0010	.0010

The digits heading the columns are additional digits for the values of the normal variable shown in the first column. Thus, the probability corresponding with the standard normal variable 1.32 is found in the row in which "1.3" appears at the left and the column in which "2" appears at the top. The probability is 0.0934 (one tail).

Table O.*   *Percentage Points of the k-Sample Rank Statistics* T'

α = .05

N \ k	2	3	4	5	6	7	8	9	10
6	52	55	56	57	–	–	–	–	–
7	69	72	74	75	76	77	77	–	–
8	88	91	93	95	96	97	98	99	99
9	109	113	116	117	119	120	121	122	122
10	132	137	140	142	144	145	146	147	148
11	157	163	167	169	171	172	174	175	176
12	185	192	195	198	200	202	203	205	206
13	215	222	227	230	232	234	236	237	238
14	247	255	260	263	266	268	270	272	273
15	281	290	295	299	302	305	307	308	310
16	317	327	333	337	341	343	345	347	349
17	355	367	373	378	381	384	386	389	390
18	396	408	415	420	424	427	430	432	434
19	439	452	459	465	469	472	475	478	480
20	483	498	506	512	516	520	523	526	528
25	740	759	771	779	785	790	795	798	802
30	1049	1075	1090	1101	1109	1115	1121	1126	1130
35	1410	1443	1462	1476	1486	1495	1502	1508	1513
40	1825	1865	1888	1905	1917	1927	1936	1943	1950
45	2291	2339	2367	2387	2402	2414	2424	2433	2441
50	2810	2866	2899	2922	2939	2954	2966	2976	2985
100	10853	11010	11102	11167	11217	11258	11291	11321	11346

α = .01

N \ k	2	3	4	5	6	7	8	9	10
6	56	–	–	–	–	–	–	–	–
7	74	76	–	–	–	–	–	–	–
8	94	97	99	100	–	–	–	–	–
9	116	119	122	123	125	126	126	–	–
10	140	145	147	149	150	152	153	154	154
11	167	172	175	177	179	180	181	182	183
12	196	201	205	207	209	211	212	213	214
13	227	233	237	240	242	244	245	247	248
14	260	267	272	275	277	279	281	282	283
15	296	304	309	312	315	317	319	320	321
16	333	342	348	351	354	357	359	360	362
17	373	383	389	393	396	399	401	403	404
18	415	426	432	437	440	443	445	447	449
19	460	471	478	483	487	490	492	494	496
20	506	519	526	531	535	539	541	544	546
25	771	789	799	806	812	816	820	824	826
30	1090	1113	1127	1136	1144	1149	1155	1159	1163
35	1463	1492	1509	1521	1530	1537	1544	1549	1554
40	1889	1924	1945	1959	1971	1980	1987	1994	2000
45	2368	2410	2434	2452	2465	2476	2485	2493	2500
50	2900	2949	2978	2998	3014	3027	3038	3047	3055
100	11105	11243	11325	11383	11428	11464	11494	11521	11543

*Reprinted, with changes in notation, by permission of the publisher from R. G. Miller, *Simultaneous Statistical Inference*, p. 252. Copyright 1966, McGraw-Hill Book Company.

Table P.*   Wilcoxon T *Values for Paired Replicates*

Probabilities of a chance occurrence of a rank total of one sign, + or −, whichever is least, equal to, or less than *T*. *T* is given in the body of the table to the nearest whole number. *N* is the number of pairs.

N	.025 (one tail) .05 (two tail)	.01 .02	.005 .01
6	0	—	—
7	2	0	—
8	4	2	0
9	6	3	2
10	8	5	3
11	11	7	5
12	14	10	7
13	17	13	10
14	21	16	13
15	25	20	16
16	30	24	19
17	35	28	23
18	40	33	28
19	46	38	32
20	52	43	38
21	59	49	43
22	66	56	49
23	73	62	55
24	81	69	61
25	89	77	68

The values in the table were obtained by rounding off values given by Tukey in Memorandum Report 17, "The Simplest Signed Rank Tests," Statistical Research Group, Princeton University, 1949.

Table Q.* Critical r Values for the Sign Test

N	Two-tailed Probability						N	Two-tailed Probability					
	.001	.01	.02	.05	.10	.50		.001	.01	.02	.05	.10	.50
1	—	—	—	—	—	—	46	11	13	14	15	16	20
2	—	—	—	—	—	0	47	11	14	15	16	17	20
3	—	—	—	—	—	0	48	12	14	15	16	17	21
4	—	—	—	—	—	0	49	12	15	15	17	18	21
5	—	—	—	—	0	1	50	13	15	16	17	18	22
6	—	—	—	0	0	1							
7	—	—	0	0	0	2	51	13	15	16	18	19	22
8	—	0	0	0	1	2	52	13	16	17	18	19	23
9	—	0	0	1	1	2	53	14	16	17	18	20	23
10	—	0	0	1	1	3	54	14	17	18	19	20	24
							55	14	17	18	19	20	24
11	0	0	1	1	2	3	56	15	17	18	20	21	24
12	0	1	1	2	2	4	57	15	18	19	20	21	25
13	0	1	1	2	3	4	58	16	18	19	21	22	25
14	0	1	2	2	3	5	59	16	19	20	21	22	26
15	1	2	2	3	3	5	60	16	19	20	21	23	26
16	1	2	2	3	4	6							
17	1	2	3	4	4	6	61	17	20	20	22	23	27
18	1	3	3	4	5	7	62	17	20	21	22	24	27
19	2	3	4	4	5	7	63	18	20	21	23	24	28
20	2	3	4	5	5	7	64	18	21	22	23	24	28
							65	18	21	22	24	25	29
21	2	4	4	5	6	8	66	19	22	23	24	25	29
22	3	4	5	5	6	8	67	19	22	23	25	26	30
23	3	4	5	6	7	9	68	20	22	23	25	26	30
24	3	5	5	6	7	9	69	20	23	24	25	27	31
25	4	5	6	7	7	10	70	20	23	24	26	27	31
26	4	6	6	7	8	10							
27	4	6	7	7	8	11	71	21	24	25	26	28	32
28	5	6	7	8	9	11	72	21	24	25	27	28	32
29	5	7	7	8	9	12	73	22	25	26	27	28	33
30	5	7	8	9	10	12	74	22	25	26	28	29	33
							75	22	25	26	28	29	34
31	6	7	8	9	10	13	76	23	26	27	28	30	34
32	6	8	8	9	10	13	77	23	26	27	29	30	35
33	6	8	9	10	11	14	78	24	27	28	29	31	35
34	7	9	9	10	11	14	79	24	27	28	30	31	36
35	7	9	10	11	12	15	80	24	28	29	30	32	36
36	7	9	10	11	12	15							
37	8	10	10	12	13	15	81	25	28	29	31	32	36
38	8	10	11	12	13	16	82	25	28	30	31	33	37
39	8	11	11	12	13	16	83	26	29	30	32	33	37
40	9	11	12	13	14	17	84	26	29	30	32	33	38
							85	26	30	31	32	34	38
41	9	11	12	13	14	17	86	27	30	31	33	34	39
42	10	12	13	14	15	18	87	27	31	32	33	35	39
43	10	12	13	14	15	18	88	28	31	32	34	35	40
44	10	13	13	15	16	19	89	28	31	33	34	36	40
45	11	13	14	15	16	19	90	29	32	33	35	36	41

*Reprinted, with a change in notation, by permission of the publisher and author from W. J. MacKinnon, "Table for both the sign test and distribution-free confidence intervals of the median for sample sizes to 1, 000," *Journal of the American Statistical Association,* 59, p. 937, 1964.

Table R.* Critical χ_r^2 Values for Friedman's Test
k = 3 N = 2, 3, 4, 5, 6, 7, 8, 9

N = 2

χ_r^2	p
0	1.000
1	.833
3	.500
4	.167

N = 3

χ_r^2	p
.000	1.000
.667	.944
2.000	.528
2.667	.361
4.667	.194
6.000	.028

N = 4

χ_r^2	p
.0	1.000
.5	.931
1.5	.653
2.0	.431
3.5	.273
4.5	.125
6.0	.069
6.5	.042
8.0	.0046

N = 5

χ_r^2	p
.0	1.000
.4	.954
1.2	.691
1.6	.522
2.8	.367
3.6	.182
4.8	.124
5.2	.093
6.4	.039
7.6	.024
8.4	.0085
10.0	.00077

N = 6

χ_r^2	p
.00	1.000
.33	.956
1.00	.740
1.33	.570
2.33	.430
3.00	.252
4.00	.184
4.33	.142
5.33	.072
6.33	.052
7.00	.029
8.33	.012
9.00	.0081
9.33	.0055
10.33	.0017
12.00	.00013

N = 7

χ_r^2	p
.000	1.000
.286	.964
.857	.768
1.143	.620
2.000	.486
2.571	.305
3.429	.237
3.714	.192
4.571	.112
5.429	.085
6.000	.052
7.143	.027
7.714	.021
8.000	.016
8.857	.0084
10.286	.0036
10.571	.0027
11.143	.0012
12.286	.00032
14.000	.000021

N = 8

χ_r^2	p
.00	1.000
.25	.967
.75	.794
1.00	.654
1.75	.531
2.25	.355
3.00	.285
3.25	.236
4.00	.149
4.75	.120
5.25	.079
6.25	.047
6.75	.038
7.00	.030
7.75	.018
9.00	.0099
9.25	.0080
9.75	.0048
10.75	.0024
12.00	.0011
12.25	.00086
13.00	.00026
14.25	.000061
16.00	.0000036

N = 9

χ_r^2	p
.000	1.000
.222	.971
.667	.814
.889	.865
1.556	.569
2.000	.398
2.667	.328
2.889	.278
3.556	.187
4.222	.154
4.667	.107
5.556	.069
6.000	.057
6.222	.048
6.889	.031
8.000	.019
8.222	.016
8.667	.010
9.556	.0060
10.667	.0035
10.889	.0029
11.556	.0013
12.667	.00066
13.556	.00035
14.000	.00020
14.222	.000097
14.889	.000054
16.222	.000011
18.000	.0000006

k = 4 N = 2, 3, 4

N = 2

χ_r^2	p
.0	1.000
.6	.958
1.2	.834
1.8	.792
2.4	.625
3.0	.542
3.6	.458
4.2	.375
4.8	.208
5.4	.167
6.0	.042

N = 3

χ_r^2	p
.2	1.000
.6	.958
1.0	.910
1.8	.727
2.2	.608
2.6	.524
3.4	.446
3.8	.342
4.2	.300
5.0	.207
5.4	.175
5.8	.148
6.6	.075
7.0	.054
7.4	.033
8.2	.017
9.0	.0017

N = 4

χ_r^2	p	χ_r^2	p
.0	1.000	5.7	.141
.3	.992	6.0	.105
.6	.928	6.3	.094
.9	.900	6.6	.077
1.2	.800	6.9	.068
1.5	.754	7.2	.054
1.8	.677	7.5	.052
2.1	.649	7.8	.036
2.4	.524	8.1	.033
2.7	.508	8.4	.019
3.0	.432	8.7	.014
3.3	.389	9.3	.012
3.6	.355	9.6	.0069
3.9	.324	9.9	.0062
4.5	.242	10.2	.0027
4.8	.200	10.8	.0016
5.1	.190	11.1	.00094
5.4	.158	12.0	.000072

*Reprinted, with a change in notation, by permission of the publisher and author from M. Friedman, "The Use of Ranks to Avoid the Assumption of Normality Implicit in the Analysis of Variance," *Journal of the American Statistical Association,* 32, pp. 688–689, 1937; and from S. Siegel, *Nonparametric Statistics,* pp. 276–277. Copyright 1956, McGraw-Hill Book Company.

Table S.* Percentage Points of the k-Sample Sign Statistics s^α

$\alpha = .05$

N \ k	2	3	4	5	6	7	8	9	10
5	-	-	-	-	-	-	-	-	-
6	6	-	-	-	-	-	-	-	-
7	7	-	-	-	-	-	-	-	-
8	8	8	-	-	-	-	-	-	-
9	8	9	9	-	-	-	-	-	-
10	9	10	10	10	-	-	-	-	-
11	10	10	11	11	11	11	-	-	-
12	10	11	11	12	12	12	12	12	12
13	11	12	12	12	13	13	13	13	13
14	12	12	13	13	13	14	14	14	14
15	12	13	13	14	14	15	15	15	15
16	13	14	14	14	15	15	15	15	15
17	14	14	15	15	15	16	16	16	16
18	14	15	15	16	16	16	16	17	17
19	15	16	16	16	17	17	17	17	17
20	15	16	17	17	17	18	18	18	18
25	18	19	20	20	21	21	21	21	21
30	21	22	23	23	24	24	24	24	25
35	24	25	26	27	27	27	27	28	28
40	27	28	29	30	30	30	31	31	31
45	30	31	32	33	33	33	34	34	34
50	33	34	35	36	36	36	37	37	37
100	61	63	64	65	65	66	66	67	67

$\alpha = .01$

N \ k	2	3	4	5	6	7	8	9	10
5	-	-	-	-	-	-	-	-	-
6	-	-	-	-	-	-	-	-	-
7	-	-	-	-	-	-	-	-	-
8	-	-	-	-	-	-	-	-	-
9	9	-	-	-	-	-	-	-	-
10	10	-	-	-	-	-	-	-	-
11	11	11	-	-	-	-	-	-	-
12	11	12	12	-	-	-	-	-	-
13	12	13	13	13	-	-	-	-	-
14	13	13	14	14	14	14	-	-	-
15	13	14	15	15	15	15	15	15	16
16	14	15	15	16	16	16	16	16	17
17	15	16	16	16	16	17	17	17	18
18	15	16	17	17	17	17	17	18	18
19	16	17	17	18	18	18	18	18	19
20	17	18	18	18	19	19	19	19	23
25	20	21	21	22	22	22	22	22	26
30	23	24	25	25	25	25	26	26	29
35	26	27	28	28	28	29	29	29	33
40	29	30	31	31	32	32	32	32	36
45	32	33	34	34	35	35	35	36	39
50	35	36	37	38	38	38	38	39	69
100	64	66	67	67	68	68	69	69	69

*Reprinted by permission of the publisher from R. G. Miller, *Simultaneous Statistical Inference*, p. 249. Copyright 1966, McGraw-Hill Book Company.

Table T.* Table of Critical Values of D (or C) in the Fisher Test

Totals in right margin		B (or A)†	Level of significance			
			.05	.025	.01	.005
$A + B = 3$	$C + D = 3$	3	0	—	—	—
$A + B = 4$	$C + D = 4$	4	0	0	—	—
	$C + D = 3$	4	0	—	—	—
$A + B = 5$	$C + D = 5$	5	1	1	0	0
		4	0	0	—	—
	$C + D = 4$	5	1	0	0	—
		4	0	—	—	—
	$C + D = 3$	5	0	0	—	—
	$C + D = 2$	5	0	—	—	—
$A + B = 6$	$C + D = 6$	6	2	1	1	0
		5	1	0	0	—
		4	0	—	—	—
	$C + D = 5$	6	1	0	0	0
		5	0	0	—	—
		4	0	—	—	—
	$C + D = 4$	6	1	0	0	0
		5	0	0	—	—
	$C + D = 3$	6	0	0	—	—
		5	0	—	—	—
	$C + D = 2$	6	0	—	—	—
$A + B = 7$	$C + D = 7$	7	3	2	1	1
		6	1	1	0	0
		5	0	0	—	—
		4	0	—	—	—
	$C + D = 6$	7	2	2	1	1
		6	1	0	0	0
		5	0	0	—	—
		4	0	—	—	—
	$C + D = 5$	7	2	1	0	0
		6	1	0	0	—
		5	0	—	—	—
	$C + D = 4$	7	1	1	0	0
		6	0	0	—	—
		5	0	—	—	—
	$C + D = 3$	7	0	0	0	—
		6	0	—	—	—
	$C + D = 2$	7	0	—	—	—

† when B is entered in the middle column, the significance levels are for D. When A is used in place of B, the significance levels are for C. The p-values are one tail.

*Reprinted with modifications by permission of the author and publisher from D. J. Finney, "Table of Significance Levels for the Fisher-Yates test of Significance in 2 × 2 Contingency Tables," *Biometrika*, 35, pp. 145–156, 1948; and from S. Seigel, *Nonparametric Statistics*, pp. 360–374. Copyright 1956, McGraw-Hill Book Company.

Table T.   Table of Critical Values of D *(or* C*) in the Fisher Test —*
continued

Totals in right margin		B (or A)†	Level of significance			
			.05	.025	.01	.005
A + B = 8	C + D = 8	8	4	3	2	2
		7	2	2	1	0
		6	1	1	0	0
		5	0	0	—	—
		4	0	—	—	—
	C + D = 7	8	3	2	2	1
		7	2	1	1	0
		6	1	0	0	—
		5	0	0	—	—
	C + D = 6	8	2	2	1	1
		7	1	1	0	0
		6	0	0	0	—
		5	0	—	—	—
	C + D = 5	8	2	1	1	0
		7	1	0	0	0
		6	0	0	—	—
		5	0	—	—	—
	C + D = 4	8	1	1	0	0
		7	0	0	—	—
		6	0	—	—	—
	C + D = 3	8	0	0	0	—
		7	0	0	—	—
	C + D = 2	8	0	0	—	—
A + B = 9	C + D = 9	9	5	4	3	3
		8	3	3	2	1
		7	2	1	1	0
		6	1	1	0	0
		5	0	0	—	—
		4	0	—	—	—
	C + D = 8	9	4	3	3	2
		8	3	2	1	1
		7	2	1	0	0
		6	1	0	0	—
		5	0	0	—	—
	C + D = 7	9	3	3	2	2
		8	2	2	1	0
		7	1	1	0	0
		6	0	0	—	—
		5	0	—	—	—

Table T.   Table of Critical Values of D *(or* C *) in the Fisher Test —*
continued

Totals in right margin		B (or A)†	Level of significance			
			.05	.025	.01	.005
A + B = 9	C + D = 6	9	3	2	1	1
		8	2	1	0	0
		7	1	0	0	—
		6	0	0	—	—
		5	0	—	—	—
	C + D = 5	9	2	1	1	1
		8	1	1	0	0
		7	0	0	—	--
		6	0	—	—	—
	C + D = 4	9	1	1	0	0
		8	0	0	0	—
		7	0	0	—	—
		6	0	—	—	—
	C + D = 3	9	1	0	0	0
		8	0	0	—	—
		7	0	—	—	—
	C + D = 2	9	0	0	—	—
A + B = 10	C + D = 10	10	6	5	4	3
		9	4	3	3	2
		8	3	2	1	1
		7	2	1	1	0
		6	1	0	0	—
		5	0	0	—	—
		4	0	—	—	—
	C + D = 9	10	5	4	3	3
		9	4	3	2	2
		8	2	2	1	1
		7	1	1	0	0
		6	1	0	0	—
		5	0	0	—	—
	C + D = 8	10	4	4	3	2
		9	3	2	2	1
		8	2	1	1	0
		7	1	1	0	0
		6	0	0	—	—
		5	0	—	—	—
	C + D = 7	10	3	3	2	2
		9	2	2	1	1
		8	1	1	0	0
		7	1	0	0	—
		6	0	0	—	—
		5	0	—	—	—

Table T. *Table of Critical Values of* D *(or* C *) in the Fisher Test —*
continued

Totals in right margin		B (or A)†	Level of significance			
			.05	.025	.01	.005
A + B = 10	C + D = 6	10	3	2	2	1
		9	2	1	1	0
		8	1	1	0	0
		7	0	0	—	—
		6	0	—	—	—
	C + D = 5	10	2	2	1	1
		9	1	1	0	0
		8	1	0	0	—
		7	0	0	—	—
		6	0	—	—	—
	C + D = 4	10	1	1	0	0
		9	1	0	0	0
		8	0	0	—	—
		7	0	—	—	—
	C + D = 3	10	1	0	0	0
		9	0	0	—	—
		8	0	—	—	—
	C + D = 2	10	0	0	—	—
		9	0	—	—	—
A + B = 11	C + D = 11	11	7	6	5	4
		10	5	4	3	3
		9	4	3	2	2
		8	3	2	1	1
		7	2	1	0	0
		6	1	0	0	—
		5	0	0	—	—
		4	0	—	—	—
	C + D = 10	11	6	5	4	4
		10	4	4	3	2
		9	3	3	2	1
		8	2	2	1	0
		7	1	1	0	0
		6	1	0	0	—
		5	0	—	—	—
	C + D = 9	11	5	4	4	3
		10	4	3	2	2
		9	3	2	1	1
		8	2	1	1	0
		7	1	1	0	0
		6	0	0	—	—
		5	0	—	—	—

Table T. *Table of Critical Values of* D *(or* C*) in the Fisher Test –*
continued

Totals in right margin		B (or A)†	Level of significance			
			.05	.025	.01	.005
$A + B = 11$	$C + D = 8$	11	4	4	3	3
		10	3	3	2	1
		9	2	2	1	1
		8	1	1	0	0
		7	1	0	0	—
		6	0	0	—	—
		5	0	—	—	—
	$C + D = 7$	11	4	3	2	2
		10	3	2	1	1
		9	2	1	1	0
		8	1	1	0	0
		7	0	0	—	—
		6	0	0	—	—
	$C + D = 6$	11	3	2	2	1
		10	2	1	1	0
		9	1	1	0	0
		8	1	0	0	—
		7	0	0	—	—
		6	0	—	—	—
	$C + D = 5$	11	2	2	1	1
		10	1	1	0	0
		9	1	0	0	0
		8	0	0	—	—
		7	0	—	—	—
	$C + D = 4$	11	1	1	1	0
		10	1	0	0	0
		9	0	0	—	—
		8	0	—	—	—
	$C + D = 3$	11	1	0	0	0
		10	0	0	—	—
		9	0	—	—	—
	$C + D = 2$	11	0	0	—	—
		10	0	—	—	—
$A + B = 12$	$C + D = 12$	12	8	7	6	5
		11	6	5	4	4
		10	5	4	3	2
		9	4	3	2	1
		8	3	2	1	1
		7	2	1	0	0
		6	1	0	0	—
		5	0	0	—	—
		4	0	—	—	—

Table T.   Table of Critical Values of D *(or* C*) in the Fisher Test —
continued*

Totals in right margin		B (or A)†	Level of significance			
			.05	.025	.01	.005
A + B = 12	C + D = 11	12	7	6	5	5
		11	5	5	4	3
		10	4	3	2	2
		9	3	2	2	1
		8	2	1	1	0
		7	1	1	0	0
		6	1	0	0	—
		5	0	0	—	—
	C + D = 10	12	6	5	5	4
		11	5	4	3	3
		10	4	3	2	2
		9	3	2	1	1
		8	2	1	0	0
		7	1	0	0	0
		6	0	0	—	—
		5	0	—	—	—
	C + D = 9	12	5	5	4	3
		11	4	3	3	2
		10	3	2	2	1
		9	2	2	1	0
		8	1	1	0	0
		7	1	0	0	—
		6	0	0	—	—
		5	0	—	—	—
	C + D = 8	12	5	4	3	3
		11	3	3	2	2
		10	2	2	1	1
		9	2	1	1	0
		8	1	1	0	0
		7	0	0	—	—
		6	0	0	—	—
	C + D = 7	12	4	3	3	2
		11	3	2	2	1
		10	2	1	1	0
		9	1	1	0	0
		8	1	0	0	—
		7	0	0	—	—
		6	0	—	—	—

Table T.   Table of Critical Values of D *(or* C*) in the Fisher Test —*
continued

Totals in right margin		B (or A)†	Level of significance			
			.05	.025	.01	.005
A + B = 12	C + D = 6	12	3	3	2	2
		11	2	2	1	1
		10	1	1	0	0
		9	1	0	0	0
		8	0	0	—	—
		7	0	0	—	—
		6	0	—	—	—
	C + D = 5	12	2	2	1	1
		11	1	1	1	0
		10	1	0	0	0
		9	0	0	0	—
		8	0	0	—	—
		7	0	—	—	—
	C + D = 4	12	2	1	1	0
		11	1	0	0	0
		10	0	0	0	—
		9	0	0	—	—
		8	0	—	—	—
	C + D = 3	12	1	0	0	0
		11	0	0	0	—
		10	0	0	—	—
		9	0	—	—	—
	C + D = 2	12	0	0	—	—
		11	0	—	—	—
A + B = 13	C + D = 13	13	9	8	7	6
		12	7	6	5	4
		11	6	5	4	3
		10	4	4	3	2
		9	3	3	2	1
		8	2	2	1	0
		7	2	1	0	0
		6	1	0	0	—
		5	0	0	—	—
		4	0	—	—	—
	C + D = 12	13	8	7	6	5
		12	6	5	5	4
		11	5	4	3	3
		10	4	3	2	2
		9	3	2	1	1
		8	2	1	1	0
		7	1	1	0	0
		6	1	0	0	—
		5	0	0	—	—

Table T.   Table of Critical Values of D (or C) in the Fisher Test —
continued

Totals in right margin		B (or A)†	Level of significance			
			.05	.025	.01	.005
A + B = 13	C + D = 11	13	7	6	5	5
		12	6	5	4	3
		11	4	4	3	2
		10	3	3	2	1
		9	3	2	1	1
		8	2	1	0	0
		7	1	0	0	0
		6	0	0	—	—
		5	0	—	—	—
	C + D = 10	13	6	6	5	4
		12	5	4	3	3
		11	4	3	2	2
		10	3	2	1	1
		9	2	1	1	0
		8	1	1	0	0
		7	1	0	0	—
		6	0	0	—	—
		5	0	—	—	—
	C + D = 9	13	5	5	4	4
		12	4	4	3	2
		11	3	3	2	1
		10	2	2	1	1
		9	2	1	0	0
		8	1	1	0	0
		7	0	0	—	—
		6	0	0	—	—
		5	0	—	—	—
	C + D = 8	13	5	4	3	3
		12	4	3	2	2
		11	3	2	1	1
		10	2	1	1	0
		9	1	1	0	0
		8	1	0	0	—
		7	0	0	—	—
		6	0	—	—	—
	C + D = 7	13	4	3	3	2
		12	3	2	2	1
		11	2	2	1	1
		10	1	1	0	0
		9	1	0	0	0
		8	0	0	—	—
		7	0	0	—	—
		6	0	—	—	—

Table T.   Table of Critical Values of D *(or* C*) in the Fisher Test —*
continued

Totals in right margin		B (or A)†	Level of significance			
			.05	.025	.01	.005
A + B = 13	C + D = 6	13	3	3	2	2
		12	2	2	1	1
		11	2	1	1	0
		10	1	1	0	0
		9	1	0	0	—
		8	0	0	—	—
		7	0	—	—	—
	C + D = 5	13	2	2	1	1
		12	2	1	1	0
		11	1	1	0	0
		10	1	0	0	—
		9	0	0	—	—
		8	0	—	—	—
	C + D = 4	13	2	1	1	0
		12	1	1	0	0
		11	0	0	0	—
		10	0	0	—	—
		9	0	—	—	—
	C + D = 3	13	1	1	0	0
		12	0	0	0	—
		11	0	0	—	—
		10	0	—	—	—
	C + D = 2	13	0	0	0	—
		12	0	—	—	—
A + B = 14	C + D = 14	14	10	9	8	7
		13	8	7	6	5
		12	6	6	5	4
		11	5	4	3	3
		10	4	3	2	2
		9	3	2	2	1
		8	2	2	1	0
		7	1	1	0	0
		6	1	0	0	—
		5	0	0	—	—
		4	0	—	—	—

Table T.   *Table of Critical Values of* D *(or* C*) in the Fisher Test —*
continued

Totals in right margin		B (or A)†	Level of significance			
			.05	.025	.01	.005
$A + B = 14$	$C + D = 13$	14	9	8	7	6
		13	7	6	5	5
		12	6	5	4	3
		11	5	4	3	2
		10	4	3	2	2
		9	3	2	1	1
		8	2	1	1	0
		7	1	1	0	0
		6	1	0	—	—
		5	0	0	—	—
	$C + D = 12$	14	8	7	6	6
		13	6	6	5	4
		12	5	4	4	3
		11	4	3	3	2
		10	3	3	2	1
		9	2	2	1	1
		8	2	1	0	0
		7	1	0	0	—
		6	0	0	—	—
		5	0	—	—	—
	$C + D = 11$	14	7	6	6	5
		13	6	5	4	4
		12	5	4	3	3
		11	4	3	2	2
		10	3	2	1	1
		9	2	1	1	0
		8	1	1	0	0
		7	1	0	0	—
		6	0	0	—	—
		5	0	—	—	—
	$C + D = 10$	14	6	6	5	4
		13	5	4	4	3
		12	4	3	3	2
		11	3	3	2	1
		10	2	2	1	1
		9	2	1	0	0
		8	1	1	0	0
		7	0	0	0	—
		6	0	0	—	—
		5	0	—	—	—

Table T. *Table of Critical Values of* D *(or* C*) in the Fisher Test —*
continued

Totals in right margin		B (or A)†	Level of significance			
			.05	.025	.01	.005
A + B = 14	C + D = 9	14	6	5	4	4
		13	4	4	3	3
		12	3	3	2	2
		11	3	2	1	1
		10	2	1	1	0
		9	1	1	0	0
		8	1	0	0	—
		7	0	0	—	—
		6	0	—	—	—
	C + D = 8	14	5	4	4	3
		13	4	3	2	2
		12	3	2	2	1
		11	2	2	1	1
		10	2	1	0	0
		9	1	0	0	0
		8	0	0	0	—
		7	0	0	—	—
		6	0	—	—	—
	C + D = 7	14	4	3	3	2
		13	3	2	2	1
		12	2	2	1	1
		11	2	1	1	0
		10	1	1	0	0
		9	1	0	0	—
		8	0	0	—	—
		7	0	—	—	—
	C + D = 6	14	3	3	2	2
		13	2	2	1	1
		12	2	1	1	0
		11	1	1	0	0
		10	1	0	0	—
		9	0	0	—	—
		8	0	0	—	—
		7	0	—	—	—
	C + D = 5	14	2	2	1	1
		13	2	1	1	0
		12	1	1	0	0
		11	1	0	0	0
		10	0	0	—	—
		9	0	0	—	—
		8	0	—	—	—

Table T.   Table of Critical Values of D *(or* C*) in the Fisher Test —*
continued

Totals in right margin		B (or A)†	Level of significance			
			.05	.025	.01	.005
A + B = 14	C + D = 4	14	2	1	1	1
		13	1	1	0	0
		12	1	0	0	0
		11	0	0	—	—
		10	0	0	—	—
		9	0	—	—	—
	C + D = 3	14	1	1	0	0
		13	0	0	0	—
		12	0	0	—	—
		11	0	—	—	—
	C + D = 2	14	0	0	0	—
		13	0	0	—	—
		12	0	—	—	—
A + B = 15	C + D = 15	15	11	10	9	8
		14	9	8	7	6
		13	7	6	5	5
		12	6	5	4	4
		11	5	4	3	3
		10	4	3	2	2
		9	3	2	1	1
		8	2	1	1	0
		7	1	1	0	0
		6	1	0	0	—
		5	0	0	—	—
		4	0	—	—	—
	C + D = 14	15	10	9	8	7
		14	8	7	6	6
		13	7	6	5	4
		12	6	5	4	3
		11	5	4	3	2
		10	4	3	2	1
		9	3	2	1	1
		8	2	1	1	0
		7	1	1	0	0
		6	1	0	—	—
		5	0	—	—	—

Table T.   Table of Critical Values of D *(or* C *) in the Fisher Test –*
continued

Totals in right margin		B (or A)†	Level of significance			
			.05	.025	.01	.005
A + B = 15	C + D = 13	15	9	8	7	7
		14	7	7	6	5
		13	6	5	4	4
		12	5	4	3	3
		11	4	3	2	2
		10	3	2	2	1
		9	2	2	1	0
		8	2	1	0	0
		7	1	0	0	—
		6	0	0	—	—
		5	0	—	—	—
	C + D = 12	15	8	7	7	6
		14	7	6	5	4
		13	6	5	4	3
		12	5	4	3	2
		11	4	3	2	2
		10	3	2	1	1
		9	2	1	1	0
		8	1	1	0	0
		7	1	0	0	—
		6	0	0	—	—
		5	0	—	—	—
	C + D = 11	15	7	7	6	5
		14	6	5	4	4
		13	5	4	3	3
		12	4	3	2	2
		11	3	2	2	1
		10	2	2	1	1
		9	2	1	0	0
		8	1	1	0	0
		7	1	0	0	—
		6	0	0	—	—
		5	0	—	—	—
	C + D = 10	15	6	6	5	5
		14	5	5	4	3
		13	4	4	3	2
		12	3	3	2	2
		11	3	2	1	1
		10	2	1	1	0
		9	1	1	0	0
		8	1	0	0	—
		7	0	0	—	—
		6	0	—	—	—

Table T.   Table of Critical Values of D *(or* C*) in the Fisher Test —*
continued

Totals in right margin		B (or A)†	Level of significance			
			.05	.025	.01	.005
A + B = 15	C + D = 9	15	6	5	4	4
		14	5	4	3	3
		13	4	3	2	2
		12	3	2	2	1
		11	2	2	1	1
		10	2	1	0	0
		9	1	1	0	0
		8	1	0	0	—
		7	0	0	—	—
		6	0	—	—	—
	C + D = 8	15	5	4	4	3
		14	4	3	3	2
		13	3	2	2	1
		12	2	2	1	1
		11	2	1	1	0
		10	1	1	0	0
		9	1	0	0	—
		8	0	0	—	—
		7	0	—	—	—
		6	0	—	—	—
	C + D = 7	15	4	4	3	3
		14	3	3	2	2
		13	2	2	1	1
		12	2	1	1	0
		11	1	1	0	0
		10	1	0	0	0
		9	0	0	—	—
		8	0	0	—	—
		7	0	—	—	—
	C + D = 6	15	3	3	2	2
		14	2	2	1	1
		13	2	1	1	0
		12	1	1	0	0
		11	1	0	0	0
		10	0	0	0	—
		9	0	0	—	—
		8	0	—	—	—
	C + D = 5	15	2	2	2	1
		14	2	1	1	1
		13	1	1	0	0
		12	1	0	0	0
		11	0	0	0	—
		10	0	0	—	—
		9	0	—	—	—

Table T. Table of Critical Values of D *(or* C*) in the Fisher Test —*
concluded

Totals in right margin		B (or A)†	Level of significance			
			.05	.025	.01	.005
A + B = 15	C + D = 4	15	2	1	1	1
		14	1	1	0	0
		13	1	0	0	0
		12	0	0	0	—
		11	0	0	—	—
		10	0	—	—	—
	C + D = 3	15	1	1	0	0
		14	0	0	0	0
		13	0	0	—	—
		12	0	0	—	—
		11	0	—	—	—
	C + D = 2	15	0	0	0	—
		14	0	0	—	—
		13	0	—	—	—

Table U.*   Table of r for .05 and .01 Level of Significance

Number of points	p = 0.05	p = 0.01
3	0·9969	0·99988
4	0·950	0·990
5	0·878	0·959
6	0·811	0·917
7	0·754	0·875
8	0·707	0·834
9	0·666	0·798
10	0·632	0·765
11	0·602	0·735
12	0·576	0·708
13	0·553	0·684
14	0·532	0·661
15	0·514	0·641
16	0·497	0·623
17	0·482	0·606
18	0·468	0·590
19	0·456	0·575
20	0·444	0·561
22	0·423	0·537
24	0·404	0·515
26	0·388	0·496
28	0·374	0·478
30	0·361	0·463
35	0·334	0·430
40	0·312	0·403
50	0·279	0·361
60	0·254	0·330
70	0·235	0·306
80	0·220	0·286
90	0·207	0·270
100	0·197	0·257
120	0·179	0·234
150	0·160	0·210
200	0·139	0·182
300	0·113	0·149
400	0·098	0·129

The probability values are for a two-tailed test.

*Reprinted by permission of the publisher from M. H. Quenouille, *Introductory Statistics*, p. 235. Copyright 1950, Butterworths.

Table V.* Significance Levels for the Medial Coefficient
Significance levels for number of points falling in any quadrant

Number of points	Lower limit 0.05	Lower limit 0.01	Upper limit 0.05	Upper limit 0.01	Number of points	Lower limit 0.05	Lower limit 0.01	Upper limit 0.05	Upper limit 0.01
8– 9	0	—	4	—	74–75	13	12	24	25
10–11	0	0	5	5	76–77	14	12	24	26
12–13	0	0	6	6	78–79	14	13	25	26
14–15	1	0	6	7	80–81	15	13	25	27
16–17	1	0	7	8	82–83	15	14	26	27
18–19	1	1	8	8	84–85	16	14	26	28
20–21	2	1	8	9	86–87	16	15	27	28
22–23	2	2	9	9	88–89	16	15	28	29
24–25	3	2	9	10	90–91	17	15	28	30
26–27	3	2	10	11	92–93	17	16	29	30
28–29	3	3	11	11	94–95	18	16	29	31
30–31	4	3	11	12	96–97	18	17	30	31
32–33	4	3	12	13	98–99	19	17	30	32
34–35	5	4	12	13	100–101	19	18	31	32
36–37	5	4	13	14	110–111	21	20	34	35
38–39	6	5	13	14	120–121	24	22	36	38
40–41	6	5	14	15	130–131	26	24	39	41
42–43	6	5	15	16	140–141	28	26	42	44
44–45	7	6	15	16	150–151	31	29	44	46
46–47	7	6	16	17	160–161	33	31	47	49
48–49	8	7	16	17	170–171	35	33	50	52
50–51	8	7	17	18	180–181	37	35	53	55
52–53	8	7	18	19	200–201	42	40	58	60
54–55	9	8	18	19	220–221	47	44	63	66
56–57	9	8	19	20	240–241	51	49	69	71
58–59	10	9	19	20	260–261	56	54	74	76
60–61	10	9	20	21	280–281	61	58	79	82
62–63	11	9	20	22	300–301	66	63	84	87
64–65	11	10	21	22	320–321	70	67	90	93
66–67	12	10	21	23	340–341	75	72	95	98
68–69	12	11	22	23	360–361	80	77	100	103
70–71	12	11	23	24	380–381	84	81	106	109
72–73	13	12	23	24	400–401*	89	86	111	114

†For N large, use $\dfrac{N}{4} \pm \left(\dfrac{1}{2} + \dfrac{Z\sqrt{N}}{4} \right)$, where $Z \begin{cases} = 1.96 \text{ for } .05 \text{ significance.} \\ = 2.58 \text{ for } .01 \text{ significance.} \end{cases}$

*Reprinted, with a change in notation, by permission of the publisher from M. H. Quenouille, *Associated Measurements*, p. 225. Copyright 1955, Butterworths.

Table W.*   One-Tail Probability of S *for Kendall's* Tau
Probability that S *(for* τ*) attains or exceeds a specified value. (Shown only for positive values. Negative values obtainable by symmetry.)*

S	Values of N				S	Values of N		
	4	5	8	9		6	7	10
0	0·625	0·592	0·548	0·540	1	0·500	0·500	0·500
2	0·375	0·408	0·452	0·460	3	0·360	0·386	0·431
4	0·167	0·242	0·360	0·381	5	0·235	0·281	0·364
6	0·042	0·117	0·274	0·306	7	0·136	0·191	0·300
8		0·042	0·199	0·238	9	0·068	0·119	0·242
10		$0.0^2 83$	0·138	0·179	11	0·028	0·068	0·190
12			0·089	0·130	13	$0.0^2 83$	0·035	0·146
14			0·054	0·090	15	$0.0^2 14$	0·015	0·108
16			0·031	0·060	17		$0.0^2 54$	0·078
18			0·016	0·038	19		$0.0^2 14$	0·054
20			$0.0^2 71$	0·022	21		$0.0^3 20$	0·036
22			$0.0^2 28$	0·012	23			0·023
24			$0.0^3 87$	$0.0^2 63$	25			0·014
26			$0.0^3 19$	$0.0^2 29$	27			$0.0^2 83$
28			$0.0^4 25$	$0.0^2 12$	29			$0.0^2 46$
30				$0.0^3 43$	31			$0.0^2 23$
32				$0.0^3 12$	33			$0.0^2 11$
34				$0.0^4 25$	35			$0.0^3 47$
36				$0.0^5 28$	37			$0.0^3 18$
					39			$0.0^4 58$
					41			$0.0^4 15$
					43			$0.0^5 28$
					45			$0.0^6 28$

Note.—Repeated zeros are indicated by powers, *e.g.* $0.0^3 47$ stands for 0·00047.

*Reproduced from *Rank Correlation Methods* (3rd Edition, 1962), M. G. Kendall, by permission of Publishers Charles Griffin and Company Ltd., London.

Index

Analysis of variance, curvilinear
  relationships and, 151–154, 174
correlation ratio, *eta*, and, 154–155
factorial design, 73–83, 102, 172
  assumptions for, 83
  crossing of independent variables
    in, 74, 102, 172
  degrees of freedom in, 75, 77, 172
  efficiency of, 75, 102, 172
  independent experiments and, 74
  interactions in, 74–75, 77–83, 102
  main effects in, 75–76
  multiple comparisons of means in,
    79, 83
  pooling of levels in, 75–77
  problems with complex designs,
    83, 103, 173
  significance tests for, 79, 82
factorial design with repeated
  measurements, 73–74, 89–101
  assumptions for, 101
  conservative *F* tests in, 96
  correlated observations in, 91
  error terms in, 95
  independent observations in, 91, 95
  interactions in, 92–101
  multiple comparisons of means in,
    103
  problems with complex designs, 101
  significance tests for, 95–97
independent groups with repeated

measurements, 73–74, 83–89
  assumptions for, 88
  conservative *F* tests in, 88
  correlated observations in, 85
  error terms in, 87, 89
  independent observations in,
    85–86
  interactions in, 86
  multiple comparisons of means in,
    89
  significance test for, 87–89
  simple main effects in, 88–89
k independent groups, 40–53
  additivity of sums of squares, 41
  adjusting significance levels in, 51
  assumptions for, 44, 171–172
  Box's study of, 51
  degrees of freedom in, 41–43
  fixed-effects model of, 43–44
  Norton's study of, 49–52
  null hypothesis in, 41
  random-effects model of, 43–44
  rationale of, 43
  robustness of, 52, 102, 172
  significance test for, 41, 43
  studentized range test and, 114
  sums of squares in, 41–43
  variance estimates in, 41, 43
k matched groups, 67–71
  assumptions for, 70
  carry-over effects in, 67, 70

conservative F tests in, 70, 172
correlations in, 69–70, 102, 172
degrees of freedom in, 68–70
efficiency of, 68–69, 102, 172
error terms in, 68–69
independent groups design and, 69
matching variable in, 68–70
randomized-blocks design and, 67–68, 172
significance tests for, 69, 70
types of designs in, 67
linear regression and, 144–149
Pearson product-moment r and, 144–149
Average. *See* Measures of central tendency
Average deviation, 15–17
interpretation of, 16
weaknesses of, 17
Auxiliary hypotheses, 30, 33

Bartlett's test, k independent variances, 44–45, 172
Binomial distribution, 116–117, 135, 138
Bivariate data, 142, 151, 174
Bivariate normal distribution, assumption of, 148–150
Boneau's study, assumptions for the t test, 36–39, 50
critique of, 39
Bonferroni t test, 71–73, 89, 102, 172
Box's conservative F test, 70, 88, 96, 172
studies on assumptions for the F test, 51, 52, 70
test of variances for k independent groups, 45–47, 53, 172

Calculations, checking of, 42, 78
Canonical correlation, 149
Carry-over effects, 64, 66–67, 70, 117, 119, 132, 134
Central limit theorem, 30
Chance, 29–30, 32–33
Chi-square distribution, 124, 126
Chi-square test, frequencies for k independent groups, 127–129, 173
degrees of freedom in, 127
significance test for, 129
small expected frequencies in, 128, 138, 173
Yate's correction for continuity in, 127–128, 138, 173

frequencies for two independent groups, 123–127, 173
assumptions for, 125, 127, 173
contingency table of, 124
degrees of freedom in, 124–125
expected frequencies in, 124–126, 138
Fisher's exact test and, 126–127, 138, 173
observed frequencies in, 124
one- vs two-tail test in, 126
sample size and, 125, 127, 173
significance tests for, 124–127
Yate's correction for continuity in, 125–127, 138, 173
misuses of, 138
Class interval, 9, 11
lower limit of, 11
midpoint of, 11–12
range and, 9, 11
true limits of, 11
Confidence intervals, 165–167
for the mean, 166
for other parameters, 167
magnitude of an effect and, 164–167
statistical hypotheses and, 164–165
Confidence limits, 166–167
for the mean, 166
for other parameters, 167
Contingency table, 124
Continuous population distribution, assumption of, 109, 111, 117
Cochran's test, frequencies of k matched groups, 135–136, 173–174
efficiency of, 136
McNemar's test and, 135
significance test for, 136
variances for k independent groups, 44–45, 172
Control group, 33
Constructive replication, 169–170, 175
Correlation ratio, *eta*, 154–155
analysis of variance and, 154, 174
limits of, 154
nonlinearity and, 154, 174
significance test for, 154–155, 174
Covariance, 145
correlation and, 145, 147
sum of products and, 145
Cross-over design, 64
Cumulative frequencies, 14

Curvilinear relationships, 150–155, 174
    analysis of variance in, 151–154, 174
    bivariate data, 151
    correlation ratio, *eta,* and, 154–155
    curvilinear regression equation for,
      154, 174
    regression analysis in, 151–154, 174
    test for linearity in, 154

Data-snooping, 60
Dependent variable, 40
Difference scores, 65–67, 115–116
Distribution-free methods, 30, 39, 47,
    105–138, 149–150, 155–160, 173–174
Distributions, chi square, 124, 126
    empirical, 8–12
    F, 35, 43
    normal, 10
    rectangular, 11, 20
    sampling, 27, 34, 36–39, 49–52, 57–61
    skewed, 20–21, 171
    "spotty" data in, 19–25, 171
    symmetrical, 11, 20, 29
    t, 29–30, 34
Dixon's test, extreme scores, 23–24, 171
Duncan's test, means for k independent
    groups, 55–61, 71
Dunn's test, differences in k mean ranks,
    112–113
    means for k groups. *See* Bonferroni t
tests

Equated-groups design, 64, 102
Error rates for multiple-comparison tests,
    54–55
    per comparison, 54
    per experiment, 54–55
    experimentwise, 54–55, 60
Errors of inference, 31
    Type I, 36, 38, 50–53, 57–60
    Type II, 36, 38, 50, 52, 57–60
Error of prediction, 142–143, 148
Experimental group, 33
Experimenter bias, 166–168
Experiments, types of, 2–3
Extraneous variable, 81, 102, 173
Extreme scores (outliers, wild shots), 13–19,
    22–24, 53
    detection of, 22–23
    Dixon's test for, 23–24, 171
    effects of, 13–19

    ignoring of, 23–24, 171
    meaning of, 22, 24
    ranking and, 111
    trimming of, 23–24
    Winsorizing of, 23–24

Factor analysis, 149
F distribution, 35, 43
Fisher's exact test, 126–127
Frequencies, analysis of, 123–138
Frequency polygon, 11–13, 14, 171
Friedman's test, locations of k matched
    groups, 117–119, 173
    assumptions for, 119
    carry-over effects in, 119
    efficiency of, 119
    interaction and, 119
    null hypothesis for, 118
    rationale for, 118
    significance test for, 119
    tied scores in, 119
F test, variances for two independent
    groups, 35–36
    degrees of freedom for, 35
    nonnormality and, 35–36, 172
    one- vs two-tail test in, 35, 43

Hartley's test, variances for k independent
    groups, 44–45, 47–49
Histogram, 9–13, 171
Homogeneity of variance, assumption of,
    19, 35–36, 38, 44, 70, 83, 88, 102
    Bartlett's test for, 44–45, 172
    Boneau's study of, 36–39
    Box's studies of, 51–52, 70
      test for, 45–47, 53, 172
    Cochran's test for, 44–45, 172
    F test and, 35
    F test for, 35–36, 172
    Hartley's test for, 44–45, 47–49, 172
    increasing sample size and, 38–39, 172
    normality and, 45, 47, 52, 172
    Norton's study of, 49–52
    Petrinovich-Hardyck study of, 54,
      57–61
    t test and, 36–39
Homoscedasticity, assumption of, 148
Hypothesis, working, 3

Independence, assumption of, 30–31, 35,
    44, 67, 73, 83, 88, 109, 111, 117, 125,
    127, 132, 138, 148–150, 160, 171–172,
    174
    random assignment of Ss and, 31
    random sampling and, 31, 64
Independent variable, 40, 74
    levels of, 40, 43, 74
Interaction, 74–75, 77–79, 86, 92–95, 102,
    119
    calculation of, 78–79, 93–94, 97
    combination of extrinsic and intrinsic,
        81, 102, 173
    degrees of freedom for, 77, 86, 95–96
    error terms for, 79, 96, 100
    extraneous variable and, 81, 102, 173
    extrinsic, 81, 102, 173
    graphical interpretation of, 80–81,
        99–101
    intrinsic, 81, 102, 173
    multiple comparisons in, 83, 89, 173
    partitioning of, 82–83, 88, 102–103
    qualification of main effect and, 79, 81,
        87, 89
    short-cut formula for, 78–79
    simple interaction effects in, 100–101,
        103, 173
    simple main effects in, 82, 88, 96, 103,
        173
    table, 78, 83, 86, 92–93, 98
    transformation of scale and, 81, 102,
        173
Interquartile range, 15–16
    extreme score and, 18–19
    reliability of, 19
Interval scale. See Measurement scales;
    Level of measurement, assumption
    of

Kendall's rank-order correlation, Tau,
    155–160, 174
    accuracy and, 157
    agreement and, 157–158
    assumptions for, 160
    correction for continuity and, 159
    disarray of ranks and, 155–156
    efficiency of, 160, 174
    limits of, 155
    one- vs two-tail test in, 156, 158
    significance tests for, 156, 158–160
    tie and, 157–158, 160

Kruskal-Wallis test, locations for k
    independent groups, 110–111,
    114–115, 173
    assumptions for, 111
    efficiency of, 111
    interpretation of, 111
    significance tests for, 110
    Steel's test and, 114–115, 173
    Wilcoxon's test and, 110

Levels of measurement, assumption of, 30,
    67
Linearity, assumption of, 148, 150, 174
Linear regression, 142–148
    analysis of variance and, 144–146
    equations for regression lines, 143,
        147–149, 160, 174
    errors of prediction in, 142–143, 148
    least squares criterion for, 143
    regression analysis and, 144–146, 149,
        174
    regression coefficients in, 148, 160
    regression lines in, 142–143
    significance tests for, 146–147
Literal replication, 169–170, 175
Location tests, two matched groups,
    115–117
    assumptions for, 116–117
    binomial distribution and, 116–117
    carry-over effects and, 117
    efficiency of, 117
    significance tests for, 116
    Sign test for, 115–117, 173
    unusually large differences and, 117
    Wilcoxon's signed-ranks test for,
        115–116
    zero differences in, 115–117

Magnitude of an effect, 164–167
    confidence intervals and, 165, 174
    value judgments and, 166–167, 174
Matching variable, 63, 65, 68–70, 132, 172
McNemar's test, frequencies for two
    matched groups, 132–135, 173–174
    carry-over effects in, 132
    efficiency of, 132
    expected frequencies and, 135, 138
    independence and, 132, 138
    inflation of number of Ss in, 133, 135,
        138
    null hypothesis for, 135

252

significance tests for, 134–135
Sign test and, 135, 138
Yates' correction for continuity in, 134
Mean, 13–14, 171
confidence intervals for, 166
confidence limits for, 166
grand, 41
extreme scores and, 13–14, 22, 171
population, 26, 28, 166
reliability of, 19
sampling distribution of, 27
theoretical, 26, 28–29
Measurement scales, 31–32
importance of, 32, 172
interval, 30, 67
nominal, 31–32, 123
ordinal, 31–32
ratio, 31–32
relations in, 32
statistical tests and, 31
Measures of central tendency, 13–15
Measures of variability, 15–19
Median, 13–14, 171
class, 14
extreme scores and, 13, 171
from grouped data, 13–14
from nongrouped data, 13
grand, 137–138
reliability of, 19
Median test, efficiency of, 138
Midranks method, 107–108, 116, 119
Mode, 14
extreme scores and, 14–15
Monotonicity, assumption of, 160, 174
Multiple-analysis, 7–8, 167–171, 174
data-snooping and, 60
facts and, 7–8, 167–171, 174
indications and, 7–8, 44, 167–171, 174
in physical sciences, 7–8, 167
interpretations of, 8, 167–170
replications and, 8, 167–171, 174
transformations of scale in, 25, 60, 167
Multiple comparisons, frequencies for k
    independent groups, 129–132
additivity of chi square and, 130
orthogonal comparisons for,
    130–132, 173
Ryan's test for, 130, 132, 173
significance tests for, 130, 132
special formula for, 132
2×2 tables as, 129–130

frequencies for k matched groups,
    136–137
Cochran's test and, 137
Multiple-Sign test for, 136–137, 174
Ryan's test for 136–137
significance tests for, 136–137
locations for k independent groups,
    111–115
Dunn's test for 112–113
Kruskal-Wallis test and, 144–115
Nemenyi's test for, 112
normality and, 113
Ryan's test for, 112–113
significance test for, 112–114
Steel's test for, 113–115
Wilcoxon's test for, 111–113
locations for k matched groups, 120–121
Friedman's test and, 121
Multiple-Sign tests for, 120–121,
    173
Nemenyi's test for, 120–121
power of, 121
significance tests for, 120–121
Sign test for, 120
Wilcoxon's test for, 120
means for k independent groups,
    53–63, 172
all possible contrasts of, 55, 60
Duncan's test for, 56–61
error rates in, 54–61
homogeneity of variance and,
    57–58, 60–61
Newman-Keuls test for, 56–61, 71
normality and, 57–59
number of treatments and, 57–58
pairwise comparisons of, 53–55, 60
Petrinovich-Hardyck study of, 54,
    57–61
power and, 58, 61
Scheffé's test for, 55–57, 59–60
t tests for, 53, 55–61
Tukey A test for, 56–61
Tukey B test for, 56–63, 172
Type I and II errors in, 53, 57–61
unequal numbers of Ss and, 57–61
means of k matched groups, 71–73
Bonferroni t test for, 71–73, 89,
    102, 172
error term in, 71, 72
significance tests for, 72–73
t tests for, 73

Tukey B test for, 71–73
variances for k independent groups,
    Tukey B test for, 62–63
Multiple correlation and regression, 149
Multiple-Sign test, 120–121, 136–137,
    173–174
Murphy's law, 5

Nemenyi's tests, mean ranks for k matched
    groups, 120–121
    rank sums for k independent groups,
        112
        critique of, 121
Newman-Keuls test, means of k independent
    groups, 56–61, 71
Noise-level of significance, 168–169, 174
Nominal scale. *See* Measurement scales
Nonparametric tests. *See* Distribution-free
    methods
Normal deviate test, 112–113, 160
Normality of parent population, assumption
    of, 19, 30, 35, 38, 44, 67, 83, 172
    Boneau's study of, 36–39
    Norton's study of, 49–52
    Petrinovich-Hardyck study of, 54, 57–61
Norton's study, assumptions for F test,
    49–52
    critique of, 52–53
Null hypothesis, 34–36, 41, 66, 118, 135, 168
Numbers, analysis of, 26–103, 142–155

One- vs two-tail test, 29–30, 34–35, 38, 43,
    66, 109, 126, 156, 158
Operational replication, 169–170, 175
Ordinal scale. *See* Measurement scales
Orthogonal comparisons, frequencies for k
    independent groups, 130–132, 173

Pearson product-moment correlation, r,
    144–149
    analysis of variance and, 144–149
    as a descriptive statistic, 149
    assumptions for, 148–149
    bivariate data, 142
    covariance and, 145
    direction of relationship and sign, 64,
        144, 149, 174
    limits of, 144
    scatter diagram for, 142, 174
    significance test for, 146, 147
    stability of, 160–161

strength of relationship and magnitude,
    144, 149, 174
    sum of products and, 145, 153
    variance accounted for and, 144,
        146–147, 149, 174
Percentile, 16
    ranges, 16, 171
        extreme scores and, 16, 18–19, 171
Petrinovich-Hardyck study, multiple
    comparison methods, 54, 57–61
Pilot experiments, value of, 5–6, 171
Population, 17, 26, 148, 166
Power of a statistical test, 39, 58, 61, 113,
    117, 121, 148
Proportion, 124, 130, 132–133, 135–137

Quartile, 16
Quenouille's medial test of correlation,
    149–150, 174
    assumptions for, 150
    coefficient of, 149–150
    efficiency of, 150
    limits of, 150
    scatter diagram and, 149–150
    significance test for, 149

Randomized-blocks design, 67–68, 172
Random sampling, assumption of, 30–31,
    35, 43–44, 83, 88, 109, 111, 117, 119
    myth of, 31
Random variation, estimate of, 34, 44, 75,
    79, 87, 89, 95, 96, 100
Range, 8–9, 11, 15–16
    class interval and, 9, 11
    reliability of, 16
Ranks and signs, analysis of, 105–122,
    155–160
Ratio scale. *See* Measurement scales
Replication, experimental, 8, 33, 167–171,
    174–175
    constructive, 169–170, 175
    facts and, 8, 33, 167–171, 174
    literal, 169–170, 175
    operational, 169–170, 175
    systematic, 170
Research errors, 4–5, 6
    detection of, 4–5
    external validity and, 4
    internal validity and, 4
Robustness of statistical tests, 39, 52, 102,
    172

Ryan's test, locations for k independent
groups, 112–113
frequencies for k independent groups,
130–132, 173
frequencies for k matched groups,
136–137

Sampling distribution, 27
of difference in means, 34
of F, 43, 49–52
of the mean, 27
of multiple-comparison tests, 57–61
of t, 36–39, 50
Scatter diagram, 142, 149–151, 174
Scheffé's test, all possible contrasts of
means, 55–57, 59–61, 71
Science, aims of, 2–4, 6
answering questions, 2–3, 171
hypothesis testing, 2–4, 171
theory development, 3
Serendipity, 8
Sign test, 115–117, 120, 135, 138, 173
Simple analysis of variance. See analysis of
variance, k independent groups
Simple interaction effects, 100–101, 103, 173
error estimates for, 100
Simple main effects, 82–83, 88, 96–97,
100–101, 103, 173
as interaction plus main effect, 82,
88–89, 96
error estimates for, 82, 89, 96–97
Spearman's rank-order correlation, rho, 155
disadvantages of, 155
"Spotty" data, 19–25, 171
characteristics of, 20, 171
kinds of departures from normality, 20
relation of mean to median in, 21
Standard deviation, 15–19, 164, 171
degrees of freedom for, 18
extreme scores and, 16, 19, 171
interpretation of, 18
population, 17
reliability of, 17, 19
sum of squares and, 18
variance and, 18
Standard error of difference in means for
two independent groups, 34
of difference in mean ranks, 112
of difference in means for two matched
groups, 64–65
of Kendall's S, 159–160

of mean, 27–29, 32, 61–62, 71, 166
Standard scores, 147
Statistical hypotheses, 34–36, 41, 66, 118,
135, 164–165, 168
Steel's test, rank sums for k independent
groups, 113–115, 173
Studentized ranges, 62, 72–73, 113–114
Summary table, 68–69, 79, 82
Sum of products, 145–148, 153
Sums of squares, 18, 41
between groups, 41
degrees of freedom for, 18
total, 41
variance estimates and, 41
within groups, 41–42
Systematic replication, 170

Tactics, research and data analysis,
102–103, 170–175
t and F, relationship of, 79
t distribution, 29
degrees of freedom for, 29
one- vs two-tail test in, 29–30
positive and negative t values, 34
Theories, multiple corroboration of,
169–170, 175
Tied scores, treatment of, 107–109
average probability method, 107–108
corrections for, 108–109, 157–158, 160
midranks method, 107–108, 116, 119,
158
probability limits method, 107
random assignment of ranks method,
107–108
Transformations of scale, 21–22
arc sin, 22, 171
homogeneity of variance and, 22, 25,
45, 51, 171
interactions and, 81, 102, 173
logarithmic, 21–22, 45–46, 171
normality and, 22, 25, 45, 47, 51, 171
reciprocal, 21–22, 171
rules for, 21
simplifying relationships by, 25, 167,
171
skewness and, 21, 171
square root, 21–22, 171
standard score, 147
t test, mean for a single group, 26–33
assumptions for, 30–32
degrees of freedom and, 29

one- vs two-tail test in, 29–30
significance test for, 29–30
standard error of a mean in,
    27–29
means for two independent groups,
    33–39, 66
    assumptions for, 35, 171–172
    Boneau's study on assumptions for,
      36–39
    degrees of freedom in, 34
    equal sample sizes and, 36, 38
    homogeneity of variance and,
      35–36
    normality and, 35, 38
    null hypothesis, 34–35
    one- vs two-tail test in, 34
    robustness of, 39, 52, 102, 172
    significance test for, 34
    standard error of difference in
      means in, 34
means for two matched groups, 63–67
    assumptions for, 67
    carry-over effects and, 64, 66
    correlation and, 64–65, 102, 172
    cross-over design and, 64
    degrees of freedom in, 66
    efficiency of, 65–66, 102, 172
    equated-groups design and, 64, 102
    limited supply of Ss and, 66
    matching variable in, 63
    null hypothesis for, 66
    one- vs two-tail test in, 66
    problems of matching in, 63
    significance test for, 66
    standard error of difference in
      means in, 64–65

t test for a single mean and, 65
t test for means for two
    independent groups and, 64–66
types of designs in, 63–64
Tukey tests, k means, 56–61
    A test, 56–61
    B test, 56–63, 71–73, 79, 83, 89, 102, 172
Type I error. *See* Errors of inference
Type II error. *See* Errors of inference

Use of equal numbers of Ss in treatments,
    8, 36, 38, 102, 172

Variability. *See* Measures of variability
Variance, 18
    degrees of freedom for, 18
    extreme scores and, 19, 22
    partitioning of, 18
    sums of squares and, 18

Wilcoxon's test, locations for two
    independent groups, 105–113, 173
    assumptions for, 109
    correction for tied scores in,
      108–109
    efficiency of, 109
    one- vs two-tail test in, 109
    rationale for, 109
    significance test for, 106, 109
    treatment of tied scores in,
      107–109
    signed-ranks test. *See* Location tests,
    two matched groups

Yate's correction for continuity, 125–128,
    134, 138, 159, 173